Spy Wars

Spy Wars
MOLES, MYSTERIES, AND DEADLY GAMES

Tennent H. Bagley

Yale University Press   New Haven & London

A Caravan book. For more information, visit www.caravanbooks.org

Published with assistance from the foundation established in memory of Philip Hamilton McMillan of the Class of 1894, Yale College.

Set in Aster Roman by Keystone Typesetting, Inc.

Printed in the United States of America.

Library of Congress Cataloging-in-Publication Data
Bagley, T. H. (Tennent H.), 1925–
Spy wars : moles, mysteries, and deadly games / Tennent H. Bagley.
p. cm.
Includes bibliographical references and index.
ISBN 978-0-300-12198-8 (hardcover: alk. paper)
1. United States. Central Intelligence Agency. 2. Soviet Union. Komitet gosudarstvennoi bezopasnosti. 3. Intelligence service—Soviet Union—History. 4. Espionage, American—Soviet Union. 5. Bagley, T. H. (Tennent H.), 1925– 6. Intelligence officers—United States—Biography. 7. Intelligence officers—Soviet Union—Biography. I. Title.
JK468.I6B345 2007
327.1247073—dc22
2006036953

A catalogue record for this book is available from the British Library.

10 9 8 7 6 5 4 3 2

Contents

Preface

Like millions of others I was riveted to my TV screen in late 1989 watching young Germans exuberantly hacking away with hammers and picks at the Berlin "wall of death." They were breaking down the most visible symbol of the Cold War—and opening up an opportunity I had never foreseen.

Long years had passed since my retirement from CIA, but old questions still nagged. The nation—and History—had been ill-served in certain encounters between CIA and KGB. In the meantime the truth had been buried under layers of lies so often repeated that they had become conventional wisdom. Now those gaps opening in the Wall foreshadowed an early end to the Cold War—and suggested a way to dig the truth back out. After the Second World War veterans had met with wartime foes to compare tactics and see their battles through the enemy's eyes. If the Cold War was really ending, might KGB veterans loosen up the same way? Their side of old events could break out some of the buried truth.

Two years later the Soviet Union collapsed and the opportunity loomed large. I grabbed it, knowing that if I didn't go after the answers to certain old questions, no one would. The American intelligence community had so unequivocally supported falsehood—and lost so much by doing so—that if any CIA people still remembered, they would probably prefer to let *this* sleeping dog lie.

It wasn't mere curiosity. I was sure that that old blanket of lies was covering traitors in our midst. More than one American intelligence officer before Aldrich Ames had betrayed CIA's secret helpers inside the Soviet bloc—and got away with it. More than one American code clerk before the infamous treason of Navy communicator John Walker had compromised America's secret ciphers—and got away with it. Today practically no one in the West is aware that they even existed.

At that late date I suppose I might have relaxed and taken comfort from the thought that our side won the Cold War despite their treason. The passage of time had probably eroded whatever damage they had done. Or had it? Maybe, instead, as had happened throughout history, old spies had led the enemy to others in a continuum of treason that might still be active today.

Either way, any history of the Cold War that ignored the role these traitors played would remain distorted and incomplete.

So I set out on my own, with no reference to my former employers, toward former Soviet bloc intelligence and counterintelligence officers who might be willing to throw light on those old mysteries. Step by step, year after year through the 1990s, I worked my way slowly from an introduction here to a visit there, sent letters, traveled to one place and another—including Russia—and sat with Eastern veterans at European roundtables discussing our Cold War.

Luck rode with me. I managed to get in through the door that opened when the Soviet Union collapsed and, before it began to close again early in the new century, to talk with almost twenty Soviet bloc intelligence veterans, a few during their visits to the West but most of them in the former Soviet bloc. I visited some of their apartments, was invited to official premises (even to see the luxurious bathroom in the Moscow residence of the infamous wartime and postwar Smersh leader Victor Abakumov), and had a look at Dzerzhinsky's statue after it had been lifted away from in front of the Lubyanka, the KGB headquarters.

These Chekist veterans, knowing that I had supervised CIA's work against them, reacted in different ways. One senior KGB general bared his teeth. When my European journalist companion mentioned some recent East-West roundtable discussions of Cold War espionage, this old Chekist snapped his disapproval of any such openness. He turned to me. "Remember," he said darkly, "we are still working against you."

He was telling it straight. Though the KGB's name has changed (not for the first time) its main elements remain intact in the same buildings, with the same mindset and many of the same objectives. As another high official affirmed—years after the collapse of the Soviet Union—"the KGB is not dead." It still hides its assets and significant parts of its history. Until its files are opened no one can tell the full story of our old skirmishes in the dark—and it will not open *these* files. The fall of the Soviet Union in 1991 caused hardly a hiccup in the KGB's handling of penetration agents inside American intelligence, like Robert Hanssen and Aldrich Ames. Today it stiffly denies that it had any other such spies or that it broke America's codes before or after the Walkers' treason. It hides the advantages it gained and the tricks it played, for it still needs those advantages and uses those tricks.

But some Chekist veterans had turned the page and spoke with candor. They seemed pleased and intrigued by the opportunity to talk with a known former adversary familiar with the people and incidents and procedures of their past. They responded spontaneously even to detailed questions (posed in a neutral context), confident that as a professional I would not ask them to betray their undiscovered spies in the West. Their answers cast priceless light on hidden activities of our past.

Some, in fact, were trying as I was to bring old mysteries out of the dark. True, most of the memoirs and histories that the KGB and its veterans published after the Cold War differed little from what they had been pumping out for decades, rehashing and exalting their known successes, telling little new and exposing no recent secrets. But some Moscow memoirs, either published without official imprimatur or cleared inattentively, gave fresh insights into their past operations.

Over the course of ten years I thus succeeded in digging out at least the broad outlines of the buried truth. Satisfied with that and aware that I would never get all the answers I sought, I might just have laid it all away on a shelf. But in September 2001 came the shock of 9/11—and some basic questions it raised.

The first question was relatively easy: How did we fail to detect it in advance? One obvious answer lies in the near-impossibility of infiltrating spies into tiny groups of closely related and fanatic alien terrorists—a task more difficult even than ours, in my time, of penetrating the near-seamless security barriers of the Soviet regime.

A second question, however, looms larger: Why did the American intelligence community fail to properly assess the information it *did* have? This stirred old memories. In the answer to that question lay some of the same defects that had buried truth in my time. I saw the same group-thinking, the same bureaucratic resistance to unpleasant warnings, the same inability to think outside the box of comfortable assumptions, the same refusal to recognize visible portents, and the same failure to "connect the dots." Perhaps, after all, my findings about that earlier time might be useful—not to correct these tendencies, for they are incorrigible—at least to haul them out again into the open where, if intelligence is to properly serve the nation, they must be recognized and fought like a chronic disease.

To describe these matters, already complicated enough, one has to disentangle threads that have been craftily woven into misleading and confusing patterns. Making sense of it all has proved too difficult even for many professionals in this recondite field. So instead of trying to explain it all, I will go back and retrace, step by step, the path I trod in this murky realm of deception and let the reader join me in unraveling, knot by knot, these twisted strands.

In the process I have depended not only on my own memory but on that of others who lived through these events, and I have been helped by some declassified documents and old notes. To narrate the course of unfolding events I have had to reconstruct conversations that took place forty years ago. I have no transcripts of them and of course I cannot remember every spoken word, but I have checked with those interlocutors who are still alive and am confident that I have accurately recorded the substance and context—and in some cases even the exact words—of these conversations.

Here, then, is the long-buried truth about certain events I lived through. As they unfold they will draw us from a sunny spring afternoon in Switzerland down into depths of deceit and treachery that have remained unlit to this day.

Acknowledgments

Some of the events and facts dealt with in this book had been so painstakingly buried that I could not have dug them out without a lot of help, from West and East. And the story could not have been told or brought to print without critical help and encouragement from friends.

William Hood used the wit and talent that has marked his own writings to help me shape the story. Without Fred Kempe's push, it might never have come to press, and he bestowed generously from his bountiful store of enthusiasm, editorial skill, and caring friendship. David E. Murphy confirmed my memories of our times together, added some of his own, and corrected some inaccuracies, as did Joseph Culver Evans, Newton S. "Scotty" Miler, and the late Peter Deriabin. John Abidian kindly shared his memories of his Moscow service. Fulton Oursler, Jr., gave essential help, and I owe inestimable thanks to the late Maurice Najman. The work is better for the thoughtful editing and comments of William Jennings. *Merci* to Pierre de Villemarest for his valuable assist. It buoyed me to have the interest and support of all those and of Henry Hurt, Owen Lock, Edmund Lazar, Alexander Rocca, and Andrew W. Bagley.

Former adversaries in the East gave precious insight into their side of the events I describe and pointed me toward helpful Russian publications. Although they reminisced only about no-longer-secret affairs, procedures, and personalities, they might be embarrassed to be named, because of the tightened restrictions in Russia today. So to them I acknowledge my debt with one broad *Spasibo!*

Memories are never enough, so I thank those who supplied or directed me toward published documentation that I would otherwise not have found, particularly John Dziak, Dan Mulvenna, Edward Jay Epstein, and Hayden Peake.

Thanks go to CIA's Publications Review Board, which reviewed and cleared the substance of this book and prevented some indiscretions from slipping into its final form.

I am grateful to Jonathan Brent of Yale University Press. It is heartening to have the support of one who knows so well the undersides of Soviet history. To my competent editor at Yale, Jeffrey Schier, go admiring thanks.

Sustaining me throughout were the integrity and courage of the tiny handful of CIA colleagues who did not bend to adverse political winds or let themselves be engulfed by the spreading flood of distortions of history. They held steadfastly to what they knew to be true even when that could threaten their careers. My hat is off to Newton S. ("Scotty") Miler, Joseph Culver Evans, Peter Deriabin, and Fritz Giesecke, though the latter two are regrettably no longer here to acknowledge this salute.

PART ONE

A Defector Like No Other

CHAPTER 1

Walk-in

When the door opened in front of him, my visitor knew he was being led into a secret CIA apartment. But which of us was really being led? As he took my welcoming hand I had no idea that it was to drag me and my service into a labyrinth so complex that even today, more than forty years later, my successors have still not found their way through its twists and turns.

On that afternoon in late May 1962 Geneva was at its springtime best. Beyond the open glass door onto a narrow balcony, red flowers glowed in window boxes and the sun shone on the roofs of the picturesque Old Town—a bright contrast to the dark doings in this little apartment. The man walking in was a Soviet official taking the deadly dangerous step of making secret contact with American intelligence. I was the CIA officer to greet him.

Two days earlier, in the marble halls of Geneva's Palace of Nations, he made his move during a break in the proceedings of an arms-control conference. He eased himself to the side of an American delegate he knew to have served in Moscow, shook hands, and, after a glance around to be sure he was out of range of fellow Soviet delegates, asked urgently for contact with CIA. The startled American—call him Edwin Dodge—said he would try to arrange it. Within hours he got the message to my chief.

By the time I had given Dodge the address and hour for the meeting, a young tech had fitted the apartment with a hidden tape recorder and microphones. Dodge was reluctant to compromise his diplomatic status by involvement in our clandestine world but was willing to lead the Russian to our door.

Dodge motioned him in and followed close behind, but obviously had no desire to stay a minute longer than necessary. "This is Mr. Nosenko of the Soviet delegation," he said. "He wants to talk to you." Turning to the Soviet and making eye contact, he shook his hand and said, "I'll leave you now. And the best of luck." With this, Dodge spun on his heel and was down the stairs before I could thank him.

Dressed in a dark, Western-style suit and conservative tie befitting his status as a first secretary from the Soviet foreign ministry, Yuri Ivanovich Nosenko was in his mid-thirties, a bit under six feet tall, and strongly built with a slightly hunched posture. His light-brown hair was combed straight back from his forehead, emphasizing his wide face with its slightly hooded eyes, broad nose, and thick lips. His eyes swept the small living room, crowded with fussy, old-fashioned armchairs, a sofa, oriental rugs, and heavy draperies. He looked through the half-open door onto the balcony and seemed content that it was higher than the neighboring houses.

I said in English, "Mr. Dodge told me you want to talk to someone from American Intelligence. I'm pleased to meet you."

"Thank you," he replied in Russian, "I have important things to tell you."

I raised my hand. "Mr. Dodge said you speak good English. I understand Russian but have trouble expressing myself clearly in it, so if it's all right with you, let's speak English. If you like you can speak Russian and I'll answer in English."

He nodded and said in easy English, "No problem." And indeed there was no problem of mutual understanding from that moment on. I motioned him to a chair and offered him a drink. "Yes, please, scotch"— following familiar Soviet drinking habits, vodka at home, whiskey abroad.

As I poured the whiskey over ice and added plenty of soda he said, "I'm in trouble. I need some money urgently." I nodded sympathetically but remained silent. He went on. "I think you'll help me, because I am here to talk about my real business. I am an officer of the KGB, and I work against your people in Moscow."

It was as if a gold brick had dropped into my lap. I had dealt with defectors and sources inside Soviet Intelligence and knew how a source inside the core of the Soviet system could contribute to our mission. Though I kept a cool demeanor, my visitor surely knew the elation I was feeling because his service, too, gave top priority to recruiting sources among its adversaries' "special services."

At that moment I knew little more about Nosenko than his name, one among seventy on the list of Moscow's delegates who had flown in to Geneva in March with Foreign Minister Gromyko. Gromyko attended the opening sessions and left, but the conference went on, as foreseen, for months.

Intelligence services the world over take a routine interest in the delegates assigned to multinational conferences. Central files are checked to see if there are any potential friends or lapsed agents of ours in the group. Or hostile intelligence officers: these delegations offered ready-made cover for Moscow-based KGB and Soviet Military Intelligence (GRU) officers to go out and meet important agents already in place. In the past, local security services tipped by us had shadowed such traveling spymasters and had occasionally identified their spies. We received no such traces on Nosenko and hence no details; our headquarters saw no need to clutter us with trivial information on every delegate to every conference. Even the truly interesting ones usually went unwatched for lack of time or facilities to do much about their presence—such as, in this delegation, Mikhail S. Rogov. This, we knew, was the well-worn pseudonym for Mikhail Tsymbal, the KGB's former chief in Paris, now heading a major Moscow operations division. It was only many years later that we learned he had come out this time to meet KGB spies high inside the French intelligence service.

Soviet delegations also brought along security officers assigned from the KGB "delegations department" that specialized in watching over Russians who might let themselves be tempted by life in "enemy territory," as the West was known in Soviet regime parlance.

"I am a Major in the Second Chief Directorate," Nosenko said, assuming correctly that I would know it as the KGB's huge counterintelligence and security organization. "I am responsible for the security of our delegation."

He glanced toward the whiskey bottle I had set on a sideboard, so I poured some more scotch in his glass and was just starting to add soda water when he raised his hand for me to stop. I went to the balcony door and closed it to emphasize my concern for the privacy of what he was going to tell me.

"I know what I'm doing here is dangerous, but I need money right now. I've been in too many bars—been with too many girls, drunk too much whiskey," he said, flicking his index finger against his neck in a characteristic Russian gesture. "Mostly with Yuri Guk of the rezidentura [Soviet intelligence station, or residency, of KGB] here. You probably know about him." He looked at me expectantly and I nodded; we knew of Guk's earlier KGB service in the United States. "We've been friends for years, even from university. We're having a great time together."

Nosenko said he had run out of his own money and had been paying for these revels with funds advanced to him for official expenses. Now, at the end of the delegation's three-month sojourn, he had to account for the advance. "I don't mind talking to you, because I don't believe in our system anymore. But it's this damned money problem that drove me here."

"How much do you owe?"

"Eight hundred francs." This amounted to 250 U.S. dollars, about a week's pay for him or his colleagues.

"I'll answer all your questions," Nosenko said, "but you must understand that I will never come over to your side, to live in the West—I won't ever leave my family or my country. I have two little girls."

He fished an envelope from his jacket pocket and pulled out two pictures from a folded letter. "Look, I just got these from my wife. Guk was back in Moscow for a few days and my wife asked him to bring them to me." He pointed at one. "That's my daughter Oksana," he said proudly. "She looks so much like me that my wife calls her my *kopiya* [image]."

I clucked approval and got back to business. "How much of a problem is it for you to come meet me? Who might notice your absence?"

"No problem," Nosenko replied. "I don't have any fixed duties in the conference and no one knows or cares when I come and go. I'm not accountable to anyone." He took a deep gulp of his whiskey and pulled a pack of American cigarettes from his jacket pocket and offered one to me. I declined but picked up a book of matches that lay on the coffee table and lit his.

"I'm not staying with the rest of the delegation. They're in the Hotel Rex but four of us are in another hotel, not even close." He identified it as the Hotel d'Allèves, a small place close to the Rhone River and at least two kilometers across town from the Rex, which I knew to be the usual habitat of visiting Soviet delegations.

"Yes, but how about those three?" I asked. "Will they notice and report your absences?"

"Absolutely not. The guy sharing my room is just a journalist with nothing to do with the KGB. Same for the other two."

"What's your roommate's name?"

"Aleksandr Kislov," he replied. I remembered having seen the name on the list of delegates as a TASS correspondent attached to the Soviet delegation. No traces had come in on him, so Nosenko's indifference seemed justified.

Nosenko continued to reassure me. He had good reason to be confident. In his routine preparation in Moscow for this stint in Geneva he had studied all the travelers' KGB files, for he was the only security officer for them all. It was his responsibility to know which delegates he should watch most closely and which others, as regular KGB informants, might help him keep an eye on the rest.

"The only person who really knows how I spend my time is Guk, but he's my friend, no problem."

"How long can you safely stay today?" I asked.

"Maybe an hour, not much longer. Guk will be waiting. We're going out again tonight."

"Tell me about your job in Moscow."

Until a few weeks before leaving for Geneva, Nosenko told me, he had been the number two man in the section operating against the American Embassy in Moscow. Just now he had become the section chief supervising KGB work against American and British tourists in the USSR. Earlier he had served in both these sections, always working against Americans. The Second Chief Directorate was trying not just to prevent their spying, he explained, but especially to recruit them as spies.

"We have a tremendous coverage of your people—surveillance, microphones, agents inside your buildings. Don't ever expect me to meet you inside the country. I'll meet you when I'm in the West but I'll never risk meeting you inside."

I shrugged and raised my hands in a gesture of regretful resignation. "Because there's so little time today, I'd like you to tell me what *you* think is the most important thing you have to tell us."

Nosenko thought for a moment, looking down at the near-empty glass of whiskey and soda that I had served him. "I know the most important American spy the KGB ever recruited in Moscow," he said.

Bingo! I leaned forward as he paused for effect. "He was a sergeant in your Embassy, a cipher machine mechanic. He had the code name 'Andrey.' I never knew his true name. He got involved with a Russian woman working for us in the Embassy's apartments. The old thing—it usually works—well, you know . . ." He paused expectantly and I nodded. He went on. "We took compromising pictures and he cooperated to get them back and save his marriage."

"A tremendously valuable source," he added, "In fact, my boss went himself all the way to the United States just to reactivate 'Andrey' after the rezidentura lost contact with him."

"Who was that who went?" I asked. He was referring to the man for whom Nosenko had been deputy until just before coming here, the chief of KGB operations against our Moscow Embassy.

"Kovshuk, Vladislav Kovshuk," Nosenko answered.

"Can you tell me anything more, that might help us identify the sergeant? When was he recruited?"

He twisted his wrist in the air, "1949 or 1950. One or the other."

Nosenko said he himself had joined the KGB in 1952 and had recently received the "ten-year certificate" honoring that service. "The bosses know me as a real operator," he said proudly. "I speak good English so I'm called on to handle a lot of things. I've recruited ten Americans and Englishmen, and have gotten commendations."

He then named an American and a British tourist, and two American tourist agency directors cooperating with the KGB, though he did not claim to have recruited them himself.

For no apparent reason, his eyes suddenly swept around the apartment and he snapped his fingers three times. He looked knowingly at me. "Microphones?" I looked at him blankly, not answering. He shrugged. "Well, it would be natural."

With the door closed it had become stuffy in the apartment, and time for a break. Drinks in hand, we stepped out onto the still-sunlit balcony in the back, away from public view. Abruptly, without context, Nosenko asked, "Did Golitsyn tell you about the Finnish president?"

This was a surprise. A CIA visitor to Switzerland had told me that KGB Major Anatoly Golitsyn had defected in Finland a few months earlier, though this was still kept secret from the public. I shook my head and admitted that I wouldn't know. What I didn't tell him is that I was aware that Finnish President Urho Kekkonen was well known for his friendly accommodation to Soviet interests in his country. It did not take vast insight to imagine what a KGB officer there might have said about the relationship.

We stepped back into the apartment and sat down. I refilled Nosenko's glass. After some more talk he glanced at his watch. "I should go now, so Guk won't wonder where I've been. But I'll come back day after tomorrow."

I promised to have his money ready by then. We agreed to meet again in the late afternoon, the best time for him to be absent from the delegation.

We rose and were moving toward the door when Nosenko suddenly blurted, "I know how Popov was caught."

This was a jolt. Lieutenant Colonel Pyotr Semyonovich Popov, a GRU officer, had for seven years delivered the highest-level Soviet military and political intelligence to CIA. His arrest in Moscow in October 1959—and his execution afterward—was a shattering blow. In the three years since then, as far as I knew, CIA had not discovered how things had gone so wrong. The sudden, unexplained loss of a vitally important agent always ignites an extensive investigation. The most closely examined possibility was that the spy was betrayed from within the operating service.

Popov's death held special meaning for me. For the three years after he first came to us in Vienna in late 1952, I had supported the operation as one of the four officers most intimately involved.

I stopped and faced him. "Tell me how."

But Nosenko backed off just as abruptly as he had raised the subject. He shook his head. "No, no, I don't have time now. Next time."

"It won't take but a minute," I said, but Nosenko could not be moved. This was another surprise. Moments earlier he had not seemed in a hurry. Now, after exploding a bombshell, he had no time at all.

He opened the door. With a quick peek into the corridor, he whispered, "Next time," and disappeared down the stairs.

I closed the door and muttered, "Damn!"—not just because I had failed to get the answer, but because I knew only too well the chilling fact of secret operations: there may never be a "next time."

CHAPTER **2**

Getting Under Way

When the door closed behind Yuri Nosenko I hardly caught my breath before jotting notes on highlights and my initial impressions for a priority cable to Headquarters. It would go with an extra code word to limit its distribution there. This affair was promising enough to merit special security precautions.

First, I noted, Nosenko gave every indication that he was really a KGB officer. Only an insider could have spoken so easily about secret Soviet places, KGB people unknown to the general public, and secret operations like Popov. This, to me, seemed to establish his bona fides. Second, he had not yet indicated any significant interest in or access to military or political information. I would mention some of the specifics Nosenko had reported and close with the suggestion that Headquarters pack a more fluent Russian speaker onto the next flight to Geneva. At no time had we had the slightest communication problem; he never had trouble finding words and never had to ask me to repeat anything. But I did not want to risk losing nuances when he slipped into Russian.

Headquarters' reply came within hours. The central file held no record on Nosenko other than a single trip to the Caribbean with a Soviet group. There was nothing on him personally nor had any other KGB defector ever mentioned his name.

The good news was that Headquarters was sending George Kisevalter. This burly, warmhearted case officer had the gift of rapport with strangers, and his idiomatic Russian was a notable plus in dealings with Soviet contacts like Popov, whom he had handled in Vienna (where we worked together).

George was born in Saint Petersburg in 1910. Six years later he and his mother accompanied his father, an official of the tsarist government, to Washington on a munitions procurement mission. After Lenin's coup d'état, Kisevalter's father prudently decided to remain in the United States. As a child, George showed such talent at chess that it was not until his sophomore year in engineering that he decided against attempting a chess career. A World War Two assignment as a U.S. army liaison officer with Soviet officers arranging American arms shipments to the USSR erased most of the tsarist flavor from Kisevalter's Russian and brought him abreast of the language's postrevolutionary, apparatchik, and military slang.

George reached the Geneva safe house scant hours before Nosenko, by our prearrangement, was to be knocking at our door. Fortunately, Kisevalter was a quick study and rapidly grasped the details of my hasty briefing.

To be available for unscheduled visits George and I bedded down in the now cramped safe house. Between the sessions we had time to discuss the latest news from the Soviet Union, catch up on Headquarters gossip, and reminisce about our days in Vienna.

By the time the conference ended in early June 1962—only a week after Nosenko first made contact with us—we had squeezed in four more meetings with our new source. His conference duties, which he described only in vague terms, seemed close to nonexistent. He was available for sessions that lasted from slightly less than an hour to three hours. The atmosphere was relaxed and loosened by intervals for drinks and snacks. The talk shifted easily between Russian and English.

Nosenko told us more about his family. His father had been Minister of Shipbuilding until his death six years earlier. His mother was still alive, as was a younger brother. He himself had studied at MGIMO, the Moscow State Institute of International Relations, where he had learned his English. He had done military service in naval intelligence in the Far East and on the Baltic. He said his present wife, the mother of the two daughters, was his second, though he later corrected this to third. He had divorced the previous one while on his naval station on the Pacific.

And in the course of our first meeting with George, Nosenko told us how Popov was caught.

"It was surveillance," he said. "Our guys were routinely tailing George

Winters, an attaché at your embassy. Some time in early 1959 they saw him drop a letter into a street mailbox. It was written in Russian with a false return address and addressed to Popov.

"That was all we needed—diplomats don't post innocent letters to GRU officers. Popov was put under twenty-four-hour surveillance. Within a few days they followed him to a clandestine meeting with [Russell] Langelle, the American Embassy security officer. They arrested Popov a few days later, interrogated and got his confession, and ran him for a while as a double agent before closing the operation down. Langelle was arrested moments after Popov handed him some reports the KGB had concocted. As usual in such cases, they tried to recruit him. Langelle refused and got kicked out on his diplomatic ass. Popov was tried and shot."

Here was poignant confirmation for Kisevalter, who knew that Popov had told the same story in a note he surreptitiously passed to Langelle a month before the fatal meeting.

"Yes," George told me after the meeting, "Winters did mail that damned letter, and that was never published in the press. This guy really has the inside story."

George and I had debriefed many a source in our careers and knew the areas of primary national intelligence and counterintelligence interest. Headquarters intervened only once, with a list of names and code names brought to Geneva by a Headquarters security officer. We weren't told their origin, and I learned only later that they were follow-ups to leads given by the recent KGB defector Anatoly Golitsyn. Nosenko drew a blank on all of them.

"We're breaking into a lot of embassies in Moscow," Nosenko said. "We have great teams that know how to get in, open locked safes, take the stuff out and photograph it on the spot and put it back without one thing showing that they'd ever been there." He named the Swedish and Indonesian embassies as victims of these practices.

"And they plant mikes, too."

"Any in our embassy?" George asked.

"Yes. I've read transcripts of conversations in maybe ten different offices. I know who was talking, so I can tell you some offices where the mikes must be." He named two.

"Do you know how and when they were installed? Their exact placement?"

"No, that's impossible. No one knows that except the guys who plant them. It's their business. We just read transcripts and sometimes hear tapes of what's being said."

This confirmed what CIA knew about the KGB's precautions in handling the take from phone taps and microphones and other eavesdropping devices. We knew that transcripts were hand-carried in special folders to the few officers having direct need to know. In fact, I was surprised that Nosenko or anyone else could have read transcripts or had occasion to listen to tapes from so many different emplacements. No one but a high supervisor could have such access, and this, I reasoned, testified to Nosenko's claim to have had overall supervision of the American Embassy section during the two years preceding his departure for Geneva.

"One thing I can tell you for sure. We have no microphones at all in the new wing of the embassy. [That was the north wing, built in the late 1950s.] We wanted to plant them during the construction, but Khrushchev nixed it. He was afraid they'd be discovered and spoil relations that were improving just then."

KGB operatives were continuing, Nosenko confirmed, their decades-long efforts to lure potential sources—diplomats, journalists, businessmen, scholars, students, tourists—into compromising situations involving sexual indiscretions, illegal currency transactions, or overfriendly, casual revelations of sensitive information. Victims were usually confronted with threats of disclosure or arrest and public trial and forced into cooperation, while others were treated leniently and eased into a sort of tacit dependency.

Through other agencies—in all of which the KGB kept its hand regarding personnel and contacts with foreigners—the KGB offered Westerners bait such as travel permits to restricted areas, rights to hunt rare game, choice interviews, and news scoops. It offered them enticing opportunities to compromise themselves by indiscretions—sexual, homosexual, financial, and other.

Much of what Nosenko reported along these lines was, like the presence of microphones, widely known to Western intelligence services, which had been coping with such operations for decades. But when he provided names and details, his data were valuable. Some checked out against reports in our files and added to our respect for his inside knowledge.

"Gribanov himself," he said (referring to the chief of the Second Chief Directorate, Oleg Mikhailovich Gribanov), "is dealing with an important

French businessman. The guy's name is Saar Demichel. He lives in Paris and has a lot of business with the Soviet Union."

"And the French ambassador, too," he added. Maurice Dejean was compromised, Nosenko said, in an adulterous affair with a KGB woman agent and brought into a relationship with Gribanov. The KGB had lured a Canadian ambassador into a compromising situation from which he extricated himself by friendly cooperation with the KGB—in this case, Gribanov again. Nosenko did not name the ambassador, whom we later identified as John Watkins.

Nosenko named some American journalists in contact with the KGB in a sort of informal barter system. "We help them and they help us," he said, remaining vague about the extent to which they were wittingly cooperating with the KGB.

He paused, emptied his glass of scotch, and glanced significantly toward the bottles on the sideboard. He showed no effects of this drinking, no facial flush, glassy eyes, or slurred speech—and not the slightest problem in understanding or expressing himself. He thus upheld a proud Russian tradition which George and I, cautious to keep alert, made no effort to emulate.

I filled his glass and was turning to hand it to him when I heard him say to George, "We recruited a member of the British naval attaché's office."

I sat down, picked up my pad, and leaned forward. "Tell us what you can."

"Our guys recognized him as a homosexual and gave him a 'friend' who worked for us. They threatened to expose him and got him to agree to work for us. It was a firm recruitment."

"Do you know the name, any details at all?"

"All I know is it happened about five years ago, maybe a bit more. But you can find him. He's in touch with the rezidentura in London. He's working in the Admiralty."

"Who told you?"

"I don't remember. Someone in the British Department."

Nosenko flicked his cigarette ash into the ashtray in front of him. "Homosexuals," he said, momentarily lost in thought. "We have a bunch of them working for us, ready for jobs like this. I recruited and handled about six of the ones we used against foreign targets—in fact, I'm considered a kind of specialist in this. I've been handling 'Shmelev' and 'Grigoriy' for more than four years."

"What were their names?"

"Guys I recruited. Homos. I can't think of their names right now. Anyway, it doesn't matter. What does matter is that we did trap some Americans. I can give you names." Over the course of these meetings he did, in fact, name a professor, a tourist-agency operator, and a half-dozen others.

In an early meeting Nosenko volunteered details of the KGB's work against Western intelligence inside the USSR. "We have all kinds of ways to spot your intelligence work," he said with pride. "Our surveillance teams are first class."

He paused, thinking of examples. "Real high-tech stuff we've developed. There's a powder we call 'Metka' that's put into the pockets of American diplomats. It leaves a chemical trace on any envelope they'd carry for posting on the street. Censorship picks up the trace."

Nosenko also described a clear liquid which, when brushed on the top of automobiles, allowed watchers at high points in the city to spot and track suspect vehicles. And a substance, code-named "Neptune-80," which, when applied to the soles of the shoes of surveillance targets, left a scent that dogs, handled by the surveillance team, could track from far behind.

Household employees of diplomats were taught to use these chemicals. Like all Soviet nationals working in foreign embassies, these workers were supplied by the UPDK, the Soviet Foreign Ministry's Directorate for Assistance to the Diplomatic Corps. It served in effect as a sort of KGB employment agency. Through the UPDK and its own officers in its ranks, the Second Chief Directorate could place informants and agents in the form of babysitters, housemaids, and administrative clerks, as sexy and lissome or as buxom and efficient as the situation might demand. These agents would report—or provoke—personal vulnerabilities of foreign embassy personnel upon which the KGB might base a recruitment.

Soviet technicians had managed the difficult task of rigging microphone transmitters into ashtrays and vases that could easily be placed at restaurant tables to which likely target personalities might be escorted. "I remember one such instance," he volunteered without our asking. "We taped the conversation of the American assistant naval attaché, Lieutenant Colonel Dulacki [later to be a general in Vietnam], as he lunched in a Moscow restaurant with the Indonesian military attaché, Zepp."

He paused. I took the opportunity to jot it down. "How do you spell that name?"

"Z-e-p-p."

As sometimes happens in secret operations, this inconsequential question was to become of considerable importance.

"As deputy chief of the American Embassy section, I myself had two personal tasks in addition to helping supervise all the other work. These were our top-priority targets, the embassy security officer and the code clerks. They were so important that they deserved my personal attention."

Nosenko leaned slightly forward, as if to emphasize the importance of what he was saying.

"We put a tremendous coverage on the security officer, [John] Abidian, following him everywhere. Because Abidian replaced [Russell] Langelle, who had been CIA's contact man with Popov in Moscow, we figured that by watching him we might uncover another Popov."

He shook his head, disgustedly. "We got nowhere. Surveillance didn't see him go anywhere interesting. And all we got was something his maid found in his bedroom."

He paused with a smile. "Some discovery—the panties of an American girl who occupied an apartment in the same building. How could that help us? Abidian was single."

Nosenko's other personal responsibility was supervising all the KGB's work against American Embassy code clerks. These operations were handled by case officers Vadim Kosolapov and Gennady Gryaznov, and they were two busy men. Nosenko named two code clerks approached for recruitment during his time in the job, whom I'll call "K" and "Will." Nosenko himself had approached K on the street in what we in CIA would call a "cold" approach—a blunt offer made without the usual careful development and staging. In the other operation Gryaznov had brought in a Finnish businessman to help with the KGB's development of Will. Nosenko had befriended the Finn, named Preisfreund. But the recruitment attempt had failed.

"We never managed to recruit any American code clerk," Nosenko said. "The closest we ever came was 'Andrey.'" He was referring to the cipher machine mechanic whom he had mentioned in our first meeting.

Kisevalter remembered that CIA's first representative in Moscow, years before, had reported that the KGB tried to recruit him. He asked Nosenko, "Do you know about the approach to Ed Smith?"

"Sure," he responded without hesitation, "I even took part in it. We gave him the code name 'Ryzhiy' [Redhead]." He paused and chuckled. "We used to call him 'Ryzhiy Khui.'" Turning to me he translated (unnecessarily in this case), "red-headed prick. He went to bed with his Russian maid, our agent, and we staged a scene that made it look like a criminal offense. You know."

Yes, we knew. The KGB did not always use the classical approach of presenting, after the event, clandestinely taken pictures or films that would compromise a marriage or a career. Sometimes, for shock effect, an indignant "husband" (or wife) or local authorities would break into the love nest at a key moment and threaten punishment under Soviet laws. A benevolent "uncle" might appear in time to smooth things out with the law—if the Westerner would demonstrate his friendship toward his hosts.

We waited, expectantly.

"Well," Nosenko shrugged, "nothing doing. Ryzhiy refused, reported it to the ambassador, and was pulled back to the States. Case closed."

This squared with what Kisevalter knew and testified once again to Nosenko's inside knowledge and authority. He grew further in our esteem.

In Geneva Nosenko had contact with local KGB rezidentura officers in addition to his pal Yuri Guk, and passed along to us a few tidbits of information he had picked up from them. One had been indiscreet enough to let slip something a traveler like Nosenko had no need to know. Boris Belitsky, a Soviet radio journalist ostensibly working as a spy for CIA when outside the USSR, was actually a double agent loyal to the KGB. Though Nosenko, merely a visiting delegation security officer, naturally knew no details, Kisevalter and I knew that Belitsky had, in fact, been met here in Geneva recently by his CIA handlers. By revealing to us an active double agent Nosenko confirmed that he was the real thing.

All of this would have merited more detailed probing, but we had only the time he could safely get free and we never knew which meeting might be the last. We had to move rapidly over each subject to ensure that others, possibly more important, would not go untouched. Our first question was always, "How long can you stay?" Whatever his answer, we were ready, for we had prioritized our questions to fit various time frames while leaving time, we hoped, for any newsworthy intelligence Nosenko might himself volunteer.

Given Nosenko's potential importance we scrupulously taped every meeting in toto, to confirm and amplify the notes we were jotting down during the meetings.

In one session Nosenko told us he urgently wanted to obtain certain medicines that might alleviate his daughter Oksana's asthma. They were not available in Moscow and he hadn't been able to find them in Geneva. This was a man we wanted to keep happy, so our urgent cable caused the Agency to scramble its worldwide assets to find the obscure potions and whisk them to Geneva.

Nothing this good could last forever, and only a few days after Nosenko had first contacted CIA the conference ended. It was a pity he had waited so long—but of course it was only because of his need to replenish his operational fund just before departure that he had come to us at all. Now he was to return with the others to the USSR.

Nosenko's new KGB section-chief job, he said, should offer opportunities for further travel abroad, so to motivate him to contact us we told him that a salary of $25,000 a year would be deposited for him in a Western bank account.

There remained the considerable problem of being sure that Nosenko could promptly let us know when he next would be in the West, and that we could make contact. The system had to be simple, easily memorized, and never committed to paper. Cryptic notes might be as sure a death warrant as a clear-text document. I devised this system: on arriving in the West he was to send a telegram signed "George" to a safe address in the United States, which Headquarters supplied in timely fashion. Two days later (with alternates) he would be met at 7:45 p.m. in front of the first movie theater listed alphabetically in the local phone book of the city from which the telegram had been sent.

With a toast to safety and to future meetings, and a sentimental Slavic embrace, George and I saw Nosenko to the door and waved him off. His plane, and the remaining delegates, took off for Moscow the next day.

CHAPTER 3

A Visit to Headquarters

"Good stuff, I'm really pleased," said Jack Maury, the Soviet Division chief, greeting me in his office on the fifth floor of the bright new CIA headquarters in Langley, Virginia, which I was now seeing and entering for the first time. "And it's a good running start on your assignment here in the fall," he added in his soft Virginia accent—a welcome confirmation that I was still booked to become chief of the division's counterintelligence section.

Within hours of Nosenko's departure for Moscow, Maury had summoned George Kisevalter and me to Headquarters. Because there had not been time to transcribe the hours of taped recordings of our sessions with Nosenko, we were ordered to take separate flights, each to carry his own notes and a duplicate set of tapes. This rather grim security precaution was evidence that Headquarters agreed with our initial evaluation of the operation.

"Is he for real?" Maury's first question went to the heart of the matter.

George answered for us both. "There's no sign to the contrary. He sure talks the way only a KGB man could. We knew some of the stuff he told us, and it all sounded straight."

"But why in hell did he take that kind of risk for a few hundred bucks?"

"I don't know," George said. "Pete [my colleagues never used "Tennent," my given name] and I have gone all around the barn talking about it and we still haven't come up with an answer. He didn't want to take a franc more than that. Maybe he's mad at someone over there. Maybe he just likes to take chances. Obviously, we didn't ask him."

We had not, in fact, gotten much further than that in pondering this strange aspect of the case. I added, "There must be more to this than a few bucks. Well, we'll take a good shot at that next time. For now we'll just have to live with it."

"And count ourselves lucky," Jack said.

George and I sat on what was certainly the only eight-foot, custom-made sofa in the new headquarters building. I later learned that it had been constructed for a long-ago defector who had convinced his Washington handlers that he did his best thinking when lying flat on his back, legs fully extended. As far as I ever learned, this worn chunk of furniture was the defector's only surviving contribution to Western intelligence.

We ran through the highlights of the Geneva meetings and responded to Jack's eager and probing questions.

Finally Maury summed it up. "This case has potential. Let's keep a tight lid on it. No more than five people here know about Nosenko.[1] Everyone thinks you're here, Pete, in connection with your assignment later this year. Let's keep it that way—strictly for our eyes only."

This raised the Nosenko operation to the rare level of the most sensitive and most productive operations on CIA's roster. Aside from the officers and clerks involved in handling these operations in the field or at Headquarters, only the most senior officers in the direct line of command even knew of their existence or, except in veiled form, of their intelligence product. In the Nosenko case the line of command went from Maury to Richard Helms, the deputy director of Plans (later to be renamed Operations), who reported to John McCone, then Director of Central Intelligence. Because this case involved penetration of a hostile intelligence service, James Angleton, chief of the Counterintelligence Staff (though outside the direct line), was also in the picture.

The source of intelligence obtained from agents at this level was masked to protect the source and to hinder speculation about how he got the information. In the White House the National Security Advisor would be informed, and possibly the president. Depending on the substance the Secretaries of State and Defense would be briefed in general terms. In no event was the source's name ever disclosed.

Maury's next question seemed rhetorical. "Should we consider trying to contact him inside?"

"Absolutely not," George said. "He left no doubt about it and he knows better than most how well they've got our people covered in Moscow."

"Yes," I said. "He made a big point of what hotshots their surveillants are and the state-of-the-art technical gimmicks they use. If we barge ahead and try something inside, even if we could pull it off safely, it would likely turn him off."

George added, "He knows how to reach us whenever he gets out."

Jack nodded. "Agree. I just wanted to hear it from you two."

Jack's secretary brought in a coffeepot and a tray of cups. Kisevalter gave a sly wink and motioned toward the porcelain cups, indeed a big step up from the government-standard Styrofoam tumblers.

Jack glanced significantly at George and said, "I think now is the time to bring Pete into the 'Hero' operation. He'll be having lots to do on it when he gets here in the fall."

George nodded, evidently prepared, and turned to me on the couch. "We've got another Popov."

That was stunning news, as he knew it would be. It meant another GRU officer had become a source of rare importance to CIA's mission.

George took a deep breath. "'Hero' is a GRU colonel assigned to the GNTK [which he rightly assumed I knew was the State Committee of Science and Technology] and has fantastic access to top-secret military data. We've been meeting with him since last year."

Colonel Oleg Vladimirovich Penkovsky had "walked in." After unsuccessfully trying to gain contact with American Intelligence through two American students, a Canadian geologist, and the Canadian commercial attaché, he finally in March 1961 got the help of Greville Wynne, a visiting British trade delegate with whom he had official contact during Wynne's visits in the course of British-Soviet cooperation in science and technology.

"Wynne immediately reported it to MI6," George said. "We had been in touch with them on this matter ever since Penkovsky first tried to get to us, so they informed us and we agreed to handle it jointly. They set up the first contact in London when Penkovsky came on official business for GNTK—with GRU assignments, of course. I met him with Joe Bulik and two guys from MI6."

The joint team met Penkovsky in a series of meetings in the Mount Royal Hotel near Hyde Park. Penkovsky then returned to Moscow where, two weeks later, he met Wynne. In August Penkovsky again traveled to

London and in late September to Paris. On both occasions he met repeatedly with the joint handling team.

Since the time Penkovsky returned to Moscow from Paris in early October 1961 every one of his five applications for further official trips abroad, though sponsored and backed by the GRU, had been turned down at the last minute—by the KGB. He was given to understand that this was merely a provisional situation, pending the KGB's clarification of doubts about the true fate of his father, a White Army officer killed in 1919 during the Russian Civil War. For some unknown reason this old question, long ago laid to rest, had been revived.

"That's worrying us," Jack said. "But it might mean nothing serious, because Penkovsky's still in his job in Moscow and making brush passes, handing microfilm rolls to our contact people in both embassies. It's great stuff: missile manuals, descriptions of current Soviet military strategy from a top-secret archive, details of weapons, and scores of other subjects."

This was exciting news. Kisevalter chimed in with details and was boiling enthusiastically along when Jack suggested that the full briefing could wait until my return when I could get into the files.

"Before you leave, Pete, you'll want to look into some new information we've got. There's been an important defection from the KGB. He's here in Washington."

This was Anatoly Golitsyn, the KGB officer whose name Nosenko had tossed at me on the balcony in Geneva. He had defected to CIA in Helsinki six months before Nosenko had walked in.

"And do check in with Jim Angleton. He's aware of Nosenko's contact with us but he'll want to have your details. He has all the Golitsyn data, too. You could read that here, but you might as well get it from Jim."

James Angleton, chief of CIA's Counterintelligence Staff, was not above an occasional bit of drama, but his office was less a stage setting than it appeared. The drawn Venetian blinds covering the wide windows behind his desk were a shield against the summer sun and not a dramatic artifact. A table lamp on the long oak desk provided the necessary light. A pile of thick files on each end of the desk framed the scene.

Angleton's bony thinness emphasized his sharp-hewn features. With his piercing eyes behind horn-rimmed spectacles, and his large, expressive mouth, it was not hard to understand why one of CIA's early leaders, thinking about a design for the new intelligence agency's official seal, pointed at Angleton and exclaimed "Hah! I have it! That face!" In the event, other designs prevailed for the seal, but Angleton's striking appearance, his habit of rather formal dress in dark colors, the air of mastery of recondite matters that hung about him, and the quick mind with which he absorbed and synthesized facts into complex perceptions embodied CIA counterintelligence of that time.

Angleton and I had built a relationship of friendly mutual trust during the years when I had supervised operations against Polish Intelligence. There had been the long, Martini-eased lunches for which he was well known, and dinner parties. Charades were often played in those days, and I still remember the desperate antics of one guest trying to convey an obscure line from Jim's favorite poet, T. S. Eliot, "clot the bedded axle tree." Jim had a select inner circle of friends, including Dick Helms and other veterans of the wartime Office of Strategic Services (OSS) that he had served in its counterintelligence branch, X-2. That I was among them despite my relatively recent arrival on the CIA scene I owed to a warm introduction years earlier by William Hood, who had been my boss in CIA's Vienna Station in the early 1950s.

Hood cared deeply for the counterintelligence aspect of American Intelligence—handling its clandestine operations with realistic appreciation of the hazards, while exploiting the openings offered by the clandestine work of our adversaries. In Vienna he had recognized and fostered my interest in this field and brought me into this personal relationship with the otherwise closeted and very busy counterintelligence staff chief. My confident relations with Angleton were to play a role in what was to come. It was no small matter at the CIA to get the attention of the right senior officers to the right matters.

Jim listened with evident interest to my account of the meetings with Nosenko and was upbeat about the possibilities. All the while his attention seemed fixed on penciling an elaborate geometric design on notepaper. As I finished, Jim dropped his pencil into his out-tray, glanced approvingly at his completed doodle, tore it to bits, and dropped the remains in the classified trash box at the corner of his desk.

He reinforced Maury's suggestion that for future meetings with Nosenko I would do well to take aboard the Golitsyn data.

Jim summoned Bertha, nominally his secretary but in actuality his de facto office manager and personal assistant, handed me an armload of files, and asked her to take me across the hallway to what he referred to as the counterintelligence conference room, where I could study the new defector's reports in complete privacy.

Conference room, indeed. It was windowless, with barely space for the worn table and six government-issue, straight-back chairs. I suspected that before its christening as a conference room it had been a comfortable closet. The fascinating sweep and detail of Golitsyn's revelations offset the absent creature comfort. My hours there were, as Maury and Angleton had foreseen, an essential background for any future Nosenko meetings.

But the reports were also unsettling. They contained repeated references to incidents and operations that Nosenko had just described in Geneva. Reading one after another I began to feel uneasy. I knew from experience that any two colleagues working in different sections of an intelligence service might glean knowledge of the same secret operations. But it stretched coincidence that two officers from such separated elements of the KGB would both know of so many, especially of a kind unlikely to be widely known within a service as tightly disciplined as the KGB. It seemed even more of a coincidence that one of these overlapping sources arrived almost on the heels of the other. And strikingly, and all too often, Nosenko's versions differed from Golitsyn's with the effect of dismissing or diverting suspicions that the earlier reports had evoked.

Golitsyn was the first source to reveal—five years after the fact—Vladislav Kovshuk's trip, the same trip that Nosenko had described at our first meeting. Had it been known at the time that the chief of KGB operations against the American Embassy in Moscow had traveled to Washington, the question would have screamed—as it still did—"Why?" It seemed more than fortuitous that shortly after Golitsyn's revelation, Kovshuk's deputy Nosenko had come and explained that long-ago trip—authoritatively, but in a banal, almost benign light.

Concerning the KGB discovery of CIA's contact with Pyotr Popov, Golitsyn's version did not square with Nosenko's. Golitsyn placed it so much earlier that it could not have resulted from the KGB's chance surveillance of a diplomat mailing a letter in Moscow.

Here, too, in these files was the KGB recruitment of the British naval attaché office member in Moscow. Golitsyn in KGB Headquarters had been handling reports from spies in NATO, and among these papers were secret documents from that office. So accurately had he described them after his defection that already, according to a note in this file, the British were on the heels of the traitor, having narrowed their list of suspects to three. Nosenko had given us something we were about to learn anyway.

There were many more similarities. Golitsyn reported that a certain

Canadian ambassador had been recruited. Nosenko reported the same case. Golitsyn, while in Vienna, had known that Gribanov came there to meet an agent, a French businessman. The French had identified him as François Saar Demichel—whom Nosenko had just named to us. Golitsyn had studied the file of the KGB's double agent case against CIA using Soviet radio journalist Boris Belitsky. Golitsyn would have had to sign, per KGB regulations, for accessing it, and after his defection KGB investigators dredged up any such files. Quite a coincidence that a few months later an unidentified KGB man in Geneva is seized by such a fit of indiscretion that he tells Nosenko, a visiting delegation watchdog, about that tightly held operation. All in all, this was hard to believe.

Even more striking was the next coincidence, fact for fact. Golitsyn recounted a visit to his KGB residency in Helsinki by Gennady Gryaznov, a KGB officer from Moscow who was targeting the American Embassy there. To facilitate his development for recruitment of an American code clerk (unnamed), Gryaznov wanted to borrow an agent. Because the American Embassy restricted socialization between its code clerks and Russians, he knew that this Finn agent, a businessman who traveled occasionally to Moscow, could more easily make friends with the American target. Golitsyn agreed and lent Moscow the agent—a certain Preisfreund.

Preisfreund? That's an unusual name for a Finn, and easy to remember. Nosenko not only had met Preisfreund but had made a drinking buddy of him in Moscow, the only such foreign friend Nosenko had mentioned. In Geneva he had recounted the same operation against the code clerk, whom he named (and whom I here call "Will").

It was only on the outcome of the venture that Golitsyn and Nosenko differed. Gryaznov later told Golitsyn that the KGB's attempt succeeded. But Nosenko reported—having been personally involved and supervising Gryaznov—that the operation had failed. Of course, I thought, Gryaznov may have simply been exaggerating or inventing to impress his colleague Golitsyn. But even so, the coincidence of such parallel reporting by two volunteer sources from widely separated elements of the KGB was enough to stir an ugly question.

On top of all that: I now saw that what I had thought to be Nosenko's unique and fresh information about KGB operations against tourists in the USSR had already been exposed. Golitsyn had reported in great detail on this subject, having had on-the-job training in early 1959 in the Second Chief Directorate's Tourist Department and long talks with an officer of the department. In addition, Golitsyn had received at his rezidentura in Helsinki a KGB Moscow study dated 7 April 1961 detailing its work against foreign visitors to the USSR—and had given CIA a copy.

It was in that tiny room, poring over thick files and busily penciling page after page of notes on a lined yellow pad, that doubts began to arise that had not occurred to me in Geneva.

Might the KGB have sent Nosenko to CIA to divert Golitsyn's leads?

On the face of it, that seemed hardly conceivable. The Soviet bloc counterintelligence services had been sending scores of false refugees to the West to mislead us, but never in the KGB's forty-five years—at least, to my knowledge—had they sent one directly out of their own halls. To do that, I thought, they must have powerful reasons. Deception is risky: if the intended dupe recognizes it he may ask himself why the opposition went to such a bother, and may perceive the truth it was designed to hide.

The morning after my final night of study, after long reflection that had left me little sleep, I went back to Angleton.

"Thanks, Jim. You were right. I needed this information. But at the same time, I've got to tell you something. We may have a problem."

I told him about the curious coincidences and persistent overlapping of the two men's reports.

Jim frowned, thought for a moment, shook his head and said, "Please jot down these points for me. I want to look carefully at this."

The next day I gave Bertha an envelope with my handwritten list of the most significant fourteen points of parallel reporting. I could have listed more, but it did not seem worth mentioning the many events and people that both sources had reported but that any two KGB officers could be expected to know.

That afternoon Jim called me back to his office. "You may be on to something here," he said. "As a matter of fact, Golitsyn himself said he expected the KGB to make some effort to divert the leads he could give us. Maybe that's what we've got on our hands now."

We agreed that there wasn't enough data to make a case and that Nosenko was to be handled as if there were no doubts. "Just leave this with me," Jim said. "We can look deeper into it when you come on duty this fall." He shook his head and added, "Pity. You'd be in for a medal for this, but that wouldn't be appropriate in this new light, would it?"

Indeed it would not. I shrugged. "Easy come, easy go."

Jim tossed another pencil aside and stood to shake hands. "Meanwhile, let's not tell anyone else about this problem."

"I have to tell Jack," I said.

"Of course."

Jack Maury had too many other operations on his mind to have absorbed the details of Golitsyn's reporting and he cared little about the practices of Soviet counterintelligence. I painted the picture for him, but because it was too early to ring alarm bells I closed on a high note. "What the hell, there's probably some innocent explanation. We should be able to clear it up next time we meet Nosenko."

"Good." Jack seemed relieved. Like many other senior officers, he disliked dealing with the minutiae of counterintelligence and viewed them as time-wasting impediments to what he considered a different and higher priority, the task of collecting "positive" intelligence. He was happy to let me cope with those details.

"Okay, you work it out with Jim and we'll go on handling the case as if it's straight. George seems to be happy with it. If he should mention any doubts of his own, I'll let you know."

Three months later my wife, Maria, and I packed up in Bern and one morning in September 1962 loaded our two little daughters into a borrowed car and drove to Zurich. There we caught a Pan Am flight that would carry us to the States to two months' home leave—and then the Headquarters job that would put me athwart CIA's worldwide counterintelligence operations against the KGB and GRU.

CHAPTER **4**

En Route

Looking down at the clouds over the Atlantic as my five-year-old daughter Christina dropped into sleep at my side, I wondered how she would adapt to her new life in Washington—and how I would, too. My thoughts ran over the life and professional experience that had brought me here and—I hoped—prepared me for the challenges toward which I was flying.

Like most lives and careers, mine had been bumped into new directions by chance encounters and unforeseen events. But one direction seemed foreordained: government service—and in my time that was bound to be military.

World War Two narrowed the "career" choices available to my generation to branch of military service ("for the duration," which then seemed forever). For my two brothers and me that choice came naturally; our lives had been spent with and by the navy. Mine literally began there, for I was born within the grounds of the U.S. Naval Academy in Annapolis.

My father was a career naval officer. His elder brother, who had preceded him at the U.S. Naval Academy (and there become one of the first of Navy's football stars), was killed in action in the war with Spain in 1898. The destroyer *Bagley* (the third named for him) drew some of the first blood of our war with Japan, downing attacking planes at Pearl Harbor. The husband of my father and uncle's sister, my Uncle Joe, was Josephus Daniels, Secretary of the Navy through the First World War, who was well remembered for having banned the drinking of alcohol on naval ships. His Assistant Secretary was Franklin D. Roosevelt, and he is the only person whom FDR, all his life, called "Chief" and one of the few who had the president's blessing to call him "Franklin."

My great-uncles William D. Leahy and Albert P. Niblack were admirals. The destroyer *Niblack* fired the first American shots (depth charges) at the Germans in World War Two, ten months before the United States formally joined the war. My brothers followed the tradition and became the first siblings to wear four stars each. Seven warships, from frigates to cruisers, have borne the names of my father and uncles. A newspaper article called our family tradition the "naviest" of all.

The sea attracted me from my earliest years. The family moved from one port or naval facility to the next, and the ships of the navy became as familiar as old friends. In those permissive peacetime days I was taken out to sea on one of the first PT boats, a destroyer, a minelayer, and an oil tanker. As the war in Europe loomed and America built up its fleet, I was watching the launchings of warships in the Mare Island Navy Yard in California.

When the Japanese attacked Pearl Harbor I was nearby in Honolulu, just sixteen and in my last year of high school. Some noises I heard from the Manoa Valley were probably the engines of the second wave of Japanese planes. That night Dad—oil-spattered—returned briefly from Pearl Harbor to tell my mother and me that he was alive. Two weeks later, after swearing us to secrecy—the extent of American losses was long hidden from the enemy—he took us to see the terrible scene, the wreckage of ships we had known where friends had died. I see them now almost as vividly as then. We drove to the edge of the narrow channel opposite the point where the battleship *Nevada* had been beached after her valiant effort to leave harbor, conned in this emergency by a young ensign, our friend Joe Taussig, who lost a leg in the action. The *California* tilted on the shallow bottom and behind her was a shocking sight, the upturned hull of *Oklahoma*. *West Virginia*, her superstructure blackened by fire, had sunk the few feet to the shallow bottom, our friend Captain Mervyn S. Bennion having died on her bridge. Moored inboard of her and thus protected from the torpedoes she took was my father's flagship, *Tennessee*. (I still have some family letters he had been keeping in a tin box in his quarters aboard, the edges singed brown from the fire that caught from the explosion of the broken and blackened *Arizona*, just aft.) The *Arizona* was still holding, and was to do so for generations, the remains of some of its crewmen who died, including our longtime family friend Rear Admiral Isaac C. Kidd. The old minelayer *Oglala*, on which I had gone to sea, had capsized. I still remember my rage and frustration—and urge for revenge.

In my life, as in all others, family experiences shaped my character. My parents were warm and supportive, my father an example of strength of character and decency, my mother of self-discipline and loyalty and with an impish sense of fun. As a naval family we were spared the economic blows of the depression of the 1930s and so never had to face hunger or financial ruin.

Our life was peripatetic, as my father shifted from one assignment to the next, and I spent the last two years of high school in four different, far separate towns. This lifestyle taught me to adapt to new surroundings, new friends, and changing rules—no doubt creating flexibility but also a certain detachment.

I had to strive harder than most because I was usually dealing with older contemporaries. For that I had my first girlfriend to thank. When I was four years old we lived on a naval base where my frequent playmate was Ida, the girl next door. But she was a few significant months older, and one fateful day in early September 1930 she came by to break the bad news that she was going off to school. "Off" wasn't far because the base school lay only a few hundred yards from our row of houses. Seeing no reason for this separation, though I was too young to start that year, I tagged along and, when we got to the school, announced that I too was enrolling. The teacher, nonplussed, phoned my mother, who thought I had been playing around the house. To my delight she said, "Oh well, if you're willing, let him stay."

No one then knew that war was coming and that this early start would impact my later life. I was already in college when I reached the age of seventeen and enlisted in the marines (my eyesight not quite sharp enough for the U.S. Naval Academy's standards of the time). At that time the marines were starting a long-range program to provide a steady input of junior officers over the coming months. Enlistees from college would be assigned (with the rank of private) to certain universities where in Marine units they would, while continuing their studies, learn basic military practice and discipline, close-order drill, and familiarization with weapons. After each semester the most academically advanced students from these "V-12" units moved on to boot camp at Parris Island, South Carolina, combat training at Camp Lejeune in North Carolina, and platoon commanders' school in Quantico, Virginia, and from there to line units as lieutenants. Unexpectedly, this route would take me to sea in the family tradition—as a lieutenant in the marine detachment on an aircraft carrier.

After the war my course seemed to veer from government and the military. What appealed most was finishing college. In my one year of "V-12" I had crammed in so many courses that on return to university after the war I was already close to graduation. The support of the G. I. Bill made it possible to go on to advanced study, so I went for advanced degrees at the University of Geneva's Graduate Institute of International Studies in Switzerland.

Events in Europe were soon to draw me back toward service—the Cold War was brewing. It could be felt in Czechoslovakia, where shortly after making friends there I had to cut off correspondence for their own safety after the Communists took power. When I was in Prague in the summer of 1947 it was possible to wangle, through an American military office there, a permit to slip into occupied Vienna, skirting the immediate postwar rules that kept tourists out. In Vienna I saw Soviet troops at the dividing line that Churchill had just dubbed an "Iron Curtain" and was becoming ever more deeply interested in the countries of Eastern Europe and the Balkans that were the subject of my doctoral dissertation.

With a new war looming I felt the call to return to service. As a U.S. Marine Reserve officer I interrupted my Geneva studies to take two short tours of active duty.

In 1949, after brief service in the Marine Corps History Division in Washington, I took the opportunity to do some research in the Library of Congress for my dissertation. At that time I became aware of the recently created, first peacetime national intelligence service. I was being provided "rations and quarters," as servicemen put it, by my beloved great-uncle in his little house on Florida Avenue. One night at dinner I mentioned that I was thinking of applying to join this new Central Intelligence Agency after completing my doctorate. Uncle Bill—Fleet Admiral William D. Leahy— was unusually qualified to comment. Three years earlier he himself— with the Secretaries of State, War, and Navy, as the National Intelligence Authority—had caused the creation of the Central Intelligence Group, the CIA's predecessor. When I lived with him he was the closest military-political adviser to President Truman and had recently been an influence at the beginnings of the Truman Doctrine and the Marshall Plan.[1] "Good idea," he said, "I'll mention it to Hilly."

Rear Admiral Roscoe Hillenkoetter, who had been the naval attaché when Uncle Bill was ambassador to unoccupied France in 1940–1941, was now Director of Central Intelligence. My 1949 application was cleared so quickly that I had to ask for a few months' delay in entering until I could complete my doctorate in Geneva.

CIA's school for spymasters was then housed in one of the ramshackle temporary buildings clustered near the Jefferson Memorial on what had been and would later again become green lawns when these "tempos" were finally cleared away. There in 1950 came the next turn along my career path, in the form of a poke in the back as I hustled along the corridor to the cafeteria for a late luncheon sandwich. I turned to see the red hair and smiling face of John Dimmer, a friend from student days in Switzerland. Neither of us knew that the other had signed on.

"You're slated for Germany?" he said. "No good—too big a station, you'll get lost in the crowd." With all the authority of his three months' seniority this veteran added another bit of advice. "You should join us in Vienna. Small station. Some good guys are going out there under a first-class new chief."

This sounded good to me, having already had a taste of Vienna. John promised to arrange a meeting with his future boss.

A week later, downtown in the bar of the Hotel Washington, I met William Hood, the heavyset mustached veteran of wartime service in X-2 (the counterintelligence element of OSS), first in London and then with Allen Dulles in Switzerland. He was about to go out as chief of operations in Vienna. After our talk he proposed to Richard Helms, the branch (later division) chief overseeing stations in both Germany and Austria, that I be reassigned. Helms interviewed me—beginning a long, friendly relationship—and the transfer was set. It was to be Vienna.

William Hood had a rare gift for stimulating the motivation and professional competence of his subordinates. In Vienna he immersed me in the counterespionage operations that were to shape my career.

He instilled rigid standards. Handling an agent under his supervision required not just concern for and response to the agent's needs and problems but also, and especially, conscientious reporting of what the agent said and anything affecting our view of him. Hood insisted, on threat of dire punishment, that no case officer ever give in to the temptation that classically hovers over all secret agent handling—to omit, exaggerate, or invent what the agent did or said, to make either case officer or agent look better. No careless slips, misdeeds, or oversights by either party were to be downplayed or go unreported. Only through honest reporting could the Agency properly evaluate the sources of the intelligence it supplied to customer agencies.

This "correctness" characterized the atmosphere of the Vienna Station in my time, especially under the leadership of the admirable station chief, Bronson Tweedy. It exemplified the dictum said to have been framed on the office wall of the World War One chief of German Intelligence, Colonel Walter Nicolai: *Nachrichtendienst ist Herrendienst*. Intelligence is a gentleman's service, in the sense that the good intelligence officer is a man of honor.

There were other practical reasons to write extensive contact reports. A detailed record of every meeting offered the handler a great advantage over his spy, who could scarcely keep such a record and thus would have a hard time keeping track of any lies he was telling. This advantage was later to serve conspicuously in the case of Yuri Nosenko.

Vienna at the beginning of the 1950s was a prime first assignment. Then and for decades afterward it was aptly described as a "turntable of espionage." The war had done relatively little damage to the physical face of this lovely city, but it had shattered the social structure. Its inhabitants had difficulty with their identity—were they defeated Nazis or victims happily liberated from Nazi tyranny? This created an ambivalent attitude toward their military occupiers. Seeing Soviet soldiers on their streets, knowing much of their territory was already a "Soviet Zone" and with Communist regimes already established on their borders, amid growing tensions between East and West, and harassed by strikes and other unrest here and further west, the people of Vienna and its surroundings found little cause for confidence in future stability or prosperity. Business stagnated and industry was stymied by postwar problems of ownership. The war's toll had left few young men to build or inspire a future. Life for many was reduced to getting along as best they could, at or beyond the edge of legality and with little room for morality. It was a climate made for adventurers, black marketers, information peddlers and fabricators, soldiers without an army, refugees from the East without prospects of going further, and former intelligence operatives with a cunning sense of what the increasingly hostile occupiers would want to know about each other.

More promisingly, the city offered extraordinary access to Soviet officials, the only potential human sources of the critical military-political intelligence the White House was desperately demanding of us in CIA.

Jointly governed by the war-winning powers, Vienna was the rare place where a disaffected Soviet soldier or civilian official could jump from East to West by stepping from one building into a neighboring one. In the normal course of events not only local citizens but also American, British, and French officials would meet and deal with Soviet counterparts and perhaps sense susceptibilities or vulnerabilities to an eventual recruitment approach.

These advantages worked in both directions—the Soviets had as much chance to get at us as we had to get at them. To operate clandestinely in four-power-occupied Vienna required strict tradecraft and caution. The various Soviet intelligence services outnumbered Western organizations three to one and at this time they killed and kidnapped as if they were operating within their own borders. This threatened only our agents and contacts, I hasten to add; they did not menace us in our official installations. Spy novels and films to the contrary, staff officers of East and West enjoyed a tacit immunity from violence by their adversaries.

This seething ferment produced rich lessons in the spy trade. Invaluable experience was afforded by dealing with agents of questionable motives, receiving information of hugely varied value and reliability, manipulating double agents, and facing provocative, deceptive operations mounted against us by the Soviet side.

This Vienna assignment shaped my life in other, more important ways, too. It was there, one gray Sunday afternoon in October 1952 in the apartment of some Austrian friends, that I found myself sitting on a couch falling under the spell of a young Austro-Hungarian lady I had just met. Her name was Maria—and the charm has never worn off.

As I gazed down at the clouds over the ocean below, with my little Christina beside me, thinking about that chance meeting ten years earlier, Maria was sitting across the aisle with our two-year-old Patricia. (In Washington we were to add our son, Andrew, and now we have bright and promising grandchildren.) Maria's good judgment and rare insight into people's characters had already helped me again and again. My absolute confidence in her devotion and support made it easy to take career-risky positions in my profession—and though I could not know it then, the job toward which we were flying would demand some of those.

The deepest lessons in counterintelligence—knowing the adversary—came from defectors, officers stepping out of the heart of Soviet bloc military and espionage services. The first I dealt with, in Vienna, was a young officer of the AVH, the Hungarian satellite service of the KGB. To me the experience was enlightenment. Others were to follow.

When an enemy intelligence officer begins to speak openly, an immense gulf is bridged. From the plodding investigations, tedious interviews, tortuous analysis, and even flashes of intuition that counterintelligence demands just to get fragments of hidden truth—fragments that would themselves demand evaluation that often bordered on guesswork—suddenly the hard-sought secrets are lying around waiting to be picked up. "Who and where are your spies?" you ask an insider—and you get the answers. "How did your service get to that man and recruit him? Who is handling him, where and how? Tell us about them."

It was good fortune in my career to deal directly with more than a dozen defectors from and within hostile intelligence staffs. Being familiar with their ways helped in recognizing aberrations, gambits, blunders—and lies. Because we never had enough sources inside the adversary's camp, such insights were precious.

In Vienna in late 1952 Soviet Major Petr Semenovich Popov dropped a note in a car bearing license plates marking it as belonging to an official of the "U.S. Mission to Austria," parked just off the Ringstrasse near the American-occupied Hotel Bristol. The driver of the car had been doing some shopping with his wife and daughter. "What's this?" his wife asked, seeing the note on the floor under the seat. He looked with surprise at the misspelled German of the addressee, the American High Commissioner, and stuffed it into his pocket; a crank message could keep until tomorrow. Next day at a staff meeting he handed it to his boss, who opened it and found a note written in Cyrillic—then gave it to CIA chief John ("Jocko") Richardson.[2]

Back in his office, Jocko handed it to William Hood, his operations chief and then to the Soviet-operations specialist. The latter was no master of the Russian language but could nevertheless understand its message: "I am a Russian officer attached to the Soviet Central Group of Forces in Baden near Vienna. I have important information to offer you if you meet me on the corner of Dorotheergasse and Stallburggasse at 8:30 P.M. on [two days later]. If you are not there I will return at the same time the following day."

Hood turned to Jocko. "We have Alex on hand if we decide to go."

Russian speakers were in short supply. Before taking over supervision of Vienna operations, Hood had fought to get one for his station. The best he could wangle after considerable effort was Alex, a Russian emigré who had earned CIA's trust in previous service abroad along with the status of career agent which gave him something approximating full officer standing. Now the eventuality that Hood had provided for had come to pass, and Alex's presence in Vienna proved to be crucial. Hood's professionalism and prescience paid off. As we who participated in this operation were aware, and as the later head of CIA's clandestine services, Desmond Fitzgerald, wrote, "There never would have been a Popov operation without [Hood] in that station."

An after-dark meeting with an unidentified person claiming to be a Soviet officer, at a place of his choosing in the international sector of midtown Vienna, was not something to be lightly undertaken. Soviet bloc agents were regularly kidnapping from Vienna streets Austrians, refugees, and almost anyone of security interest. Alex was especially vulnerable. Only seven years had passed since he had escaped Soviet custody, and, although recently naturalized as an American citizen, he would have no chance of release if taken by Soviet authorities. He deserves much credit for the role he played in getting this operation going.

On that cold night on a narrow street in the center of Vienna, my job was to watch, without making myself noticeable, for anything suggesting that the letter writer might be accompanied to the scene. I saw the man who must be Popov approaching, entirely alone.

Led to a nearby safe apartment, Popov left no doubt in Alex's mind, or in those to whom Alex reported, of Popov's good faith and inside knowledge of Soviet military affairs, of the work of Soviet intelligence in Austria, and, to a degree, of Soviet foreign policy.

A few days later a Russian-speaking case officer was moved into Vienna to take over from Alex. George Kisevalter continued to meet secretly with Popov there for nearly three years, until the four-power occupation ended in September 1955.

My role was to deal with everything having to do with Soviet Intelligence personnel and activity in our area, setting the questions and follow-up queries and assimilating Popov's information in forms that might be used without compromising him. Already in the first two meetings Popov exposed to us the whole GRU staff in Austria and later, on his routine watches as night duty officer in the residency offices, managed to get into the work folders of his colleagues—using our copies of their wax seals he had provided—and identified many of the spies they were handling.

But these revelations were almost useless, because our overriding duty and interest lay in protecting him, this uniquely precious source. We could do nothing that might alert the Soviets to the presence of a mole in their midst. This meant that a number of GRU agents went on spying untroubled by our secret knowledge—that is, after we determined none of them had access to vital strategic secrets of NATO countries. As for Austria itself, it had no secrets from its Soviet occupiers, who controlled many of its government and police officials almost openly.

In the precious time available for meetings with Popov, questions about GRU spies held a deservedly low priority alongside the vital military questions flowing in from Washington. One memorable day, while taking a walk after a boiled-beef lunch at the Bristol Hotel, I happened to glance across the Ringstrasse and spotted Popov. I was aware that he was to meet Kisevalter in about an hour, and I suddenly remembered what he had promised to bring to this meeting. For years the Pentagon had been hammering at the Agency for a copy of the Field Service Regulations of the Soviet army, virtually their operational bible. If all had gone well, this treasure was at this moment bundled beneath that dark blue overcoat across the street. Our time with Popov that day would be better spent reviewing that document than with him responding to my hard-wrought questions.

Popov continued to meet us until the end of the occupation of Austria in the fall of 1955. Later, the Soviets discovered this operation—in a way that was to impact heavily on my new Nosenko operation.

Of outright defections, as contrasted to volunteers who became secret collaborators of CIA while remaining in their official positions, one that was to bring lasting benefit to America's counterintelligence capabilities— and to mine—was that of KGB Major Peter Deriabin.

On the wintry 15th of February 1954 a stocky, nondescript figure in a dark coat approached the corporal standing guard at the entrance to the Stiftskaserne, a cluster of buildings housing American military offices in the busy shopping area of Vienna's Mariahilferstrasse. Speaking no English, he mumbled incomprehensibly to the sentry, who tried to shoo this nuisance away until he caught the words "Soviet officer" and thought, this poor guy has mistaken this place for a Soviet army installation.

"You want me to call a Soviet officer?" He turned to the phone at his booth.

"No! Stop!" the man whispered. "American—American." The corporal called the duty officer. Minutes later Peter Deriabin managed to make known that he was a Soviet intelligence officer defecting to the Americans. The captain called military counterintelligence and within the hour a Russian-speaking CIA officer, Ted, was questioning Deriabin.

Fifteen minutes into the preliminary questioning Ted bolted out of the room. "He knows I'm Captain Peterson!"

Ted had used that pseudonym when meeting Sergey Feoktistov, a Soviet economic official, whom we too casually had assumed was in our employ. Ted was taking notes in a characteristic left-handed manner, which Deriabin observed with a growing smile. Tongue in cheek, he asked if Ted knew a Captain Peterson. "If you should happen to see him, you might mention that his agent Feoktistov is actually working for us."

These few words blew Feoktistov out of our stable and proved that Deriabin was for real and that we had an important defector in our hands.

In the past we had flown less-important defectors from a small airfield in the U.S. sector of Vienna to the U.S.-occupied zone of Austria. But Deriabin was such a loss to the Soviets that they might risk a serious international incident by "accidentally" knocking down the light aircraft as it carried him over the Soviet zone.

The only other exit from Vienna, aside from highways subject to roadblocks, was the "Mozart Express," an American military train making daily trips from Vienna through the Soviet occupation zone to Salzburg in the American zone. Aside from what was usually a pro forma exchange of documents between the American train commander and the Soviet army officer at the zonal border, there was no inspection of the train—which was not to say that the Russians might be sufficiently provoked to insist upon checking the passenger list once the train was within the Soviet zone.

Deriabin was boxed as "machinery" and loaded into the train's cargo car. Along with armed troops, Bill Hood and I boarded the train. We sat alone in a passenger compartment playing chess to keep our minds off the consequence—a gunfight? surrender?—if the Soviets exercised their right to stop and inspect the train. At one point it screeched to an entirely unexpected halt in the middle of the Soviet zone. Bill and I exchanged glances and shrugs and prepared for the worst, but after ten minutes the train started up again, to our sighs of relief. No chess game I've played since was nearly as tense.

The Bavarian Alps offered a calmer setting for the next phase. The snow-laden fir trees and glistening slopes seemed an incongruous setting for the dark affairs of spies and kidnapping that Deriabin and I were discussing in a little chalet looking down over the white roofs of the village below. Elsewhere, others were arranging his flight to and entry into the United States.

An officer detailed to help us was enjoying the vacationlike atmosphere of the chalet. As we sat at the kitchen table while Deriabin took a nap, the scene reminded him of a similar one. "Look, here's a picture I took near here a few years ago." From his wallet Vic plucked a little snapshot taken in a rustic chalet kitchen like ours. He had been part of the U.S. army's post-war search in the salt mines and other hiding places of the Salzburg region for looted art treasures that the Nazis had stashed to protect or conceal. Of those they found, Vic had placed two on the kitchen table's checked table-cloth as if they had been nothing more than pottery figurines and snapped their picture. I gasped.

Vic smiled. "You recognize them."

Who wouldn't? There on that simple table, together for the first and last time ever, stood two objects that are today the heavily guarded center-pieces of major museums, one in Berlin, the other in Budapest. I recognized the three-thousand-year-old bust of Nefertiti despite the small-scale, low-quality photo. And the bent cross on top of the object alongside her left no doubt that this was the thousand-year-old crown of St. Stephen, the national treasure of Hungary. I handed the photo back to Vic, too awed to think of asking him to have a copy made for me. I've regretted it ever since and wonder if the photo still exists today, years after Vic's death.

When all the clearances and preparations were done—and we had covered a decade of KGB operations in Austria—Deriabin and I were driven over icy roads to the American military airfield near Munich. Under gloomy skies in bone-chilling cold we boarded a C-54 transport plane and spent the long flight cramped in austere seats. Though warmed occasionally by a cup of coffee and sandwiches handed us by the friendly aircrew, we were re-lieved when the plane made its fuel stop on the island of Terceira in the Azores. We stepped out under a warm sun, an abrupt change from the cold darkness we had left in Germany. A scent of flowers and greenery wafted across the tarmac and I took it as a happy augury for Deriabin's future.

In the Washington area a pleasant neighborhood split-level had been arranged for his reception, and he and I continued our talks for another week to cover the essentials of what he had to say about Soviet activities in Austria. Others took over and Deriabin began a long and distinguished career with CIA. He later became my friend, a highly valued professional associate, and, much later, my collaborator on a book about the KGB in the Soviet system.[3]

An incident in Vienna's Gartenbau Café demonstrated the importance of paying heed to seemingly trivial anomalies in an adversary's behavior. In the absence of a mole in his camp one has to take advantage of any small hole in his curtain of secrecy that might be opened by carelessness, oversight, or blunder on his part. It would be a mistake if, glimpsing something unpleasant or undesirable through that hole, one were to shrug it off as irrelevant or insignificant—as happened here.

In this episode the hole was opened by one KGB officer's excessive curiosity to see for himself a scene of action. That permitted a glimpse of nothing more than a man on a street—but it could have been enough to prevent a debacle.

The occasion was our attempt to recruit the senior KGB officer Boris Nalivaiko. It gave a new sense to the term "recruitment pitch" when Nalivaiko pitched his beer into the face of our would-be recruiter as a signal for armed Soviet soldiers to crash into the Gartenbau Café on Vienna's Ringstrasse.

Our recruiter, who had known Nalivaiko years before in Berlin, phoned him to arrange a get-together of old acquaintances. Nalivaiko agreed cheerfully but warned that he should not set out the time and place by phone. He suggested instead that we pass a note to his chauffeur, who could be trusted not to open the envelope. This strange arrangement—it's a brave Soviet official who would trust to his KGB chauffeur what might be construed as illicit contact with Westerners—didn't deter my high-spirited colleagues. From a nearby hotel window I watched the note being passed to the chauffeur, who was waiting in his parked car on the Ringstrasse just down the street from the Soviet Headquarters. I left the hotel and walked away—only to see Nalivaiko's KGB deputy Georgy Litovkin walking not far away. Odd coincidence, I thought—perhaps a bad augury for our operation.

But our eager recruiters brushed this off. After all, why shouldn't this Soviet official be walking so near his office? The meeting took place at the appointed spot in the Stadtpark. I was cruising the area in a car checking for KGB surveillance when I saw a familiar figure walking along the edge of the park, his head turned directly toward the meeting site at the precise moment of the meeting. Familiar, indeed: Litovkin!

That did it. At least we wouldn't be sucked in any further.

By the time I got back to the office, however, our recruiter was already there, thrilling the station leadership with juicy prospects. Nalivaiko, he said, had been nearly weeping with emotion and, after a few days to think it over, would be likely to come over to our side. "And he's telling the truth, or he's a consummate actor!" When I walked in saying, "Pity it's a washout, isn't it?" I was received with the welcome of a dog on a bowling alley.

"What do you mean?" my chief asked.

"Well, you got my call. Litovkin was there again!"

They hadn't understood my message. Because of the low-tech car-radio equipment of those days, or of city interference, it had been garbled. In the throes of hopeful enthusiasm, they preferred to brush aside and ignore this bad news. "So you've seen Litovkin again!" said one. "Ha!"

Wishful thinking prevailed and the meeting took place—exactly where Nalivaiko had instructed us, the Gartenbau Café on the Ring in the central, international sector of the city. It was perilous to accept the target's choice of site, and more so to overlook the fact that the Soviets controlled the international sector that month and had a motor pool just back of that particular café.

At the scene that evening my post was outside the café, ready to warn the team inside of anything untoward. Sure enough, I spotted some unusual movements and darted in to warn our recruiters to get out. A Soviet soldier, his submachine gun at the ready, stepped in just behind me.

Clearly, I was too late. Across the crowded café our recruiter stood, still too stunned to wipe the beer dripping from his face. Nalivaiko, that consummate actor, in the role of a lifetime, stood center stage shouting his lines in outrage. Bewildered but up to their bit parts, the armed Soviet troops blocked all the doorways.

I dropped into the only empty seat in a booth along the window wall. I glanced casually at my three tablemates—and had to suppress an "oops." Both men, and their woman companion, were members of the KGB rezidentura! Evidently, I had walked onto a prepared stage. "What's going on?" I asked innocently in German. One of my tablemates, whom I recognized as the young KGB case officer Vitaly V. Korotkov, who was later to handle the KGB's mole in German Intelligence, Heinz Felfe, was not to be distracted from the unfolding drama. He gently shushed me and the four of us watched the scene together.

The station, by no means entirely sanguine, had taken precautions. In addition to me outside, we too had people at other tables inside the café. A phone call by a quick-thinking CIA officer speaking perfect Viennese

German brought speedy intervention from the Austrian police—the KGB had overlooked the fact that the police had an emergency command post close to this café. Whereas the Soviet soldiers might have marched our recruiters off to some interrogation point and sharpened the debacle, the affair came to a neutral end. The International Patrol arrived and after a brief session at their center, our now soggy recruiters were released.

Perhaps our public embarrassment was all the KGB sought. A Soviet-controlled Vienna newspaper shouted its outrage at this scandalous provocation against an innocent Soviet diplomat. A pro-Western paper gave it a more friendly spin, stressing the other side of the coin, the Soviet entrapment, under the headline "Soviet Consul Used as Decoy."[4]

We learned in Vienna, too, that (as many CIA scoffers later took excessive comfort in repeating) the KGB was indeed "not ten feet tall." Their guiding principle in counterintelligence work, "aggressivity" (*nastupatelnost'*), taught them to take the operational initiative. They mounted sophisticated operations to lure and entrap and mislead Western intelligence services. But such operations require careful attention to detail—a deception exposed is like a boomerang—and as we perceived in Vienna, the KGB's execution could be less sophisticated than its plan.

Among the false agents they strewed in our path in Vienna, like Feoktistov mentioned above, was Olga, a half-Russian interpreter from Austria whom we duly recruited to spy on the Soviet military command where she worked.

After a number of meetings which netted us mediocre tidbits about the Soviet city command in the Bellaria building on Vienna's Ring, Olga told us she was being avidly pursued by a young Soviet officer named Sasha, and she rather liked him, too. Over the next weeks the affair blossomed into love. And now, she announced one day, her Sasha decided he wanted to defect and live with her in the West.

But with the Soviet lieutenant added to Olga's earlier inability to supply the sort of information that had to be available to her in the Soviet city command center, it had become clear to us that Olga must be a KGB-controlled double agent. We told her so, rejecting the offer of her Sasha. Because William Hood always preferred to leave even lousy agents with a smile—one never knew when one of them might get lucky, and why make unnecessary enemies anyway?—we politely showed her to the door.

Off she went, only to slink back a few days later to confess that we'd been right. Now she recounted how she had been manipulated against us by a KGB military counterintelligence unit under Colonel Serdyukov in the Bellaria. But her lieutenant Sasha, she insisted, had nothing to do with all that.

I did not believe it, and wrote a memo outlining the signs that Sasha's defection must have been an integral part of the original KGB plan. Our headquarters took no issue with this, but rightly judged that even if he were a plant it would be interesting to debrief Sasha. So we told Olga to go ahead and bring him to us.

Olga's original CIA case officer and I met the two of them in a Vienna safe house. When we left the room to get them drinks while they tried to identify pictures of Soviets we had taken clandestinely, I glimpsed them paying no attention to the pictures themselves but instead poring over penciled notes on the back of the photos, evidently looking for signs left by other Soviet defectors. This betrayed their real interest and demonstrated a lack of sophistication—shortcomings in the KGB's agent selection and training.

We escorted them out of the country and interrogated Sasha in West Germany. He could not answer our probing questions and finally confessed and told us in detail of the KGB's handling and long-range plans for him to get employment in an anti-Soviet organization in West Germany.

In the midst of his debriefing Sasha had second thoughts and slipped away one night under the noses of his guards (who had no brief to hold him by force anyway) and slipped into the Soviet Military Mission in Frankfurt. I never heard how he fared back in the Soviet Union. Olga returned to Austria, and I doubt she ever heard from him again, either.

The KGB had made an aggressive plan to use their double agent "game" with Olga to plant a more important agent, with a long-term mission—but had carried it out ineptly. I was to encounter this heavy hand later. Visibly, KGB counterintelligence was not "ten feet tall."

Our proximity to Soviet installations in Vienna presented ways to observe their intelligence activity and patterns. We came to know the individual spymasters by sight because we had photos of many and the sources to identify them. With official pictures submitted by all allied official personnel for passes to travel to or through the zones of the other powers, we knew them and most of them by their operational specialty, thanks to identifications by Deriabin, Popov, and others. The Soviet High Commission had its headquarters in the Imperial Hotel, including the principal KGB rezidentura. Its workers lunched in the nearby Soviet-occupied

Grand Hotel, so we put a helper of the station nearby on the street as they walked to lunch and back, to snap photos of them through a small camera hidden behind his tie. When we learned that the KGB residency would reserve blocks of seats at football matches played in Vienna by visiting Soviet teams—especially Dynamo Moscow, which was the club of the KGB and Ministry of Internal Affairs—we placed a "sports photographer" at the edge of the field, who would surreptitiously reverse the direction of his high-quality Hasselblad camera for an instant to take in the KGB-reserved section.[5] Our sources identified practically all of those in the photos, including some unexpected visitors from Moscow. As a result we could select the targets for foot and automobile surveillance that managed to uncover some assets of both GRU and KGB.

After my more than four years in Vienna ended in 1955, along with the four-power occupation, good fortune put me in a spot where I could apply these lessons on a broader scale—and learn much more. Assigned by William Hood, who had become operations chief of the Middle-Europe (later to be renamed Eastern Europe) Division, my new job was to head the counterintelligence section of the Poland Branch. Though the section made up just a tiny part of a small branch, the job gave me the responsibility for planning and overseeing our worldwide efforts against the KGB's Polish satellite service and also against the Soviet-dominated Polish Military Intelligence. And by great good luck, just at this time—in the loosening that followed Stalin's death and Khrushchev's denunciation of Stalin—we were acquiring productive new sources from inside the Polish government apparatus, some inside the intelligence services. This job prepared me and gave me a taste for my 1962 assignment, similar but on a broader front.

It was pleasant to get back to those old, familiar offices in the fall of 1955. CIA's Office of Special Operations (OSO) then occupied some long, low temporary buildings from the Second World War that stretched for hundreds of yards along the Reflecting Pool at the Lincoln Memorial end. They were flimsy affairs that had long outlived their planned longevity. In the still evenings, after most people had gone home, I used to count the rats climbing the hollyhock stalks just outside my office window—four on one stalk was my record. A mouse would sometimes come up through holes in the floor into my office, looking for the bits of food I'd laid out for him from my brown-bag lunch.

Dilapidated as they were, those little buildings had advantages. For one thing, they had an inspiring location. Of all the monuments in Washington the Lincoln Memorial was my favorite. Sitting just across the road, it was a fitting reminder of our responsibility and our cause. But more importantly, the very smallness of these old, stretched-out two-story buildings gave me the feeling that if I didn't make decisions in my domain—my little corner of one corridor off the long central alley—there would be no one else around to do it. And their very shabbiness and informality gave little room for pomposity or self-promotion, fakery, or bureaucratic intrigue. I think that was a healthier base for our business than the ponderous structure the Agency was later to occupy up the Potomac River in Langley, Virginia.

From the relatively small OSO that I had left five years earlier, the operations side of the Agency had expanded to become CIA's "Clandestine Services." OSO's tasks had been limited to clandestine collection of intelligence and counterintelligence abroad, but while I was serving in Vienna it had merged with a younger organization with quite different missions, blandly dubbed Office of Policy Coordination (OPC). Willy-nilly, we had become associated with its broad and sometimes flamboyant operations which later came to characterize (and damage) the public image of the whole CIA.

OPC had been created in response to a growing fear that war with the Soviet Union might soon break out. It was designed to implement the policy of containing international Communism and, if possible, "rolling it back." OPC had been tasked with conducting political action (influencing or even subverting hostile governments), black propaganda, and paramilitary operations. In the latter field it was trying to build up sleeper networks inside Soviet-controlled countries of Eastern Europe that, if war were to break out, could wage guerrilla warfare and send intelligence from behind Soviet lines. War seemed imminent in those days, so OPC had to work under intense political pressure with an urgency that impelled it toward haste and disregard of the obstacles in its path.

This paramilitary mission was doomed. To succeed, relatively inexperienced Americans would have to help émigré organizations—never unified, seldom efficient, with agendas of their own, and susceptible to hostile penetration—assemble large numbers of people for subversive purposes under police-state conditions. My predecessors in the counterintelligence section of OSO's Poland Branch had recently undertaken a detailed review of one of these operations and concluded—oh so correctly—that our OPC colleagues had fallen into a Soviet trap. In a later chapter I describe that operation (dubbed "Cezary" by its Eastern instigators, meaning "Caesar") as a classic example of Soviet deception of Western intelligence services and a telling example of the KGB's "aggressivity" that I would be facing from 1962 on.

It was not only from studying the Cezary disaster that the new job was instructive. It gave me another deep look into the functioning of the KGB itself, because the Polish security service, an obedient satellite of the KGB, was organized and working in the same ways as their Soviet creators and overseers. We got inside information thanks to some Polish State Security (UB) officers who were cooperating secretly with our side. (Happily, they were never uncovered.)

My job offered the opportunity to discuss Cezary with the Polish State Security defector Josef Swiatlo, who had come over to our side two years earlier. His extraordinary revelations shook the Polish leadership following Stalin's death and began the evolution of Poland into a lever that eventually helped bring down the Soviet empire. Swiatlo had been close to the handlers of Cezary, and his insight into their thinking was later to help me understand things about Yuri Nosenko.

In that Polish Branch job I got an early look into the problem of possible hostile penetration of our own ranks—and a burning lesson in how significant details, though reported, can go unrecognized. For years, from West Germany and Berlin the CIA had been sending spies across the border into Poland. These operations had been failing so consistently that operations chief William Hood asked me to examine the old records to see whether a mole in our ranks might have been the cause of the debacle.

I delved into a mass of files and by comparing reports from different operations I found unmistakable signs that one of our operatives must be a Soviet and/or Polish agent. He wasn't a CIA staff officer but a Polish refugee named Gustav Gorecki, who, after making a successful clandestine reentry to and return from Poland himself, had been handling other agents for us in Berlin. He had been using as a safe house on the other side of the border a farmhouse that—as another case showed—must have been UB-controlled.

Emerging from my researches, I asked John, a veteran on the Polish desk, what ever became of him.

"Oh, I think Gus lives over in Georgetown," John answered casually, "but I haven't seen him for a while."

"What? He's here?"

"Sure! Didn't you know he'd immigrated to the States? Why do you ask?"

John's next words mitigated my shock. "Oh, by the way, Gus recently mentioned to Stan [a CIA crony from Berlin days] that he's about to go back to Berlin to visit old friends. This will be his first trip back since he's been here."

I got Gorecki's travel details and sent a cable asking our Berlin Base to put a watch on him.

Hardly had Gus's plane landed before our surveillants spotted him going into the Soviet sector. Confronted on his return, caught in flagrante delicto where, in those days, he could only be guilty, Gorecki confessed. After he had told us about his work against us on behalf of both the Soviet KGB and its Polish satellite service, we turned him loose to return to Poland. There his masters set him up as a hotel manager in a Baltic beach resort and I suppose he lived happily ever after. Years later, in one of those rare moments of Cold War happenstance, my Polish Branch colleague John traveled to that resort and coincidentally met him.

But throughout all that time poring over the records of so many failed operations—even finding suspects like Gus—I never found the slightest reason to suspect that any staff-level mole might have betrayed any of them. What had doomed each and every one of these cross-border ventures was the CIA handlers' disregard of Eastern bloc counterintelligence capabilities and inattention to visible indications that all was not well.

How unlikely it seems that an assignment to bucolic Switzerland, land of my postwar student days, would lead into the deepest realms of Cold War counterintelligence. Once again, when I left the Polish Branch in early 1958, fortune led me to the right place at the right time.

Its neutrality and its image of mountain beauty might give the impression that Switzerland lay outside Cold War rough-and-tumble. In reality it remained a crossroads of international espionage, only somewhat less busy than when it had been an island of neutrality in a sea of Second World War belligerents. Our Soviet bloc adversaries were operating in and through Switzerland into the surrounding NATO countries. CIA had very few people there, which meant I would be involved in everything that went on.

And as fate would have it, a lot went on.

A walk-in volunteer from inside the Soviet establishment was rare anywhere, yet Nosenko was not the first in my time here. In 1960 a Soviet diplomat expressed interest in defecting and I persuaded him, perhaps too easily, to remain in place. In his position he should have had insights into

Soviet policy and access to secret documents, so we started with high hopes and careful attention. But the information he gave fell far short of expectations, and his responses were generalized and sluggish to the point almost of reluctance, contrasting starkly with his stated motivation. He did not inspire confidence. When he was transferred home we set up means for future contact, but as far as I know he never reappeared or produced any useful intelligence. Perhaps the KGB had planted him on us, but they could surely not have derived much benefit from the effort.

Two operations in Switzerland were to impact heavily on my future.

The "Sniper" case began with the arrival of an anonymous letter mailed in April 1959 in Zurich, addressed to the American ambassador in Bern, who passed it to my chief. The writer claimed to be a Soviet bloc intelligence officer writing from "behind the Iron Curtain." His letter was typed in good German and signed "Heckenschuetze" (Sniper).

This first letter, before he began giving really sensitive information, evoked my suspicions. But adopting his proposal we ran an ad in the *Frankfurter Allgemeine Zeitung* that provided him an address to which he could safely send his subsequent letters. It took only one or two more letters from him to persuade me that "Sniper" was not only genuine but also invaluable.

His letters were several pages long, single spaced. They dealt with separate cases, each under its own paragraph heading. Under "Lambda," several letters in succession pointed vaguely but inescapably toward a KGB mole inside British Intelligence. Under "Hacke" he told of KGB exploitation "under false flag" of an organization of former Nazi bigwigs and operatives. "Boxer" was his heading for news of an American military officer recruited and run by Soviet Intelligence.

Though our "Sniper" rarely knew the names of the Soviet spies about whom he reported, he occupied a special position of trust with the KGB and thus learned a lot from his KGB friends, mostly but not all involving operations with connections to Poles and Poland. As a result we were able to identify several active and dangerous moles in Western governments. One was Heinz Felfe, the counterintelligence chief of West German Intelligence (*Bundesnachrichtendienst* [BND]), who for a decade had been exposing to the KGB West Germany's spies in the Soviet Union and its satellite states.

Even more dangerous was the British Intelligence officer George Blake, finally identified after a wide British investigation into Sniper's

Lambda. For eight years Blake had been exposing British secret operations, including the famous Berlin tunnel, which the British ran jointly with CIA.[6]

Because the Poles had recruited a member of the British naval attaché's office in Warsaw and turned his handling over to the KGB, Sniper had heard his name and gave a rough approximation that made it easy for the British to identify him as Admiralty employee Harry Houghton—by now a specially valuable source of the KGB. While the British were tailing him (and his lady friend and treasonous accomplice Ethel Gee) the British discovered the KGB's London KGB handling group, the now-famous Illegals Conon Molody ("Gordon Lonsdale") and Morris and Lona Cohen (the "Krogers").[7] Among other spies identified by Sniper were Israel Beer, an intimate of high Israeli officials, and American State Department official Irwin Scarbeck.

But somehow the KGB got wind of our anonymous source in the UB. To identify and root him out they went for discreet help to their man of confidence inside that service—who by great good luck happened to be Sniper himself. Forewarned, he managed to escape before they finally closed in on him. At the end of 1960 he arranged for himself an operational mission to Berlin, where he defected. Now Sniper identified himself as the Polish UB Colonel Michal Goleniewski. An experienced counterintelligence officer of rare sharpness and professionalism, he had worked closely with the KGB, enjoyed its confidence, and was confided many of its secrets. He had cached secret documents in Poland that CIA later recovered.

It was a great loss to our side when, all too soon after his defection, this sharpest of counterintelligence minds slipped into delusion and his information became confused and misleading.

But how did the KGB get onto him? How did it know where to look? These questions rankled. In my new job I would tackle them.

In Geneva in late May 1962, only months before I was to leave Switzerland to take over the Soviet counterintelligence responsibility in Headquarters, Yuri Nosenko walked in. During my recent visit to Headquarters shadows had been cast over this new source.

Now, high over the Atlantic, I was being carried toward a position where I would have to evaluate and deal with Nosenko, the shadows over him, and, though I could not yet know it, a swarm of other new sources.

My reflections over my past life suggested that my experience would indeed serve me well in the maze of mirrors I was about to enter. It had given me enough familiarity with Soviet counterintelligence practices to distinguish between real and unreal, enough detachment to call things as I saw them (independent of group-think), and enough confidence to face the consequences of uncomfortable calls.

CHAPTER **5**

New Job, Under Clouds

"Hero's been arrested."

Jack Maury was standing by a window staring out at the gray November sky as I stepped into this dark welcome regarding one of our top spies, Colonel Oleg Vladimirovich Penkovsky. My new job was beginning on an ominous note.

After only a year and a half that great operation had ended.

"We don't know when he was arrested. The last contact was September 6th. Then Penkovsky missed scheduled brushes in mid-September, so it must have been about then. But we didn't know, so we didn't call off Greville Wynne's scheduled business trip to Budapest. The KGB kidnapped him there a few days ago."

With Wynne jailed, the KGB closed the case with a bang. Using Penkovsky's arrangements, the KGB signaled that his "dead drop"—in an apartment house lobby on Pushkin Street—should be unloaded. Just as our case officer Dick Jacob, as instructed, pulled a matchbox from behind the radiator, KGB thugs jumped him. Their leader made a show, maybe for the benefit of a hidden camera, of opening the matchbox and feigning shock to find microfilm in it. (When shown photos later, Jacob identified the actor, who was Vladislav Kovshuk, chief of the American Embassy Section of the KGB's Second Chief Directorate and a major figure in our story.) Jacob and others were expelled from the Soviet Union, and the "scandal" was now bursting into headlines.

Ironically, just when we were lamenting Penkovsky's loss, his information was making its most critical contribution to Western security. Thanks largely to secret documents he had provided, the Cuban missile crisis had cooled, nuclear war was averted, and the world breathed more easily. His information, combined with observations on the ground and from the air, showed that the missiles the Soviets were installing in Cuba, which they had assured the White House were for anti-aircraft defense only, were in fact surface-to-surface missiles—equipped with nuclear warheads—with Washington well inside their range. Moreover, by informing the Kennedy White House how long it would take the Soviets to make the missiles fully operational, Penkovsky had given U.S. officials sufficient time to force the USSR to remove them before it could confront the United States with the fait accompli of a first-strike capability.

Penkovsky's contribution was "invaluable," "essential," and "critical," in the words of top-level government insiders. He was later said to have "saved the world."[1] No less than Attorney General Robert Kennedy, a member of his brother President John F. Kennedy's tiny inner circle for the crisis (dubbed "Excomm"), observed that Penkovsky's contribution to the missile crisis had justified every penny the United States had spent on the whole CIA throughout its fifteen years of existence.

The active phase of the Penkovsky case, and any involvement I might have had in it, had thus been cut off. But the aftermath was at hand. No longer needing to protect Penkovsky, we could begin exploiting his leads to potentially recruitable Soviet Military Intelligence people and could inform Western security services about spies he had uncovered.

Later, after Penkovsky's public trial and the announcement of his execution in May 1963, another line of action emerged. At the highest level the decision was taken to publicize Penkovsky's exposures of machinations among the Soviet leaders, their aggressive military strategy, their missiles and their espionage operations and personnel abroad. Some favored adding spicy elements to sharpen the blow and to exacerbate KGB-GRU frictions by telling more about how the KGB controlled GRU work and interfered with GRU efforts to inform the Soviet military about Western plans and capabilities. A wiser course prevailed: to preserve unchallengeable authenticity, nothing would be fabricated. The book was constructed entirely from Penkovsky's own words as taped at the meetings, supplemented by official documents he had provided. The job of transcription and editing was assigned to Peter Deriabin, onetime KGB officer, who worked with a Russian-speaking officer of the Division. It was published in 1965 and had the hoped-for impact on Western views of Moscow and caused dismay there.[2]

While the Agency's heaviest hitters were thrashing through the political exploitation of Penkovsky's contribution, there remained a problem at my level. How had the Soviets tumbled so fast to Penkovsky's secret contact with us? These would be among the questions I would be facing in my new position—along with the signs that this loss was somehow connected with the near-simultaneous arrival of fresh new—but suspect—sources.

Arriving in the late fall I had been spared Washington's soggy summer and the long hassle that accompanied the Agency's move into its new premises in Langley. I also missed the "drama of the doors." Corridor gossip had it that the funds budgeted for constructing CIA's new headquarters were so tight that only a single shade of paint could be afforded for the interior. An allegedly cheerful Civil Service–mandated monochrome beige covered the entire interior—office walls, hallways, closets, and doorways from top to bottom, front and back. Aside from arrows pointing vaguely toward stair-way fire escapes and marked doors to toilet facilities, there was no in-dication whatsoever of who or what might be behind any closed door. By now, however, things had brightened a bit. According to hallway chat-ter we could thank a resident CIA psychiatrist, who for the sake of the staff's emotional stability had strongly recommended that funds be some-how scraped up to permit rendering at least the inner doors in varied colors.

Missing that hassle and having a royal blue door to my office were simply the luck of the draw. Far better was the job I would be doing behind that door.

Heading the Soviet Russia Division's counterintelligence section, which counted only a dozen members, was a job short on prestige and bureaucratic clout but long on the substance that had fascinated me from my early years in the Agency. It carried the responsibility to plan and guide the Agency's operations to counter Soviet espionage and subver-sion. That required a command of all we knew of the secret doings of the KGB, Moscow's central instrument of internal repression and action abroad, and of the Soviet military intelligence service, GRU. The practice of counterintelligence gave me, personally, a more immediate sense of defending the nation against its adversaries than did the broader task of collecting strategic intelligence on those adversaries' political, economic, and technical capabilities and intentions.

At the same time, counterintelligence was an integral part of the collection of so-called positive intelligence and a more promising one than it might seem. This was no simple game of "spy vs. spy" as sometimes depicted. Even in its "defensive" aspect—countering the subversive work of adversary intelligence services—counterintelligence's ultimate goal was to penetrate those services. While protecting our own intelligence-collection process from contamination, diversion, or negation by hostile forces, counterintelligence needed eyes and ears inside the adversary's intelligence staffs to expose his intentions, capabilities, and targets. And these could be rich sources of political, scientific, economic, and military intelligence.

The officers of KGB and GRU could be knowledgeable sources on technology, military matters, and foreign policy, and they were surely the most accessible: knowledgeable because they were briefed on what information their regime sought and thus still needed to learn, accessible because while most Soviet scientists and military staffs were forbidden foreign contacts and many were isolated in remote regions, the raison d'être of KGB and GRU officers was to seek such contacts abroad.

This proved out when we succeeded in establishing a secret relationship with military intelligence officers like Popov or Penkovsky. Their intelligence product was spectacular. Penkovsky turned over thousands of pages of top-secret scientific and military-strategic secrets and gave information on missiles that played a key role in the Cuban missile crisis. Of Popov, a middle-level field officer of GRU, a top CIA insider wrote,

> He provided technical specifications on Soviet conventional weapons, including the first information on several new Soviet tanks . . . detailed order of battle data and tables of equipment for Soviet tank, mechanized, and rifle divisions . . . large increases in the number of amphibious vehicles and armored personnel carriers a full eighteen months before they were spotted by other sources. His other firsts included the description of several tactical missile systems and reports on the existence of Soviet nuclear submarines, a new heavy tank division, and Soviet Army tactics in the utilization of atomic weapons. [Here, the author could have added, details of a fighter-bomber years before it first flew.]
>
> This one man's reporting had a direct and substantial effect on U.S. military organization, doctrine, and tactics, and saved the

Pentagon at least a half billion dollars in its research and development program.[3]

KGB operatives, too, were potential sources of political and scientific information. Because they were seeking and using sources of intelligence and influence inside the political establishments of the West, their instructions from Moscow often gave insights into Soviet policies and intentions. And one of the largest sections of KGB foreign intelligence was devoted to collecting scientific and technological intelligence. Their instructions from Headquarters exposed areas of Soviet ignorance and incapacity, and main lines of their research and development.

To get closer to Soviet intelligence officers and their operations, the first step was to take stock of what we knew and what assets we had.

This required a long look backward. The past pervades counterintelligence work—or it should. The Soviet intelligence services that CIA faced were the product of a long history. By this time the KGB's people had been building their assets in foreign countries for forty-five years and using their active spies to spot and recruit new agents in an unbroken continuum.[4]

They had been accumulating vast experience and developing their methods of work for thirty years by the time CIA was born—and born, in fact, of the remnants of a wartime creation (the Office of Strategic Services, OSS) that had neither collected intelligence on the USSR nor devoted any effort to checking the work of the Soviet secret services. On the other hand, those Soviet services, as if they didn't have enough to do in dealing with the Third Reich, had the time and foresight to continue operations against the United States and Britain. (They not only stole the secrets of the atomic bomb but also planted agents in OSS, a dozen of whom—all, we hoped—were identified and out of service before some OSS remnants joined the new CIA.)

CIA's Counterintelligence Staff had a lot of catching up to do. It was not enough just to take in what allied services with longer experience could tell us. We now had the resources to unearth the all-but-forgotten testimonies of veterans of the international Communist movement and of former intelligence services of countries that were no longer independent in Eastern Europe and the Baltic.

Bales of captured German files dating from 1920 to 1945 on operations against Soviet Intelligence were studied. As weak as Nazi military intelligence had proven to be in Russia, the Gestapo and related security services had detected major Soviet intelligence networks throughout Europe, principally the Rote Kapelle (Red Orchestra) and Rote Drei (Red Three, based in Switzerland), and German files on these cases contributed importantly to CIA's nascent understanding of Soviet espionage. From evidence of massive radio deception operations against the invading Germans CIA gained insights into this aspect of Soviet counterintelligence work, including an appreciation of the KGB's willingness to sacrifice blood and assets to support deceptions.

A rich source of knowledge reposed in the veterans of KGB and GRU who had fled and resettled in the West. I sought them out not only to talk but also to enlist them for active participation. The counterintelligence talents of former KGB Major Peter Deriabin—deep inside knowledge, disciplined attention to detail, and sharp instinct—were particularly valuable. As I revived our relationship that had begun on the evening of his defection, it was readily apparent that he had been finding his advisory role too passive and saw many ways he could help more actively. Yuri Rastvorov, a KGB lieutenant colonel who had defected in Japan in January 1954, had come to feel underemployed on the outside economy and was eager to rejoin and apply his boundless energy to our task. On the GRU side was the impressive, dignified personality of former Colonel Ismail Akhmedov, known also by his other name, Ege. He had been in the GRU assigned to the Soviet Embassy in Berlin when the Nazis attacked the Soviet Union. When Germany and the USSR allowed the exchange of diplomats after the outbreak of war, Akhmedov, en route back to Moscow, was assigned to the GRU residency in Turkey (he was of Turkic ethnic origin). There he defected and, after years in Turkey and West Germany, had now been nearly ten years in America.

It was a stimulating experience to seek out and convert these and other veterans from occasional sources of answers to regular sources of questions and proposals for operations, based on their special understanding of our adversaries. What did they think might be done? What ideas did they have to do it? Our section set them up in offices with assistants and, to stimulate their imaginations, did not hesitate to put into their hands, for the first time, information that came from others. For this breach of accepted practice I was admonished by older colleagues who stiffly kept Agency documents from them, mistrusting "turncoats." I never had any reason to doubt their loyalty, and they produced results beyond expectations. One, for instance, started us out on a path long trodden by our adversaries, the "false flag" approach. Posing as an active KGB officer, he recruited a top Communist Party leader in a Third-World country.

Here we were following a tradition from the early days in the American West, when the army had used Indian scouts against warring tribes. These people were better trackers and were instinctively aware of how the enemy lived, worked, reasoned, and planned.

The most recent defector had no part in this, but his reports were of immense interest and value to us in the months that followed.

KGB Major Anatoly Golitsyn had walked in to the CIA chief in Helsinki on 15 December 1961. For more than two years he had been preparing this break but, fearing leaks, had never taken the risk of contacting us or giving any hint of his intention. During this time he took pains to memorize details from hundreds of reports that crossed his desk and conversations with KGB colleagues, and as a result he was nearly as productive as if he had been operating in place. And he was also alive and safe here in the United States.

In his KGB position Golitsyn had wide access to operational secrets because his job entailed analyzing reports on NATO coming into Moscow from KGB spies in at least eight countries. Additional information came from his indoctrination periods in several KGB departments, and from his service in two KGB residencies abroad. In the process Golitsyn had learned the precise identities of some spies but, most remarkably, had heard and seen and remembered things that would point us to many more whom he couldn't directly place. His information led to identification of important KGB spies still active in Western governments: senior diplomats, intelligence officers, and prominent businessmen. Many were later arrested or fired from their positions of trust, including two NATO officials, a Norwegian intelligence official, a Canadian ambassador, a former CIA principal agent, a double agent misleading CIA, and some highly placed French intelligence officers. Others who could not be firmly identified or, if identified, could not be prosecuted for lack of evidence included West German intelligence officers, French diplomats, and American code clerks.

Each of Golitsyn's leads had been listed as a "serial," divided by nationality and shared with the security services of the friendly countries involved. These serials might sometimes have stemmed from fragmentary hearsay—for example, "My KGB colleague X in the Y section told me in [year] that he was handling as a source a diplomat serving in Z Embassy in

Moscow who kept a large dog there." Or they might be descriptions of specific intelligence reports he'd handled that emanated from an unidentified source in a certain NATO country. Some serials were sharper and included the spies' names or KGB code names. Two or more serials might apply to one and the same spy; the diplomat with the dog, for instance, might have been the source of one or more of the intelligence reports.

The number of these serials was phenomenal: more than one hundred fifty British and about one hundred French, of which more than ten pointed to spies in French intelligence and security staffs. Because so many of his leads were fragmentary and could not be verified, some outsiders later criticized Golitsyn for causing turmoil and tension between allies and even suggested that this was his purpose. Shocked and feeling attacked by his revelations, some Western European officials accused him of paranoia and dismissed his information as mad ravings.

They were wrong. Golitsyn was not easy to deal with, but those who did over the years attested to his effort to separate fact from supposition. When he was later shown Western files to help him identify spies about whom he knew only fragmentary facts, he erred in two or three cases and pointed in wrong directions (though the leads themselves were later found to have been valid). But what he told in the first months after his defection proved to be accurate and priceless. Those of us who worked with those leads came to call them "vintage Golitsyn," in contrast to his later, more speculative pointers and notions.

The new job brought me back into close professional and personal relations with James Angleton, chief of the Clandestine Services' Counterintelligence Staff, though we occupied clearly demarcated areas of responsibility. His staff gave advice on the counterintelligence operations of the area divisions but had no authority over the conduct of those operations. It handled liaison with other U.S. agencies and a few foreign intelligence and security services, and maintained relations with some defectors from Eastern intelligence services. Its research group studied the past and published the results. Jim and I had a forthright and productive cooperation, and our differences of opinion, even disputes, were always conducted in good spirit and often with amusing banter.

Scores of books and articles have presented Angleton in such distorted form as to be unrecognizable to those of us who worked closest with him. They describe a man of mystery sensing dark plots and spinning paranoid webs of confusion. We noticed, instead, his love of his country and his deep-felt interest in and sympathy for his friends. He was indeed secretive, imbued as he was by World War Two experience in dealing with the ultrasecret material stemming from the breaking of Nazi codes and ciphers. And he was deeply aware of the danger of hostile penetration and the resulting need to compartment information within our service—at times applying this principle of "need to know" with excessive zeal to me and others.

Angleton has been publicly accused of conducting a paranoid hunt for moles—seeking spies in our midst on the basis of wild theorizing that some must be lurking somewhere. In reality, his staff (in conjunction with the Agency's Office of Security) looked only into *specific indications* of possible hostile penetration of the Agency's staff. This was justified by any professional or even moral standard. Not to have done so would have been criminal negligence in the face of the unending efforts of the KGB throughout the world to infiltrate the ranks of Western intelligence and security services. That some such specific pointers to possible moles might turn out to be unfounded or misleading, or that they might be wrongly interpreted—and that as a result some innocent officers might unjustly suffer harm to their careers—was an inevitable hazard of our profession to be recognized and accepted by anyone entering it. The Counterintelligence Staff and the Office of Security customarily tried, even if not always successfully, to mitigate this danger. They dealt discreetly, for example, with the wild accusations of treason that were flung—against me among a lot of others—by a couple of spiteful and underendowed colleagues.

My arrival in the new job coincided with the arrival of a surprising flow of new sources—surprising in more than one way.

Within the space of a few years, from the late 1950s to the mid-1960s, encompassing my time heading counterespionage against the Soviet intelligence services, more volunteers emerged from inside those services than ever before in any comparable period, including even the time of purges in the first half of the 1950s just before and after Stalin's death and the rise and fall of Beria.

Here was something entirely new: KGB officers who dared to remain in their KGB jobs while establishing a secret relationship with Western intelligence services. In all the forty-five years of Soviet history before 1962, not a single officer in any KGB installation—where there was general awareness that their service had eyes and ears inside Western intelligence services—had ever dared work in place for the Western adversary. Before and after World War Two two or more KGB officers mailed letters to Western intelligence services—but anonymously.

It was safer for a Communist official to jump outright to the West, but even this act was rare. For seventy years, until just before the final collapse of the Soviet Union, full of events that would encourage disaffection—civil war, famine, forcible and painful social change, bloody purges of their ranks, a stupendous war, repression of whole nationalities, abrupt changes of leadership, economic decline, and growing disillusionment—only some fifty KGB officers ever fled to the West. This number averaged fewer than one a year from among the many hundreds of Soviet State security officers abroad at any one time.

Of the KGB or GRU officers who did defect, the wise ones made their move without giving any advance notice to anyone, East or West. To let their intention become known to either side even a few days in advance could be fatal—and, in several cases, was. In Japan GRU officer Vladimir A. Skripkin made contact with British Intelligence and was still preparing his defection when the KGB arrested and executed him. He had evidently been betrayed by a mole inside British Intelligence, possibly (but not certainly) Kim Philby. In 1945 KGB officer Konstantin Volkov, involved in operations against Great Britain, contacted British officials in Istanbul, promising startling news about KGB infiltration of the British secret services. His approach became known to KGB mole Kim Philby, who caused delays in British reaction in order to give the KGB time to spirit Volkov away before he could unload his trove of revelations. He was taken to Moscow and shot. Several other such incidents smeared the history of the Cold War.

The years 1961–1962 saw a notable change in this picture. After the trailblazing Popov operation came to its end in 1959, compensated to some degree by our all too short contact with Penkovsky from April 1961 to the fall of 1962, in the volunteers flowed. Our new sources were remarkable not only for their numbers and their unprecedented willingness to spy in place but also for the questions they brought with them. From 1917 to 1961 not a single defector from inside the staff of the KGB or GRU had been suspected of having been sent out on KGB instructions. Now, from 1961 to 1966 serious doubts arose about the genuineness of *eight*. They were remarkable, too, for the interconnections between them—and with the Nosenko operation, as would become more striking by 1964 when he came West again.

Amid these successes a few of us were noticing signs that there might be a mole in our midst. Was this incongruous situation merely coincidence, or might it suggest that a single Moscow hand could be directing a program of provocation and deception, based on penetration of our staff?

As ominous as distant thunder, these signs were accumulating.

- When "Sniper," the high-ranking Polish counterintelligence officer and KGB confidant Michal Goleniewski, started sending anonymous letters to the Americans in Europe in the spring of 1959, he carefully contrived the way he did it to bypass CIA, because his KGB friends let him know that they had CIA penetrated. And the KGB did entrust Goleniewski with such sensitive information. His letters led us to uncover now well publicized Soviet moles in key places inside the British and West German intelligence services.
- Goleniewski's fears proved well founded. After he found himself in touch with CIA despite his efforts to avoid it, the KGB did learn about his contact with us. Because his letters were anonymous the KGB didn't know any better than we did who the writer was. But despite his efforts to hide his country of origin—he wrote "from behind the iron curtain" and focused mainly on Soviet operations— we figured out that he must be a high-ranking officer of the Polish security service. *And that is where the KGB looked.* The questions hung there. How did the KGB learn that someone was passing high-grade information to CIA, and how did it know where to look for him?
- In 1961, when Oleg Penkovsky made secret contact with American and British Intelligence, the KGB detected him with astonishing— and suspicious—speed, in fact within weeks, as I describe in Chapter 14. Strangely, they then let him continue to spy for more than a year before arresting him. As in Popov's case, they took pains to make us think they had detected Penkovsky only later, and by chance when routinely shadowing Western diplomats in Moscow.
- In late 1961 someone other than he used Penkovsky's secret method to call CIA to service (unnecessarily) an emergency dead drop in Moscow. As Nosenko's information revealed, the KGB knew who, from

the American Embassy, went to the drop. How did the KGB learn of this signaling system and dead drop, known only to a few outside the small group handling Penkovsky? And how did they know who went there?

- In December 1961 KGB officer Anatoly Golitsyn defected and pointed toward spies within NATO governments, some of whom were subsequently identified and arrested. He had reason to believe the KGB had spies in CIA, too. Though he knew specifics about only one nonstaff agent handler (who was found), other circumstances he described—had they been properly assessed and investigated— pointed toward a KGB penetration of the CIA staff.

- CIA's operations against Soviet targets in various parts of the world were failing so often and so oddly that more than coincidence (or our ineptitude) was at play. When we planted a microphone in an important Soviet office, it would be discovered "by chance," or the office would soon be used for other, innocuous purposes. Recruitment efforts came strangely unstuck. By the mid-1960s over fifty such incidents had been counted.[5]

- The KGB had somehow uncovered CIA's best secret source, Pyotr Popov in the GRU. *When* and *how* did the KGB do that?

That Popov question now became a burning issue, because the story purveyed by Nosenko and by another of our new inside sources, Cherepanov (see Chapter 16) was falling apart. Their tale—of the KGB's stumbling onto Popov's trail in February 1959 thanks to a chance sighting of a diplomat mailing a letter in Moscow—was beginning to look like a ruse designed to hide the real betrayer of our great agent.

It began with the discovery of "the three musketeers."

CHAPTER **6**

Bombshell

"Here are the traces on that Russian you asked me about yesterday," said the analyst Sally as she slipped into my office brandishing a slim sheaf of papers. "They're stuff the FBI passed to us years ago."

I nodded thanks and, without taking the phone from my ear, pointed to my in-box. Sally dropped the papers, waved an apology for the interruption, and hustled away.

It was late afternoon before I got to the bottom of my in-box. It didn't matter; I felt no urgent need to scan old FBI reports. They would most likely be typical of the material the Bureau and CIA routinely exchanged.

The door opened and Mary, the section's senior secretary, reminded me that it was five-thirty and that she had an early date. I raised my right hand and promised to "take care of things." As Mary knew better than most, that meant I would put all my files in the safe, make a final check of the office and other safes, and initial the security sign-out roster. Mary managed a grin and fled.

I picked up the first FBI report.

It was November 1962. Soon after taking over the new job I started looking into the nagging questions raised by the strangely parallel reporting of Nosenko and Golitsyn—and the marked differences in their evaluations of the importance, even portent, of identical incidents.

They had both reported on Kovshuk's trip. Golitsyn had given the West its first inkling that the head of the KGB's counterintelligence work against the American Embassy in Moscow had traveled to Washington. Because Kovshuk had been outfitted with a new name for the purpose, neither the FBI nor CIA had recognized him. Golitsyn hadn't known why Kovshuk went to the United States but he had picked up insiders' boasts that the trip contributed to the KGB's discovery of Popov's treason.

In any event such a trip would raise questions. Why would this man with no overseas responsibilities leave Moscow for Washington? Surely not to give him a personal glimpse of his primary targets on their home ground or a breather from his Moscow responsibilities. Surely he came on business—and his business was to know and thwart American intelligence collecting from the Embassy in Moscow. Could someone in Washington be helping him in that business?

That question was intriguing enough by itself. But it had sharpened when Nosenko, on his own, had now brought up the same long-ago trip. More to the point, by claiming to have been Kovshuk's deputy, Nosenko had endowed himself with the authority to explain its purpose. According to him, Kovshuk had gone to Washington to restore contact with an American army sergeant whom the KGB had recruited in Moscow and code-named "Andrey." Though we had not yet been able to identify this "Andrey," Nosenko's report let us live more easily with Golitsyn's information. A sergeant-mechanic working on cipher machines—but not himself dealing with ciphers—could not endanger American security as might, for instance, a higher military, diplomatic, or intelligence officer.

But the question hung there. Was it just another of those fortuitous circumstances that, a few months after Golitsyn had rung the alarm bell in Washington, there arrived one of the few KGB men who could explain the trip, and so blandly? Or was Nosenko's story covering some other, more important target?

The first step in digging into this mystery had already been taken for us. When, as a matter of routine, Golitsyn was shown photos of Soviet officials who had visited or served in the United States, he immediately identified Kovshuk. According to our records, however, this was a photo of someone called "Vladimir Komarov," who had come to the United States in early 1957. Armed with this identification, Sally began searching the files for any clue to what Komarov-Kovshuk might have been up to in Washington.

Now, as my secretary waved goodnight, Sally's findings lay in front of me.

After one look, a bright light seemed to flash across my desk—and change the whole color of the Nosenko matter. There was nothing dramatic in the first report; it was just another of the hundreds of documents passed between the Bureau and CIA, routinely scanned and routinely consigned to the central files. Now, however, coincidence played a role: another person would not have seen what lay in it, or in the other reports accompanying it.

"Komarov" was here described not as a temporary traveler but as a diplomat who in January 1957 had arrived on *permanent* assignment to the Soviet Embassy in Washington.

Just a minute! I thought. Golitsyn had talked only of a "trip"—because he, like Nosenko, had known that Kovshuk retained his leadership of the Moscow section while away. As the FBI reports revealed, Kovshuk had actually stayed in Washington for ten months of what would normally have been a two-year assignment.

If the Soviets assigned Kovshuk to an ostensibly normal two-year tour abroad, they knew his mission would require an extended stay. This could not be squared with Nosenko's story that his boss had gone off simply to restore a lost contact with a recruited sergeant-mechanic. But Kovshuk's mission must have been pertinent to his Moscow responsibility—penetrating our Moscow Embassy and opposing American intelligence work in the Soviet Union. Why else would they have held his Moscow position open for him?

Then what? One possibility, among others, sprang to mind: might Kovshuk have recruited an American working in the Embassy who had then been reassigned home before Kovshuk had time to fully establish the relationship and debrief him in Moscow?

But the length of the "trip" was only the first shock hidden in these "routine" FBI reports. What was to come would knife even deeper into the heart of the heretofore-promising Nosenko operation.

I now learned for the first time that Kovshuk had not worked alone during his trip to Washington. The FBI had no reason to take special interest in "Komarov," a nondescript diplomat with no previous record. But while they were tailing a known KGB operative from the Soviet Embassy, FBI surveillants saw him making furtive maneuvers in the company of "Komarov" and a third Soviet official. In the weeks that followed the FBI watchers saw the trio so often together that, according to these reports, they dubbed them "the three musketeers."

The third man was a TASS news agency correspondent in New York who, like "Komarov," had gone unreported in the West. Why would a TASS man from New York be working in Washington, where other TASS representatives were stationed, and consorting there during office hours with two KGB "diplomats," neither of whom had even ostensible press functions?

The musketeers' pattern of activity convinced the experienced FBI watchers that the threesome was meeting a spy.[1] After casually glancing at the reflection of shop windows to see who might be behind them, the Russians would separate and then rejoin, and spend working hours in or around movie theaters. Only one or two of the Russians would enter and none of them would sit through a film. But the troika worked with such professional skill that the FBI, with all its surveillance competence, never spotted their spy. With time the affair had become just one more unresolved counterintelligence mystery.

It was the identity of Kovshuk's fellow "musketeers" that floored me. The KGB man the FBI had been tailing when they came upon the "three musketeers" was Yuri Guk, nominally a diplomat assigned to the Soviet Embassy.

"What?" I exclaimed aloud.

This was Nosenko's chum in Geneva—with him just before and after his meetings with Kisevalter and me—who "happened" to have visited Moscow and returned to Geneva a few days before Nosenko had asked to meet a CIA officer.

And the third "musketeer"—the TASS man from New York? His name was Aleksandr Konstantinovich Kislov.

My jaw dropped. Here "coincidence" stopped. Comrade Kislov was the chap who had shared the Geneva hotel room with Nosenko. From the first it had seemed strange that Nosenko, the security officer responsible for watching over the delegates, had been quartered in a hotel far away from his flock.

This could no longer be coincidence. Kovshuk's deputy Nosenko was highlighting a trip Kovshuk had taken five years earlier. At the moment Nosenko was telling us about it, alongside him there in Geneva were precisely the two KGB operatives who had worked with Kovshuk during that trip. Nosenko had failed to mention that astounding fact, which of course he might, conceivably, not have known. But, with the authority of having read Kislov's KGB file he had certified that Kislov had no connection with the KGB. Might he not have known it? Or would he have remembered it had we given him more time in Geneva? Each line of thought ran up against a wall.

If it was not coincidence?

Then it would look as if the KGB had sent Nosenko to us, perhaps (given that strange overlap in their reports) to divert us from Golitsyn's dangerous revelations.

This we would look into—right away.

CHAPTER 7

Popov's Ghost

Nosenko's story of Andrey—his "most important" story—could not be true. The facts of Kovshuk's trip made that clear. It was possible, of course, that Nosenko had heard of Andrey and separately heard of Kovshuk's trip and made a false assumption, adding one and one to get three. No matter. It was not to restore an old contact that the KGB had sent one of its key counterintelligence officers away on ostensibly permanent assignment while holding his Moscow job for him.

So why *did* Kovshuk travel to Washington?

He had not gone alone—another sign that his mission was important. He and Aleksandr Kislov applied for their visas within two days of one another, in early November 1956. Then, in early January 1957, again at a two-day interval, they had flown to the United States, Kislov as "journalist" to New York, Kovshuk as "diplomat" to Washington—yet within weeks the FBI saw them working together in Washington with KGB operative Yuri Guk.

We adopted the working hypothesis that they had gone out to follow up a recruitment of someone in the American Embassy in Moscow successfully begun but left unfinished because of the target's departure. Going off on ostensible two-year assignments—instead of brief temporary missions—these KGB officers must have been confident that their target would talk and had much more to tell. They would debrief their target and turn over his subsequent handling to the local residency.

Their target must have been residing in Washington. That is where they were seen operating and where Kovshuk, under diplomatic cover, would need State Department clearance for any trip beyond the twenty-five-mile radius allowed to Soviet diplomats.

We dug up the records on departures of Embassy personnel prior to Kovshuk's visa request. On the assumption that the KGB would want to quickly recontact a new recruit to forestall his or her change of mind about cooperating, we limited our search to three months, from August through October 1956.

This search would test our hypothesis. We were highly unlikely to find anyone who fit this exact picture—someone of great interest to KGB counterintelligence who happened to leave his station in Moscow within this narrow time frame and was in Washington through the following spring. If there were no fit, we would discard this hypothesis and look for some other, hopefully innocent, explanation for Nosenko's reporting. On the other hand, in the unlikely event that we should find some such person, it would indicate that the KGB fed us Nosenko's Andrey story to hide a more important KGB target—perhaps someone able to put them onto Popov's track, as Golitsyn's information suggested.

We sorted through the military and civilian records and produced a list of everyone who left the Moscow embassy from August to November 1956. It wasn't a long list—ten or so—and one reading sufficed.

There it was.

Among names of no special intelligence interest one stood out—the man whom CIA had sent to Moscow to support the Popov operation. The man whom Nosenko, as Kovshuk's deputy, had helped try to recruit for the KGB and whom the KGB had code-named "Rhyzhiy," "Redhead."

Edward Ellis Smith was the only CIA operative in the American Embassy at that time and had been the first one ever assigned there.[1] Smith was instructed to find dead drops for Popov's eventual use—and had chosen them so ineptly that when they were proposed to Popov, in Vienna, he exclaimed, "Are you trying to get me killed?"

This had dimmed Smith's professional prospects even before he fell into the KGB's trap.

Kovshuk's section had planted as Smith's maid an attractive KGB agent and, as embassy security officer, ignoring his own warnings to others about this sort of thing, Smith grabbed the bait and began trysts with her in her apartment. There, in September 1956, the KGB stormed in and caught him in flagrante delicto. Kovshuk confronted Smith with his "criminal adultery" (as defined by Soviet law) and, using the shopworn technique, offered him an easy way out—all he had to do was collaborate with the KGB.[2]

Smith hesitated for some days before informing an Embassy superior, then asked whether he need report it officially. Astonished at such a question from a security officer, the diplomat instructed him to submit a report forthwith.

CIA recalled Smith to Washington where Paul, a security officer, questioned him in detail. He found Smith evasive and got the firm impression that before reporting to his Embassy superior Smith had met at least one more time with the KGB man or men who had confronted him. As a result, CIA decided not to let him return to Moscow and, to Smith's disappointment, fired him in October.

With help in Washington designed to sweeten this bitter pill, Smith obtained a research position at the Hoover Institution at Stanford University in California. There he would study the just-opened files of the Tsarist security service, the *Okhrana*.[3]

While waiting for his job in California Smith remained in Washington until the late summer of 1957. We found in the files a note written that spring by a Soviet (SR) Division officer (call him Frank) who had chanced to encounter Smith on the street. Because he knew that Smith had been fired Frank asked, "What are you doing these days?"

"Nothing much," Smith replied, "just killing time, waiting to go out to California. Spending a lot of time in the movies."

The fit was stunning. It had been Kovshuk himself, as Nosenko had told us and as would be logical in his position, who had confronted Smith in the KGB boudoir. The KGB's threat or offer had swayed Smith to the point that he hesitated to report it. CIA recalled him from Moscow before a relationship with the KGB could develop. He did not tell a full or convincing story to CIA Security in Washington, and by October it was clear that he would not return to Moscow. (Kovshuk and "Kislov" asked for their U.S. visas on 7 and 9 November.) Smith was embittered by what he considered an unfair dismissal. He remained in Washington through the spring of 1957, spending a lot of time at the movies while the "three musketeers" were operating around movie houses—and, as Golitsyn had heard, learning things that put the KGB on the trail of Pyotr Popov.

That the "musketeer" activity was connected with the KGB's Popov investigation was further indicated when we discovered from a routine note in our Moscow files that in February 1959 George Winters had chanced to meet Kislov socially. At that precise moment Kovshuk's KGB section was targeting Winters because it determined that just three weeks earlier he mailed a letter to Popov. All social encounters between Soviet officials and American Embassy personnel were being watched, often instigated, and wherever possible exploited by Kovshuk's section. So it was surely no coincidence that just at that point, Kovshuk's colleague Kislov, only two weeks after stepping off the plane from his minimum (two-year) stint in the United States, should "happen" to meet Kovshuk's target Winters.

Nosenko had shown inexplicable familiarity with the Smith case, to the point of claiming personal participation—though this was impossible. Kovshuk confronted Smith in the second half of 1956, whereas Nosenko had transferred nearly a year earlier to a department having nothing to do with operations against the Embassy.

And Smith was one of a mere handful of CIA officers who knew of the Popov operation.

Much later, the KGB admitted that it had, in fact, recruited Smith. A book published in 2001 with KGB authorization, and containing its official file data, listed Smith as the first CIA officer recruited by the KGB.[4]

So Golitsyn had heard right: Kovshuk's 1957 trip had indeed led the KGB onto the track of Pyotr Popov. Nosenko's stories of the trip and of the surveillance of the letter mailing looked more and more suspicious. Could it have been a KGB attempt to draw American counterintelligence off Smith's track?

When the occupation of Austria drew to a close in September 1955, Popov went back to Moscow. In early 1956 he was posted to the GRU tactical intelligence unit in Schwerin, East Germany, where CIA reestablished contact via a courier. He was shifted in 1957 to East Berlin to support GRU Illegals (Soviet intelligence personnel, either KGB or GRU, serving abroad under assumed foreign identities), and that made contact simpler. From then on he would slip into West Berlin to meet his case officer from Vienna days, George Kisevalter, who was occasionally accompanied by another CIA officer.

There in the second half of 1957 things were seen to go wrong.

Popov began to notice a disturbing influx of KGB acquaintances from his Vienna days arriving for duty in Berlin and resuming social contact with him. He knew at least two of them to be involved in security and counterintelligence work. This worried him, and with reason. As we learned much later from Golitsyn, by September 1957 the KGB had begun assigning personnel to establish a watch over Popov.

Other things might have attracted unfavorable KGB attention to Popov —enough, in fact, to permit a CIA analyst to reach the happy finding that Popov need not have been (and from there to jump to the conclusion that he *was* not) betrayed from within CIA:[5]

- In March 1957 Popov witnessed a secret speech by Marshal Georgy Zhukov, who came to East Germany to address Soviet troop commanders. Popov's report, though disseminated only to a few American and British officials, apparently fell into the hands of a mole, because the KGB learned of it and investigated those who had been present.
- Popov continued to correspond with his Yugoslav girlfriend in Austria, Mili Kohanek, and brought her to Berlin on a visit, drawing unfavorable attention. Earlier he had even proposed her as an agent for the GRU, which raised the eyebrows of his chief in Schwerin.
- In October 1957, Popov dispatched to New York from Berlin a GRU Illegal, Margarita Tairova. (She had been escorted to Berlin from Moscow by a GRU officer whom Popov had, to his surprise, never heard of—but who will become prominent later in this book.) CIA alerted the FBI to her coming and despite stern injunctions, the FBI put such heavy coverage on her that she noticed it (as later reported by Popov in a controversial note to CIA—see below). She and her fellow-Illegal husband, already in the United States, became frightened and fled back to Russia. Since Popov was one of the very few who could have known her travel plans and identity, he came under suspicion and was questioned, along with others. But the cloud seemed to blow over and Popov was left in his Berlin post.
- To give a much-needed boost to Popov's GRU career (he had made no recruitments and feared he might be recalled for poor performance), CIA arranged in the summer of 1958 for him to meet an American student whom he could ostensibly recruit. The GRU later came to suspect this case was not genuine, which reflected discredit if not suspicion on Popov.[6]

On 17 November 1958 Popov was recalled to Moscow "for consultation" about the student operation, and left Berlin within a day or so. He never returned.

On 8 December 1958 it was announced that the chief of the KGB,

Ivan A. Serov, would be leaving his post and assume leadership of the GRU. Lieutenant General Mikhail Alekseyevich Shalin, who had been GRU chief, was abruptly removed from his post.

Toward the end of December CIA got a prearranged signal from Popov indicating in coded language that he was safe but no longer in the GRU and unable to leave the USSR. Now, according to the contingency plan, CIA was to make a brush contact with him in Moscow on a date (with alternates) prearranged in Berlin. Failing that, CIA would arrange contact through an innocent-appearing letter to Popov's home in the city of Kalinin. Popov's CIA contact would be Russell Langelle, under cover as American Embassy security officer. Popov had been introduced to him in Berlin for just this contingency—a sudden recall to Russia.

Popov made the brush contact in early January, then another in mid-month. Then confusion played a potentially fatal role. CIA's contingency letter to Popov had been prepared in advance and put into the hands of the man who would mail it if it were to be needed, a co-opted official of the American Embassy, George Winters. By some misunderstanding, Winters dropped the now-unnecessary letter into a Moscow mailbox on 29 January even though by then Langelle had already met Popov twice.[7]

On 18 March 1959, nearly two months after the letter mailing, Popov came to a meeting in the uniform of a full colonel in the Transportation Corps, to which he had been transferred from the GRU. He gave Langelle a booklet of notes and said he was soon to be transferred to the Sverdlovsk region. In July CIA passed him questions about missile launch facilities in that area. Popov's information was now noticeably less valuable than what he had supplied in Germany. This worried CIA, of course, but could be explained by his reduced access to top-level information.

The real reason became clear in September. The KGB had arrested Popov and doubled him back against us.

In the men's room of the Aragvi Restaurant, after motioning Langelle to be silent and indicating that he was wired for sound, Popov passed to Langelle a cigarette-sized roll of paper. On both sides of seven or eight narrow pieces of toilet paper—about half the size of a square of Western toilet paper, and of a rough brown texture—Popov had neatly block-printed in pencil a message that I present here translated and paraphrased:

- I was arrested as a result of KGB surveillance of the mailing of the re-contact letter.
- I was under suspicion and recalled from Berlin because of my rela-

tions with Mili and because of the Illegal woman in New York [Tairova], who fled after she noted that her baggage had been tampered with in her U.S. hotel. She claimed that she'd been tailed all the way from Germany.

- I told them that you recruited me at the end of November 1953, and that I had given you no documentary material and nothing in writing except during the Schwerin period. Apart from these two lies, I told them the whole truth.
- Because the KGB believed I had confessed fully, they are using me in this double agent game. I was told that if I cooperate, my sentence might be only fifteen years. Thus I beg you to act as if you know nothing about the trap.
- I will keep you informed about my situation and the KGB's intentions.
- I hope that if this meeting and the next one go well, the KGB will trust me and maybe let me go to Berlin, where I may have a chance to escape.
- Do not take any chances. When you go to a meeting with me, take plenty of cover.
- In the December meeting I will supply a detailed report.[8]

This KGB game, said the note, was being handled by KGB officers Zvezdenkov and Sumin under the direction of counterintelligence chief Oleg Gribanov. It added gratuitously that the KGB "knows a lot about the American Embassy" and mentioned by name, for no apparent reason, some of Popov's former GRU colleagues.

The note claimed, quite improbably, that Popov himself and not the KGB had provided some (unspecified) parts of the information he had passed to CIA while under KGB control. It also speculated that the KGB might be planning to use Popov in a propaganda coup.

CIA was of course willing to carry on playacting to protect Popov, but at the next brush pass on 9 October 1959—the meeting that his note had begged CIA to attend with "plenty of cover"—the KGB brought the play to an abrupt halt. As Langelle stepped off a Moscow bus on which Popov had slipped him some written information, the KGB arrested him. After Langelle had refused their offer to help him out of his trouble if he would cooperate, the KGB expelled him from the country. They left George Winters untouched and unmentioned to the end of his tour of duty more than a year later.[9] Only years later did the Soviet press begin vilifying Winters as a spy and even then without referring to the Popov case.

On 20 October 1959 *Izvestiya*, as always the voice of the government, briefly noted the expulsion of Langelle, without naming the spy he had been meeting. It was not until a year later that the Soviet press mentioned—without connecting this to Langelle—that an "Army Lt. Col. P." had been executed. In publications through the 1960s and as late as 1979 they still withheld his name, giving it variously as "P" or "Petrov." Through the 1960s, writings by leading KGB officials intentionally distorted the details of the affair to convey the impression that the KGB did not even know when CIA recruited Popov, giving dates varying from 1951 to 1956.

If CIA were to accept Nosenko's (and the Popov note's) account of the letter mailing—and Nosenko's version of Kovshuk's trip to Washington—it could breathe a sigh of relief in the confidence that Popov's tragic downfall was due to mischance—not something more sinister, like a mole.

But Nosenko's version clashed with known facts. Even high-level KGB sources later said GRU chief General Shalin was fired because of the revelation of Popov's treason—and he was fired in early December 1958, right after Popov's return to Russia and *seven weeks before the letter mailing* to which Nosenko had attributed Popov's downfall. And surely the KGB would not have left Popov free, perhaps to run away, when alerted to his danger by the (published) news of Shalin's fall.

The KGB itself admitted after the Cold War that it had Popov under tight surveillance (more likely, under control) and that the surveillants saw him meet Langelle more than a week before the letter mailing.[10]

Veterans conversant with the KGB's detention procedures stated categorically that Popov could not have genuinely written, hidden, and passed this note undetected—much less with such excess verbiage and without any strikeover or sign of haste.

A picture was taking shape. One could see the KGB taking pains to protect its real source (Smith) by delaying Popov's recall from Berlin and using him, after a secret arrest, as a double agent in Moscow. This would draw a CIA person from the Embassy to contact him so he could ostensibly be exposed by "routine surveillance of diplomats"—the story told by Popov's note and by Nosenko.

Indeed, Kovshuk did *not* go to Washington for the cipher-machine mechanic. When Andrey was finally identified and interviewed by the FBI, his account made that clear.

Leaving his wife and children in the United States, Andrey had arrived in Moscow in the fall of 1951 to serve as a cipher-machine mechanic. That work involved only repairs to and testing of exterior parts of the machines, like input and output connections. Only visiting specialists did deeper repair and maintenance. Andrey would never see the rotors, the secret parts in a sealed housing, and if they should happen to break down, the cipher clerks themselves would send them to the United States for repair. Whenever Andrey was admitted to the code room, a code room official closely accompanied him—"like a Siamese twin," as he put it—even to the toilet.

In the winter of 1953, some months before his tour of duty was to end, he accepted his good-looking maid's invitation to visit her little apartment —where hidden KGB cameras recorded their lovemaking. The KGB called him to a meeting on the river embankment, where two operatives showed him photos, one of which had been touched up to be even more ruinous to his marriage. They would give him the photos and negatives, they said. All he had to do in return was "steal the keys to the Embassy codes."

Shocked, he agreed to meet them again, and at this second meeting one of the KGB officers gave him a special paper and flashlight, instructing him to put the paper against the list of rotor settings and shine the flashlight on the paper. But even if he'd been willing, Andrey would never have had an opportunity to do any such thing, so at the next meeting he returned the paper, blank. For months thereafter there were no more meetings. Andrey thought this might have had something to do with Stalin's death at that time.

Then the KGB called him to a last meeting just before his tour ended in the late summer of 1953. He didn't yet know where he would next be stationed but expected to learn before he left. So the KGB man told him to write his next assignment on a piece of paper, put it into a crushed empty cigarette package, and drop it into a trash bin at the airport on departure. Presumably under KGB surveillance, he dropped the package, but he had left the paper blank.

From then on, in the United States, Andrey lived in fear that the KGB would get back in touch, especially during the first year or so when he worked in the Pentagon War Room sorting and posting clear-text messages from a teletype machine. So when he was offered a transfer to an army recruiting station in the Washington area, where he would have no access whatever to classified information, he happily accepted.

But in his new job, as in the old one, he heard nothing from the KGB— for four years. Then, one evening in October 1957 at an American Legion post, he was called to the phone where a Russian-accented voice reminded him of the Moscow maid and the pictures, and proposed a meeting. The KGB must have been tailing him to know he was there, and if they knew that they presumably also knew how insignificant was his job.

Andrey remembered the date of the call because it came at an unpropitious moment. Public attention had just been paid to people like himself by the revelation in the press that an American sergeant named Roy Rhodes had confessed to being recruited by the KGB while serving in Moscow. Rhodes, said the papers, would appear as a surprise witness in the forthcoming trial of the Soviet Illegal operative Rudolf Abel. Rhodes's name was never mentioned publicly before October 1957.

Andrey went to the designated restaurant in the Washington suburb of Falls Church, where a short, heavyset Russian met him. He offered to return the compromising pictures, but demanded documentary information in return. Andrey agreed and for the next meeting he grabbed a handful of unclassified recruitment pamphlets from his office, the only documents kept there. At this second meeting the short man was accompanied by another Russian, older and more authoritative. Andrey had never seen either of them before these Washington meetings, but recognized them from photographs the FBI showed him. The older man was "Komarov"—Vladislav Kovshuk.

Kovshuk never spoke during the meeting, merely nodding whenever the other Soviet looked to him for approval. Evidently, they knew Andrey was close to retirement, for the short Soviet asked him to look for a job in a company working on government contracts.

But he never heard from them again. Now, seven years later, the FBI came to him armed with—but not disclosing to him—Nosenko's information.

Andrey had retired from the army in late 1961, six months before Nosenko first reported on him. Now, as a civilian, he had no access whatever to classified information. Sacrificing him cost the KGB nothing. Evidently it considered him a worthless source, and the Americans likewise saw him as no security risk. Even before interviewing him the FBI had determined from army records that Andrey could not have delivered sensitive information, and during hours of questioning they became convinced of his sincerity. The FBI did not charge or arrest him, and army security authorities saw no reason even to question him further. He was left to live out his retirement in peace.

Many years later, by then an old man living alone in a trailer camp,

Andrey told a visitor that he had been baffled by the KGB's actions and inaction. "I've never stopped thinking about it," he said, "and I finally decided that I had somehow been used as a pawn. The KGB knew I hadn't been helpful, and decided to give me away to the FBI. But why? Maybe I was used to promote a Soviet agent who came here? I just don't know. I don't suppose I ever will know."

It was surely not for this unnecessary and silent one-time appearance to a dormant and useless agent with whom he had had no previous contact that the Moscow section chief had been sent to Washington on ostensibly permanent assignment nine months earlier.

The identification of Edward Ellis Smith as the near-certain target of Kovshuk's trip posed a vexing question. Smith had left CIA five years before Golitsyn defected and told the Americans about Kovshuk's trip. By then he would presumably be of less interest to the KGB. Why then did it go to the trouble as late as 1962, through Nosenko, to throw CIA off his track?

We never found out, but one possible answer troubled us. Might Smith have helped the KGB recruit another CIA official—one still active?

My colleague Sid and I were returning from lunch at a restaurant in nearby McLean, Virginia. Like every American of a certain age I remember where I was at that moment. The date, to be graven in history, was 22 November 1963. I had one foot in an elevator in the CIA building in Langley.

"Isn't it terrible?" said Jerry, as he stepped out of the elevator.

"Probably not as bad as all that, Jerry," Sid said flippantly. Jerry stopped. "No, listen. Haven't you heard?" he said, "The President has been shot in Dallas!"

We rushed to our offices on the fifth floor where radios were on. Sickened, we talked in subdued voices, stirring each other's hope for that brief moment before the sad, final news was flashed. Soon the radio announced that the assassin had been captured and, not long after that, identified him.

A later news bulletin galvanized us: Lee Harvey Oswald was an ex-Marine who had defected to the Soviet Union in 1959 and had returned to the United States only a year and a half ago.

The Counterintelligence Staff, with its established liaison with the FBI and other government agencies, was quickly designated as the Agency's coordinating point for all Clandestine Services efforts to collect information on Oswald and his connections. Among the traces that James Angleton's shop first uncovered was a recent report from Mexico City on

Oswald's contact with the Soviet Embassy when he applied for a visa to return to the USSR. The "consular officials" he met were both KGB officers. By itself this was no surprise, because the KGB occupied almost all consular slots throughout the world. But one of those whom Oswald met was Valery V. Kostikov, whom we knew to have been a member of the First Chief Directorate's 13th Department, the one responsible for sabotage and "liquid affairs" abroad—murder.

The Counterintelligence Staff handled the microscopic search of Agency files, but everyone stretched to make any possible contribution. It was Lee Wigren, our Counterintelligence section research chief, who made the section's first contribution. On his own initiative he leafed through the Agency's photographic files on the remote chance that some detail of Minsk, where Oswald had lived, might assist in visualizing his environment in the Soviet Union.

Photo in hand, Lee burst into my office.

"Look at this," he exclaimed. "I asked for pictures of landmarks and public buildings in Minsk and got this one of the opera house." An American tourist had taken photos in August 1961 during a trip to the USSR and thinking they might be of some interest, he had turned them over to a CIA representative he knew. In due course, the snapshots were filed. Among them was the one in Lee's hand, of the opera house in Minsk.

"So, what do you think?"

I thought as Lee did. Standing there, undeniably, was Lee Harvey Oswald himself. This useful confirmation of Oswald's presence there was passed on to the investigators and later appeared in the Warren Commission Report on the assassination.[11]

The circumstances—Oswald's defection to the USSR, his return to the United States with a Soviet wife, his contact with Kostikov only two months before the assassination—opened the question of whether the Soviet government had had a hand in the assassination. It seemed entirely unlikely but could not be disregarded.

Incredibly, it was only a few weeks later that I would be listening to a denial of any Soviet involvement in the assassination, delivered with rare authority by my agent at work in the USSR.

CHAPTER 8

Defection

"Come in, Pete. There's news," said David Murphy over the internal phone line. I hurried along the corridor to the corner office of the chief of the Soviet Russia Division.

It was 23 January 1964, eighteen months after George Kisevalter and I had said farewell to Yuri Nosenko. Meanwhile, Jack Maury had been assigned abroad, Howard Osborne had held the post for a short time, and in August 1963 David Murphy had taken over as division chief. His appointment added hugely to the professionalism of CIA's operations against the USSR. He had a keen interest in and deep knowledge of the Soviet Union, he spoke Russian, he had long operated in the field against Soviet bloc targets (and had overseen the handling in Berlin of Pyotr Popov), and he came to this job directly from years of supervising our operations against the Eastern European satellites of the Soviet Union. He brought to the task a unique verve, activism, and initiative—tempered by a well-informed, realistic insight into Soviet bloc counterintelligence capabilities. It was one of those rare cases of the right man in the right job, and a major influence on the course of events I will describe here.

As I stepped into his office I saw that George Kisevalter was there. Dave greeted me with a smile. "Nosenko's back."

Kisevalter, in evident good cheer, added, "The telegram came in last night, exactly as we arranged it. Even better, it's Geneva again."

I clenched my fist and faked a short right-hand punch. "We're off." We were ready. In the months since Nosenko had left Geneva, George and I had had time to prepare and update meeting plans and questions for future encounters.

Dave reviewed our communications arrangements. No one would be told where we were going or why we were away, and we would book separate flights to avoid notice that we had gone out together. Our messages to Headquarters from the field would carry a special indicator to ensure that the smallest possible number of people would become aware of this source.

As we left his office Dave said, "Let's hope he can stay for a while."

"Amen to that," I muttered, and, as we went off to pack for the trip, I reminded George that Geneva was cold and wet in January.

Thirty-six hours later we were in Geneva, checking the safe house accommodation. This time we had a larger apartment in a handsome building in the residential district in which I had lived as a student. The techs had already rigged the audio equipment, and an administrative clerk was providing the food and drink supply. (Neither they nor other officers in Geneva knew whom we would be meeting in the apartment they so carefully arranged for us.) The problem of getting the safe house address to Nosenko was more to the point. All things being equal, according to plan he would be expecting to meet us tonight at seven forty-five.

"The first movie theater in the phone book is the ABC," I told George. "I know it well. I'll go there tonight, slip him a paper with this address, and we'll assume he can get here on his own. If he arrives before I can get back, you'll be here. And if he doesn't show up I'll phone you and then hang around in town for the alternate meeting an hour later."

An hour before the appointed time, I bundled into my overcoat and donned a black Styrian hat. With the horn-rimmed glasses that I rarely wore, this minimal effort would at least lessen the chances of being recognized by someone who might know me from my earlier years here. I strolled awhile in the chilly air, caught a bus to the town center, and got off a few blocks from the theater.

Walking toward the brightly lit open foyer by the ticket booth of the "ABC," I spotted Nosenko standing off to the left, a typical moviegoer waiting for his date. It was movie time and others were milling about, so he didn't see me coming. I brushed quickly past, thrusting a paper with the address and phone number into his hand and moving without pause out of the foyer into the darkness of the street.

Nosenko must have found a taxi immediately because by the time I got back to the apartment he and Kisevalter were standing in the living room chatting. I left my coat and hat in the vestibule and, rubbing my hands from the cold, walked into a warm reunion. But right off, Nosenko asked with apparent concern, "Who was it that passed me the note?"

"Didn't you recognize me?" He shook his head in disbelief as I led him out to the vestibule, opened the closet, and pointed to the black hat. He continued to shake his head, surprisingly upset that he had failed to spot his own contact.

"Yuri has a bit of a surprise for us," said George with less than his usual enthusiasm. "He wants to stay."

"What?" I exclaimed. "Stay where?" I turned to Nosenko, "You don't mean defect, do you?"

Nosenko nodded. "Yes, and right now. I don't want to go back."

"Well, well," I said. "We'd better sit down and talk about this—and let's have a drink. I could use one." On a scale of safe house surprises, this ranked close to the top. But higher was yet to come.

George had already put *zakouskies*—snacks—on a tray, and I served Nosenko the scotch whisky that he preferred. We raised our whisky glasses to this reunion, and I broke the silence. "I don't understand. You said you would never leave your country and family. Is something wrong?"

"Yes, I don't know exactly what, but I've been getting the feeling that they might be onto me. It would be too risky to go on."

Odd, I thought. He had left the USSR three days before, again to act as security officer for the Soviet delegation to the resumed disarmament talks. We knew—and as a KGB officer, he knew much better—that if there had been the slightest reason for distrust, the KGB would not have signed off on this assignment abroad, especially for a mission unrelated to his Moscow responsibilities.

"Can you give us any specifics? This is damned important."

"No, nothing special. Just the way people look at me. I'm worried."

Suppressing my astonishment I said, matter-of-factly, "Of course, you can come over any time you want, and we will welcome you. But I still don't understand. What about your family, the little girls?"

"Oh, they'll be okay," he answered offhandedly. Doubts flashed through my mind. We knew how the regime treated the families left behind by defectors, and it was anything but "okay." Close relatives were fired from responsible jobs and ostracized by friends and colleagues. The family would be kicked out of their apartment and probably be exiled to a distant city, the children shunned as the offspring of a traitor. They would never be allowed to join him in the West, and he would never return to Russia, for he would be under sentence of death for treason.

After a glance at Kisevalter, who just shrugged, I turned to Nosenko, "Okay, but give yourself and us a little time. Stay where you are, at least for a few days. If you sense any real danger, you can come here any time. They won't kidnap you in Switzerland. We'll need the time to make arrangements with Washington for your entry into the U.S. And we want to know what you might learn here."

George and I knew that CIA would strongly have preferred that he stay where he was. An agent in place has a future and offers opportunities, while the value of most defectors is finite. But as we sipped at our drinks and nibbled at the snacks I began to see the brighter side of Nosenko's decision. At least now there would be the opportunity to question him in detail about things we had barely touched upon in the hurry of spy meetings abroad. There would also be the chance to plumb any knowledge of political and strategic matters that he might have learned during his years in the inner core of the system.

He agreed to wait "maybe for a week or so," and we settled down to our meeting.

On the register of operational surprises, Nosenko's next remark scored a perfect ten.

He had personal, not to say intimate, knowledge of the stay in the Soviet Union of Lee Harvey Oswald, who two months earlier had assassinated President Kennedy.

For weeks the Warren Commission had been turning Washington inside out in investigating every conceivable aspect of the crime. High on the list were the circumstances of Oswald's bizarre decision to defect to the Soviet Union, his apparent change of heart and return to the United States with a Soviet wife; his pro-Cuban political activity; and his visit to the Soviet consulate in Mexico City two months before the assassination. Now, in this most timely fashion, CIA's only source inside the KGB had come out with direct knowledge. If President Johnson himself had been sitting in this safe house, his first question would have been, "What can you tell us about the assassination of President Kennedy?" And George and I had spent all this time discussing Nosenko's future!

"I was personally involved in this case," he said. "When Oswald came to the Soviet Union in 1959, he told his Intourist guide he wanted to stay in the country and become a Soviet citizen. I was deputy chief of our section dealing with American and British Commonwealth tourists to the USSR. Krupnov, one of my case officers, was handling the young guide. When Krupnov reported to me, I called up everything we knew about Oswald— from the guide, from his visa application, and from the staff at the Hotel Berlin, where he was staying. On the basis of this, Krupnov and I judged that Oswald was of no interest and would probably just be a nuisance. So, I decided to reject his request."

George and I listened without interrupting Nosenko's story. It seemed unlikely to me that a KGB officer at Nosenko's level would be allowed to make such a decision but this was not the time to mention it.

"When Oswald was told he couldn't stay, he went back to the hotel and tried to commit suicide. They found him in his room with his wrist cut open, and got him to a hospital. We still didn't want to let him stay, but higher-ups decided it would be too embarrassing if he should really succeed in killing himself in our country. So they let him stay. But we saw to it that he would not be allowed to stay in the Moscow area. The Red Cross found him a job in Minsk."

As I moved to top off Nosenko's glass with soda water, he motioned me to stop, took the whiskey bottle himself, and poured more on top of the soda. "Didn't you even suspect he might be an American spy?" I asked.

"We thought of it, but it was clear he was somehow abnormal, and not the type. Anyway, that sort of thing would be looked into only if he was to be allowed to remain in the country. And we didn't think that would happen."

"Didn't any KGB people at least interview him, to get their own impressions? To see if he might be useful to the KGB? After all, he had just left the marines. Even if that was of no importance to you, wouldn't the GRU have an interest?"

"No. No one ever bothered. He was obviously low level, just a corporal or something. And after the suicide attempt it was even clearer that he was not normal."[1] George and I took notes (neither waiting for nor relying on the tapes that were recording everything) and avoided interrupting Nosenko's account with detailed questions.

"Then came the news about his assassination of President Kennedy. When the top people found out that the killer had recently lived for three years in our country, they went into a spin. The Americans might get the idea that they had something to do with it. So Khrushchev himself asked my boss Gribanov if the KGB had had anything to do with Oswald. Immediately, Gribanov told me to get the KGB file from Minsk. I phoned Minsk and they flew a man right away with their file on Oswald.

"The guy from Minsk delivered it to me, and as Khrushchev had ordered, I personally reviewed it to see if the KGB there had had any relationship whatever with Oswald."

George and I leaned forward, expectantly. "And?"

"And nothing. There was no sign whatever that the KGB in Minsk had taken any interest in him."

"Didn't they watch him, or bug his apartment, or put agents next to him?" George asked.

"No, nothing of the sort."

"What did the file look like? How big was it?"

"One volume, thick like this," Nosenko answered, holding his thumb and index finger about an inch and a half apart.

"Did you read it all?"

"I had to. I had to be absolutely sure of my answer to Gribanov and Khrushchev. I read it carefully."

He paused, then added, "If anyone wants to know whether the Soviet government was behind Oswald, I can answer. It wasn't. No one in the KGB paid any attention to him."

Yes, I thought, you can damned well be sure that the Warren Commission and just about everyone else will be interested. George and I exchanged glances, but did not interrupt our guest.

After a long swallow of his drink, Nosenko recalled another contact with the Oswald affair.

"A few months ago, in September, long before the assassination, I happened to be visiting an office in the First Chief Directorate. One of the guys said it was good I was there, because I might be able to throw some light on a cable that had just come in from the residency in Mexico City. They showed it to me. The cable reported this guy Oswald had come in to the consulate saying he had lived in the USSR and wanted to go back. He was asking for a visa to return here. I told them I vaguely remembered something about his visit and request to stay, and the problems we'd had with that."

"How long was the cable, exactly what did it say?" George asked.

"About half a page, no more. As I remember, it just gave the identifying data on Oswald and his Soviet wife, and told what he had said about having lived in the USSR and gone back to the States. I heard the guys talking it over. They decided there would be no good reason to let him come back. So they sent a cable telling Mexico to refuse the request."

By any measure we were getting a most extraordinary break—and witnessing a stunning coincidence. CIA's only source among the thousands of KGB officers in the USSR arrives straight from Moscow two months after the JFK assassination, to report having had no fewer than four points of contact with the case of Lee Harvey Oswald in the USSR. First, he'd been a key figure in 1959 in the initial refusal (later rescinded) to let him stay. Second, he had personally observed Moscow's refusal to let Oswald return to the USSR in September 1963. Third, he had personally intervened to get the file from Minsk, and fourth, he had reviewed the entire KGB file on Oswald.

The Nosenko operation had clearly taken a major turn. Now our agent in place had placed himself as a witness—probably the only one—to a question facing the American government concerning one of the most dramatic and potentially dangerous incidents of the Cold War. This overwhelmed all the questions and doubts and shadows that had fallen over this case in the preceding months, all the reservations that piled up about Nosenko's truthfulness. I doubted that this sensational turn of events was coincidence—new doubts added to so many—but that didn't matter. Now it was certain: his defection would be accepted and he would be brought into the United States.

We took a break from this talk and once again I filled the glasses and brought more food from the kitchen. Nosenko sat comfortably and had evidently made his peace with the idea of staying in place for a while. He showed no flicker of anxiety at the prospect of abandoning his family, career, country, or way of life, and no hint of the concern that all defectors feel for their future. Defection ranks high on the list of personal traumas. Nosenko appeared to have weathered his move as easily as if he had chosen between a vacation at the shore or in the mountains.

I was less relaxed; I was composing in my mind a cable to report Nosenko's stunning account of Oswald. My attention snapped back when I heard him say, "I attended the trial of Penkovsky, your agent. And I know how he was caught."

George, who had been Penkovsky's case officer, could not restrain himself. "Great! That's important to us. How did it happen?"

"Surveillance in Moscow. Our guys were tailing a British diplomat and saw a contact with an unknown person who looked like a Russian. They took after him and identified him as this GRU colonel."

"How did you find this out?" Kisevalter asked, not revealing his own role in the case.

"One of the guys in our [Second Chief Directorate] British Department told me about it. They were very proud of their work. Surveillance did a great job."

"When did it happen?" I asked.

"I'm not sure—some time at the beginning of 1962."

"Who was it that told you?"

"I don't remember. Someone in the department. Maybe [Yevgeny] Tarabrin, the department chief. I know him well."

Then, abruptly, Nosenko changed the subject. "Did you get the papers?"

I looked questioningly at him, and at George, who shrugged.

"I mean the KGB documents that were sent to the American Embassy in Moscow."

"Oh yes," I said. I realized that he was talking about a newspaper-wrapped bundle of documents handed to an American in Moscow two months earlier by a former KGB officer named Aleksandr Cherepanov. The Embassy, fearing provocation, had turned the papers back to Soviet authorities. "We managed to photograph them before the Embassy sent them back. But sending them back was a stupid mistake."

"Yes, we had no trouble identifying the guy who sent them. He got wind of the suspicion and ran away. I went out on the hunt for him." Nosenko then told about it and showed us the official authorization for his travel during that hunt (see Chapter 16). The document was issued to "Lieutenant Colonel Nosenko."

"Yes," he said proudly, "my promotion came through last year. And what's more, I'm now first deputy chief of the whole Tourist Department." Our agent's career was blossoming—ironically, just at the moment he decided to bring it to an end.

George and I raised our glasses in congratulations.

"I've learned about an important case. We have a man in the middle of your secret courier center in Paris. He has given a lot of secret American air force documents."

We probed for details. Here was something far more important than what Nosenko had been telling us about, tourists who had no access to secrets. The KGB had recruited an army sergeant, Nosenko said, who was now working in the U.S. courier center at Orly airport south of Paris. He occasionally had night duty alone in the center, where dispatches arrived for onward flights to and from air force and army bases in Europe. Nosenko did not know his name.

"He comes out of the center and hands our boys envelopes full of documents to photocopy. They have a car waiting and speed to the Embassy, where technicians open the envelopes, photograph the documents, replace them, and reseal the envelopes so there's no trace that they had been opened. Then they rush them back to Orly to get them to the sergeant before he goes off duty in the morning. It's close timing. They're really proud of the way it's running."

"How did you learn about this?"

"From the boys themselves."

"Who are they?"

"Guys I know. The technicians. They were boasting to me. I can't remember which of these guys it was who told me. I know several of them."

Despite our questions, Nosenko could not identify his source, though he had been our willing collaborator when "one of the boys" committed this flagrant violation of the KGB's tightly enforced rule of "need to know." Well, I thought, perhaps he is just being protective of the friend who told him. Perhaps.

"When was all this going on?"

"I heard it recently. As far as I know it still is. Maybe you can catch the guy."

Nosenko volunteered another item. He had heard that the KGB had recruited an American army officer in Germany, a captain. The KGB code name was "Sasha."

"Tell us what you know, please," I said. "There are a lot of captains in Germany." He seemed not to remember that we had asked him about this code name among others in 1962, when he drew a blank on it.

"That's all I heard, just that," he shrugged.

"How did you hear about this?" He could not remember.

A couple more questions made it clear that he could add nothing, not even to specify whether the case was still active. This was too vague even to begin investigating.

Nosenko recalled an incident from his time in the American Embassy Section. "We were watching a dead drop of yours. I was keeping a close watch on Abidian, the Embassy security officer. Our surveillance saw him setting up a drop on Pushkin Street. We set a watch over it so we could catch whoever would come there to use it. Week after week for three months the watchers' reports came over my desk—all negative. We never did spot any-one coming there."

"When was this?" Kisevalter asked. I figured that he was having some of the same thoughts I was. We knew something about that dead drop (the one at which Dick Jacob had been trapped).

"I remember exactly. It was late in December 1960."

This piece of information was later to cause immense puzzlement.

Nosenko emptied his drink. "If I'm going to stay with the delegation for these next days, I'd better go back now."

We assured him that one of us would always be in the apartment to receive him any day, at any time he felt able to get away from his official duties or whenever he might feel himself in danger. Otherwise, we would meet in two days.

I no longer remember how long it took us to get the details of this memorable session into a cable to Headquarters, but it seemed only min-utes before we received an urgent instruction to keep our man in place as long as possible. Aside from the advantage, as we were gratuitously in-formed, of having an eye into the local Soviet installations, it would take time for Headquarters to arrange to bring our prize legally into the United States. If Nosenko had to jump before Washington could get its act to-gether, we were to drive him to an American military installation in West Germany for debriefing and evaluation.

Two days later Nosenko told us more about KGB activities, including some information he'd picked up from chats with colleagues while visiting the lo-cal rezidentura in connection with his delegation security responsibilities.

"I was there yesterday, and the guy I was talking to had a file on his desk. I saw its code name, 'Scorpion.' He told me it was the rezidentura's file on CIA in Geneva. It was real thin, couldn't have had more than a couple of sheets of paper in it. Obviously they don't know much about you here."

Strange, I thought, for a couple of reasons. Earlier sources had told CIA that traveling KGB officers were admitted into residency premises only if they had a specific need to come inside there. Contacts between the local KGB and their visiting colleagues on conference delegations were customarily maintained outside the sacrosanct KGB enclave.

Even the existence of such a file as this "Scorpion" was questionable. To our knowledge, no KGB rezidenturas in the West retained subject files of this sort. Aside from occasional special requirements from Moscow, their safes held little more than the individual officers' working files, and even those were usually reduced to cryptic notes. Well, I thought, maybe the Geneva residency does. But if it does, this file sounds too thin. The KGB knew more than that about CIA in Geneva. Nosenko himself had told us in 1962 that the KGB was running a double agent (the Soviet radio reporter Boris Belitsky) against CIA. Belitsky was sometimes in Geneva, and that alone should have told them more than they could put on a couple of sheets of paper. One more oddity to tuck away.

I did not discuss these oddities with George Kisevalter. He was clearly reveling in his role, once again, as case officer to an important source inside Soviet Intelligence. He seemed primarily concerned with projecting his own avuncular image and impressing the agent with his knowledge. (I had winced internally in 1962 each time he tossed out to Nosenko details about senior Soviet regime figures that could only have come from another secret source, though I did not then know about Oleg Penkovsky.) In our friendly talks between meetings George never evinced any suspicion of Nosenko. In fact, he gave no sign then or later that he had noticed the contradictions and anomalies popping up in this case.

While he and I—on orders—were keeping from our colleagues the existence of this operation, I was keeping from George and others my growing suspicions. (I was sharing them only with a few of my section mates, with the Soviet Division chief, and with Counterintelligence Staff chief Angleton.) I still clung to a shred of optimism that we might eventually be able to discard them as coincidence or see them in a different light, so why spread doubts prematurely?

"We haven't been able to identify the sergeant 'Andrey' that you told us about last time," I told Nosenko in the second or third meeting. "We didn't have enough detail. Can you remember anything more that might help us?"

Nosenko paused, presumably refreshing his memory. "No, I don't think so. All I learned was from hearing the case officers talking about it when they came back to the office from meetings with 'Andrey.' That was when I was in the American Embassy Section in the 1950s. I could only hear fragments of what they were saying, so I don't know anything more. Sorry."

I shrugged. "Well, maybe this will help some." Indeed it would, I thought. Now the investigators can begin to look for cipher-machine mechanics who served in the Embassy three to five years later than 1949–1950, the dates Nosenko had given us in 1962.

Strange. According to what he had said back then, the Andrey case had taken place years before Nosenko had even entered the KGB. Now he had become an eyewitness. I shoved it to the back of my mind. More inconsistencies.

George and I were still sorting out answers to Headquarters' follow-up questions on our cabled reports when, on 4 February 1964, Nosenko arrived unannounced. His news was urgent. A member of the Geneva rezidentura had tipped him off that a telegram had arrived at the Soviet Mission that morning, recalling him to Moscow.

"This must mean they've found out about our contact," he said. "Look, I have to leave, and right now. I don't even want to go back to the hotel."

By this time Headquarters had agreed to accept Nosenko's defection but had not decided whether to bring him to the United States. We togged him out in an American officer's uniform and had him driven in a car that was politely waved through the border controls en route to the Agency's facilities in Frankfurt, West Germany.

There the Soviet Division chief, David Murphy, arrived from Washington to talk to Nosenko, get his own impressions, and reassure him about his entry into the United States and about CIA's readiness to fulfill its promises of financial remuneration ($25,000 per year) that had been made to him in 1962. From things Nosenko said, Murphy got the strange impression that Nosenko knew of him and had expected to meet him.

After Murphy's return to Washington, we were told that Nosenko would be brought into the country as a "parolee" under the terms of Section 7 of the Central Intelligence Act of 1949. This specified that "in the interest of national security and the furtherance of the national intelligence mission, as many as one hundred individuals a year can, with the authority of the Director of Central Intelligence, and the concurrence of the Attorney General and the commissioner of immigration, be admitted permanently to the United States without reference to other laws and regulations."

This law made the Agency responsible to determine—and to certify to other agencies—that the individual was the person he claimed to be, that he had plausible reasons to defect, and that there were no data suggesting the involvement of any foreign intelligence service in his defection.[2]

Under these terms Nosenko entered the United States on 11 February 1964.

CHAPTER 9

Impasse

Yuri Nosenko and his CIA companion stepped off the plane at the New York airport that six weeks earlier had been renamed for the assassinated John F. Kennedy. He was welcomed by CIA security officials, spared any customs or immigration formalities, and escorted to the gate for his onward flight. In Washington he was bundled into a waiting car and driven to a split-level house in suburban northern Virginia that would be his home and workplace for a period of initial debriefing and settling in.

Only a few people knew that questions had arisen about his bona fides. The officers who came to debrief him were not told, nor were his security guards or household staff. Nosenko would be given the same chance as any other defector to demonstrate his good faith.

Questioning began slowly. To help him get accustomed to his new surroundings he was taken on sightseeing drives and on shopping trips to buy clothes and personal effects to replace what he had left behind. He spent evenings, at his own request, in bars and nightclubs—in outlying areas as far away as Baltimore, to minimize the chance that he might be spotted by KGB operatives who would presumably be looking for him.

The Soviet Embassy in Washington demanded an opportunity to interview him to ascertain whether he had come of his own volition. (This was standard procedure for every defection.) In an hour-long session in the State Department the Soviet interviewers seemed satisfied by Nosenko's unequivocal statement of intent to renounce his Soviet citizenship and to settle in America.

Like every defector Nosenko was asked to sit down and take as many hours or days as he needed to write about his personal life—family, schooling, military service, and professional career. These leisurely considered reflections, we hoped, would correct things he might have said carelessly in the haste of safe house meetings in Geneva. He might have led himself into contradictions by boasting to impress us but now, firmly accepted in the West, he would have little reason for self-puffery.

What he now wrote did indeed contradict things he had said before but instead of clarifying old discrepancies it created new ones. His stories of his marriages and divorces rang false, his military service made no sense, and his manner of leaving military service and entering the KGB clashed with the administrative requirements known to us from other sources. When we called him on such anomalies he readily shifted details, but this produced further contradictions and questions.

Even his accounts of his career varied, beginning with the date he entered the KGB. In Geneva he had written in an autobiographical note that he had entered in the spring of 1952, and told us he had received a ten-year certificate. Now he placed his entry in the spring of 1953, but could not remember whether before or after the death of Stalin. This was as easy for a Soviet citizen to remember as for an American asked when he learned of President Kennedy's assassination, especially given the near-chaos that reigned in the service when Beria rose and fell at that time.

Nosenko said he had come, without training or preparation, directly into the American Department of the Second Chief Directorate. His first job was to spy on (and recruit as spies) American press correspondents in Russia. A year afterward he was shifted within the same section to work against the personnel of the military attaché offices of the American Embassy.

Preparing to debrief him on this critical subject, we checked the American Embassy security records to see what American personnel had said about KGB attempts to recruit them. We turned up incidents that had occurred in Nosenko's time and sector, but, strangely, he did not know about them. The KGB had staged two provocations against Nosenko's own military attaché targets and expelled them in a loud press campaign of outrage—scandals that were the talk of the whole service (one veteran later referred to them as "famous" affairs) and not just among the officers working directly against those attachés. But Nosenko had never heard of either of them.

Moreover, we could find no mention of anyone resembling Nosenko in American Embassy reports of contacts with Russians.

Charles Bohlen, the American ambassador in Moscow from April 1953 to April 1957, remembered that during this period "there were about twelve cases, mostly of [our] clerical personnel but in one instance of a security officer, getting into trouble, usually with women. The secret police [KGB] took incriminating infrared pictures, then tried to recruit the Americans for espionage. All of these people were out of the country in twenty-four hours."[1] Nosenko knew of none of these cases except (he said in 1962) that of the security officer Edward E. Smith.

The KGB was well aware that the Americans were collecting intelligence from their Embassy premises via long-range photography, radio intercept, and other techniques. To thwart these efforts the KGB was using sophisticated countermeasures which the Embassy people could perceive.

"What measures do your people take against American intercept work from inside the Moscow Embassy?" I asked Nosenko.

"I don't know anything about that," he answered.

"Well, anyone who looks at the Embassy can see the antennas. In your coverage of the Embassy, did you never look into this?"

"No, never."

"The antennas were on the roof," I said. As you've said, the top floors held the substantive sections where only the Americans were allowed. How many such classified floors were there?"

Nosenko answered confidently. "Two. As I've told you, we had mikes in there."

How could a supervisor of the section working against the Embassy not know that there were in fact three classified floors?

Nosenko was queried about KGB officers and their work against Embassy personnel. Whenever our interviewer would ask which colleague was responsible for work against a targeted American, Nosenko had a ready answer. But it became apparent that he was relying not on personal memory but on some sort of memorized table of organization. When his answers were collated they presented an absurd imbalance in the workloads of his section mates and sometimes contradicted what he had said earlier.

We asked Nosenko about his previous travel abroad but were unable to get a coherent or believable explanation for trips that made no sense in his career. While overseeing in Moscow some of the KGB's highest priority counterintelligence work, he was off at least eight times on the unrelated task of security-watchdogging various types of Soviet groups traveling abroad. He escorted boxing teams to London in August 1957 and October 1958 and to the Caribbean in 1959, and during the period 1960–1961 did things impossible for someone actually supervising work against the American Embassy as he claimed to be doing (see Chapter 15). Only a month after moving back to the Tourist Department with a promotion to section chief, his name was submitted for a Swiss visa to watchdog a months-long conference in Geneva. On his return to Moscow, having spent hardly three months on the job, he was promoted again. A year later—having had no apparent professional success—he was upped to a still higher post as first deputy department chief. But mere days afterward, off he went again on an extended delegation-watchdog assignment to Geneva. Such a career had no relation to the real KGB, or indeed to any functioning organization.

As we probed into KGB internal procedures, Nosenko proved to be ignorant of routine practices that he supposedly practiced daily, like sending telegrams or checking files.

Doubts arose about Nosenko's important insights into Lee Harvey Oswald's sojourn in Russia. On this subject FBI representatives came to question him for any slightest detail he could supply. He had hardly a word to add to what he had said in the Geneva meetings, and we later learned that what he was telling the FBI was not exactly the same as what he was telling us. Much later, more inexplicable contradictions were to come to light when he testified before the House of Representatives Select Committee on Assassinations: When the Committee compared his statements with what he had told CIA and FBI in 1964 (and observing his manner of answering questions), it concluded flatly that "Nosenko was lying." For example:

- He told the FBI he didn't know how the Soviet Embassy in Mexico City had informed Moscow of Oswald's September 1963.
- He told us that the Soviets performed no psychiatric tests on Oswald after his suicide attempt, but later said he had seen the written report of such tests.
- He told the FBI that he did not know how the Soviet Embassy in Mexico City had informed Moscow of Oswald's September 1963 application to return to the USSR—but he told us that he witnessed the arrival of the cable and even described its length.[2]
- Nosenko told us in 1964 that he had "thoroughly reviewed" the KGB's

"one-volume," modest-sized file on Oswald—but told the House Committee in 1978 that he had only *cursorily* read the *first of eight thick volumes.*

- He told us and the FBI in 1964 that Oswald was not surveilled in Minsk, but told the Committee fourteen years later that *seven* of those eight volumes consisted of surveillance reports and transcripts of bugged conversations.[3]
- He told us that the KGB had not known that Oswald was going around with Marina Prusakova. "There was no surveillance of her" until he applied to marry her. But a KGB file reported by KGB Colonel Oleg Nechiporenko (see below) revealed that the KGB checked on Marina as soon as she first met Oswald, on 17 March 1961.
- He told us and also the FBI that he learned of Oswald's 1959 request to stay in Russia and his attempted suicide from his KGB colleague Kim Krupnov. By 1978 this had become a different colleague, named Rastrusin.

KGB file material published in November 1993 by KGB Colonel Nechiporenko revealed that *Nosenko could not have read Oswald's file,* for he knew nothing about several striking and unforgettable facts in that file that bore directly on Nosenko's pretended purpose in reading it, including:

- An experienced KGB foreign-intelligence operative interviewed Oswald to judge his suitability for use as a spy. It didn't matter that this KGB officer talked to Oswald under some guise, for the file would have revealed to Nosenko the KGB officer's involvement, just as it had to Nechiporenko.
- The KGB had placed Oswald in its highest suspect category, as a possible American agent, and for that reason had put "maximum" surveillance on him, bugging his apartment, following him, and recruiting his contacts in Minsk.
- Oswald boarded a streetcar with a rifle "in plain sight."
- Oswald's correspondence with the American Embassy was intercepted and its contents became known to the KGB.
- Oswald was "making bombs," and although he later got rid of the material, the KGB feared "another weird act before his departure."[4]

Another top priority in the debriefing was to learn what, if anything, Nosenko could tell us of Soviet military, economic, and scientific matters that were not publicly available. When we asked in varying contexts what he might have picked up, even from gossip, about Soviet policymakers and their relationships, we came up with nothing worth reporting. This caused no great surprise because a counterintelligence officer at his level need not know details about military weapons or strategy, and he need know even less about scientific or technological matters. That said, most reasonably intelligent and informed citizens around the globe were likely to have some notion of national political developments and foreign policy issues. Nosenko appeared to have none, although he claimed to have deserted the Soviet Union because he disagreed with its system and policy. He never explained what specific aspects he most disliked.

High on the order of business was our attempt to draw out details of those KGB activities Nosenko had reported that seemed (in contrast to a dozen or more trivial tourist operations) of potential importance. We delved again into the Orly Airport courier center case, the army captain code-named "Sasha," the KGB's recruitment inside the British naval attaché office, its uncovering of Popov and Penkovsky, and the Belitsky double agent case. It seemed odd that Nosenko had little or nothing to add. Asked to amplify things he had said earlier, he would repeat the same generalities, sometimes word for word, as if reciting a memorized story.

Unlike any other KGB defector, Nosenko could not explain consistently how he had learned about these more important cases. He was invariably vague. "I heard it from one of the guys," he would say, or "Someone in the Department told me"—and offered different explanations at different times. He could not have forgotten, for he had learned some of these things after he had taken up contact with CIA and only shortly before reporting them.

Nosenko said that he had managed the KGB's arrest in Moscow of Yale professor Frederick C. Barghoorn in late October 1963—a blatant provocation designed to charge Barghoorn falsely with "espionage," apparently to trade his freedom for that of a Soviet official who had just been arrested for espionage in the United States. It was an ill-considered and short-lived affair. Barghoorn was a personal friend of President Kennedy, who in a press conference proclaimed his outrage and Barghoorn's innocence. The red-faced Soviets quickly released him. Barghoorn's description of the events contradicted Nosenko's and though he recognized that a person fitting our description of Nosenko had once sat in the background, silent and glowering, during an interrogation, this person had nothing to do with the events themselves. It looked as though the KGB had stuck Nosenko out there to show CIA that he was a real operative—shortly before he would reappear in Geneva.

Nosenko was questioned about his earlier report of having recruited in Kiev in 1956 a visiting American professor "B." In this, which was the only other event in which Nosenko's presence was ever confirmed, his version clashed with that of the American. He proved ignorant of key events and the role "B" ascribed to him was that of a low-level agent, not a staff officer (see Appendix A).

Though Nosenko professed wholehearted cooperation, in practice he persistently diverted our efforts to get at details. Even in apparently relaxed, off-duty moments he would deflect seemingly insignificant questions. One evening in a bar we were idly commenting on some women customers who appeared to be off-duty secretaries. A question popped into my mind. "How about the KGB's secretaries? Are they assigned to individual officers, or do they work in a pool serving everyone in the section?" Nosenko ignored the question. Thinking his attention had wandered, I repeated the query and again he brushed it off. Now, any professional could easily answer such a question in a few words. This was not boredom or disinterest. Either he didn't know or he didn't want to tell.

FBI officers questioning Nosenko did not get much, either. He knew little about KGB operations in the United States. He told them of two or three American travel agents informing the KGB about clients traveling to the USSR, and he named some tourists (without access to government secrets) recruited by homosexual compromise, and a few unsuccessful KGB tries to recruit American government officials.

This ignorance didn't surprise or bother us; Nosenko had always worked inside the USSR. More troubling was the claim by an FBI source inside the KGB in New York that it had to suspend its operations because Nosenko knew so much. This discrepancy needed looking into.

Nosenko was becoming edgy and unwilling to sit still for debriefings. No sooner would a systematic questioning begin when he would ask to break it off and do something else. It became increasingly difficult to hold him to a regular debriefing schedule even when we limited the sessions to a few hours.

On one such day he said, "That's enough questioning. Let's get out for a while and drive around. I'd like to see more." Off we went, driven by his security guard into the Virginia countryside. He had already been given tours of the city, and according to his escorts he had shown complete indifference; his only comments were to compare Washington's tourist attractions unfavorably to Moscow's. On this occasion, I thought, we'll show him the countryside instead. To left and right we passed new housing tracts under construction, and as we drove further out I showed him the surviving farmland, pleasant now even in its winter bareness and under the vestiges of snow. He sullenly faced forward, refusing to look even when things were pointed out. Odd, I thought. It was he who had asked for this outing, and this was going to be his new homeland. Perhaps, I thought, this is understandable in someone who's been forced to leave his country—but I was later to come to see his disinterest in a different light.

On another occasion he asked that we stop "all this questioning" and get on with active operations. "We can recruit people in the KGB."

"Good idea," I said, readying pad and pencil to record his ideas. "Whom do you have in mind?"

Nosenko named a former colleague.

"Tell me about him. Why would he be vulnerable or susceptible to a pitch from our side? How would you propose that we go about it?"

Faced with the need to justify his recommendation, Nosenko admitted that he had no reason to suppose the man would ever cooperate with the West, no matter what conditions we might create around him.

He named another—but had no idea on what grounds he might be recruited. We were up against a blank wall and dropped the subject.[5] Nosenko was drawing attention to himself in public with noisy and boisterous conduct, flouting our efforts to protect him from the searching eyes of the KGB. Drunk in a Baltimore nightclub he assaulted a barmaid and started a fistfight with a stranger. When the manager called the police, Nosenko's security escorts had to talk their way out of a situation made all the more ticklish by his tenuous legal status in the United States.

We were getting insights into the man's personality. Here too there were contradictions. Whereas in Geneva in 1962 he proclaimed his devotion to his daughters and concern for their health and welfare, when he returned to Geneva in 1964 he dismissed the problems his defection would cause them with the offhand remark, "They'll be okay." Now, after his defection, they seemed to have been wiped out of his memory. Neither I nor others who dealt with Nosenko in his first years in the United States ever heard him mention them, much less express concern about their fate.

To ease his transition to a new life, his Agency contacts sought to indulge his interests and preferences, to encourage him to do whatever he enjoyed. And that became clear and remained constant: he was interested only in drink and sex. He was taken to good restaurants, but he seemed to pay little attention to the food. We offered him any books, in Russian or English, he might like to read—and he did not want any. Years later, when the person who knew him best was asked what Nosenko read, he answered, "Nothing—well, he occasionally looks at a newspaper or magazine, but no serious ones."[6] He did not want to go to movies or the theater, he showed no interest in music, and though he said he played chess and was interested in boxing, he showed no desire to play or watch either.

Nosenko's conduct led me to query an Agency psychologist, John Gittinger. From his own conversations with Nosenko and the accounts of Nosenko's handlers, Gittinger recognized signs of a sociopathic personality and handed me some published works on the subject by reputed psychologists. I was startled to find them veritable lists of Nosenko's characteristics. His superficial charm, insincere smile, and frequent touch on his listener's hand or arm fit the descriptions of a sociopath's manipulative behavior. These texts noted the sociopath's self-centeredness and apparent incapacity for real attachment, which fit with Nosenko's evident forgetting of the family left behind. Nosenko's striking absence of remorse, anxiety, or other emotions struck a chord. So too did his quick mood shifts, another recognized sociopathic symptom. Especially striking was his indifference to truth. Nosenko would readily and quickly change his stories whenever they were challenged by contrary fact, sometimes shifting to blatant improvisation. His rude and vulgar behavior in public places after a few drinks also fit the mold.

Nosenko's CIA handlers were in a quandary. This case was unique. Never before had a defector from an Eastern intelligence service told us so much that overlapped the reporting of an earlier defector—and so consistently contradicted or deflected that earlier reporting. Never had one been unable to give details of operations he had personally conducted or of daily procedures of his service. Never from earlier defectors had it been impossible to get a straight, in-depth, or consistent story even about such seemingly benign subjects as schooling, travels, vacations, and marriages. Never had so many contradictions arisen.

With these shadows deepening and the information well running dry, it was with little regret that six weeks after Nosenko's arrival in the United States his CIA supervisors agreed to his long-standing request for a vacation in Hawaii, a place of his dreams. This was pampering: defectors were sometimes taken on trips to see something of their new country, but none that I know of had been invited out to a Pacific island. But for those handling his case in CIA, Nosenko's absence was welcomed. It got him out of the Washington area, where his tendency toward public troublemaking could have immediate consequences, and while he was away (spending his days drinking on the beach at Waikiki and his evenings with a flaming-red-haired prostitute) there was time to deliberate the problems he had posed and what to do about them.

Those problems were potentially grave. Nosenko's stories had raised the specter of major security problems. His false tale of his boss Kovshuk's trip to Washington pointed to a possible mole in CIA. So too did his account of the KGB's bugging a conversation in a Moscow restaurant and his jumbled tale of a certain dead drop in Moscow. His claim to have supervised the KGB's work against American code clerks—by now thrown into question—might be hiding KGB success in breaking American ciphers, a dire threat should war break out.

The KGB had sent false emissaries to the West before. We would do well to look behind Nosenko's stories and try to discern whether the KGB might have written them—and if so, why.

For that, the long bloody history of KGB deception operations, by now well known to us, could throw light.

PART TWO

Deadly Games

CHAPTER 10

"Guiding Principle"

For more than forty years before Yuri Nosenko's advent in Geneva, Soviet State Security had been sending out false defectors and handing fake sources to those they perceived as working against their rule or opposing their objectives from abroad.

To tighten the Communist Party's clutch on power at home the Chekists set out aggressively to attract, neutralize, and criminalize dissidents under their power. They created fictional movements, ostensibly militant and treasonous, that would attract potential regime opponents and put them under an all-seeing eye and controlling hand. They dispatched emissaries abroad in the name of these invented "resistance movements" to seek the support of Western opponents, to bring their work, too, under the Chekists' eye and hand.

By the late 1930s the KGB had eliminated any serious threat at home. It shifted the aim of these creative and aggressive operations more directly toward Western intelligence services, but never stopped or reduced them.

Why should it? The KGB had come to consider such practices the "basic" and "essential" principle guiding its counterintelligence work through the 1970s and beyond. Labeled as "aggressiveness" [*nastupatelnost*], it was defined in the KGB's own top-secret lexicon as "the mode of counterintelligence that takes the offensive and seizes the initiative and thereby gains the greatest success in the struggle with the adversary. This is the guiding principle directing [our] counterintelligence. All other things being equal, the side taking the offensive will get the best results."

One form this took was the "operational game" *(Igra operativnaya)*: "The counterintelligence system by which Soviet State Security gains control of and manipulates its adversary's apparatus by means of its agent (usually a Soviet citizen) posing as a collaborator of that apparatus. That agent systematically supplies the adversary with carefully prepared and backed-up disinformation and false activity reports. . . . Operational games may also use captured agents when the enemy is unaware of their arrest, or manipulate exposed agents without their knowledge. The best results are achieved by KGB agents working within the structure of the enemy apparatus."[1]

CIA did not really need this latter-day documentary confirmation. For decades Western intelligence services had been thwarted by elaborate hoaxes that had taught them, the hard way, that this is how the KGB worked. There was nothing new about many aspects of the Nosenko case. To persuade the adversary of the value and goodwill of its false emissaries, the KGB had long been sacrificing real secrets (and friendly human lives) as well as former secrets known to have been betrayed by earlier defectors. Its provocateurs had been vouching for one another. And the KGB had long been demonstrating its ability to hide such deception operations even from its own personnel not directly involved. CIA had heard from earlier defectors of the KGB's scorn for Western gullibility and arrogant confidence that these aggressive hoaxes would succeed. Two of them (Golitsyn and Goleniewski) reported that they had heard that the KGB's Second Chief Directorate was brewing a major deception in the late 1950s, though neither knew details.

By the early 1960s the Chekists were not only admitting their use of these practices but also vaunting their successes. It was they themselves, they now boasted, not the malevolent Western plotters they had been blaming for decades, who had created the scandal they called the "Ambassadors Plot" or "Lockhart Affair."

After the Bolshevik coup d'état of late 1917, while the British diplomatic agent Robert Bruce Lockhart was busily collecting information from Russians of all persuasions, the Chekists slipped in and twisted his intelligence gathering into subversive plotting. Two provocateurs—the heroes of the KGB's story, under the directing brain of Felix Dzerzhinsky—drew Lockhart into an anti-Bolshevik conspiracy that the Chekists themselves had cooked up. Then the Bolsheviks arrested him, splashed the affair in the press, and for decades afterward cited this dastardly "plot" as a prime example of capitalist conniving and ill will. They used it to stir anti-foreign sentiment, to excuse their own harsh rule (explaining, among other things, why the regime was preventing contact with foreigners), and even to justify their own secret subversive work abroad.

A Soviet history of Russian foreign intelligence notes, "Within days of taking power the Chekists began agent penetration into hostile organizations to see what they were secretly doing and to decompose them from inside." Within weeks the Chekists "were regularly undertaking such dangerous operations."[2]

It might seem unlikely that a newly born counterintelligence service could so quickly launch such sophisticated operations, but this newborn had a running start. By the time they took power the Bolsheviks not only had long experience in revolutionary conspiracy, but also had inherited provocative techniques from their predecessors, the Tsarist political police, or *Okhrana*.

By the late nineteenth century the Okhrana had refined the age-old agent provocateur into a formal system emphasizing "internal" observation of its opponents alongside the "external" methods commonly used by all police—shadowing, file investigations, interviews, etc. To the Okhrana, "internal" meant more than merely worming agents into opposing groups to identify their activists and to spy out their plans and methods. Any police service might do that, and the universal term *agent provocateur* comes not from Russian practice, but from the French. The Okhrana had taken a step or two beyond that and laid foundations that the Chekists were to build on.

Tsarist penetration agents not only stirred dissension inside opposition groups ("decomposing" them), but also sought to gain *control*. The police would arrest their leaders not only to rid themselves of the regime's most effective opponents but also to clear the way upward for their own agents within. Once these penetration agents reached the top, the Okhrana, having gained the power to manipulate, could turn resistance into an instrument of social control. Supposed "resistance" organizations would now attract (and expose) potential opponents and lure them into actions that would promote the rulers' interests, not theirs.

With these techniques, though sometimes applied clumsily, the Tsarist police succeeded in pulling the teeth of every political organization that opposed the Tsar. The militant arm ("battle organization") of the most active opposition party, the Socialist Revolutionaries (SRs) came to naught because their leader, the now infamous Yevno Azev, worked secretly with the Okhrana. Also rendered impotent were Lenin's clandestine Bolsheviks. In their underground leadership in Moscow were four police agents, in Saint Petersburg three out of the seven, including Lenin's top lieutenant inside the country, Roman Malinovsky. Their clandestinely printed newspaper *Pravda* was set up with Okhrana funds and edited by a secret Okhrana agent, Mikhail Chernomazov. Other Okhrana agents were "secretly" smuggling into the country the tracts that Lenin's people were printing abroad.

Enjoying this much control over their opposition—and this was loose and lenient compared with what the Communists later developed from it—the Tsars might have stayed in power indefinitely. Even Lenin thought they would, until he changed his mind only a month before Nicholas II abdicated. What brought the Tsar down were not these mole-ridden revolutionaries, but the disastrous losses of the First World War.

When Lenin's men grabbed power from the weak hands of a feckless, infant democracy a few months after the Tsar had fallen, they quickly started applying the techniques of the hated Okhrana against people who dared oppose *them*. They found the methodology spelled out in captured Okhrana files. As the KGB's own history put it, "the whole arsenal of techniques used by the earlier [Tsarist] special services were at the disposal of the newly formed [Cheka], which developed them on the basis of its own experience."[3]

The Chekists were applying Lenin's own thinking. Soon after taking power he enjoined Communist revolutionaries abroad not to shun the bourgeois institutions of their countries—governments, parties, parliaments, labor organizations, and such—but instead to join them and destroy them systematically from within: "resorting to all sorts of stratagems, maneuvers and illegal methods, to evasions and subterfuges, in order to penetrate [them] and stay inside them."[4]

Unlike their Tsarist predecessors the Chekists were not content merely to penetrate and manipulate opposition groups. They made a leap forward and created false ones of their own. Within months, according to their first Internal Affairs minister, Grigory Petrovsky, "the Chekists were seeing what they wanted to see, conspiracies and threats everywhere, *and when they could not see them they would manufacture them*."[5]

This sort of sting quickly became official policy when Felix Dzerzhinsky formally instructed his Chekists "to organize pretended [opposition] associations in order to detect foreign agencies on our territory." As its own secret history put it, the KGB "set up false [opposition] organizations and, using them as bait, began operational games with enemy intelligence agents and foreign anti-Soviet centers. By drawing enemy attention to these false organizations, the State Security organs distracted the outside enemy from real hostile groups within the country and at the same time tried to convince him that such interference was futile."[6] Already in January 1923 was established a unit whose whole purpose was to mount operations to pass misleading information to Western intelligence organizations.

Mythical "opposition organizations" sprang up, and the remnants of crushed ones were pumped into artificial new life. The classic example is the "Trust."

This was a group of supposed anti-Bolsheviks calling themselves the "Monarchist Organization of Central Russia." The name "Trust" stemmed from its cover as a business conglomerate. No such organization had ever existed. The Chekists invented it and used as its key figure an agent of theirs, Aleksandr Yakushev, who was expiating some earlier anti-regime plotting, for which he had been caught. Its real leaders were Chekists working in their own headquarters building, but this pseudo-organization did recruit rank-and-file members who were never told that their "resistance" was a sham.

In 1921 this Chekist creation sent Yakushev to the West posing as a Soviet trade official, first to Estonia, later to Berlin and Paris, to tell émigré leaders and their Western intelligence friends about the Trust's existence and to solicit their support for it. Yakushev told his eager listeners, who trusted him because some had known him earlier as a true anti-Bolshevik, that his organization was but one manifestation of a growing opposition to Soviet rule inside the country. Influential dissidents inside the country, he reported, were getting secret support from within government agencies— even from among the Chekists themselves—and were preparing for a post-Bolshevik future. He managed to convince his listeners, who as émigrés were instinctively receptive to any signs propitious to their return home. They in turn sought help from the several Western intelligence services that hungered for information from inside Russia, notably Polish, Finnish, and Estonian, but also French and British.

The KGB's deception began, and for six years "Trust" dispatched couriers to the West, some of them unaware that their organization was a Bolshevik tool, carrying out reports on the internal political, military, and social situation, and carrying in money and questionnaires. The KGB slanted this "secret intelligence" so as to discourage Western activism inside the still-turbulent country, conveying the message that "the Bolsheviks are weakening anyway so don't rock the boat." The information the "Trust" sent out to the West was of such low quality that several Western intelligence services became suspicious, but this is not what finally killed the operation. The Chekists themselves staged its final demise, to contribute to yet another provocation: Stalin's "war scare" of 1927 aimed at his internal rivals for power.

Some historians treat the Trust as an isolated phenomenon. In fact, it differed little from dozens of similar operations. The main difference was that the Trust's story has been told and retold in Russian and Western publications whereas the others have been ignored. By its very fame the Trust has, in a sense, cloaked the fact that it exemplified a general and permanent practice that the KGB applied against all sorts of enemies up to and throughout the Cold War.

The Trust was just the "game" the Chekists used to attack one particular target group, the monarchist opposition, and its associations abroad. Against other targets they used similar techniques and gained control of national-patriotic movements in the Ukraine, Armenia, and Georgia, among others, and came to "represent" émigré political parties and church organizations to their followers inside the country. When we in CIA's Soviet operations division later reviewed old files we identified about twenty-five such Trust-type games that had been played before the Second World War. One inside source heard in 1927 that more than forty "lines" were then active.

This "aggressive counterintelligence" quickly propelled the Chekists abroad. "It was hard," their own history noted, "to separate our fight against internal opposition . . . from our intelligence work abroad where counterrevolutionary organizations were getting support."[7] As Stalin put it in 1927, the capitalist states lurked out there as the "base and the rear for the internal enemies of our revolution."

Thus the KGB's claws stretched out to Paris, Berlin, and Vienna and sank into the groups of émigrés trying to weaken or overthrow Soviet power in the homeland. As the threat from those émigré groups declined, the Western intelligence services behind them became the KGB's prime target.

Chekist agents, some sent out by false "resistance organizations," wormed their way into the ranks of anti-Soviet émigré groups and into contact with the intelligence services. These penetration agents helped the

KGB spot other émigrés who would cooperate with the Chekists to protect their families left behind in Russia or to gain forgiveness and permission to return home to their native land. Every émigré organization became riddled with Chekist penetration agents.[8]

These claws drew blood. KGB games lured bothersome anti-Communist émigrés back into the Soviet Union to prison or death, or sent out emissaries to kill or kidnap them. The Trust, for instance, drew the British operative Sidney Reilly and others into Russia to their doom, while a parallel game called "Sindikat-2" sucked in the heroic Socialist Revolutionary (SR) leader Boris Savinkov, longtime foe of tsars and commissars alike. Chekist agents snatched off a Paris street the head of the monarchist emigration, General Alexander Kutepov. Later in Paris they took out his successor, General Yevgeny Miller—not just to rid themselves of an opponent, but mainly to clear the way to the top of his organization for Miller's deputy, their mole General Nikolay Skoblin. This part failed—Skoblin had to flee to Russia a step ahead of the French police—because Miller had left a note before going out to the fatal rendezvous with Skoblin, telling whom he was going to meet.

But more commonly these Chekist talons sank invisibly into the flesh of their victims, leaving those organizations bleeding internally from penetration agents like Skoblin and only dimly aware of it.

Not everyone was duped. There were skeptics in the victimized organizations who, seeing their actions fail repeatedly, sensed that they were penetrated and were being manipulated. But when they spoke up, their voices were usually drowned out by colleagues who scoffed at their worries.

Then came the German attack on Russia in 1941 that shifted "aggressive counterintelligence" to new targets.

11

Deceiving in Wartime

Fighting along huge fronts after smashing into the Soviet Union in June 1941, the German army needed intelligence from behind the Soviet lines so absolutely, so urgently, that it took its spies wherever and whenever it could find them.

German intelligence units selected candidates among the hundreds of thousands of prisoners of war and deserters to their side, trained them for missions, and then parachuted them or infiltrated them behind the battle lines. Some carried radio transmitters. Some went on short missions with instructions to come back through the lines, others to reestablish themselves in Soviet society.

Through the four years of the war in the East the Germans dispatched tens of thousands of such agents. Many, they knew, accepted German missions simply to win freedom and get back to their own side. Tight nets of security waited to capture the spies. Some of the recruits had been sent out by Soviet Counterintelligence in the first place, to get themselves recruited by the Germans. Many who tried to carry out German orders were betrayed even before they could begin spying. Others, having begun to transmit radio messages, were pinpointed by Soviet radio-detection apparatuses and caught in massive search operations by NKVD (earlier name of KGB) troop units. German intelligence veterans said after the war that they counted themselves successful if even ten percent survived and produced useful intelligence.

They knew, too, that the Soviets, having captured some of their agents, were playing them back and passing false information. The Germans concluded, for example, that of some two hundred reports received by one intelligence unit, all but one in ten were disinformation or rumor and "caused the greatest possible confusion."[1]

Despite all this awareness of Soviet security measures and Soviet tactical deception, the Germans failed to understand—just as postwar Western intelligence services would fail to understand throughout the Cold War—the Soviets' ability to deceive on a strategic level. A postwar study of German wartime documents revealed "a surprising lack of appreciation for the principles guiding Soviet Counterintelligence."[2] When Nazi security chiefs Himmler and Heydrich were confronted with evidence that the Soviets were infiltrating provocateurs behind the German lines to incite the occupation authorities to harsh reprisals against the population—which the Kremlin hoped would encourage more partisan activity—they refused to believe that the Soviets had "the time or ability to work out such complicated ideas."

The postwar memoirs of German intelligence leaders reflect this incomprehension. They thought they had done very well indeed. Their intelligence chief on the Soviet front, Reinhard Gehlen (later the founding head of the West German Intelligence Service, BND), remembered his subordinate Hermann Baun, head of espionage operations at the front, as a "first-class intelligence procurer [. . . who] was able to maintain contacts in the heart of Moscow until the very end."[3] Other German military intelligence (*Abwehr*) veterans shared this view. "Disguised as Soviet officers, Baun's agents insinuated themselves into Red Army headquarters; they led a perfectly legal existence in Russian civilian life; they made their niche in factories and offices, in the administration and even in the Communist Party. Baun's tentacles reached even to Moscow. [. . . Baun] had a radio group known as 'Flamingo' operating just outside the walls of the Kremlin. Its leader, a man named Alexander, joined a Soviet Reserve Signals Regiment as a captain, thus obtaining access to Red Army military secrets."[4]

Veterans of the other major intelligence unit on the Eastern Front, the *Sicherheitsdienst* (SD), intelligence arm of the Nazi Party (which in 1944 took over the Abwehr), also remembered their work as successful. "From the end of 1943," they said, "the information produced was of considerable value. . . . The so-called activists of Operation Zeppelin were working at numerous points far behind the Soviet front. They included for instance: a three-man team in Moscow which infiltrated the Soviet Ministry of Transport and photographed reports on Red Army movements [and several groups watching Soviet rail lines, others doing sabotage behind Soviet lines]." SD chief Walter Schellenberg boasted, "Through one of [our spy] centers—the existence of which was known only to three persons in the central office—we had a direct Secret Service connection with two of [Soviet] Marshal Rokossovsky's General Staff officers."[5]

From the Soviet side these German successes looked quite different.

According to the KGB's own top-secret internal history, its territorial offices arrested thousands of German agents. Of those captured by Soviet territorial units (not counting as many caught by frontline counterintelligence), more than six hundred had radio transmitters. They had to make a stark choice: either face the firing squad or cooperate with Soviet Counterintelligence.

Moreover, every agent that the Germans thought most successful—those who had supposedly wormed their way into Soviet official positions, like "Alexander" and his "Flamingo" group, and Rokossovsky's staff officer—were in fact working under the control of Soviet Counterintelligence.[6] Although SD chief Schellenberg probably believed in his postwar boasts of success, the Abwehr's Hermann Baun knew better. He admitted after the war to an American interrogator that he had been aware at the time that *every one* of his productive sources behind Soviet lines was under the control of Soviet Counterintelligence. Because he couldn't get anything better, and because Germany's Army High Command (OKH) liked his reports, it would have been politically dangerous for him to call them into question. So he had gone on pretending to his superiors that all was well.[7]

The Chekists used these controlled agents not only to deceive the enemy. Their ultimate target was those who had sent them. In war as in peace, penetration of the adversary's staff was the KGB's objective. "To successfully combat German-fascist intelligence operations," KGB historians later wrote, "we had to work in the enemy's rear where its intelligence, counterintelligence and sabotage units and schools were located. We conducted active operations behind the front lines to penetrate the enemy agent network, its intelligence and counterintelligence organs, police and administration, and to decompose anti-Soviet formations from inside. We first set out to acquire a secret agent network within the most active enemy departments. We did this mainly by offering the enemy our own agents for recruitment [some posing as escapees from the partisans], by doubling their agents back against them . . . by offering up female agents to work for them as interpreters or typists, and by recruiting their staff personnel."[8]

This sort of thing was also going on elsewhere in the war, of course. On both sides, security services were capturing enemy radio agents and turning them back against their masters. In the classic "Fortitude" operation the British misled the Germans about plans for the D-Day invasion, using, among other deceptive tricks, several doubled German radio agents. On the other side of the channel the Nazis captured and played back agents whom the British had parachuted into France and Holland. In "games" like the famous "North Pole" operation the Germans pretended that these agents had set themselves up safely, and sent messages that nullified Allied sabotage efforts and drew in more doomed agents, supplies, and money. On the Eastern Front, too, it went both ways: the Germans caught Soviet-sent radio operators and turned them against their sponsors.

But the sheer scale of the Soviet effort overshadowed the others. The KGB played many such "games" and frequently in combination. In the summer months of 1942 captured radios sent out false information on the locations of hundreds of Soviet rifle divisions, six tank corps, and scores of artillery regiments. In little more than a year and a half, from the end of 1941 to September 1943, no fewer than 80 captured agent radios were used. The KGB's Partisan Directorate alone operated 40 such radio deception games. In all, the KGB ran 185 radio games.[9]

To shift the enemy's attention from their forthcoming offensive in 1943 at Kursk, the Soviets brought nine controlled enemy agent radios into one coordinated action from five different cities. In a single game at the turn of the year 1944–1945, each of *twenty-four* agent radio transmitters from different parts of the country pumped out its part of a plan to lull the Germans into confidence that no Red Army attack was imminent in Poland and East Prussia. They succeeded: the Germans, with so much "confirmation," felt able to move many of their tanks from that front shortly before the Soviets attacked.[10]

The Germans especially liked the reports they were getting from a spy they had code-named "Max." But, unknown to them, "Max" had another code name. The KGB called him "Heine." Heine was the key figure in a KGB deception operation code-named "Monastery" *(Monastir)* that takes its historical place alongside "Trust" and "Syndikat-2" as a classic of the genre. Not until after the collapse of Soviet Communism did the KGB release the facts. Here is the story.

When the German invaders set out to insinuate spies behind the lines into Soviet military, communications, and supply centers, the KGB instinctively turned to its "basic" practice. To suck the Germans in, they invented an anti-Soviet organization in Moscow named "Throne" *(Prestol)* under the leadership of a well-known intellectual named Glebov. It ostensibly collected together opponents of Communism because of their religious faith and aristocratic origins. Their apparent motive was to obtain leading positions in the postwar German administration of the country after the inevitable Nazi conquest was complete.

At the end of 1941 this pseudo-organization sent a purported deserter through the battle lines. The Germans already knew him. Alexander Demyanov—code name Heine—had hobnobbed in Moscow with German diplomats and had even visited and made friends in Germany before the war. Thus German Intelligence was quick to give him their confidence when he now told them that Throne had sent him to get German help. Within six weeks the Germans parachuted him back behind Soviet lines, now carrying the German code name Max, asking Throne to recruit secret helpers in large Soviet cities and to step up sabotage and propaganda.

Max radioed back to the Germans that he himself had become an officer in a Red Army staff. By late 1942 he was able to send more good news: Throne had recruited a communications official able to report Red Army rail movements.

The Throne organization asked for and got the Germans to parachute couriers equipped with radios and other equipment to ensure their communications. The couriers sailed down into KGB hands and some survived (at least for a time) by cooperating with their captors. One of them ostensibly set up networks of his own inside Soviet local administrations—a part of the operation that the KGB code-named "Couriers" *(Kuriery)*. In all, twenty-three couriers were caught, with money, spy equipment, and their inside helpers.[11]

The KGB allowed some of the couriers to land and make contact with (and get the thanks of) Throne activists, and then helped them return safely to the West, giving German Intelligence comforting evidence that all was well.

The Soviet regime made almost inconceivably cruel sacrifices to build the Germans' faith in these radio agents. "The information supplied by Heine always contained elements of truth," said a top Chekist who had supervised some of these operations. And that is why "the German high command used it in critical situations."[12]

This work was bloody—and highly secret. Not even the commanding generals whose troops would be sacrificed were told of these deception schemes, to avoid their resistance. In 1942 the KGB let the Germans know (through Heine) about a forthcoming Soviet attack by Marshal Zhukov's forces. They portrayed it as a main thrust whereas, in reality, it aimed to divert German forces away from Stalingrad. "When [Heine's] information about the attack proved to be true, his credibility rose," wrote a KGB chief. "Zhukov, not knowing this disinformation game was being played at his expense, paid a heavy price in the loss of thousands of men under his command. . . . He knew his offensive was an auxiliary operation, but he did not know that he had been targeted in advance by the Germans."[13]

The same Heine fed the Germans disinformation that, with another dreadful sacrifice of blood, contributed to the Soviets' decisive victory at Kursk in April–May 1943. So believable, so provably correct was his information that even after the war SD chief Schellenberg was still boasting about it—for his "communications officer on Marshal Rokossovsky's staff" was none other than the KGB's agent Heine.

Among the side effects of this immense effort was the training of a whole new generation of practitioners of "aggressive counterintelligence." Chekists who learned and honed their skills in "games" against wartime German Intelligence would apply them afterward in the sovietization of Eastern Europe and—especially—in Cold War struggles against Western intelligence services.

As the Soviet armies moved westward these experienced deceivers turned to the new tasks that faced the Soviet regime in consolidating control over newly occupied Eastern European countries—and in combating the Western intelligence services which they would now confront in Germany and Austria.

It was they who mounted, in Poland, a carbon copy of the Trust that, like Trust, succeeded, fooling even the same people who had fallen for that earlier sting.

CHAPTER **12**

Postwar Games

As the Soviet armies moved westward over the territory the Germans had taken, they faced the task of reimposing their rule over people who had been living outside it for years.

For this task Stalin now strengthened State Security's military-security component and gave it a new name that he is said to have coined personally: "Smersh," short for *Smert' Shpionam*, "Death to Spies." In every recaptured town Smersh, using the NKVD troops at its disposal, arrested and interrogated those suspected of collaboration with the German occupiers, shot or hanged most of them, and deported their families eastward. Whole towns and ethnic groups—Tatars, Chechens, Ingush, Balkars, Volga Germans, Karachai, and Kalmyks who had welcomed the German invaders as liberators from Soviet tyranny—were rounded up and dumped in remote areas of Kazakhstan and Siberia.

Further west they faced more complicated situations and called into play the techniques of "aggressive counterintelligence." In the Ukraine they had never fully quashed anti-Communist, nationalist resistance movements, even during the prewar decades. And their rule over the Baltic nations, eastern Poland, and Romanian Bessarabia had lasted hardly a year before the Germans had rolled in. Now they faced resistance from organized groups that had fought them before, then fought the German occupiers, and now, knowing their fate if they were to surrender to the oncoming Soviet forces, took to the hills and forests and marshes to oppose their new—old—conqueror.

The arriving Soviets arrested, killed, deported, or put under special observation all who fit into their categories of potential opponents—merchants, employers, former police, military and intelligence officers, judges and prosecutors, members of non-Communist political groupings, ethnic and political patriots, and anyone with foreign connections.[1] How widely this deadly broom swept can be seen in its performance in eastern Poland, occupied according to Stalin's 1939 accord with Hitler. In the twenty months before the Germans invaded in June 1941, Soviet security authorities had managed to list, locate, arrest, and ship eastward more than a million Poles, nearly a fifth of the entire population of the areas they occupied. Later, in 1944 and 1945, they moved hundreds of thousands from the Baltic States alone.

In Poland a special problem awaited the Chekist experts in "aggressive counterintelligence." The Polish underground "Home Army" (*Armija Krajowa,* or AK), a patriotic force loyal to the Polish government-in-exile in London, stood as a major obstacle to Moscow's planned sovietization of the country. It was an old enmity: already in September 1939, when some twenty-five thousand Polish officers and prominent government and intellectual figures fell into their hands—men who would form the backbone of Polish patriotic resistance to *any* occupier—the NKVD, on orders from the top, simply massacred them all, some five thousand in the Katyn Forest, the rest elsewhere.

They used more devious ways during the war of 1941–1945. Thanks to the defection of Polish state security officer Josef Swiatlo to CIA in late 1953, the West learned things known only to a handful even within the Polish Communist leadership. Of these things perhaps the most sinister was the history of the "disinformation cell." Inside the Polish Communist underground (set up as a counterweight to the AK) the KGB (then called NKVD) set up a little group with an incredible mission—to collaborate with the Gestapo to destroy non-Communist Polish resistance.

The NKVD parachuted its agent Marceli Nowotko into Poland in late 1941 to assign this terrible mission to a Communist named Molojec. Molojec (understandably) found the order so outrageous that he assumed it must have come from the Gestapo itself—so he murdered Nowotko. (On Soviet orders Molojec was later killed for this.) The cell was activated nevertheless, and the NKVD parachuted a radio-equipped agent named Skonieczny to maintain its contact with Moscow.

The cell infiltrated an agent into an AK-related anti-Nazi resistance organization called "Sword and Plow" *(Miecz i Plug)*. The NKVD furnished Boguslaw Hrynkiewicz, a leading agent of Soviet Intelligence, with falsified "evidence" that the organization's two leaders were Gestapo agents, to give him the pretext to shoot them both. Then, taking command himself, he led "Sword and Plow" into *real* contact with the Gestapo, using as his channel an NKVD agent within the Gestapo. In Gestapo uniforms he and three men raided an apartment in Warsaw where they knew the Home Army was storing its archives. They found the names of its members and *turned them over to the Gestapo.*

All of these Gestapo collaborators later became party functionaries in the postwar Communist Polish regime, even the Gestapo man, who adopted a Polish name. The Soviet invaders installed the overseer of the "disinformation cell," Boleslaw Bierut, a longtime NKVD agent, as president of Poland.[2]

In January 1945, after the Soviet armies had taken all of Poland, the puppet government they had set up in Lublin formally disbanded the AK and urged its surviving members to come out into the open, assuring them that they would have freedom and safety. Some did—and were arrested on the spot and deported to the east. Those who didn't were hunted down by security services and special killer squads.

The survivors, having lost hope for a normal life, started to regroup in a clandestine association to oppose the new occupiers. They called it "Freedom and Independence" *(Wolnosc i Niezawislosc*—WiN). But before they could even get started their plan was compromised and in March 1945 the Polish State Security service UB arrested WiN's proposed chief, the former AK commander. In August of that year WiN managed to start work under his successor, another top AK commander, and sent an emissary to London to explain their efforts to the Polish exile staff. But in November WiN's chief was arrested. A third leadership arose in Poland, and this one sent to London a delegation *(delegatura)* of three men, headed by Jozef Maciolek, to stay there and arrange regular communications between the exiles and WiN and to drum up financial support from Western institutions. The delegatura was also to try to set itself up as the coordinating center for *all* emigration activity against the Polish Communist regime.

Maciolek succeeded in getting some money from the Polish government-in-exile and persuaded British Intelligence (MI6) to provide illegal documents and secret writing materials to help the delegatura com-municate with WiN inside Poland. The Belgian government let them use its diplomatic pouch for messages into and out of Poland.

But again the inside leadership was discovered and arrested. So too were their successors, who took over in the early fall of 1947, along with the men in touch with the Belgian Embassy in Warsaw, ending that connection.

When yet another leadership arose in early 1948, it was the fifth. To set up communications with them the delegatura member Adam Boryczko went into Warsaw illegally in the spring of 1948 and met with the new leader's deputy, Stefan Sienko, a man whom Boryczko had known before and who was well known, even family-connected, to Maciolek. WiN's new leader, working under the alias "Kos," preferred to stay in the background, unidentified, said Sienko.

Now, finally, WiN got going, and gained Western recognition as the nucleus of all anti-Communist resistance in Poland.

At this point the Americans came into the picture. In November 1950 the young Office of Policy Coordination (OPC) signed an agreement with Maciolek in Washington and took over from the British as WiN's principal supporter. It offered only a small budget at first ($10,000 a month for the first six months of 1951, according to the account by Polish Communists), to be increased if WiN performed as Maciolek claimed. In the ensuing months OPC became satisfied and upped the payments until, within two years, they had invested several million dollars.

Maciolek moved his headquarters from more skeptical London to the American-occupied zone of Germany, keeping some people in London and other European centers, including a group in Mannheim that coordinated communications with the inside. In each of these places the WiN represen-tatives kept in touch with the parties of the Polish emigration that had fol-lowers inside the country, dealt with intelligence services that were seeking information from Poland, debriefed refugees, and identified those refu-gees who might be willing to go back to Poland on WiN missions.

The delegatura, working with OPC, kept in touch with WiN inside Poland mainly by couriers slipped surreptitiously across land borders. Once or twice a month letters were cached in international trains or mailed openly (with secret writing) to postal addresses of WiN adherents. Begin-ning in 1951, when OPC sent agent transmitter-receivers and radio opera-tors into Poland, they used wireless communications.

Though OPC's aim was to set up wartime sabotage assets behind the Iron Curtain, it also tried to get intelligence. But they were tapping a dry well. WiN's reports looked no better to Western analysts than what they themselves could derive by reading Polish newspapers and debriefing refugees. WiN in Poland had a ready excuse: it was unwilling to let its "sleepers" risk their necks by nosing out real secrets now because, after all, their real purpose was to be alive and ready when war broke out.

After OPC and CIA's Office of Special Operations (OSO) merged, CIA sent detailed questionnaires to stimulate WiN to produce better intelligence—but got no response. Soon thereafter, on December 27, 1952, WiN came to an explosive end.

"Foreign spy centers discovered!" screamed Soviet bloc headlines. Military aggression being prepared against the socialist states! Emigrés in the pay of the "special services" of capitalist powers! Parachute drops into northern Poland and nearby Lithuania! Some of these traitors had seen the light and had turned themselves in, the papers reported, and they published interviews with the individuals (some of whom had been sent in from abroad) with photos of their weapons and radio sets.

Then the Polish Branch of CIA's OSO did the first thorough review of the OPC's operation. As I found when I arrived soon afterward at the Branch, they concluded that WiN must have been under Polish control from its inception.

How right they were!

WiN was never really a Western operation. It was a Soviet deception, run by the KGB in collaboration with its Polish State Security satellite, the UB. The initials UB stood for *Urzad Bezpiecestwa*, or Security Directorate, inside the Ministry of Public Security, which later (following the Soviet model) became part of the Ministry of Internal Affairs. Whatever its subsequent designations, it was commonly referred to by those earlier, infamous initials. In its organization and methods it followed the Moscow example. Its departments paralleled (and were supervised by) equivalent ones in the KGB in Moscow. At the outset KGB officers wearing Polish uniforms, some speaking Polish imperfectly if at all, occupied UB command positions (just as Soviet Marshal Rokossovskiy, now spelling his name in the Polish way as Rokossowski, had become Polish Defense Minister) and though by this time they had stepped back to become mere "advisers," they kept offices within the UB building and close to the sections. All operational decisions had to be cleared with these KGB officers, and their decision was law. It richly illustrates how the KGB conducted "aggressive counterintelligence"—as it was to do later with Nosenko. CIA learned the inside truth from Swiatlo in late 1953 and in greater detail later from Goleniewski, who provided the UB's own study of the operation.

It began, as these things often did, with the chance acquisition of a trustworthy agent. Already in the last months of the war in their sweeping arrests of AK veterans, the KGB got wind of the plans to set up WiN. It was easy for them, with their Polish satellite UB, to plant spies in its ranks and to identify and arrest the first four leaderships of WiN.

Not long after the UB arrested the fourth leadership, they learned that Adam Boryczko of the delegatura was planning a clandestine trip to Warsaw to meet the new leadership and solidify communications arrangements. The UB prepared to arrest him.

At that point their Soviet masters, under the direction of the KGB's counterintelligence chief Yevgeny Pitovranov—veteran of KGB wartime deception operations against the Germans—stepped in, saying in effect, "Don't even *dream* of arresting him!" Sure, it was a good thing that the UB had wiped out the genuine WiN leadership, but to the aggressive-minded KGB this appeared not as the end but as the chance for a beginning. Pitovranov instructed the Poles to revive WiN—under their control—and use it to draw under their wing all Western subversive activity in Poland.

The operation that resulted was to be code-named by the Poles "Cezary" (Polish for Caesar)—and by the KGB "Arsenal 2." The details of this operation come from Josef Swiatlo and from the UB's own top-secret internal report on their Cezary operation. I was told the KGB code name after the Cold War.

To hide Arsenal 2 from their own people who weren't involved, the KGB created a super-secret section inside the UB's Department III (Nationalities) with the innocuous name "Special Branch" *(Wydzial Specyjalny)*. It was headed by Soviet KGB (at that time called MGB) officers, one of whom had been involved in its prewar "Trust" and "Syndikat" operations and another in wartime radio "games" against the Germans. With them worked UB officers headed by Colonel Roman Wysocki and including Colonel Roman Werfel.

Now the KGB urgently needed someone who could pose as a WiN leader to meet Boryczko. To be convincing, their candidate had to be someone already known to the Londoners as a member of the former leadership. Moreover, as Wysocki later put it in his report on the operation, the candidate would have to be "intelligent, cool-headed, and have the flexibility and initiative to deal with surprises." But more importantly, he had to be "fully checked out, completely reliable, and properly motivated"

—and it was no small trick to find such a person among these bitter anti-Communists, even though the UB had the entire WiN leadership sitting in its jails.

By luck they found the right man, in the person of a former WiN activist named Stefan Sienko. This young man had maintained WiN's contact with its letter drops (individuals in Poland who were receiving mail from the delegatura). He had close personal and operational connections with Maciolek and was known to Boryczko. And luckily, no one outside the UB knew he had been arrested. (After raiding his WiN group in Krakow, the UB had secretly captured him far away in the mountains near Zakopane, where he had been hiding out in a girlfriend's house.) Best of all, from the moment of his arrest Sienko had told all, helped the UB investigators, and convinced them of his genuine repentance.

They released Sienko and thereafter he loyally played the UB's game, becoming, as Wysocki wrote, the key to the whole success. Like many other aspects of Cezary this echoed the KGB's Trust operation of the 1920s, in which the KGB recognized the essential role of the original agent, Aleksandr Yakushev, also a repentant.

Sienko's meeting with Boryczko took place in April 1948 in a Warsaw room set up and wired for sound by the Special Branch. Too young to pose convincingly as overall head of the organization, Sienko told Boryczko that he was deputy to the leader, alias "Kos." He declined to name him—not, as he pretended, to protect Kos's security but for a much simpler reason: the KGB/UB had not yet found anyone to embody the fictional Kos. Boryczko pressed Sienko to expand WiN's regional groups and told him that prospects were good for getting Western support. Then Boryczko returned to London—unhampered—bringing the happy report that WiN was back in business.

The secret was tightly kept. No one else in UB had any idea what the Special Branch was doing, and not even the branch's own officers knew all the others working on the case. Inside the "resistance movement" itself never more than about five key figures were aware of UB control, and none of these was allowed to go to the West or to meet visiting Westerners. For tasks that required contact with outsiders, the UB would most often use its own deep-cover staff officers.

Just how tightly the UB kept the secret can be seen in their treatment of one of their own agents inside the WiN leadership. Although they trusted him completely, they let him believe he was simply a mole inside a *genuine* anti-Communist underground. And the few survivors of the old, genuine WiN—real resisters against Communism—went about their sub-versive work, sometimes enlisting like-minded friends, unaware of the watchful eye and guiding hand above.

From time to time some in the West had their doubts. The UB handlers in Warsaw worried when they heard that one delegatura member had sardonically asked a courier, who had just made his third safe trip into and out of Poland, "Who gave you your travel documents, the UB or the NKVD?" Another émigré party courier who had gone into Poland through WiN channels became convinced, and spread the word, that WiN simply had to be infiltrated by UB agents if it genuinely existed at all. Two other émigré leaders spoke more vaguely of the "mystery" surrounding WiN.

Getting wind of these suspicions, the UB/KGB decided to send out an emissary to calm them. But this posed a problem: should the emissary be witting of UB control? No, they decided, it would be too risky to send someone who, if he made a slip of the tongue while abroad—or worse, if he changed camps—could undo the whole operation. It would be more con-vincing if the emissary truly believed WiN was genuine. So the Special Branch dispatched a real WiN activist named Jerzy Cichalewski. This did the trick: Cichalewski's evident honesty, the fact that WIN had been able to get him safely out of Poland, and the reports he carried with him, carried the day for those in the West who *wanted* to believe in WiN. For them it was clear: all was well with their "resistance organization."

To Warsaw's dismay, Cichalewski decided not to return to Poland. The UB leaders cursed themselves for not having "set up conditions guarantee-ing his return." But a year later they were feeling more confident and did send to the West a *witting* emissary named Wedrowski, who by then had been chosen to play the part of Kos, and also another, code-named "Karol," both of whom played their parts loyally and fooled the outsiders.

The KGB/UB knew, of course, practically every one of the couriers the delegatura sent into Poland but, to avoid alarming the outside group, usu-ally let them make their contacts freely and return to the West in peace.

But there were exceptions, like the courier Mieczyslaw Klempa (WiN code name "Mietek"). The UB had too many reasons to arrest Klempa. First, he had expressed his suspicion that the UB was controlling the WiN elements inside Poland. Second, he had come across the border without inside help from WiN, a practice the UB wanted to discourage. And third, the UB wanted to prosecute him for his earlier involvement in armed underground activities. So they moved against him. But to make it look innocent, they didn't arrest him in Poland but only later in Czechoslovakia, on his way back toward the West. And then they rebuked the delegatura for causing Klempa's downfall and carelessly endangering the operation by letting couriers use routes other than those guaranteed by WiN.

At the outset the UB's aims abroad had been limited to neutralizing the hostile activity of émigrés. Inside the country they saw WiN as creating a safety valve in the form of a "resistance" organization which would attract, expose, and compromise their most determined opponents—for later liquidation.

The UB aimed to get all émigré parties to use the WiN delegatura as their sole channel by which to communicate with their secret adherents inside Poland. So WiN informed the outsiders that it had a "Political Committee" that was harmoniously coordinating the whole gamut of secret parties inside. Some émigré leaders fell for it, and as a result the UB, by watching the delegatura couriers, could identify anti-Communist groups being set up in Poland by several different émigré political parties. This was double insurance: through other WiN-type "games" they were already controlling other parties inside the country, including the clandestine National Party (*Stronnictwo Narodowa*—SN) and the Ukrainian Insurrection Army (*Ukrainska Powstancza Armia*—UPA), the latter in a KGB/UB operation code-named "Arsenal-1."

WiN enhanced internal Communist security in other ways, too. When one or another UB repressive department got hints from its informants that a particular citizen might be disloyal, the UB's top leadership, aware of Cezary, could pass the name to the Special Branch. Its WiN would then send operatives to get acquainted with the suspect and try to recruit him for WiN. If he accepted the offer, one more potential opponent would have come under the eye of the authorities and opened himself to charges of treason.

But these priorities changed when British Intelligence and later (in November 1950) the fledgling American OPC began to support and exploit WiN through the delegatura. Now these Western agencies became the primary target. As the UB's own postoperational report described it, Cezary's first priority was "to neutralize Western special services' activities by planting agents from Poland into their operating centers abroad, to mislead and disorient them, and to lead them into fruitless operations and blunders."

To shield themselves from pressure to take real action, the KGB manipulators of WiN stipulated that its command lay inside Poland with complete political independence. It was cooperating with the West only to prepare secret networks for long-range wartime contingencies, not for immediate results. In this way the KGB sought simultaneously to prevent the West from carrying out peacetime sabotage and to give WiN an excuse to avoid active spying.

To keep the Westerners interested, the insiders pretended that WiN was taking actions on its own initiative. They kept an eye out for real accidents, explosions, or incidents and told the outsiders that WiN had done it. And they boasted of progress in preparing for wartime, too. Their "military department," they reported, had cached arms in five provinces and now numbered some six hundred recruits, some of them veterans of partisan fighting. As their greatest achievement they claimed to have lined up, with great difficulty, a couple hundred white- and blue-collar workers in positions they could keep in case of war, to serve WiN's cause.

When CIA began to send queries about Polish war planning and military order-of-battle, the Special Branch rejoiced at the opportunity to misinform the West. But the Polish Defense Minister (and Soviet Marshal) Rokossowski was unwilling to give away defense secrets, so they had to fend off CIA's queries. They passed out nonsecret (though usually authentic, sometimes already compromised) information in great masses, to overwhelm the outside analysts with useless work. They slanted it to discourage Western attempts at subversion, reporting for example that the regime's achievements were winning it popular support and stressing the power and effectiveness of the security services. Still, the UB considered this intelligence reporting to be the weakest part of the Cezary operation.

Some in the West remained skeptical, notably those British and American officers who knew the history of the Trust and other Soviet deceptions, and a few former intelligence officers of prewar Poland, now in emigration, who remembered Trust and recognized the parallels.

But by and large the Polish émigrés trusted the insiders. They sent to them their "Plan X," directives for wartime spying, sabotage, and communications, along with the estimates of possible future situations upon which they had based it. The UB gloated over OPC's contingency plan, code-named "Vulkan," for wartime sabotage to hinder Soviet use of Polish road and rail lines. (They later trumpeted this publicly as "irrefutable proof of aggressive intentions.") The Americans sent detailed plans and maps for distribution of agent radios and for landings on the Polish coastline, and parachuted agents to test WiN's ability to handle such drops and eventual airborne landings in wartime.

The Poles running Cezary learned a lot of KGB tricks, some of which they passed along to the colleagues who would run similar operations in the future:

- When the couriers from the West would ask for samples of up-to-date Polish official documents, WiN would supply them—but afterward would change the format to render them invalid.
- When one courier spotted someone (from the UB, of course) shadowing him on a Warsaw street, the WiN leaders restored his confidence by supplying him varied coats and hats "to help shake the tail."
- To cut short the time available to a genuine courier from outside to question Kos, the Special Branch staged a "coincidental" police visit to the courier's boardinghouse, where Kos was to brief him.
- When they discovered duplicity by an agent of theirs, the KGB/UB usually didn't arrest him. Wysocki expressed the lesson thus in his summary of Cezary: "When a double agent is discovered, we needn't eliminate, arrest, or re-double him. We can manipulate him without his knowledge to mislead and neutralize our adversaries."

In late 1952, to the surprise of the UB handlers, the KGB suddenly ordered the Poles to close down the WiN operation and to make a public splash of its juicy details of "aggressive Western war preparations."

The UB handlers were dismayed. Their game was working well and they thought it had a lot of productive life ahead—indeed, they foresaw using it to prevent wartime sabotage. They argued against the order, but the Soviets were adamant.

By way of explanation, the KGB told its Polish subordinates that Moscow now considered it more urgent to demonstrate to the Eisenhower administration, with its new "liberation" policy, that the West had no real fighting assets in Poland and no real internal opposition to exploit. Exposing WiN would have a triple effect. By ridiculing these feckless plots the regime would discredit the Americans. It would dishearten true Polish dissidents. And it would impress the West with the power of the security services. This would discourage the Eisenhower administration from launching subversive operations against Eastern European regimes.

But the Poles weren't convinced. They sensed that something deeper lay behind the KGB explanation.

Judging from a later perspective, they were surely right. It happened at the precise moment that Stalin was pursuing aims that, to him at least, far outweighed either the operational successes of Cezary or any "messages to the Eisenhower regime." Namely, his own internal Kremlin intrigues.

At just that moment Stalin was preparing a new blood purge in Russia. As in 1927—when he had blown up a similar deception operation (Trust) to feed an artificial "war scare" that would help him topple his competitors for Kremlin power—Stalin evidently saw Cezary as offering useful evidence of Western war planning. Combined with the "Doctors Plot" that he was about to unfold, it would add weight to Stalin's planned accusations—of lack of vigilance, among other things—against those he saw as rivals, notably Beria and Malenkov.

This seemed even more likely when I learned, in talks with a KGB veteran after the Cold War, that Stalin had personally ordered the KGB's former counterintelligence chief Yevgeny Pitovranov to publicly close out WiN and the similar deception operations in the Ukraine. In November 1952 he had Pitovranov released from jail and assigned him this as an initial task before moving him, on its completion, to head the KGB's foreign intelligence directorate. He needed Pitovranov because it had been Pitovranov himself who had begun these Polish and Ukrainian Arsenal operations years earlier.[3]

Now Pitovranov's orders went out to the KGB controllers of the UB in Warsaw. Close it out! Reluctantly but dutifully the Special Branch's Colonel Werfel sat down to work out plans for the blowup, including mass arrests, press conferences, radio interviews, and planted articles—while trying to avoid any hint that the regime had controlled WiN from the outset.

At Christmastime the Polish regime loosed the blast of publicity which went on for weeks and served for years afterward as fodder for anti-Western propaganda.

Then the Soviets and Poles dissolved the Special Branch they had set up for this one operation. Few officers even within the KGB or UB knew it had ever existed.

Operation Cezary was over, leaving a residue of penetration agents abroad and thus a Soviet eye into the Western intelligence services that worked with the Polish emigration.

Operation Caesar was not unique. The KGB's similar manipulation of Ukrainian resistance, Arsenal-1, has still not been exposed in its full dimensions. And the KGB has admitted, in its own top-secret internal history, its similar work in the Baltic states. "In the years 1947–1952 we carried out important operations to halt the subversive activity of nationalists in the Soviet Baltic republics. In this work we drew widely on the earlier experiences of the Vcheka and OGPU [earlier designations of KGB] against nationalist underground movements. We successfully ran operational games against Western intelligence services, set up false subversive organizations *(legendirovaniye)* and disinformed the enemy."[4]

Behind those dry words lay subtle intrigues, cunning traps, and dark betrayals that illustrated the KGB's commitment to aggressive counterintelligence—and got it closer to the American and British intelligence services that had become its prime target.[5]

While quelling this "nationalist" opposition in Eastern European countries, the Soviets were facing a special security problem in Germany. There as in Poland and the Baltic states they applied their aggressive techniques.

Occupying eastern Germany, bordering on American and British zones, the Soviet army feared the defection of soldiers getting their first glimpse of the better life in the West. A less aggressive regime might think security adequate with the harsh restrictions the Soviets imposed on the soldiers' movements and contacts in this foreign environment—but not the KGB. It set out aggressively to identify anyone entertaining disloyal thoughts, and to entice and entrap the foreign "special services" that might encourage them. It not only set provocateurs among them to entice them to reveal their thoughts, but also provoked them into treason—using, for instance, the time-tested method of the "false border."

As early as the 1930s at a few selected points along their international borders the Chekists had erected fences or markers looking like a real frontier and just beyond, apparent border posts flying the flag of the bordering country. A provocateur would lead a would-be escapee to this "safe" point, where he would successfully cross over and be welcomed by foreign-uniformed border police needing an interpreter to communicate in Russian. Relieved at finally getting free, the new refugee would unburden himself to these interviewers and perhaps name friends with similar intent to flee. Then a hitch would arise to prevent his new hosts from accepting him—a regrettable treaty clause, perhaps, that compelled them to turn back refugees. With ostentatious reluctance they would return him to a more obvious Soviet custody, whence he (and friends he had named) would be carted off to the Gulag. He might never become aware that he had never really been free, even for those few days.

In Berlin in the early postwar years one could move freely between the

Soviet and Western sectors of the city, and the sector limits were not every-where marked. Here, on the suggestion of its Colonel Ivan G. Pavlovsky, the KGB set up one of these false borders.

"Pavlovsky's Trap" began with a Soviet agent in East Germany suggesting to the suspect soldier that, if he were truly fed up with Soviet life, a trip to Berlin could be arranged. When he arrived in East Berlin a German would lead him by a safe route to an American installation in "West Berlin," a luxuriously furnished estate where he was "surrounded by people in American uniforms speaking English (with varying proficiency)." The rest followed the well-worn pattern.[6]

These aggressive "games" remained the basic Soviet counterintelligence practice from the beginning to the end of Soviet rule in Russia, with an unbroken succession of practitioners. Chekists who ran Trust and Syndikat-2 in the 1920s raised the next generation, who went on to deceive the German army by similar fake organizations—Throne modeled upon Trust, by sending fake defectors through the battle lines and by manipulating captured German radio spies. At the end of the war and immediately thereafter these experts and their apprentices created or took over resistance movements in postwar Ukraine, Poland, and the Baltic. Then, brought face to face with American forces in Germany, they applied their craft and developed young successors who would carry on through the Cold War.

Yevgeny Pitovranov exemplifies the continuum. He directed some of the wartime radio deceptions against the invading Germans and then went on, as head of Soviet Counterintelligence, to create postwar Polish and Ukrainian deception operations. Later, as head of worldwide KGB operations, he promoted the use of these methods. As chief in Germany he oversaw sophisticated deceptions of the West based on penetrations of West German and other intelligence services. His successor as head of Counterintelligence, Oleg Gribanov, proved himself hungry to emulate Pitovranov's deceptive deeds. He was the sponsor of Nosenko, among others.

Working under Pitovranov was Arkady A. Fabrichnikov. Having run radio "games" against the German armies in Smersh under Viktor Abakumov, he then ran part of the Arsenal game in the Ukraine. Later, from East Berlin he planted provocateurs in American Intelligence in Berlin and West Germany and ran penetration agents in the leadership of the anti-Soviet radio stations Radio Liberty and Radio Free Europe. Afterward, in the First Chief Directorate's foreign counterintelligence department, he conducted "complicated counterintelligence games, offering false targets and recruits to Western Intelligence, identifying their people, methods and plans and disorienting their work." In the mid-1970s the Second Chief Directorate (SCD) needed his expertise and arranged his transfer as deputy chief of the SCD and head of its operational deception department. There, according to his KGB biography, he developed aggressive methods that "uncovered several Soviet officials" spying for the West. Then, to further the continuum, he moved to the KGB's Higher School to train new specialists in this field of "aggressive counterintelligence"—carrying it on through the fall of the Soviet Union until retirement in 2000.[7]

Specialists in this aggressive practice offered alluring targets to divert and mislead CIA in Berlin. One such target was Yuri Krotkov, a Soviet propaganda officer and budding writer. He met with a CIA officer there in 1948, pretending to be on the verge of cooperating or defecting. The contact dwindled and was abandoned by both sides, but Krotkov evidently stayed on the roster of KGB deceivers. Though he did not "defect" this time, he did fifteen years later, after working in Moscow under Oleg Gribanov.

Among the KGB counterintelligence officers springing Pavlovsky's Trap in postwar Berlin was the young Yuri Guk, who, a decade later, was to be one of the "three musketeers" handling a mole in CIA in Washington and, five years after that, was to work in Geneva at the side of Yuri Nosenko. Not only does Guk exemplify the continuum, but he also illustrates the intimate connection between these "games" and the penetration of Western intelligence services—"moles."

CHAPTER **13**

Symbiosis
Moles and Games

The KGB has from its earliest days given top priority to penetrating the staff of Western intelligence services—planting "moles" in the enemy camp. As a result, they have similarly raised aggressive counterintelligence operations to the same top priority, for moles and deception feed off one another. Lacking the other, one may fail, even die.

The interaction takes many forms. Games, for example, can produce moles. Again and again through the years the KGB put out lures to draw hostile intelligence officers into dangerous or compromising situations where they might be pressured into cooperation. And once recruited as a mole, an officer in an opposing intelligence service, by his very existence, produces games. A KGB ploy might expand his access to secrets, for instance. And if the KGB is to act on his revelations, it must do so in a way that will not alert the adversary to his existence—so games are used to create innocent excuses for action. To "safely" arrest a spy whom a mole has uncovered, a game is mounted to persuade the adversary of some other cause—for example, that "routine surveillance of diplomats" had stumbled upon the spy.

The KGB recognized and emphasized this symbiosis. In its top-secret history of its own operations it noted that aggressive games "achieved the best results" against Western intelligence services. And these games required moles in those services: "our need for timely information required penetration into the enemy's camp. We achieved this by recruiting Western intelligence personnel."[1]

They started early. As soon as Chekists first put *rezidentura* in Soviet diplomatic and trade missions abroad, each chief (*rezident*) was ordered "by Party instructions of 1920" to give highest priority to "inserting agents into the enemy's intelligence and counterintelligence organs by recruiting people working there."[2]

They succeeded, profiting early from Western sympathy for the bold Russian-Communist "social experiment" that grew when the great depression of the 1930s eroded faith in Western institutions. With Hitler's rise to power there arose the image of Communism as an anti-fascist bulwark and, after his invasion of the USSR, as a gallant ally desperately needing help. Numbers of Western intellectuals, journalists, filmmakers, workers, and university students moved from leftist idealism into active conspiracy, and of these some joined the intelligence services of their own countries to spy there for Moscow. Inside CIA's predecessor, OSS, about a dozen such Communists and Soviet sympathizers were subsequently identified as Soviet agents. A leading Chekist claimed, in his memoirs after the Cold War, "Yes, we had agents in [the OSS]. Moreover," he added in a mischievous and probably unfounded dig, "when CIA was created in 1947, some transferred there."[3]

In Britain, Kim Philby, John Cairncross, Guy Burgess, and Anthony Blunt joined the secret services and exposed their work to the KGB. They also gave the KGB insights into the newly founded CIA, where British Intelligence for a time maintained a near-parental liaison.

In France the KGB infiltrated so deeply that even the KGB's foreign-counterintelligence chief was surprised when he took command in the early 1970s. "Though I knew before that we had an impressive network of agents in France, I was nevertheless surprised at the sheer number of high-ranking moles we had in French Intelligence, Counterintelligence, and the military. During my time we boasted about a dozen excellent spies in France, most of them operating at the top rung of their agencies."[4]

The KGB focused its postwar games against CIA and British MI6 after the Second World War. "Using the rich experience gained in the struggle against German-fascist intelligence during the war," they said in their top-secret official history, "we conducted operational games, plots, and other actions against American and British Intelligence."

So well had this KGB penetration work succeeded that, by the late

1970s (according to Oleg Kalugin) the KGB had moles inside *fifty* Western intelligence and security services, including those of every major power.

A rare confluence of circumstances enabled CIA to get a look behind one of these KGB mole operations that illuminated the interplay between moles and deceptive games.

A tip from Michal Goleniewski in the "Sniper" letters exposed Heinz Felfe as a KGB agent and led to his arrest in 1961 and later imprisonment. Felfe was a key officer of West German Intelligence Service, BND (*Bundesnachrichtendienst*) that had earlier been the "Gehlen Organization," known as the "Org."

CIA had set up, and cooperated with, the Org, so it knew a lot about the secret activities that Felfe had been betraying.

There was little that Felfe had *not* known. He supervised all the BND's counterespionage operations against the Soviet Union. No sooner had he entered the Org in November 1951—already a KGB agent—than he was plunged straight into the very heart of those operations. He started as deputy and soon became chief of the base in Karlsruhe that handled counterintelligence operations. In 1953 he moved up to the Org's Pullach Headquarters to oversee, first as deputy and from early 1957 as chief, the BND's whole counterintelligence effort against the Soviets. He supervised its double agents—spies of the Soviet services who had been caught and turned against their handlers or who had turned themselves in and agreed to spy on under BND control. He got his eye on the BND's intelligence-collection operations as well, and through liaison with American and British Intelligence he learned some of their secret activities. (In fact, it was his visit to CIA in a BND group that led to his downfall. Goleniewski learned that two of the six BND delegates to Washington were KGB agents, and Felfe [though not the other] was identified.)

Thus the KGB had achieved every counterintelligence service's dream: to know practically everything its adversary was doing against it. But it would have to be cautious in exploiting those insights. In order for the goose to keep laying golden eggs, the KGB would have to hide her existence.

Not long afterward I came to supervise CIA's work against the KGB and saw a way to profit from this unfortunate affair. The uncovering of Felfe had given us a marvelous gift—the power of hindsight. Knowing about some BND activities during Felfe's time of treason, we could look back and see them with new eyes. Questions sprang to mind. What steps had the KGB taken to exploit—and hide—the inside knowledge that Felfe had given them? How did the KGB deal with the spies whom Felfe had betrayed? Did it manipulate them without their knowledge? And if it arrested them, how did it manage to do so without alerting the BND to a leak? Had the KGB mounted games to promote Felfe in his own service and to extend his reach into new fields? Had any of the German handlers of BND agents, exposed by Felfe, noted any sign that his operation might be known to the Soviets? Here was a rare window into a super-secret, tightly compartmented field of KGB activity.

Above all, what might we learn that could help us detect signs of trouble in *our own* operations against the Soviet Union?

With such questions in mind, we dug into the recent German past.

We saw, for one thing, that the KGB was ready to make cruel sacrifices to protect or promote a mole in the enemy camp.

KGB defector Peter Deriabin had disclosed to CIA in February 1954 the presence inside West German Intelligence of two important KGB spies, though he knew only their code names "Peter" and "Paul." In Moscow a special commission of the KGB feverishly assessed what Deriabin might reveal about its spies in the West, poring over files he had handled and interviewing colleagues with whom he had talked. Examining his service in the German-Austrian Department they could not have failed to learn that he knew of the existence of Peter and Paul—though Deriabin did not know that Peter was Felfe.

That, it seems, is what lay behind some extraordinary events in the early summer of 1954 around a lamppost in Ludwigsburg, north of Stuttgart in West Germany.

In a crevice in a wall near that lamppost, West German police found a report detailing the structure and operations of the Gehlen Org's Karlsruhe base, where Felfe had recently been chief and which he still oversaw from the Org's Headquarters. These were secrets known only to Org insiders, and the only reason they would be lying out here, in an obvious dead drop, was that someone had deposited them for the enemy to pick up.

A mole was at work. Might it be Deriabin's Peter or Paul?

West German Counterintelligence (BfV) set a hidden watch over the spot and code-named this vigil "Operation Lili Marlene," for the lonely lady under the lamppost of the famous song.

A lucky coincidence had led them there. A townsman passing by had glimpsed someone inserting a packet in the crevice. In spy-ridden postwar

Germany this kind of thing looked suspicious, so he had loyally reported it to the police, who quickly retrieved the report. Seeing its shocking contents they called in the BfV, whose experts quickly recognized that they had been handed a rare opportunity. They photographed the report, resealed it, put it back by the lamppost, set up a vigil, and waited to pounce on whoever might come to pick it up.

One evening a man approached, loitered near the lamppost for a moment, then quickly moved to the crevice and extracted the packet. The watchers alerted a nearby patrol, and the man strolled off into their waiting arms. They took him to a police station, where he first protested that he had found the package by chance and pocketed it, but when confronted with its damning contents, he confessed. Though carrying West German identity papers he was an East German citizen acting as a courier for the KGB in East Berlin. He had no idea what was in the packet; his job had been simply to pick it up and carry it unopened to the East.

Analyzing the report with the help of the BND's Karlsruhe base, the BfV narrowed down the possible writers to one insider, an officer named Ludwig Albert. They arrested him and searched his house—and found evidence of his spying.

Before he could be brought to trial Ludwig Albert committed suicide, leaving a note confessing his treason. Thus was resolved the mystery of at least one of the two moles Peter and Paul. Or so it seemed at the time.

Seven years later Goleniewski gave pointers that led to the arrest of BND officers Felfe (who was Peter) and Hans Clemens (Paul). Those earlier events around the lamppost began to look different.

Surprising new light fell on that episode. The BfV came to suspect the loyalty of the Ludwigsburg townsman who had "chanced" to see the packet being deposited near the lamppost. They called him in for questioning, and he confessed to being a KGB agent. His handler, he admitted, had told him to report to the police this fictitious sighting.

Thus the KGB itself had planted the incriminating report, purposely letting the West know that it possessed secrets from inside the BND's Karlsruhe office—secrets that Ludwig Albert provided, or could have provided. They were throwing Ludwig Albert into the sacrificial fire (causing his death, as it happened), evidently to protect the more important mole, Felfe.

The KGB could afford the loss. So well stocked were they with spies inside the BND that when Hans Clemens (as he later confessed) had told his KGB handler that he was to be transferred to the BND office in

Cologne, the KGB instructed him to refuse assignment to certain sections but to accept certain others. They obviously had the base covered, so why have two or more spies in the same section?

Why was Ludwig Albert chosen to be thrown onto the sacrificial fire? Perhaps it was because he had become an enemy of Felfe within the Karlsruhe base and was even accusing him of being a Soviet agent. But perhaps also it was because Albert was cooperating with American military counterintelligence, and the KGB may have come to suspect (wrongly) that he was playing a double game against them.[5] Whatever their reason, the KGB had sacrificed him in a cruel and cunning game to protect Felfe.

Albert was not the only sacrificial victim of "Lili Marlene." Another was the courier the KGB sent into a trap they themselves had set for him.

The KGB played other games to protect their moles.

Our review of Felfe's years in the BND showed that in 1961 he learned —and told the KGB—that the BfV was planning to compromise and recruit a Soviet trade official, Dmitry Kirpichev, during his forthcoming trip to a North German port city.

What should the KGB do? They could not let Kirpichev step into the BfV trap. Yet they did not trust Kirpichev enough to forewarn him, for that would reveal that they had inside information from the West German side. They concluded that they must cancel his trip but worried that a last-minute cancellation might make the BfV suspect a leak. That would be dangerous because any BfV investigation would inevitably point toward Felfe, who had been officially consulted on their plan against Kirpichev.

To resolve this dilemma the KGB played an old game. They knew (through moles) that the BfV was tapping certain Soviet telephone lines in West Germany but—following standing orders—the KGB had left things unchanged. They regarded enemy phone taps or microphones on their premises more as opportunity than menace—as ready-made channels through which they could pass deceptive information to the West.[6] This was the channel they now chose to protect Felfe while at the same time removing Kirpichev from danger.

KGB-trusted Soviet colleagues of Kirpichev were instructed to stage phone calls over the tapped lines. A wife phoned a friend and gossiped about complications in Kirpichev's life. In a call to a West German client in the northern city, a Soviet shipping official gave a similar story to explain why Kirpichev could not come as scheduled but reassured him that Kirpichev would come as soon as he could. It worked. Kirpichev's trip was cancelled. The danger from the BfV was averted. No alarm bells rang, because now the BfV had the inside story from a secret source of their own—the phone tap.

I was to encounter this ploy more than once. CIA was preparing to make recruitment pitches in two different parts of the world to Soviet Military Intelligence officers "Ivan" and "Boris," whose susceptibility Penkovsky had signaled to us. The KGB somehow got advance knowledge of our plans. They thought it prudent to remove our targets from temptation but feared that we would suspect a leak if they were inexplicably to depart just before we moved in. So they played games to allay such suspicions. As we were preparing to move in on Ivan we heard over tapped phone lines a Soviet wife chatting with another and deploring the accident by which dear Ivan had broken his leg—what a pity that the poor fellow had to go home for treatment. Over similarly known tapped lines, an Embassy officer phoned the Soviet doctor about Ivan's leg, and then Western surveillance saw Ivan being bundled onto a plane to Moscow with a very visible cast on that leg.

This subterfuge was hiding a secret source. In Kirpichev's case it was Felfe, but we never discovered who had betrayed our plans to approach Ivan and Boris. (In at least one case it might have been a KGB penetration of the local security service that was cooperating with CIA in the pitch.)

After the BND had sorted through the rubble of the Felfe disaster its chief, Reinhard Gehlen, expressed awe at the massive efforts and sacrifices the KGB had made to support and promote this mole within his service.

"Felfe had been given secrets to feed to us," Gehlen wrote in his memoirs, "which were unique [as far as Gehlen was aware] in the history of the intelligence war between East and West. This was their way of insuring that he would be rapidly promoted."

"Felfe was kept well supplied with priceless political intelligence to feed to us," Gehlen continued. "These reports sometimes contained important state secrets of the East German government; the Russians sacrificed their satellite government's secrets for one purpose alone—to build up this traitor's prestige within the BND and to give the impression that he was one of our most dependable intelligence procurers."

Gehlen gave an example: "To speed up his promotion still further and to enhance his access to classified material, the KGB sacrificed one of its own political agents in West Germany without the slightest compunction. Through Felfe they fed us in cleverly regulated doses the clues that led to the arrest and conviction of C. A. Weber, the editor of the magazine *Die Deutsche Woche*. He was an agent who acted for the Russians out of mistaken idealism and had long been under observation. Thus, the agent who was of the greater value to Moscow was permitted to deliver his less important colleague to the sword."[7]

Barely recognizable behind Gehlen's sketchy account was a subtle and ramified KGB operation that boosted Felfe's BND prestige and opened mouth-watering possibilities for his KGB masters.

The central figure was an East German publisher and party official whom the BND thought was spying for them but who in fact was operating under KGB control as a double agent. He had the BND code name "Lena." The case had been running for three years when Felfe arrived in October 1953 for duty in Pullach to oversee counterespionage. Remarkably, Lena's activity now changed. He came to his BND handling officer with astonishing news: the KGB had recruited him to develop a spy network in West Germany! Lena was to recruit others to assist him in spotting likely targets for KGB recruitment among officials of the West German Foreign Ministry and the Office of the Federal Chancellor.

This offered the BND rich possibilities to deceive the Soviets—but it changed the nature of their Lena case. From an effort to collect intelligence on the East German ruling party and leading personalities it had now become a counterintelligence case against the KGB. Logically, the BND turned the case over to Felfe's supervision. Soon the case expanded and became the BND's most important counterespionage operation—and made Felfe's reputation as an authority.

Lena reported that he was enjoying unusually friendly and informal relations with his KGB handlers, primitive souls who seemed awed to be talking with such a well-connected, experienced politician. It caused them to become so indiscreet that they "inadvertently" gave Lena insights into Soviet policy toward West Germany and exposed to him officers from KGB Headquarters in East Berlin and several of their safe houses and automobiles. The KGB handlers even dropped clues to other spies in West Germany, like the C. A. Weber whom Gehlen mentioned. All this redounded to the benefit of Felfe's reputation.

These KGB officers were not only indiscreet but also ignorant and indolent. They knew little about the Foreign Ministry and the Chancellery and were not energetic enough to get much more. The BND handed them through Lena some names of West German officials as potential recruits, but the KGB was content to move against only one, though this functionary of the Press Office (who was of course under West German control) supplied them with little more than the contents of wastebaskets.

Felfe argued to his authorities that they had better provide Lena with genuine secrets that would build KGB confidence in him. To this end he negotiated a ruling by the attorney general that secrets, if already exposed, could be passed to the enemy to build up double agents (like Lena).

Having created this loophole, the KGB now exploited it. A KGB case officer would "indiscreetly" tell an agent (whom he knew through Felfe to be working for the BND as a double agent) that the KGB already knew certain West German secrets. Under Felfe's rules, that made those secrets legally "disposable," so other double agents could then expose them legally.

The KGB needed only tell Lena that one or another German official was a target for recruitment, and Felfe, the counterintelligence chief, would have an excuse to check West German files to find out *why*. What did the files really show about him or her—perhaps money or marital problems or family members in the East, just what the KGB needed to shape a recruitment pitch to that individual.

Felfe thus served as a KGB entrée into West German government personnel files. The KGB also used this tool for other purposes.

We came across the case of a West German businessman whom I will call "Karlik." He traveled frequently to Moscow and was notably more active than most businessmen there. Indeed, he had developed such a large circle of contacts among Soviet trade officials that he had aroused the suspicions of the KGB's internal counterintelligence directorate. They asked the foreign-operations directorate whether Karlik was associated with West German Intelligence. A check with Felfe certified that the BND had no contact with him. So might Karlik be working with CIA or some other Western spy service? The KGB saw a way to use their mole Felfe to find out.

Their game proceeded in two steps. First, they recruited Karlik themselves. They rightly assumed he would pretend to cooperate with them in order to keep his Russian business going—and that if he was a CIA agent he would report it and act thereafter as CIA's double agent against the KGB.

Then the KGB instructed their new agent Karlik—whom of course they did not really trust—to develop contacts in the West German Embassy in Moscow and to report on their potential vulnerability to KGB recruitment as spies. If Karlik was indeed a CIA agent, the KGB calculated, his CIA handlers would now have to bring the BND into the operation, which meant, in this sort of counterintelligence problem, Felfe.

It worked. Karlik was in fact working for CIA's Berlin Base, and CIA now did inform the BND, and even turned Karlik over to Felfe's handling. And Felfe did inform the KGB of all this.

That wasn't the end of the KGB's game. It recruited one of Karlik's Soviet trade contacts (who as a loyal Soviet citizen could hardly refuse) to act vulnerable and open himself to CIA's recruitment—in order to expose CIA assets and handling methods in Moscow.

Using this tool the KGB could even test the reliability of Soviet citizens. Felfe would instruct Karlik to contact and develop people whom the KGB suspected—then observe and report to Moscow their reactions.

When the KGB told Karlik to assess a certain West German Embassy official in Moscow, it would give Felfe an excuse to check the official's personnel file in the Foreign Ministry in Bonn. Thus the KGB got access to sensitive personal information that might give them a handle over person X—or Y, or Z.

The KGB used Felfe to expose yet another CIA agent. A West German woman was conducting a love affair with a Soviet official in Moscow. The KGB suspected that she was developing him for recruitment, on behalf of CIA. So it had Felfe pass a message to CIA, in a routine liaison meeting. The BND, he would say, thought that CIA might be in contact with this lady. If so, it should be warned that she was conducting herself loosely with a man in Moscow and exposing herself to KGB compromise and recruitment. CIA's reaction should tell whether it was behind the affair. It worked: CIA told Felfe it was okay, the lady was doing this on CIA's behalf.

Upon learning this from Felfe, the KGB proceeded to recruit the official themselves. As a loyal citizen he could not refuse if he wished to maintain his clearance to meet Western contacts. The KGB encouraged him to continue the love affair—and to let himself be recruited by CIA.

Now the operation had boomeranged. From a CIA effort to recruit a Soviet official it had become a KGB game to draw CIA into a trap to expose its methods in Moscow, and expose a CIA case officer to compromise and recruitment. But in this case the KGB lacked the time: Felfe was arrested and the game was exposed and came to an abrupt end.

These were just a few of the complicated intrigues—and sacrifices of their own assets and secrets—that the KGB used to protect and promote this one mole, Heinz Felfe. Felfe was not alone; even inside the BND the KGB had other moles. To hide (and in some cases to promote) each of them the KGB had to apply the same rigorous care. We learned some of these techniques by uncovering and studying the Felfe case, but who knows what other ploys were used to (successfully) hide the others. Scores of such cunning gambits and sacrifices remain unknown, perhaps forever.

We learned all this thanks only to an unsolicited stroke of luck. Had it not been for the secret letters from Michal Goleniewski, Felfe might never have been uncovered. Deriabin's leads to Peter and Paul were too vague. In fact, Felfe left tracks afterward that were noted and could have been followed, some of them in the operations I have described. But, lacking "proof," Westerners were inclined to shrug these things off as "anomalies" and finally to forget them.

Deriabin was frustrated and came to suspect that no one *wanted* to find these West German moles. Goleniewski must have felt the same, for he had told us there were *two* KGB moles on Felfe's six-man BND delegation to Washington—and the second was never uncovered. (Hans Clemens, the Paul to Felfe's Peter, was not a member of this delegation.)

Westerners are loath to suspect treason and even more loath to investigate clues to it. Our human penchant to reject what we don't want to believe affords a great protection to moles in our midst (see Appendix C). Clues, even fairly precise ones, can be shrugged off.

As I look over the history of the Cold War I see few exceptions to a rule I developed from my own observations: *it takes a mole to catch a mole.* In this (unprofessional) term "mole" I include other forms of staff-level penetrations of the enemy such as defectors like Goleniewski and Deriabin and Golitsyn, and cipher breaks like "Venona."

As far as I know every traitor uncovered inside intelligence services, East or West, during the Cold War was caught only because of tips from sources inside the enemy camp. That applies to every one of the KGB's famous moles in Great Britain: Kim Philby, Anthony Blunt, Guy Burgess, Donald Maclean, John Cairncross, and George Blake. It includes the Americans Aldrich Ames, Earl Pitts, Robert Hanssen, Harold Nicholson, Edwin G. Moore, David Barnett, Edward Lee Howard, William Kampiles, and Larry Wu-tai Chin. It applies as well to traitors inside major Western military services including Robert Lee Johnson, Jack Dunlap, Clyde Lee Conrad, Nelson Drummond, and the Walker family inside the U.S. Navy.

To protect the moles, the captors of these spies gave out innocuous versions of how they had come upon them: by a denunciation, for instance, or by the alertness of security officers who happened to spot suspicious contacts or learn that they were spending beyond their means or taking strange trips. Sometimes these other clues really did appear, but only during investigations following a mole's tip. (In the Walker case, for instance, the wife's denunciation did play a role—but an FBI mole inside the KGB had given a tip that made the denunciation believable.)[8] The real story could almost invariably be found in the underlying, super-secret "war of the moles."

Despite the more rigorous security precautions in the Soviet bloc, this rule of thumb applies as truly to the Soviets' discovery of the few important American spies in their midst, like Pyotr Popov, Oleg Penkovsky, and, of course, more than a dozen arrested in the 1980s, betrayed, as we later learned, by Aldrich Ames in CIA and Robert Hanssen in the FBI.

We never had enough such inside sources in the East, so the KGB succeeded in hiding moles by careful compartmentation and by skill in "games" that diverted attention from them. Robert Hanssen got away with spying from inside the FBI for some twenty years, Aldrich Ames inside CIA for nine. And earlier ones were never detected at all.

PART THREE

Hidden Moles

CHAPTER 14

Dead Drop

Nosenko's accounts of the KGB's watch over the American Embassy security officer in Moscow, John Abidian, were baffling.

In 1962 Nosenko told CIA that this watch was so important that it called for his personal supervision as deputy head of the section. The KGB tailed Abidian wherever he went and Nosenko kept a close eye and guiding hand on the surveillance. Because Abidian had succeeded Popov's CIA handler Russell Langelle as Embassy security officer the KGB hoped thus "to catch another Popov." (We thought this a far-fetched and unlikely supposition.) In the event, Nosenko told CIA, this blanket coverage had flopped; its most important find, he said, was an American girl's panties left behind in Abidian's bedroom.

In 1964 Nosenko told a wildly different story. Without referring to anything he had or had not said in 1962, Nosenko recounted the success of that KGB surveillance. In late 1960 they had spotted Abidian "setting up a dead drop" for CIA on Pushkin Street. The KGB had set a watch over the site and week after week for at least three months the watcher's reports came across Nosenko's desk—always negative.

We could find no innocent explanation for this startling contrast. In 1962 Nosenko was becoming our agent and knew that any KGB detection of CIA work in Moscow—regardless of its importance to his new CIA friends—could affect his own future security. He could not have failed to mention this discovery, infinitely more significant than a girl's panties.

We knew about that dead drop—CIA had had only one, ever, on Push-kin Street. And neither Abidian nor anyone else working with CIA "set up" that drop. Oleg Penkovsky did.[1] At no time in 1960 or earlier had Abidian or anyone else from the Western side even approached that building, much less entered its lobby, where, behind a radiator, the drop site was located. There was no reason to do so and CIA was careful *not* to go near it. Even in mid-1961, when CIA wanted to confirm to Penkovsky in Paris in September that it could safely service the drop, Abidian was asked only to look over the general area to see whether he could eventually go to that address without moving outside his normal pattern of daily life. He walked past but didn't enter the building, and saw that it would be easy. Not only was his regular barber on the next side street but on that corner was a book-store where he sometimes browsed—a bookstore with entrances onto both streets.[2]

The first time Abidian actually stepped inside the building to check that drop site occurred at the end of December, just as Nosenko had said—but of December 1961, not 1960.

Crash! went Nosenko's career story. He claimed to have finished his service in the American Department at the end of 1961, only a few days after Abidian first went to the drop, so he could not have received reports of a stakeout over the weeks and months that followed.[3] Even less because during those weeks and months he was preparing for his departure for Geneva in March 1962.

Even more startling was the *reason* Abidian went there in December 1961, which Nosenko evidently did not know. Someone had triggered Pen-kovsky's signal arrangement—and it was not Penkovsky.

The plan had been worked out at a meeting in Paris on 2 October 1961: "Penkovsky was given two phone numbers of American Embassy person-nel, either of which he could ring. When a man answered the phone, Pen-kovsky was to blow into the mouthpiece three times, then wait one minute and repeat the procedure. The Americans would then go to telephone pole number 35 on Kutuzovsky Prospekt and look for a freshly marked letter X on the pole. This signal meant that Penkovsky would leave a detailed mes-sage in the dead drop."[4]

On one of those two phones, at about 9 p.m. on 25 December 1961, the wife of the American Assistant Military Attaché, Alexis Davison, received two voiceless calls in succession. She could not hear any blowing into the phone, and she counted three minutes between the calls instead of one.

But it coincided closely enough with the planned signal, so she passed the word.

At that moment the CIA station chief and Abidian were at a Christmas party at the ambassador's residence. Station chief Garbler was called out to take a phone call and was told by prearranged code that the signal had been received. He went back to the party and, after a delay so that no one would associate his departure with the phone call, told his host he was feeling ill from the drinks and that Abidian had offered to drive him home. On the way to Abidian's car Garbler wove drunkenly for the benefit of the inevitable KGB surveillance. En route they stopped twice so Garbler could vomit for the benefit of the KGB tail, the second time close to telephone pole number 35. The CIA file account states that no mark was visible, but in fact Garbler told Abidian that although he had not seen any mark, he could not be absolutely sure in the dark. So he asked Abidian to check the drop, just in case.[5] (Strangely, Garbler later told an investigative reporter, incorrectly, that there had been no mark on the pole and that he had opposed sending anyone to the drop.)[6]

Abidian duly went to the area in the last days of 1961. His ever-vigilant KGB surveillance team drove behind him to his barbershop and as usual, while he had his hair cut, waited in their car, which was parked thirty or forty meters behind his. Afterward he strolled into the nearby bookstore, but they did not race up to see if he had gone through and out onto Pushkin Street. Abidian quickly checked the drop, found nothing, and went back into and out of the bookstore to his car. The shadows were still with their car, one of them standing outside smoking.

It must have been the KGB—who else?—who triggered the visit by using Penkovsky's signal system. Voiceless calls were rare; any voiceless calls coming coincidentally to this particular phone number were as unlikely as being struck by lightning, and two such calls in quick succession left no reasonable doubt.

Sinister questions loomed. First, how could the KGB have known the signaling system? (Probably not ten people in the world knew about it.) And how did the KGB know (as Nosenko's story revealed) that it was Abidian who went there? Abidian's KGB shadows didn't follow him on his quick trip into and out of the bookstore onto Pushkin Street, so if surveillants had been placed in advance around the corner, they must have known about the drop. Yet in the publicity surrounding the Penkovsky trial in May 1963, it was said that the KGB learned about Penkovsky's communications arrangements—including the signaling arrangements and the Pushkin Street dead drop—only when they searched his apartment in September 1962.

Nosenko could not have simply fabricated this story to look more knowledgeable and important, because Abidian's name was never publicly mentioned in connection with the Penkovsky case. And Nosenko demonstrated his inside knowledge when he told CIA in 1962 of finding the girl's panties (a finding, by the way, that Abidian later told me was not unlikely).

Thus the KGB had earlier, inside knowledge. That raised the specter of deep penetration of CIA or MI6—a mole knowing what only a handful of our officers knew. Now something Nosenko had said in 1962, which had seemed innocent at the time, took on new meaning. Only three or four months before the KGB arrested Penkovsky—and *after* they had detected his secret contact with Western intelligence—Nosenko had said that by following Abidian the KGB hoped "to catch another Popov."

New information tied Nosenko even closer to Penkovsky's downfall. A British intelligence officer brought news from their debriefing of Greville Wynne—and mentioned the strange name "Zepp."

Wynne had set up MI6 and CIA's initial contact with Penkovsky, had served as an occasional courier to him in Moscow afterward, had been kidnapped in Hungary and brought to Moscow, and was given an eight-year sentence at the joint trial with Penkovsky in May 1963. Wynne had been jailed in Vladimir prison north of Moscow, but in the spring of 1964 he returned to England, his liberty obtained in trade for that of Conon Molody (alias "Gordon Lonsdale"), a KGB Illegal jailed in Britain. Once safely back in England Wynne told his British friends what had befallen him. The British intelligence officer James Garth (as I will call him) told of one aspect of the story that was charged with portent.

In October 1963, after Wynne had spent five months in prison, the KGB transported him back to Moscow for further interrogation. This time their main concern was whether he had had contact with other spies during his business trips to Eastern Europe.

"Out of nowhere," James said, "the KGB interrogator suddenly asked him, 'Who is Zepp?' Wynne was baffled—he didn't know anyone by that name." Wynne described the interrogator's reaction: shaking his head in mock disappointment with a low "tsk, tsk," he switched on a tape recorder. Wynne heard his own voice and after some clinking of tableware, Penkovsky's voice asking "And how is Zepp?" The interrogator stopped the tape and looked Wynne in the eye.

"Now Wynne remembered," James continued. "He even remembered the conversation. 'Zeph,' not 'Zepp,' as it sounded on the tape, was a nickname he and Penkovsky had given to a bar girl they had met in a London night club. This was the only time Penkovsky ever asked Wynne about 'Zeph,' which was normal because they had just met her."[7]

"So there's the problem," James said. "The conversation took place in a Moscow restaurant while Wynne was visiting Moscow—and that was in May 1961, only a couple of weeks after our first series of meetings with Penkovsky in London!"

I saw his point. This meant that the KGB had specific reason to bug Penkovsky's lunch conversation just after our operation began—and more than a year before it ended. It was no accident. Even Nosenko had confirmed that these portable microphone-transmitters were purposely placed on specific tables that were to be used by targeted personalities. Moreover, the KGB was informed that Penkovsky was working officially with Wynne, and in such cases it was not supposed to tail GRU people, much less to listen in on their working conversations.[8]

The implications were staggering. Here was evidence that the KGB was aware of Penkovsky's treason *sixteen months* before they arrested him. Sixteen months during which the KGB allowed him to go out to London again and then to Paris and then, even after stopping any further travel abroad from October 1961, left him with his dangerous access to secret archives for nearly a year more.

Why?

In professional jargon the answer is "source protection"—the KGB's need to hide the very existence of the secret source that had exposed Penkovsky. That source must have been so close to the (tightly compartmented) Penkovsky case that he or she or it would inevitably become suspect if the West investigated how Penkovsky had been caught. So before arresting him (or even removing him from access to secrets) the KGB had to provide some innocent explanation—like "routine surveillance of Western diplomats in Moscow." To warrant leaving Penkovsky with access to high military secrets the hidden source (or sources) must have been exceptionally valuable, with the potential to remain valuable or become even more so in the future. That source was most likely a mole, because a cipher break would not have exposed the dead drop arrangements that the KGB knew about.

By preventing Penkovsky from traveling abroad after September 1961 the KGB was not only reducing the time he could spend with Western intelligence representatives, but also, and perhaps more to the point, forcing his Western handlers to meet him in Moscow—and be "routinely surveilled."

Nosenko claimed high authority to confirm that it was indeed by chance surveillance of British diplomats that the KGB had tumbled onto Penkovsky's treason. He had this truth from the horse's mouth—in fact, from several different horses. According to his varying versions he had been told by "a member of the British Department" (whose name he had forgotten), or by his friend the Department chief Yevgeny Tarabrin, or "personally by [counterintelligence chief Oleg] Gribanov himself."

Nosenko's use of the name "Zepp" in 1962 showed the KGB was using him in conjunction with their Penkovsky investigation. That name had been puzzling the KGB from May 1961, when they got it off the taped restaurant conversation, until at least October 1963, when they interrogated Wynne about it.[9] In June 1962, smack in the middle of this period of the KGB's concern, Nosenko had raised the name "Zepp" with no prompting—and in the context of a bugged restaurant meeting, just as Wynne's KGB interrogator had. Nosenko even spelled it out just as the KGB interrogator later pronounced it for Wynne.

Now Nosenko was here among us in Washington, so I went and asked him. "Tell me more about Zepp, the Indonesian military attaché."

Nosenko looked at me blankly. "Who's that?"

"You know, the guy who was having lunch with Colonel Dulacki in Moscow. You told me about that in 1962."

"No, I never said that. Don't know that name. Sure, I told you about our bugging a conversation of Dulacki's, but that was with Colonel Ongko, the Indonesian military attaché. That was in the written summary I gave you." He had indeed provided a KGB document summarizing counterintelligence matters of one year, and it did mention the (insignificant) Ongko-Dulacki luncheon meeting.

The Moscow diplomatic list had confirmed that the Indonesian military attaché at the time was Colonel Ongko and his deputy, a Lieutenant Colonel Zen.

"Maybe your tongue slipped. Maybe you were referring to Zen."

"Never heard that name," Nosenko said. "Couldn't have said it."

Could it be coincidence that just when the KGB was concerned about this most unusual name, Nosenko had tried it out on us? And that he had since forgotten it? It seemed more likely that Nosenko in 1962—put up to it by KGB handlers on the scene—was trying to get our reaction to the name of Zepp. It made sense. If he was describing Kisevalter and me to KGB handlers in Geneva, they would have recognized that Nosenko was face to face with Popov's eminently recognizable case officer. They could reasonably assume—if they did not already know—that Kisevalter was Penkovsky's case officer as well and might in his garrulous way let slip something about "Zepp."

Nosenko's "Zepp" gambit, added to his bizarre and manifestly fabricated story of the Pushkin Street dead drop, forced our attention onto other connections between Nosenko and the downfall of Oleg Penkovsky.

For instance, the timing. Nosenko was sent to Geneva (where he was later to contact CIA) in early 1962 (visa requested mid-February, departed mid-March), after the KGB had stumbled onto Penkovsky's treason. By that time, too, it had blocked Penkovsky's further travel abroad, forcing CIA and MI6 to contact him in Moscow. By late spring the KGB in Moscow —preparing to arrest Penkovsky—was tailing him so crudely that it looked as if they *wanted* the surveillance to be noticed. At this moment Nosenko made contact with CIA in Geneva and impressed us with his insider description of the KGB's vast and effective surveillance of Western diplomats in Moscow—and how it had uncovered Popov, CIA's earlier GRU source. He even said, explicitly, that the KGB hoped thus "to catch another Popov."

This correlation of dates suggested powerfully that the KGB had sent Nosenko to prepare CIA to accept the "surveillance" version and not look deeper into how Penkovsky had been detected. Afterward, in 1964, Nosenko endowed himself with insider's authority to confirm the official version.

The official Soviet version came out around the time of the Penkovsky trial in the spring of 1963. The KGB spread the word in a secret briefing paper (*obzor*) for its own personnel that in late 1961 and early 1962 its operatives, routinely tailing the wife of a British intelligence officer of the Embassy, had spotted her in successive contacts with Penkovsky. Several KGB officers with authority later confirmed this story, adding details that lent it authenticity. No doubt Mrs. Chisholm *was* seen in apparent clandestine contact with Penkovsky; the KGB even supplied photographs of the two of them together, taken surreptitiously.

But this was not the whole story.

After the Cold War KGB insiders admitted that the surveillance story was a ruse. "Don't believe for a minute that old story that we detected Penkovsky by surveillance," a retired KGB colonel confided to a former adversary as they reminisced over a glass of wine. Then the former deputy chief of KGB foreign intelligence, General Vitaly Pavlov, spilled the beans. He neither denied nor belittled the skillful surveillance work but resented the fact that counterintelligence people were seizing undue credit. *"It was Foreign Intelligence that got the first indication,"* he wrote in his memoir. "All the rest, as the saying goes, was a technical matter."[10] He meant, of course, that the Moscow surveillants had known whom to follow, and perhaps when, thanks to a source of Pavlov's foreign-intelligence directorate —presumably a mole in American or British Intelligence. And informally he later confided to a Westerner that the KGB knew about Penkovsky's secret collaboration with the West even before Penkovsky's trip to Paris in the summer of 1962, before it cut off his further travel abroad.

Even when repeating the official version KGB insiders tacitly admitted that surveillance explained only part of the story. A leader of the surveillance directorate itself, who would be the first to claim credit if he could, admitted that Penkovsky was uncovered also "by a confluence of circumstances."[11] Another KGB spokesman went further. While trying to convince a Western interviewer that surveillance and only surveillance had detected Penkovsky—taking pains to supply street photos to prove it—he found himself unable to answer some probing questions and blurted an admission that blew his whole story apart: *"Counterintelligence even now cannot disclose how Penkovsky was uncovered."*[12]

Thus came, belatedly, confirmation of our deduction thirty years earlier: Penkovsky was betrayed by a mole—and Nosenko sought to hide this fact. Might Nosenko have been merely passing on (with personal embellishment) an official briefing that he believed to be true? No—he had inside information. He knew Abidian had visited Penkovsky's dead drop though this never appeared in any briefing or press report. And even before Penkovsky was arrested Nosenko was probing Kisevalter and me about "Zepp."

Nosenko's stories, and the KGB's delay in arresting Penkovsky, combined (inadvertently) to show there was a mole in one or both of the handling services, MI6 and/or CIA—and shortened the list of suspects:

- The hidden source must have been so close to the operation that he or she would inevitably come under suspicion in the West if

Penkovsky were to be arrested for no known reason—causing a Western investigation of a possible leak.

- The mole would have to be someone who knew the dead drop arrangements (as few did).
- This person must be someone who did *not* know about the bar girl "Zeph."

That mole remains unknown to this day.

CHAPTER **15**

Code Clerks

"We never recruited any American code clerk in Moscow," said Yuri Nosenko in 1962 with the authority of having personally supervised such KGB work for two years. Even before he started that job at the beginning of 1960, "the closest [the KGB] got to recruiting communications people was Andrey"—the cipher-machine mechanic whom he had exposed in our first 1962 meeting and labeled as the Moscow KGB's most important American recruit.

Joe Westin had reasons to doubt this. Of the members of our section Joe was the most dogged and determined. Put him on a track and nothing could dampen his determination. He had been pursuing the leads the defector Golitsyn had provided from his recent KGB service in Helsinki, and had found indications that Moscow might have been more successful than Nosenko was telling us.

"What's up?" I asked with anticipation as he dropped by my office one day. He usually brought some sharp insight or funny story.

"It's time we did something about Mott," he said. "I've got some new stuff."

My face must have registered the fact that I hadn't the slightest notion of who or what Mott might be.

"M-o-t-t," he said, "for man-on-the-train." He scowled. "You know, on the way from Helsinki to Moscow."

I remembered. Golitsyn had told us, a few months before Nosenko walked in to us in Geneva, that a Moscow-based KGB officer had come to Helsinki, where Golitsyn was stationed, in late 1960 for the sole purpose of catching the train back the following night in order to chat up an incoming American Embassy communications man. I had been impressed that the KGB knew an American cipher clerk would be traveling alone from Helsinki to Moscow, and that they already knew him to be a gambler, a boozer, and involved in some problem with a woman. On the down side, I had found it depressing that any American agency could have selected such a person for a high-risk assignment to Moscow. From the ancient day that a monarch had first communicated on parchment, every intelligence service has given top priority to finding an opportunity to read the other fellow's mail. I admired this KGB action, however, a textbook example of operations tradecraft. There could hardly be a better venue than a night train ride for a deft case officer with a bottle of booze to make friends with a lonely fellow passenger. I was impressed, too, with the arrangement of reservations that put them in the same compartment.

Joe reminded me that Golitsyn, though he had not learned the code clerk's name, had taken care to note the exact date. Joe had signaled CIA in Helsinki, and they had managed to check the train's passenger manifest. Now the result had arrived. "Sure enough," Joe said with a satisfied smile, "there they were. The American pigeon 'Mott'—the only identifiable American on the manifest—and the KGB cat. Name of Kolosov."

"Kolosov," we knew, was a pseudonym used by the KGB man who had come to ride the train, Vadim Kosolapov. The similarity of the alias and true name was typical of KGB practice. On the chance that a passerby might recognize and hail a friend who was traveling under the false name, the phonetic similarity might make it pass unnoticed. A bit strained, and in this case counterproductive.

Joe continued. "Two things. First, State Department Security has no record that 'Mott' ever reported any contact with Sovs, on the train or elsewhere. Let's get this over to the FBI—they might want to find out why not. And second, you might ask the new defector if he knows anything about this." Joe knew that Nosenko claimed to have supervised all operations against American Embassy communications personnel and that he had named Kosolapov as one of the two case officers handling these priority targets.

"Thanks, Joe, I'll get to Nosenko on this. Before I do, please work up a list of Embassy communications people who reported approaches by the KGB."

Nosenko was in a cheerful mood, having spent what his guards called a boozy evening in some bars. The guards were less cheerful. One grumbled about his having been more of a handful than usual—loud talking, aggressive behavior, and some bottom-patting that narrowly missed causing a confrontation. Business as usual, he muttered.

We sat down for coffee in the sunny living room. I reminded Nosenko of what he had said in Geneva about his operations against American Embassy communications personnel. In the meantime, I said, we had checked American files for reports of KGB approaches to State or military cipher personnel. I handed him Joe's list, to which Joe had added a few extras, including notional names that might produce a reaction or stir a memory.

"Here, take a look and see if it reminds you of anything. Let's discuss each name."

Nosenko went over the list carefully. He read each name aloud, sometimes saying, "Never heard of him."

He pointed to the name of "K." "I pitched him myself." I nodded and Nosenko went on to remind me how he had approached K on a Moscow street with an unvarnished proposal that the astonished clerk sign on as a KGB agent. The young American brushed him aside and rushed back to the Embassy to report the incident.

"What made you think it worthwhile to try this cold approach?"

"Oh, I don't really remember. Just because he was a code clerk, I guess. You know, take a chance, you never can tell."

Nosenko's flippant remark and the approach to K made no more sense this time than it had when he first described it in Geneva. I suppressed a derisive comment and asked, "How did you choose the place to do it?"

"We had him under surveillance and knew his usual routes. I placed myself along where we figured he would be."

I did not tell Nosenko that his account did not match K's report to the Embassy security officer, or that K's description of the KGB sales rep bore no resemblance to Nosenko.

He chuckled pleasantly when his eye came upon the name I here call "Will." This was the code clerk whom the Moscow KGB officer Genady Gryaznov approached with the help of a Finnish agent, Preisfreund—an approach Gryaznov told Golitsyn had succeeded. "There's old Will."

Nosenko shook his head, remembering his own involvement. "That was a good try even if it didn't work."

As he moved down the list, I noticed with surprise that he passed over, without apparent recognition, the names of two code clerks who had reported KGB approaches—precisely in the period of Nosenko's claimed supervision.

When Nosenko had finished with the list I asked if any of the activity had required Gryaznov or Kosolapov to go abroad.

"No, of course not." Nosenko seemed surprised. "Their work was inside the USSR."

"Not even to follow up, or to hit people after they left Moscow?"

"Nope," he said confidently. "I would know—I had to sign off on any travel abroad."

"Okay," I said. "Just checking to make sure we haven't missed anything." With this I went on to other subjects, while mentally flagging a few queries for some future, sharper questioning.

Joe, ever the skeptic, was not impressed by my account. I asked, "You have a problem with this?"

"You know damned well I do. I saw the train manifest. Kosolapov was in Helsinki. And another time, Gryaznov went there, too, to borrow the Finn to work on the other code clerk, 'Will.'"

A thought struck him and he added, "Of course, these guys might have traveled at a time when Nosenko wasn't there to supervise them."

I shook my head. "No. Nosenko is categorical. He closely supervised both Gryaznov and Kosolapov from the beginning of 1960 to the end of 1961. If he happened to be away, he would have known in advance of the travel plan and would have been apprised of its result afterward."

Joe got up and paused as he reached the door. "Makes you wonder, doesn't it? I guess the next step is to get the FBI to interview my Mr. 'Mott.'"

I just nodded. This wasn't the moment to go into detail.

The shadows over Nosenko's code-clerk stories turned blacker a few days later. Murphy called me to his office.

"Jim Angleton has been talking to Golitsyn," he said, as I passed up the leather couch and took a seat beside his desk. "Now that Nosenko's defection is public, Jim passed Golitsyn the facts of Nosenko's personal history and KGB career—nothing more—and Golitsyn hit the roof."

"Just because of the personal history?"

"Especially the KGB career—Nosenko's claim to have been deputy chief of the SCD's [Second Chief Directorate's] American Embassy section in 1960–61. Golitsyn visited the section in Moscow during that time and talked with the chief. He *knows* Nosenko was not a member then."

"He's sure?"

"Absolutely," Dave said. "He had heard of Nosenko, says he met him once, but knew him only as a minor figure, certainly not as any kind of supervisor." Dave hunched toward me over his desk. "In fact, Golitsyn doubts that anyone below the section chief would have been supervising Gryaznov and Kosolapov. He isn't even sure the section *had* a deputy chief at that time."

"Damn it to hell," I said. "That explains it. You remember, we've been having trouble with that story, too. We couldn't see how Nosenko could possibly have held that job. Looks like Golitsyn was right about this."

Our debriefings of Nosenko were producing strange results. Nosenko did not know some things that he should have, if he had held the American Embassy section job. Even stranger, he had been describing things he himself was doing in 1960 and 1961 that made no sense whatever for someone supervising operations against the Embassy in Moscow—entrapping homosexual tourists, for example, and escorting delegations.

"Moscow isn't that much different from here," Dave said. "People in key jobs don't run around on dumb errands. Remind me."

"I've forgotten some of it, Dave. Wait a minute while I go get my notes on this." Five minutes later I was back, and started to run through the things we had noticed.

"When Tom was debriefing him the other day on his operations against tourists, Nosenko boasted that he had recruited an American tourist in Sofia by homosexual compromise, and even named the guy [call him "L"] and gave the date: May 1961. Tom was surprised and asked what the hell he was doing in Sofia when he was supposed to be working against the American Embassy in Moscow. Nosenko was taken aback. He came up with an explanation—he just happened to be in Sofia instructing Bulgarian State Security how to operate against the American Embassy in Sofia. Tom was sure he was improvising but just nodded and went on. I had told him not to pin Nosenko down on his contradictions."

If Nosenko was in Sofia on embassy-operations business, how could he get diverted there to the homosexual compromise of an American tourist? We knew that KGB pitches to foreigners need a plan and advance approval. In Sofia, moreover, the Bulgarians could handle that sort of thing without any help from Moscow.

Dave interjected, "Some homosexual provocateur would have had to set up L. Where the hell did he pop up from at just that moment? I can't swallow this story."

"I can't either, Dave. And that's just one. Here are some others."

I read out for Dave some (but not all) of the other activities in 1960 and 1961 that Nosenko had described, any one of which would be hardly imaginable for a person in his claimed position:

- In mid-1960 Nosenko was to be security watchdog for a group of Soviet automobile manufacturers visiting the American industry in Detroit. The only reason he did not go was that the trip was cancelled at the last minute.
- Later in 1960 he accompanied some Soviet metallurgists to Cuba, acting as their security watchdog.[1]
- Nosenko told us he had handled two homosexual provocateurs code-named 'Shmelev' and 'Grigory' from the time he recruited them in the 1950s until his defection. Dave stopped me here. "We're being asked to believe that a supervisor of KGB operations against its top-priority American Embassy target is handling the *tourist* department's street-level homosexual provocateurs?" I could only shrug, and went on with my list.
- He traveled to the port of Odessa with V. D. Chelnokov, chief (he said) of the *Tourist* Department, to meet Chelnokov's agent, an American travel organizer ("F") coming in on a cruise ship. The FBI had interviewed F, who confirmed Nosenko's presence—as a junior, almost menial, assistant to Chelnokov. *But this was late 1960.*
- Nosenko's mistake about the date of Abidian's visit to the Pushkin Street dead drop (see Chapter 14) revealed that he could not have held the job he claimed.
- Nosenko remembered clearly that he was in the Tourist Department when Anatoly Golitsyn defected in Finland. That was in mid-December 1961 (though Nosenko insisted it was mid-January 1962).
- The final item on my list was Nosenko's proud account of compromising and recruiting two homosexual American tourists—he had even jotted notes of the date and names. But the date was 2 January 1962 and he had left the American Embassy section on the last day

of 1961. In those forty-eight hours in the middle of the holiday season he could hardly have got into a new supervisory job, spotted and planned and got approval for provocative sexual compromise of two Americans, and then carried out both jobs. "He must have been in the Tourist Department for a lot longer than one working day," I pointed out, "if he did it at all."

We both saw that no member of the American Embassy section, least of all a supervisor, would or could do the things Nosenko claimed. He wasn't there—and Golitsyn was right.

Dave grasped at a straw. "You don't suppose he was just embellishing his own career to look better in our eyes, do you?"

"No. This Embassy-section job is at the very heart of his story." I didn't need to repeat what Dave knew all too well: that Nosenko had stressed his two personal responsibilities in that job, directly supervising work against the security officer and the code clerks. The two code clerks who did *not* report to the Embassy any KGB contact were precisely the two—"Will" and "Mott"—implicated in the events Golitsyn learned about in Helsinki.

"Moreover," I added, "That's the job that gave Nosenko authority to tell about the Pushkin Street dead drop and about 'Zepp'—and those things relate to when and how the KGB really uncovered Penkovsky."

We sat in silence for a moment.

"So many mistakes," Dave mused, shaking his head. "It looks to me like this job was tacked onto a career legend—maybe at the last minute. That could explain why he's fouling it up so badly, mixing up work against tourists with work against the Embassy and getting his dates all askew."

"I agree. Let's face it, we've got a problem. This job claim is what gives him the authority to cover up successful KGB recruitments of code clerks. If the KGB has gained the ability to read enciphered American military communications, they sure would want to hide the fact. Maybe that's what this is all about."

Murphy sighed tiredly. "Fine. But enough for today. There's a lot to think about."

CHAPTER 16

Connections

After Nosenko defected CIA began to hear from within the Soviet establishment about what an important piece of luck had fallen into its lap and what a severe blow had been dealt to the Soviet side.

Until now the Soviet regime had been quick to vilify and belittle the importance of those who defected from its ranks. Now, strangely, it set out not to mitigate but to emphasize its loss.

In France a Soviet journalist named Korolev, who could not have acted without KGB sponsorship, offered to the magazine *Paris Match* an article on "the greatest defeat the KGB had ever suffered—the defection of "Colonel Nosenko," with photos of his abandoned family. (For its own reasons, *Match* rejected the offer.)

Out from Moscow and Soviet representations abroad floated stories of a massive flap in the KGB—punishment of senior officers by expulsion from the Communist Party or demotion or reprimand—and firings in such numbers as to deplete the internal-security directorate. "Hundreds" of KGB officers abroad were said to have been recalled and disqualified for further service outside the country—although in reality this Moscow-based defector could identify only a handful of officers serving abroad and CIA stations abroad could not verify any such exodus.

Among the voices in this chorus was that of a KGB officer in New York who was secretly cooperating with the FBI. Aleksey Kulak had walked boldly into the FBI office there in March 1962 to volunteer his services.

Now he reported that inside the KGB residency it was said that Lieutenant Colonel Nosenko had fled to the West when he got wind of a KGB telegram that was recalling him from Geneva to Moscow. Among those fired as a result was Nosenko's boss and sponsor, Oleg Gribanov, the head of Soviet Counterintelligence. So widely informed was Nosenko that the KGB suspended all its New York operations. Not long afterward the New York staff was assembled to mull over ways to find and murder him.

Strange, we thought. Nosenko had never served in the foreign-operations directorate, had never set foot in the United States, had never held a job which let him know about KGB work in America, and he could identify only a handful of recruited American tourists and travel agents who had even lived in New York—none with access to classified information and none active for the KGB at the time.

Our wonderment grew when we compared this with Switzerland, where Nosenko had recently served twice on extended assignments, knew local KGB officers, and had often visited the KGB office. From there, however, the KGB recalled no one. Nor did it suspend its operations.

Quite the contrary, it revived and heated up the one operation Nosenko had known about. He had told of a Swiss woman who worked in a hospital who on a tourist trip to the USSR was blackmailed into cooperating with the KGB. As we learned later from Swiss authorities, to whom we had passed Nosenko's information, the lady never had access to any secret information—and the KGB had dropped the contact more than a year before Nosenko defected and exposed it. After Nosenko had defected from Switzerland the KGB, which customarily put compromised spies on ice, chose this extraordinary moment to revive this useless contact. And more vigorously than ever: hardly had the Swiss police begun tailing her after our tip than they saw her meeting not just once but twice in quick succession with Aleksey Sterlikov—one of the two KGB officers in Bern with whom Nosenko had had official contact. (After interviewing the lady, who told them the whole story, the Swiss police saw no reason to charge her with any crime.)

Kulak's report of a general assembly of KGB officers to discuss how best to assassinate Nosenko was a first in our experience. Such "liquid affairs" were normally kept tightly compartmented within the special KGB department responsible for them.[1]

Kulak's grotesque hyping of Nosenko's importance looked like an attempt to build up Nosenko's image in American eyes—and even more so when, a decade later, the FBI itself concluded that Kulak had been a KGB plant, deceiving them throughout their long association.[2]

Kulak's support of Nosenko typified an interlacing of Soviet sources that became especially visible after Nosenko's defection and suggested a centrally controlled campaign of KGB deception. Our Mr. Nosenko came to look like one figure in a populated landscape.

Signs appeared even before Nosenko's defection. In September 1963 a KGB agent, who had played a KGB cat-and-mouse game against CIA in postwar Berlin, defected in England. In the intervening years this Russian dramatist and film writer, Yuri Krotkov, had been luring Western diplomats and journalists into KGB traps in Moscow.[3] Now, as a defector, Krotkov said that he had worked under the direct supervision of KGB Counterintelligence chief Oleg Gribanov in 1958 in the sexual entrapment of the French ambassador Maurice Dejean in Moscow. Was it coincidence that four or five years after the event, this longtime KGB provocateur was exposing a case that Nosenko had so recently reported? Odd, too, was the way Nosenko had learned of the Dejean case. Contrary to known KGB practices, Gribanov had informally taken Nosenko along to a diplomatic reception where Gribanov was to make contact with Dejean after his compromise.

That coincidence might be shrugged off, but it would not be so easy to shrug off the even greater coincidences underlying the Cherepanov incident.

On 4 November 1963—after Nosenko had told CIA about the power of KGB surveillance in Moscow and how that surveillance had discovered CIA's contact with Pyotr Popov—another Moscow source chimed in to confirm the story.

A KGB retiree named Aleksandr Cherepanov handed a newspaper-wrapped bundle of papers to an American visitor to his office at the book concern, International Book (*Mezhdunarodnaya Kniga*), asking him to pass it to the American Embassy. Opened there, it disgorged a stack of reports and drafts from inside the KGB.

The top American diplomats' reaction was astonishment—and dismay. Fearing a KGB provocation, they decided that the papers were too hot to handle, so they ordered that they be turned over to the Soviet Foreign Ministry. CIA's Moscow representative Paul Garbler tried unsuccessfully to prevent it but managed to have the documents photographed before they were taken away.

When the photos arrived in Langley, we recognized the handwritten and typed KGB drafts as having originated, about four years earlier, in the American Embassy section of the KGB's Second Chief Directorate—where our new source Nosenko, still in place in Moscow, had worked.

The Embassy's pusillanimous and pointless act robbed American intelligence of a rare opportunity. These papers were outdated but their source had obviously been in the KGB and was willing to cooperate with us. Now, before we could even contact him, Cherepanov would have been identified and arrested.

Our examination of the documents, however, raised more questions than despair.

Until two years ago, when Golitsyn had told CIA of the organization and activities of the KGB's Second Chief Directorate—handling counter-intelligence inside the USSR—the West had gleaned only fragmentary information about it from its victims, refugees, and informants, but had never had a source from inside. Now in rapid succession we had Nosenko and Krotkov and Cherepanov. Krotkov had just reported on the same French operation as had Nosenko. Cherepanov and Nosenko had worked in the same section, reported on the same time period, told about KGB observation of the same American officials, and volunteered information about the same KGB surveillance techniques.

And these "Cherepanov papers," as we came to call them, told the same story of how the KGB caught Popov: a routine street surveillance in January 1959 had chanced to see George Winters posting a letter to Popov. In fact, Popov was the focus of Cherepanov's packet. No fewer than half its documents dealt with him, with his Moscow contact Russell Langelle, and with the letter mailer George Winters. They included 1) a summary of the KGB's arrest of Popov and his use as a double agent against Langelle, 2) a short handwritten note stating explicitly—in case the first document had not made the point clearly enough—that Popov had been caught by surveillance of Winters, and 3) a bundle of surveillance and operational reports on Winters, dating from the summer of 1959. These were the *only* raw surveillance reports among the Cherepanov papers and somehow—I thought strangely—they did *not* include the allegedly fatal January observation of his letter mailing. But they made the point: that Winters was routinely tailed.

Nosenko on his return to Geneva told of the incident (as already mentioned). "Everyone was amazed when they saw the papers the Americans had turned over. We had no trouble finding out who had sent them. It was a guy who had worked under me in the American Department, Cherepanov. As they were closing in on him he got wind of the suspicions and ran away before they could arrest him. We launched a nationwide search for him. I was sent out on the search myself."

"How come you got involved?"

"Someone near Gorky had reported seeing a person they thought might be Cherepanov. I could identify him because he had worked for me in the American Department, so Gribanov sent me there."

"Look," he said, taking a small sheet of paper from his pocket and laying it in front of us. "Here's the authorization for my trip." It was the original of an official KGB travel authorization for Lieutenant Colonel Nosenko's travel to Gorky Oblast, signed by Second Chief Directorate chief Oleg Gribanov and duly marked with certifications of his arrivals in Gorky and Shakhuniye on 16 and 17 December 1963.

"I saw the guy. It wasn't Cherepanov," he said. "But he got caught later as he tried to get across a border in the south. They brought him back to Moscow."[4]

How had Nosenko managed to keep that travel authorization and bring it to Geneva to show to us? KGB procedures require an official traveler to turn in this authorization upon return before receiving his next paycheck and before he could be authorized for further travel. When we cited these procedures Nosenko confirmed that our information was correct—but could not explain how he still had it.

We knew Cherepanov, like Krotkov, as an earlier provocateur. Under diplomatic cover in Yugoslavia five years earlier, this KGB officer had led a British intelligence officer to think he was contemplating defection and might cooperate secretly. His behavior finally persuaded the British that he was provoking them on behalf of the KGB and they backed off—whereupon Cherepanov abruptly disappeared from the scene.

Nosenko told, straight-faced, an impossible story perhaps designed to explain away Cherepanov's earlier—provocative—brush with Western intelligence (though we had not mentioned it to him). The KGB, he said, had detected an effort by Cherepanov to defect to the West from his KGB post in Belgrade. They recalled him to Moscow and, to punish his treasonous act and remove him from the temptations of the West, General

Gribanov moved him out of foreign operations—into the Counterintelligence directorate, to work in Moscow against the top-priority American Embassy target.

Nosenko's story was not only ludicrous but also demonstrably false. Those in Soviet enterprises, like International Book, who are allowed to deal with Westerners—as Cherepanov was—were not only fully trusted by the KGB but often KGB officers or reservists themselves.

Moreover, Nosenko could not have been supervising Cherepanov in the first place, because, as pointed out in the previous chapter, he had not held the American Embassy position that he claimed to have held.

Another source of ours chimed in. The KGB Illegal Yuri Loginov had walked in to CIA in 1961 and had since been met in Western locations as he prepared for Illegal missions. Now he offered both an eyewitness account of the KGB's search for Cherepanov and eyewitness evidence of the genuineness and importance of Nosenko's defection.

A friend of Loginov's father had a dacha next door to Cherepanov's and in November saw KGB cars roaring up and men encircling and searching the dacha. Cherepanov, he learned, had hoarded KGB documents through the years and passed a sample to the American Embassy through a tourist, hoping to sell them all—but the Embassy had returned the papers to the Soviet government.

It was an extraordinary coincidence that CIA should get even one eyewitness confirmation of such a secret event, but it defied coincidence that we now had *two*. It seemed even more unlikely when Loginov, on another occasion, attributed the dacha observation not to his father's friend, but to his own KGB radio trainer.

Loginov also told of the events of a day in February 1964 while he was undergoing radio training in Moscow for a mission abroad. His KGB trainers appeared disturbed, whispered among themselves, came and went excitedly, and finally suspended his training for several weeks. One of them confided that the whole KGB was in turmoil as the result of "a tremendously important defection" from its ranks. They did not mention any name (nor did Loginov to his CIA case officer afterward), but CIA could not fail to recognize that "tremendously important" defector as the only person who had defected at that moment—Nosenko.

This tale made no sense. The KGB need not interrupt the training of an Illegal—outside the headquarters building and walled off even from other parts of the foreign directorate—because someone defected from an entirely separate directorate. Like Kulak's bizarre exaggerations of Nosenko's importance, Loginov's story smelled of an effort to build up Nosenko in CIA eyes.

Indeed, suspicions had accumulated. For instance, Loginov blundered in Africa by telling his CIA case officer of a radio message he had received from Moscow—before it was actually transmitted. And the dénouement of Loginov's case left no doubt that the KGB had planted him on us.

He had originally come to the Americans saying he wanted to defect and live in the West, but CIA had ostensibly talked him into staying in place. Now he revealed his true colors. He was arrested by South African authorities and told his story, exposing KGB activities and personnel in Belgium and Africa, and won headlines in the Western press. Now, instead of defecting after this "treason" had become publicly known, he preferred to be spy-swapped back to Russia. Had the KGB not sent him out in the first place, his return would have been fatal—but as it happened, he went unpunished and in 2004 was still living and doing business in Moscow.

Other cases entwined with these—like the bizarre affair of "Z." This supervisory-level KGB officer walked in on CIA in the mid-1960s shortly after arriving for service in a Soviet installation in the West. He professed a desire to help us but we could not get any clear idea of why he was taking this dangerous step. Despite his claim to be overseeing some KGB activities in that country, he could not tell details about actual spies. He gave no information that measured up to his claimed status and access—in fact, nothing that the KGB could not easily have given away.

Z soon made it clear that the KGB *knew* he was taking up this apparently treasonous contact. Soon after establishing this relationship he traveled back to Moscow and on his return told us that he had been in touch with a faction inside the Soviet leadership that wanted to start an unofficial cooperation with American Intelligence against "the common enemy," China. The group had appointed him to act as their channel to ask for information on Chinese military technology. In return they would give details about China's military buildup and even about factional feuds in the Kremlin.

We played along briefly but could not supply the kind of information he and his sponsors were looking for. Recognizing that his (surely the KGB's) plan was getting nowhere, Z told us bitterly that we had "let him down." He walked out in a huff and went back to Moscow—apparently forgetting his assignment abroad—and was not seen again.

Z did provide one hot lead. He confided to CIA that KGB attempts to recruit Americans were failing everywhere. But he had heard in Moscow about one KGB officer who was being considered for a medal for his successes in this field. He had a helpful suggestion: because that officer was operating in America itself, why not have the FBI tail him and identify those important spies?

In a spirit of warm cooperation, Z named that one bright star in the dark picture of KGB failure. Mirabile dictu, it was none other than Aleksey Kulak, the FBI's spy inside the KGB in New York.

Z promoted Nosenko's image, too. Nosenko's defection had done vast damage, he said, and the KGB was looking for ways to find and assassinate him.

A figure now appeared on the landscape with an intriguing connection to our Popov case and Nosenko's account of it. Nosenko certified that the KGB had stumbled upon Popov's treason in late January 1959 by happening to see an American diplomat in Moscow mailing a letter. But for reasons already described, Popov must have actually been arrested upon his return to Moscow in December 1958 after being uncovered in 1957. In that mysteriously long interim period a GRU officer from Moscow escorted the Illegal Margarita Tairova to Popov in Berlin for onward dispatch to New York. Popov felt uneasy that he had not previously known or heard of this officer as a colleague in Illegal support operations.

Against this background one can understand my surprise that day in 1963 when James Angleton revealed the true name of a secret source of the FBI in New York dubbed, for liaison purposes, "Bourbon." For months Jim had been handing me bits and pieces of inside GRU information, not identifying his source (both of us tacitly respecting the principle of "need to know"), but one day it became clear that I did have that need, so he told me.

His name was Dmitry Polyakov.

"Impossible!" I exclaimed.

Jim was taken aback. "You know him?" I nodded emphatically. He checked a paper on his desk. "He arrived in 1959. After leave in Moscow he returned in late 1961 and volunteered to us. What's the problem?"

"Jim, Polyakov could not have been genuinely assigned here in 1959. This is the guy who escorted the Illegal Tairova to Popov in Berlin on her way to New York. You remember, you warned the Bureau to be especially careful, but she detected their tail and decamped for Moscow. Maybe that's what brought the house down on Popov—he was about the only person in the West who knew her false identity and travel details."

Jim shook his head ruefully. He remembered. I went on.

"Look at that date. 1959 was when the GRU was *pulling back* GRU officers exposed by Popov. You're telling me that just then the GRU chose to *send out* this guy—who had worked directly with Popov? In Illegal support? To, of all places, New York, where Tairova had been tailed? The FBI would have been all over any known Illegal-support officer there. Can you imagine any GRU supervisor signing off on such an insane assignment—taking responsibility if anything went wrong?"

Jim was silent, doodling busily.

I shook my head in wonder. "And then, of all the Soviet officials in the U.S., it happens to be *this* one who volunteers to become a spy for the Yanks. Sorry, Jim, I just can't believe it's straight."

Angleton didn't, either. For us the shadows over Polyakov never dissipated (and, after the Cold War, they were confirmed). But CIA continued to handle the case for another quarter-century, and profitably, for a strange and probably unprecedented reason (see below).

My suspicions at least won me a bet.

In 1964 I learned that a captured GRU Illegal had confessed to the FBI that Polyakov had trained him in Moscow—way back in 1958. Kaarlo Tuomi, papered as a Finn, had been discovered by chance, "turned," and subsequently controlled by the FBI since the spring of 1959.

Having in mind Polyakov's inexplicable assignment to New York, I suspected that he was a KGB plant and also, in view of Popov's doubts about him, that he had never been a genuine Illegal support officer.[5] But now I was being told that back in 1958 Polyakov had trained Tuomi, so I must be wrong.

I could not believe it. Tuomi must be lending credence to Polyakov's career legend, on the KGB's behalf. Having been caught as a foreign spy under false identity, Tuomi had been forced to cooperate with the FBI and was doing so only reluctantly. His story about Polyakov suggested to me that Tuomi had turned back against the FBI. I made a bet with our Illegals specialist Joe Westin that Tuomi had *not* identified Polyakov back in 1959 when he first confessed after the FBI caught him, nor even mentioned him before Polyakov walked in to American Intelligence at the end of 1961.

Joe went off to check with the FBI and returned, grinning, to tell me I had won my bet. His liaison partners had told him that in *September 1962*

Tuomi surprised his FBI handling officer by announcing, because of his warmhearted and hospitable FBI handling, that he had decided to come over fully to the FBI's side. Now, finally, he was ready to tell all—and one stone had lain particularly heavily on his heart. He had pretended not to recognize a Soviet official's photo shown him by his FBI handlers. Though he had truthfully identified other GRU Moscow trainers, he had pretended not to recognize one whom he had specially liked. Out came the mug books again and now, *for the first time,* Tuomi pointed to that man's picture. It was Polyakov.

Tuomi was, in fact, under KGB control at the time he had this "fit of honesty." Nearly twenty years later, on Canadian Television, he admitted that some three months after his 1959 arrest he had managed to communicate to his Soviet controllers that he had fallen under FBI control.[6] Evidently KGB Counterintelligence then took over the Soviet side of the operation.

In 1962 Tuomi was called to a direct meeting in New York's Central Park with a Soviet official—something normally avoided by Illegals in the West. In this case, however, the KGB would need a face-to-face meeting to show him Polyakov's photo and prepare his "confession" to the FBI and his new "re-doubled" role in a game of KGB Counterintelligence.

The FBI itself entertained doubts about Polyakov's good faith. In the mid-1970s they reviewed their New York relations with him and concluded that Polyakov might have been deceiving them. That they could not draw a definite conclusion was, by itself, evidence that Polyakov had never supplied the FBI with any information truly harmful to Soviet interests (beyond what Popov had already betrayed)—no active, valuable, previously unknown or unsuspected GRU spies.[7] Although Polyakov had exposed to the FBI some GRU Illegals who were operating or who had operated in the United States, these had all been previously known—and were *all the ones the FBI knew.* This was not only suspicious but also worrisome: if the KGB had fed this information through Polyakov, how had they known what the FBI knew? Was there a mole in the FBI?

After leaving New York in 1966 Polyakov safely continued spying for CIA for more than twenty years, mainly outside the USSR—and this despite being exposed to the Soviets as an American spy in 1979 by the FBI traitor Robert Hanssen and in 1985 by the CIA traitor Aldrich Ames. (This contrasted starkly to the rapid downfall of Oleg Penkovsky, who was detected within weeks after beginning his cooperating with the Americans in the same year, 1961.)

The KGB finally arrested Polyakov some time after his recall from abroad in 1986 and before January 1990, when they announced his arrest. The Soviets reported that he had been secretly tried and shot for treason. In a unique departure from precedent they published close-up films of his face while he was being arrested and of him being marched into prison. In the late 1990s Russian Intelligence was even preparing a TV series on his case. They had devoted no such attention to Popov or to other genuinely harmful defectors like Deriabin or Golitsyn.

It was a mystery. Why would the KGB arrest and execute its own planted provocateur?

Something obviously changed after Polyakov left New York and was transferred to handling by CIA. At first, CIA's handler felt certain that Polyakov was a KGB plant. As time passed, however, the quality of Polyakov's reports took a marked upturn and the handler's view changed. Twenty years later, after his arrest, CIA insiders called Polyakov the most valuable source of the Cold War—meaning, to the degree that they were making a serious comparison, that his production must eventually have surpassed that of either Penkovsky or Popov.

Apparently, some time after leaving the United States Polyakov (without telling the Americans that he had been sent out as a KGB plant) began to cooperate genuinely. When the traitor inside the FBI in New York, Robert Hanssen, exposed Polyakov in 1979, he could speak only about Polyakov's performance in New York—and the Soviets already knew that.

I was told by KGB insiders after the Cold War that the KGB later learned (perhaps from Ames, perhaps from another mole in CIA) that Polyakov was telling the Americans more than he was supposed to. So Polyakov was tried and sentenced to death—in secret proceedings that hid the fact that the KGB itself had sent Polyakov out to do the very thing he was being accused of.

Many aspects of this case remain to be clarified, but already it takes a unique place in Cold War history for its drama, mystery, and poignancy.

Never before had we seen so many interconnections between ostensibly separate penetrations of Soviet Intelligence. We could not fail to sense a common guiding hand behind them, and that this was the hand of Oleg Gribanov, head of the SCD. Gribanov was Nosenko's sponsor, was responsible for strange parts of Nosenko's story (and signer of his inexplicable travel document), was directly involved with Cherepanov and Krotkov and others of these interconnected sources, had headed the investigation of

Popov and Penkovsky, and had overseen the recruitments of American Embassy officials in Moscow that Golitsyn had partially exposed. Sources had told us, too, that Gribanov had been actively proposing some sort of bold counterintelligence gambit at about this time.

By now the questions Nosenko had raised had multiplied and coalesced into reasonable suspicion that the KGB had sent him to CIA. This forced us to look behind the case and ask ourselves why. It looked as if they were trying to prevent us from uncovering KGB moles who were betraying America's secret communications and intelligence.

PART FOUR

Confrontation

CHAPTER **17**

Crunch Time

The expression on Dave Murphy's face reflected that he knew I had come in to present him a problem—one he had hoped would simply go away.

I confirmed his apprehension. "We have to do something about Nosenko," I said. "The debriefing is winding down. There's not much water left in the well. Almost every day it looks more like we have a bad one on our hands. The time has come, Dave. We've got to decide what to do next."

Dave took no pleasure from this. He was aware of the mounting mass of anomalies in Nosenko's reporting and of the contradictions we were finding on the side. We had both hoped that with time we could find some innocent explanation, but none had materialized.

"Of course," I added, "we might just walk away from this." Only a few people were aware of our suspicions. We could resettle Nosenko somewhere, get him a job, try to keep an eye on him, and remain alert for any new data we might uncover. "Maybe that's our only course, but it would cost us our chance to clarify what's behind all this—and that will come back to haunt us."

"Yes," Dave said. "Certainly his story about Lee Harvey Oswald will."

Dave was right. As we requestioned Nosenko about President Kennedy's assassin, it was becoming ever more likely that his story was a message from the Kremlin to reassure the American government that the KGB had not commanded the deed. That message might well be true, but Nosenko was wildly exaggerating the KGB's indifference to Oswald. He was saying and repeating (with claimed but unlikely authority) that neither KGB nor GRU had paid the slightest attention to this, their first Marine defector who moreover had been a radar operator at a U-2 spy plane base in Japan and was eager to help the Soviets any way he could. This tale was so hard to believe that it might cause someone to jump to the conclusion that Nosenko was covering up a contrary truth—that the KGB did form some relationship with Oswald and that the Soviet Politburo really did order JFK's assassination.

We paused, thinking no doubt along the same lines.

"The Oswald story is one big question," I added, "but there are others—the code clerks." Nosenko had certified, with an authority that we now saw was spurious, that the KGB had failed to recruit any American code clerks. Golitsyn's information had given us reason to think the KGB may have nailed two of them—and Nosenko seemed to be diverting us from precisely those two. "If the Sovs are deciphering U.S. military communications, we'd better find out about it."

Dave nodded. "Yes, and about CIA security, too." He remembered how Nosenko's phony story of Kovshuk's trip to Washington had hidden the betrayer of Popov. He remembered, too, Nosenko's screwy account of Penkovsky's dead drop that could be hiding a KGB penetration agent inside CIA who betrayed Penkovsky.

We lapsed into silence. Dave sighed. "No other explanation? Maybe he was just boasting? Pretending he did things he didn't? Claiming personal involvement in operations he'd only heard about in corridor gossip? That he's a congenital liar, a con man?"

"Hell, Dave, we've been through this before. You know we've tested every one of these propositions over and over again. I've had Joe and Sally argue them as persuasively as they can. They all collapse."

"How about all the KGB spies he's uncovered? Would the KGB sacrifice them?"

"Try to name *one* who was previously unknown and had access to secrets at the time Nosenko uncovered him. There aren't any."

Dave knew that we had looked into each of Nosenko's ostensibly important leads and they had all come up dry. Nevertheless, I ran through them again.

- The most important suspect, "Andrey" the sergeant-mechanic of cipher machines, left service six months before Nosenko fingered him —and had never had access to cipher secrets even while active.
- The spy in the Orly courier center, Sergeant Robert Lee Johnson, had been very important indeed—when active. But by the time Nosenko told us about him, Johnson had lost his access to the courier center, and his mentally unhinged wife was broadcasting her knowledge that he was a Soviet spy. The case was stone-cold dead, and the KGB knew it before Nosenko handed it to us.
- Microphones in the American Embassy? Everyone from the ambassador to the janitor knew they existed—as they do in every embassy the Politburo might be interested in. Golitsyn had confirmed that well-known fact.
- Nosenko had heard that a U.S. army captain had been recruited but knew nothing that could single him out from the thousand or more fellow captains in Germany.
- The Belitsky double agent case had already been exposed by Golitsyn—and the KGB knew it.
- By the time Nosenko walked into CIA in Geneva and pinpointed the British naval source William Vassall, the KGB already knew Vassall to be compromised by Golitsyn's defection. They even played a game to build up Nosenko in Western eyes: *after* Golitsyn's defection, against all logic, they *restored* their contact with Vassall, which they had suspended while the British investigated an Admiralty lead from an earlier source.[1]

"Okay," Dave said, "So Nosenko didn't expose any active or valuable spies. But all the same, a lot of people around here believe the KGB would never send out one of their own staff officers as a defector."

"That may or may not be true," I answered, and reminded him that Nosenko was not deputy chief of the American Embassy Section in 1960–1961, where he ostensibly got all his more important information. "He can only tell us what he's been briefed to pass along. That's a far cry from 'sending out a KGB officer as a defector.' " When asked about the general run of stuff any KGB officer would have to know, Nosenko had proved unbelievably ignorant—or was pretending to be. He either could not or would not give sensible answers to our questions on internal KGB procedures. "When he can't dodge these questions," I added, "he says stupid, impossible things."

Moreover, it was no part of the original KGB plan to put Nosenko into our hands as a "defector" who would have to undergo detailed questioning. In 1962 he insisted that he would never defect and told why. He would meet us only when he happened to travel abroad. That way the KGB could limit the frequency and duration of face-to-face meetings and prevent our getting too deeply into any subject.

Obviously something unexpected had caused the KGB to change its plan and have Nosenko defect. It was not hard to guess what that was. The assassination of the American president by a recent resident of the USSR would have panicked the Politburo. If the U.S. government became persuaded that the Kremlin had ordered the assassination it might even cause war. This panic was confirmed after the Cold War. KGB General Oleg Kalugin recalled the Kremlin's reaction when they learned that the assassin Oswald had enjoyed their hospitality and had a Soviet wife. They turned to the KGB. In the Soviet Embassy in Washington, "We began receiving nearly frantic cables from KGB headquarters in Moscow, ordering us to do everything possible to dispel the notion that the Soviet Union was somehow behind the assassination. . . . The Kremlin leadership was clearly rattled by Oswald's Soviet connection, and in cable after cable the message we were to convey was clear: 'Inform the American public through every possible channel that we never trusted Oswald and were never in any way connected with him.' "[2]

The Soviet leaders were known to turn to the KGB when they wanted to slip an "inside" message to the American government. For years they had been establishing back channels during international conferences. One tactic was to have KGB diplomats "confide" in journalists as they did during the Cuban Missile Crisis. To put American minds to rest about Lee Harvey Oswald, the Kremlin's message—that they had nothing to do with the killing—needed to be more authoritative and convincing than diplomatic chitchat.

That would require defection, even if only temporary, of someone with convincing authority. The Warren Commission could not be satisfied with a written report from some (necessarily unnamed) CIA agent-in-place whom they could not question or from whom they could not ascertain how he had obtained the information.

Dave nodded. "I can see it. Just when they needed a channel like this they found it, ready-made: a KGB officer already established as a trusted CIA agent."

"Yes, but he would have to 'defect.' "

Dave chuckled at the thought. "Wouldn't the KGB guys who set this up hate to see their long-range operation go up in smoke just to pass Khrushchev's message to the Yanks. I can feel their pain. But they sure couldn't say no."

"Moreover," I added, "I don't think Nosenko intends to stay long as a defector." I reminded Dave of the lack of interest that Nosenko had shown toward the country he had ostensibly chosen as his new home. "After he's done his gig with the Warren Commission, he'll probably find some excuse to get mad at us and return to the USSR."[3]

"At least we'd be rid of him," Dave observed with a smile.

"And of any chance to get behind his stories," I said. "That's what it's all about. We should confront him and at least try to get a better idea of what's behind all this. Then maybe we can persuade the FBI to dig into the code clerk cases we think Nosenko's stories are covering up."

"Okay," Dave said, "go ahead—confront him."

Again he was joking but I still reminded him, "We've been tiptoeing all over the place just to keep Nosenko from getting wind of our suspicions," I said. "Once he does, he'll split—fly the coop. He steps out the door and sells his story to a newspaper, and there goes the ball game. Even with all we know, we're having a hell of a time evaluating his stuff. Can you imagine a journalist even trying?"

Dave groaned. "Okay, so how can we confront him? What's *ever* to stop him walking out the door?"

"The only possibility I see is to put him under guard while we put the tough questions to him. Depending on his answers we should learn enough to either clear him or decide beyond question that he is a plant."

"And in that case?"

There was the problem. We had no realistic options.

There was no way even to expel him. The U.S. government would not turn Nosenko back to the Soviets unless he himself asked for that, in writing. The Swiss would have no reason whatsoever to allow him back into their alpine republic—he wasn't their problem. The West Germans would not be interested. Neither would any other Western democracy. One by one, we reviewed and eliminated the possibilities. We would have to admit that CIA could not establish the bona fides of this defector whom we had brought from Europe—and resettle him as an immigrant in the United States. "Far from Washington, I would hope."

After a moment's reflection Dave remarked, "But that still leaves the problem of his legal status in the country. He's on parole to CIA and the law says we have to certify that he is who he said he is, that he had real access to the information he gave, and that we believe the reasons he gave for defecting. I couldn't certify a single one of those points."

"Nor that 'we have no information that any foreign intelligence service influenced his defection.' Hell, we're up to our ass in just such info."

Any discussion of resettling Nosenko outside the United States was probably pointless—because of Nosenko's claimed knowledge of Oswald. We could not send away the only source allegedly able to throw light, even if false light, on the Soviet role in the assassination.

"We will have to tell the Warren Commission how we evaluate Nosenko's information," I said. "That alone would be cause to detain and confront him—to assess whether his Oswald info is invention or a KGB message."

Dave summarized. "It boils down to this: either we hold and confront him, or we drop the whole thing and pretend to take Nosenko at face value." After a long pause, Dave said, "Okay, let's try. I'll take the question to Dick Helms to see whether there's even a possibility of the first alternative."

To put the question and, if the answer were yes, to get the necessary authority, Helms, Murphy, and the CIA's legal counsel went to Attorney General Nicholas Katzenbach on 2 April 1964. Although they did not ask for any specific length of time, they presumably delivered the impression we had given them, that by holding Nosenko for two or three weeks of interrogation we should be able to throw more light on the validity and probable background of his information.

The attorney general considered the terms of Nosenko's parole that made CIA responsible for ensuring that Nosenko's presence would not harm U.S. interests. In the light of our current opinion that his presence was in fact specifically designed *to* harm those interests, the Attorney General gave the go-ahead.

Now we prepared for the confrontation that, we hoped, would throw light on this extraordinary affair.

CHAPTER 18

Face-off

Every defector to American Intelligence is re-
quired—and every defector from the KGB expects—to submit to a polygraph test as part of the process of gaining acceptance by the American
government. This presented an occasion to confront Nosenko with his lies
and contradictions, with the aim of clarifying them or learning what they
were hiding.

CIA was in a bind. We had the attorney general's authority to hold
Nosenko for questioning, but it was implicit that this would be for a short
time—perhaps on the order of two or three weeks. But that would not allow
sufficient time for a systematic interrogation, especially of someone with
strong reason not to tell the truth. We saw as our only hope the possibility
of shocking Nosenko into a quick confession.

It was decided to run the polygraph test straight and then, whatever
the actual result, to accuse Nosenko of lying, to lay out his mountain of
contradictions and palpable untruths, and to demand his explanation.
This might lead him to admit the KGB had sent him to us.

Two days after Nosenko returned from his vacation in Hawaii, a car
pulled up in front of the Virginia split-level on the bright spring morning of
4 April 1964. Nosenko was perfectly amenable to the testing. Like any KGB
counterintelligence officer, he knew about the lie detector device and was
aware that CIA used it to test not only defectors and foreign agents but

even its own employees. Nosenko cheerfully stepped into the car and was driven off with one of his CIA interviewers.

The car entered the driveway of a secluded house surrounded by large woody grounds in a Maryland suburb of Washington. In one room a long table and chairs had been set up, with the polygraph apparatus standing at one side of the table. A bedroom in the attic stood ready to house Nosenko between questioning sessions.

The polygraph apparatus, as is well known, tests physiological reactions to questions: breathing, sweating of palms, and blood pressure and heartbeat. The subject faces away from the operator, who asks the questions and observes the reactions as recorded by a needle on a revolving roll of graph paper. A qualified CIA operator, previously unacquainted with Nosenko's case, was assigned the job. After we explained our points of doubt, he devised the questions that would best test them by permitting a simple "yes" or "no" answer. Contrary to some movies and TV shows, the machine does not measure the truth of discussion-type answers.

To the three pieces of test equipment normally strapped onto the subject we added a fourth that, we told Nosenko, would measure his "brain waves." If, like so many false refugees the KGB sent to the West, he had been trained to beat the machine, this additional equipment might increase his apprehension and reveal his true reactions.

The polygraph examiner concluded that Nosenko was in fact lying. He reacted suspiciously when asked whether he intended to deceive the Americans, whether the KGB had sent him, and whether he was still under Soviet control.[1] A particularly strong "lie" reaction came when he was asked, "Did you tell us the truth about Lee Harvey Oswald?"[2] What mattered to us was not the validity of the measurements, the interpretation of which was always subject to question, but how Nosenko, rocked by our accusations, would then explain the contradictions and anomalies.

Nosenko was left alone while the test results were examined and discussed in another room. After a long break, I entered with an officer of the section and expressed my shock and disappointment to find that he had lied.

"I never lied!"

"You have lied—and this time, you've put us on the spot. This test was an official requirement. Now your whole position in this country is in doubt. We'll have to go over these problems one by one. We'll stay here until we straighten them out."

"Okay. I'll prove that I've been telling only the truth."

He was led off by guards to the prepared bedroom, a bare cell-like attic room, where they had him change into an army fatigue uniform to underline the seriousness of his situation. They led him back to a chair in front of the long table where I sat with Serge, a Russian-speaking member of the section.

We launched into some of the sticking points in his story.

To our consternation he couldn't explain *any* of the contradictions. He would either mechanically repeat earlier versions or, when we gave him the facts that showed them to be false or impossible, he would improvise new versions so unlikely—sometimes so absurd—that we could hardly imagine them to occur to an experienced KGB officer.

"Tell me why Kovshuk went to the U.S."[3]

"I've told you. To restore contact with Andrey."

"How long did he stay?"

"I don't remember, maybe a week. What difference does it make?"

"It makes this difference. He stayed ten months. And he didn't contact Andrey for more than nine months. What was he doing all that time?"

Nosenko looked stunned. He evidently had no idea that Kovshuk had been gone for so long. He fell silent, then brightened. "Now I remember. He couldn't find Andrey and had to search for him."

This thoughtless improvisation hardly merited comment. The interviewer asked Nosenko the unanswerable question why, if the KGB had not known where Andrey was, did they send a key Moscow supervisor to Washington to hunt for him, and under a diplomatic cover holding him within a twenty-five-mile radius? And what took so long, since (as was true) Andrey's name and address were listed in the Washington area phone book of the time?

Nosenko hunkered down and refused to say more.

Nosenko insisted that no one from the KGB had even talked to Lee Harvey Oswald in Russia, much less used him as an agent. Nothing in this interrogation got him to budge an inch from his wholly unbelievable story about President Kennedy's assassin. The KGB must have implanted a holy fear when instructing him to tell (and stick to) this tale. It was probably their need to deliver this message that caused the Soviets to have Nosenko physically defect to the West, changing the whole basis of an operation that originally had entirely different aims. Nosenko stuck to his tale, then and forever, to the uniform incredulity of his hearers.

"Tell us about KGB relations with the president of Finland."

"I know nothing about that. Why should I?"

"Remember," I told him, "you asked me whether Golitsyn had told us about him. What were you referring to? What might Golitsyn have told us?"

"I never heard anything, ever, about this. I could never have asked any such question."

"You recently told about tailing Embassy security officer John Abidian and observing him setting up a dead drop on Pushkin Street."

"Yes, we staked out the place but no one came. I was getting the reports week after week."

"When was that?"

"I remember exactly. At the end of 1960."

"And you left the American Embassy section at the very end of 1961?"

"Yes, I've told you that."

"But in 1962 you were telling us about your systematic coverage of Abidian. Why didn't you tell us then about seeing him set up a dead drop?"

Nosenko looked blank, speechless.

We resumed. "Are you absolutely sure of the date?"

"Absolutely."

"But you're wrong, and so is your story. Abidian went to that drop at the end of 1961, not 1960. How could you be getting the stakeout reports if you were no longer in the American Embassy Section?"

"That's not true. I know it was 1960."

"No. We know. It was our dead drop."

Nosenko was flabbergasted. He fell into a sullen silence.

"Your job was to watch over John Abidian. Would you know of any trips he took outside Moscow?"

"Of course. We had him under full-time surveillance. Any travel by Embassy staff was reported in advance to us. In the case of Abidian, and of the code clerks, I would be told and we would prepare coverage where they were going."

"Did Abidian make any trips outside Moscow?"

"None."

"Think hard."

"Of course I would have to know."

"He made a very big trip. Where did he go?"

"He did not travel."

"Not only did he travel, but he traveled to the land of his Armenian ancestors, to Armenia itself."

"Impossible. That would be big news to us. It would offer opportunities."

Silence. Nosenko, morose, remained sunken in thought. We waited. Suddenly we heard him muttering, as if talking to himself. "If I admit I wasn't watching Abidian, then I'd have to admit that I'm not George, that I wasn't born in Nikolayev, and that I'm not married."

That strange sentence—recorded on tape—might have been nothing more than rhetoric, but to all evidence Nosenko was *not* serving in the American Embassy Section and of course was not watching Abidian. Such were the contradictions in his life story and his seeming forgetfulness of wife and children that we doubted he was telling the truth about them. His odd reaction suggested that now, for some reason, we had struck a chord that might impel him to confess.

The silence continued. Finally, perceptibly, he shook himself out of his near-trance and refused to answer any more questions. He tucked himself into a sort of crouch on his chair, his face closed and grim.

Asked repeatedly how he had learned about each of the more important cases he told us about—Penkovsky's uncovering, the Belitsky double agent case, the Orly courier center, and British Admiralty cases, even Andrey—Nosenko changed his stories again and again. Each new version raised new questions, for which Nosenko would devise yet other explanations.

The impossible circumstances of Nosenko's rapid promotions in the KGB hierarchy—neither having accomplished any verifiable professional successes nor for the last two promotions having even been in Moscow most of the time—led us to probe his claims.

Here Nosenko cracked, and admitted that he had lied. He was not now a lieutenant colonel, nor had he been a major as he had claimed when meeting us in Geneva in 1962. He was and had remained a captain—though he insisted on his rapid advance in the hierarchy to first-deputy department chief.

Asked to explain, then, how his travel authorization for the Cherepanov search in October 1963 had been made out to "Lieutenant Colonel No-senko," he said it had been a clerk's error. Then why had General Gribanov signed off on this error? No explanation. (And later, questioned again on the discrepancy, he attributed the error to a careless duty officer, not to a careless clerk.)

"You defected because a telegram was recalling you to Moscow just after you had arrived in Geneva?"

"Yes. I was afraid they had found out about our contact."

"We have analyzed all the radio traffic during that period. The So-viet representation in Geneva received no telegram from Moscow in those two days."

After his initial insistence before becoming convinced of our facts, Nosenko admitted he had lied. "I was afraid, and wanted to get out as fast as possible. I invented the telegram because you would have insisted that I stay in place."[4]

"You told us in 1962 that you participated with Kovshuk in the recruitment approach to Edward Smith, the Embassy security officer. But this hap-pened in 1956. How come you were there? You have said and written that you transferred to the Tourist Department in 1955."

Nosenko looked at the interrogator blankly. "Who? I never heard that name. I could not have told you that."

Our interrogator sighed in frustration, and called for a tape recorder and played back for Nosenko a clear recording of his statements in the Geneva safe house.

Nosenko thought for minutes, then said in a low voice, "Mr. Bagley was making me drunk then."[5] Again he sank into morose silence, his lips tight, unwilling to say a word.

The interrogator, aware that drink does not grant second sight, and having just heard Nosenko's voice on the tape giving firsthand details, recognized this excuse as ludicrous. But he had no choice but to move on with his questioning.

It was at points like this that time pressure squeezed us. Doing a proper interrogation disposing of the time needed, we would never have let him off any one of the hooks on which he impaled himself. Day after day, if necessary, we would hammer at the single point. But here, faced with his refusal to talk and with no means of pressure at our disposal, we had no choice but to move on to learn, in the short time given to us, how he would deal with the remaining oddities.

At times the interrogation descended into a shouting match, as no interrogation should, when we called his ludicrous stories what they were: nonsense, crap, bullshit. Our aim was to shake his composure and force some sort of admission. But even when he'd been shown—and admitted— that his stories were impossible to believe, he never confessed.

The interrogation didn't break Nosenko's resistance—*but it broke his story*. It demonstrated that no other explanation of his lies—vain boasting, invention, passing off actions of others as his own, self-glorification, or sociopathic disregard for truth—could explain how he knew what he had told us.

No private reason or self-seeking boast had led Nosenko to add the two years' service in the American Embassy Section 1960–1961. All his proud accomplishments and promotions occurred not there but in a different department, working against tourists. But his claim to have supervised work against the American Embassy enabled Nosenko to divert Golitsyn's leads to KGB recruitment of American military code clerks and to mislead us about Kovshuk's recruitment of CIA officer Ed Smith and about how the KGB caught our spies Popov and Penkovsky. Thanks to that alleged service he could gain our confidence by confirming information about the American Embassy that had already leaked out through Golitsyn—about the microphones, for example, and about the British Admiralty case (identified as William Vassall).

It was our responsibility to get the truth behind these stories, loaded as they were with implications—of penetration of U.S. cipher communications and of the CIA staff and even of Soviet involvement in the assassination of President Kennedy. Nosenko's implausible reporting on Oswald looked like a message from the Soviet leadership—that they had had no hand in Oswald's act—and though we might think this message true, we did not know.

What were we to do now?

Our only choice was to either give up and leave these politically charged and ominous questions hanging, or try to get at the answers in a more systematic interrogation. But for that we would have to hold Nosenko longer—a drastic change in plans.

Faced with the consequences and the possibilities, our superiors granted us more time.

Nosenko himself recognized how badly he was doing and made no request to be released. So often was he caught in inexplicable contradictions that he admitted he was "looking bad." In our position, he said, *he* wouldn't believe what he was saying, either.

We set out again. Over the ensuing months in that Maryland house we questioned him in detail, then periodically confronted him with the new discrepancies that kept arising.

Nosenko participated willingly despite the Spartan conditions of his detention, evidently considering it a necessary process to get at the truth. After some months he wrote a letter confessing that he had been unable to tell the truth up to that point. He added that we had been right to (as he put it) separate him from women and liquor and force him to buckle down to real work. He saw his situation as the result of his own lies. But on no occasion did he explain why he was lying. Nor could we get him to specify which lies he was referring to or what truth might lie behind them.

Try as we might, we could not piece together any coherent or consistent story of the personal life or career upon which all his reporting depended.

On two separate occasions when tangled in his own contradictions, Nosenko said he "could not" confess. A psychologist, John Gittinger, who had observed the questioning over closed-circuit television, thought it possible that Nosenko had been psychologically conditioned à la *Manchurian Candidate.*

At one point, desperately trying to persuade his skeptical questioner that he had really held certain KGB positions, Nosenko blurted out, *"You have a source in New York—ask him!"* How could he have learned of Aleksey Kulak, the FBI source in the KGB in New York? Barring the near-impossibility that FBI debriefers had indiscreetly revealed to this new defector the existence and location of a treasured in-place source, the KGB must have told Nosenko, perhaps to assure him of support in the United States. (The support proved counterproductive for the KGB. Kulak confirmed elements of Nosenko's legend—that he was a lieutenant colonel and had defected when recalled by telegram from Geneva to Moscow—that Nosenko later said were his own inventions.)

After our people had been driving for months into and out of the grounds of that house in Maryland, CIA security specialists recommended a move to prevent neighbors from becoming curious. They arranged to improve security and cut expenses of rent and guards by building a little house of their design in an Agency training site near Williamsburg, Virginia. Nosenko was moved there and questioning continued. (Nosenko's supporters in CIA later attacked it as a "torture vault" or "dungeon," whereas the Office of Security designed it simply to permit a minimum guard force to prevent escape.)

We had been bewildered by Nosenko's ignorance of things any KGB officer would know about his own workplace. To throw light on this question I decided to have a KGB veteran talk to him directly.

Peter Deriabin had served in KGB Headquarters at the time Nosenko claimed to have entered the KGB, and he knew the organization's procedures and regulations in detail. Since his defection ten years earlier Deriabin had proven fiercely loyal to his new country, had kept up to date on KGB procedures and personnel through later sources, and had given priceless counsel to our Soviet operations. After Nosenko's defection Deriabin was told of it and was asked to review the recordings of Nosenko's Geneva meetings of 1962 and early 1964. He corrected the Russian-language portions of transcripts that Kisevalter had made. He had also listened to tapes of all debriefings since Nosenko's defection. Deriabin had submitted scores of pages of comments on details and suggested questions to be put to Nosenko.

Now I asked him to conduct his own interviews face to face, using his own questions. This amounted to staging a dialogue between colleagues about the daily life in their common KGB workplace. They would inevitably know some of the same things and could talk without interruption by outsiders, who might misunderstand the jargon or ask for clarification.

Deriabin questioned Nosenko in twelve sessions, each of two hours or more, and emerged convinced beyond doubt that Nosenko was a KGB plant. So too, he added, would be any real KGB veteran who should come to know the details. (He was proven right about that when, long after the Cold War, I showed some questions and answers to a senior KGB veteran. He laughed, called Nosenko's ignorance "impossible," and asked me an unanswerable question: "How could your service *ever* have believed Nosenko's story?")

Deriabin concluded—and so reported to CIA—that Nosenko did not enter the KGB when or how he said and did not hold the KGB positions he claimed (and did not handle Lee Harvey Oswald's file). The way Nosenko explained his presence in Geneva could not be true, and his descriptions of his education and military service were impossible in the real Soviet world. (Deriabin's later summary of this report is in Appendix A.)[6]

As a result of our interrogation and side investigations, CIA now had enough facts and insight—without waiting for proof that might never become available—to justify a *working hypothesis* that the KGB had dispatched Nosenko to us.

By adopting that hypothesis as a basis for investigation, CIA would gain an asset comparable to a penetration of the KGB's staff. Assuming Nosenko to be a plant we could look behind each facet of the story he had been told to tell to CIA and perhaps root out the truths it was shaped to hide. This promised to disclose KGB recruitment of CIA officers like the target of Kovshuk's Washington trip (almost certainly Edward Ellis Smith) and the betrayer of Penkovsky, as well as communications men like "Mott" and "Will."

If these investigations produced no result, they would discredit the assumption but cause no harm. If on the other hand the investigations unearthed Soviet assets (moles, cipher breaks), the hypothesis would prove to be as valuable as a defector from the KGB—the rare insider who could throw light on the very operations the KGB guarded most carefully, that they considered worthy of protecting by a "bodyguard of lies."

But other elements of the U.S. government would have to accept that assumption, and be willing to act on it. Outside the Soviet Bloc Division, the will was lacking. The FBI saw no reason to doubt Nosenko's bona fides. Indeed, their source Kulak in the KGB was vouching for Nosenko's genuineness, and they did not—yet—recognize Kulak as a KGB plant. Thus they saw no reason to doubt Nosenko's versions of such matters as Mott and Will.

Within CIA's leadership, too, the tendency was in the other direction—to search for other explanations that might permit them to shake off this "incubus" and accept Nosenko as genuine.

By 1966, our records on Nosenko's interrogations and related matters had grown so huge that anyone arriving new on the case would have a hard time absorbing its details. So the counterintelligence section (notably Joe and Sally, and one other officer) collated this mass of material, summarizing what Nosenko had said on each subject and what we had found in our parallel investigations, and describing the related cases and incidents. It grew to more than eight hundred single-spaced, long-form, mimeographed pages, with two parts still being written. It was not intended as a report, and when I last saw it in its incomplete state, it expressed no general conclusions. My only conclusion—and even that not explicit in the file summary—had been that a tightly compartmented section within the KGB had sent Nosenko to us as a provocateur. We had *not*, with certitude, got at the truth that lay hidden behind his lies.

In the summer of 1966 the head of the Clandestine Services, Desmond Fitzgerald, aware that I had already been four years in Headquarters and would eventually, in the normal course of events, be expecting to return to a field assignment, told me that I was in line to become chief of station abroad and asked which one I would like. I named Brussels as best suited to my qualifications. Des said it was a pity that the post had just been occupied, but I assured him, wholeheartedly, that I was in no hurry. In December, however, came a surprise: the new chief at that station had become ill and could no longer continue, and the job fell to me. I accepted and began to phase out of Soviet operations. Our departure was delayed for several months because of my son's illness, but we arrived in Brussels in the second half of 1967.

I regretted leaving the Nosenko case still undecided. With Dave Murphy slated for transfer to Paris the following spring, I was aware that those best knowing the intricacies and implications of the case, and best able to sway events, would no longer be in a position to influence future decisions. But already it was clear that Nosenko was not going to confess, that the FBI (believing him to be a genuine defector) would not dig behind his lies for the spies he was hiding, and that Nosenko himself would have to be released in a cloud of equivocation. Essentially, the game was over and we had lost, but I comforted myself with the thought that the KGB and Nosenko had not really won. With people like Joe and Sally keeping the picture clear, things would turn out without further loss.

How wrong I was!

The autumn of 1966 was Nosenko's low point, but the tide was about to turn in his favor. By then our chiefs' patience had worn thin and their confidence in our assessment of Nosenko had been eroded by a new source, then unknown to me, who was somehow persuading them that Nosenko was a genuine defector. Nosenko could not be held indefinitely, and, after I left, CIA's top people finally took the only practical course: to ostensibly clear him and let him go.

Had I been there, I would have recommended that Nosenko be resettled far enough from Washington that he would find it more difficult to harm U.S. interests. But I was not there, and things turned in a quite different direction.

Our doubts were not just put in a closet, they were swept clean away. Unbelievably, the CIA leadership certified formally, in writing, its wholehearted belief in Nosenko. They brought him into collaboration with CIA. Later the director sent a personal envoy to Congress to publicly vilify those who had distrusted Nosenko.

Nosenko's release became his exoneration.

PART FIVE

Too Hot to Handle

CHAPTER 19

Head in the Sand

In June 1966 the earth began to move under the Nosenko case. The resultant tsunami swept away all the doubts and cleared Nosenko's path to acceptance and success in America—for the KGB.

The first tremor came one Sunday morning with the ring of a telephone at Richard Helms's house. The caller, in accented English, identified himself as a KGB officer on an operational mission in Washington and anxious to take up contact with CIA. Helms agreed that CIA would meet the caller at his designated place and time.

Helms was then in the process of taking over as director of Central Intelligence. He called for an urgent meeting with Clandestine Services chief Desmond Fitzgerald and Counterintelligence Staff chief James Angleton. They assembled that afternoon.

Their first decision was easy—to inform the FBI, responsible for operations inside the United States—but not the second. The caller had asked for CIA and was based in Moscow, so the Agency should participate. Who then? Wary of recent indications that the KGB might have a mole inside our Soviet Bloc Division (SB), they decided to assign CIA's handling of the case to others. It did not matter, apparently, that only in the SB lay the experience and knowledge needed to assess and draw the maximum from a source at this level. Operational security would take precedence.[1]

Instead, they called on a security officer—Bruce Solie, who had been following up clues to hostile penetration of the Agency staff. This was a strange, and in the event fateful, choice. Solie had only a shallow knowledge of the Soviet scene, knew little about the KGB, and possessed no experience in handling foreign agents. Perhaps they comforted themselves with the thought that Solie would be guided by Angleton's Counterintelligence Staff and accompanied by the FBI's man.

The FBI assigned an experienced operative, Elbert ("Bert") Turner, and together he and Solie made the scheduled meeting. No details of the operation that ensued, code-named "Kitty Hawk," have been officially revealed to this day. Its outlines eventually became public knowledge, and I learned more from KGB veterans after the Cold War.

The KGB visitor identified himself as Igor Kochnov of the foreign counterintelligence component of the KGB's First Chief Directorate (foreign intelligence). He could expect eventual promotion to head that department's work against Americans, he said, if he were to succeed in at least one of his missions in Washington. The first of these was to recruit for the KGB a Soviet navy defector named Nikolay Artamonov, who was living in Washington under the name of Nicholas Shadrin.[2] In return for CIA's help in achieving his goal, Kochnov was willing to act as its agent inside the KGB staff.

Almost as exciting to the Americans was Kochnov's other mission in Washington: he had been sent to locate the KGB defectors Golitsyn and Nosenko, presumably so they could eventually be lured back or assassinated. Wonderful news for CIA! Since the KGB evidently regarded Nosenko as it did Golitsyn, there's an end to the doubts about Nosenko's bona fides!

So juicy were Kochnov's future prospects that the Americans decided to play along and get Artamonov to pretend to cooperate with the KGB. Artamonov loyally accepted the role of double agent despite the danger and despite the unpleasant condition that he take a lower-level job with U.S. Naval Intelligence, to remove him (and the KGB) from access to the sensitive information he had been working with.

Thus began a double agent operation with Artamonov that was to last nearly nine years and bring little profit to the Americans—and death to Artamonov.[3]

From the outset, members of the Counterintelligence Staff looked with a skeptical eye on Kochnov. Why would the KGB send a traveler from Moscow to do jobs for which the KGB's Washington rezidentura was better qualified and equipped? They sensed that the KGB had sent Kochnov to CIA in order to hide a KGB penetration of American Intelligence, to convince CIA of Nosenko's genuineness, and perhaps to find out why Nosenko had dropped off the KGB radar screen.

But this skeptical view was not held by all. The participants came to this case with varying views and objectives. The Counterintelligence Staff treated it as a KGB provocation and sought to use it to test whether and where the KGB may have penetrated the ranks of CIA's Soviet operations. To this end they designed questions to be put to Kochnov to provoke revealing answers or actions. On the other hand the FBI case officer Turner and CIA's Solie firmly believed that Kochnov was genuine. Believing in Kochnov's message, Solie became unshakably convinced that Nosenko was a genuine defector—and did not even pose the questions the Counterintelligence Staff had concocted.

CIA was soon left with little reason to believe in Kochnov. His golden promise of promotion to the top of KGB American operations proved to be a will-o'-the-wisp. After recruiting Artamonov he turned over the contact to a Washington KGB man and went back to Moscow—and was never met again. (According to one report, he was spotted once or twice in Moscow.) But CIA and FBI continued the double agent case hoping that it might eventually offer a way to restore contact with Kochnov and hoping that the KGB would, as the Washington KGB handler had told Artamonov, turn Artamonov over to handling by a KGB Illegal.

The KGB later claimed it never discovered Kochnov's "treason" until his case was exposed in American publications in 1978, around which time he coincidentally died of a heart attack. However, after the Cold War KGB veterans gave me reason to believe that the KGB had indeed dispatched Kochnov to contact CIA and that the game was connected with penetration of Western intelligence services. It is a deep and complex story waiting to be told.

The Counterintelligence Staff, concerned for Artamonov's safety, recommended in writing that he never be allowed to meet the KGB outside the United States. But the KGB's lures proved too strong for Solie and Turner. They permitted Artamonov to meet the KGB in Canada, and then even in Vienna, infamous as the site of kidnappings and close to Soviet-controlled territory. Again in Vienna in December 1975, Artamonov went off to a scheduled meeting with the KGB and never returned. KGB foreign counterintelligence chief Oleg Kalugin later reported that he saw

Artamonov die as he was carried into Czechoslovakia, accidentally over-dosed with sedatives during the kidnapping.[4]

A signal success of the KGB's operation with Kochnov—in addition to elim-inating the defector Artamonov—was the restoration of Yuri Nosenko's fortunes in the West. Although I knew none of this at the time, I sensed in the second half of 1966 the CIA leadership's growing skepticism, not just impatience, concerning our case against Nosenko. It was evident that some unknown factor was influencing them. This became clearer at the end of that year when they ordered a fresh review of the case—not so much to get new insights as to find ways to rationalize the doubts and to whitewash Nosenko to prepare his release.

Deputy Director Rufus Taylor called in Gordon Stewart, a CIA veteran and old friend of Helms, to take a fresh, detached look at this forbid-ding can of worms. Stewart enjoyed a reputation for integrity and had the added quality of knowing nothing of the Nosenko case and little about KGB deception.

To simplify Stewart's review I organized the essential file materials (including my "1000-page" file summary) with an explanatory table of con-tents, and turned them over to Stewart in early 1967. This was my parting shot, for I was already preparing my assignment abroad.

After my departure the SB—without telling me—condensed this huge file summary into some 440 pages, lumping together many separate points of doubt into broad categories, each category to support a "conclusion." In effect, they transformed justifiable points of doubt into debatable (and unnecessary) conclusions, making a case against Nosenko. He did not have the naval service he claimed, it said, adding that he did not join the KGB when or how he said, did not serve in the KGB's American Embassy Section, and had not been deputy chief of its Tourist Department.

Stewart thus found himself faced with a mass of material loaded with indications of Nosenko's bad faith and lacking any innocent explanation. To his professorial eye, these papers looked "unscholarly" (as he said to associates) and "more like a prosecutor's brief." Indeed, a file summary is not an academic dissertation, and the SB report's conclusions were un-proven. So he called for a critique of the SB report. In mid-1967 Helms selected for this task the same Bruce Solie who had learned from Kochnov, the KGB volunteer, that Nosenko was a genuine defector.

Solie submitted eighteen pages of critique of the 440-page SB report and of the previous handling of Nosenko. He recommended a new and "untainted" questioning in a friendlier, less confrontational, and "more objective" atmosphere. So Helms and Taylor picked him to do the job himself.[5]

Solie was a taciturn, cigar-smoking man whose lean features gave him an air of the American farmlands. He had sat in on some of our interrogations of Nosenko prior to Kochnov's advent, not contributing but maintaining a generally approving if reserved demeanor. Now, with Nosenko's earlier interrogators removed from the scene and being himself convinced by Kochnov of Nosenko's genuineness, Solie set out to prove that we had been wrong.

Behind Solie's effort lay the hopes of CIA leaders that he would find ways to believe in Nosenko and rid the Agency of what Director Richard Helms later called this "incubus," this "bone in the throat."

They had picked the right man: Solie delivered the goods. Starting in late 1967, sometimes accompanied by FBI Special Agent Turner, Solie talked in a friendly manner for nine months with Nosenko and together they worked out ways things might—somehow—be made to look plausible. One who read the transcripts of these interviews described to me the way they were conducted:

Solie: "Wouldn't you put it this way, Yuri?"

Nosenko: "Yup, yup."

On another sticking point, Solie: "But you really meant to say it differently, didn't you?"

Nosenko: "Sure."

Solie: "Wouldn't it be more correct to say, for example, that . . . ?"

Nosenko: "Yup, yup."

Solie submitted his report on 1 October 1968. That whitewash had been the purpose from the outset was revealed by the speed with which the CIA leadership adopted its conclusions. They could not have studied it and had perhaps not even read it before, *three days later,* Deputy Director Taylor informed Director Helms that

> I am now convinced that there is no reason to conclude that Nosenko is other than what he has claimed to be, that he has not knowingly and willfully withheld information from us, that there is no conflict between what we have learned from him and what we have learned from other defectors or informants that would cast any doubts on his bona fides. Most particularly I perceive no significant conflict

between the information Nosenko has provided and the information and opinions Golitsyn has provided. Thus, I conclude that Nosenko should be accepted as a bona fide defector.[6]

So well had Solie done the job that CIA gave him a medal for his travails. One can only concur in their assessment of him as a "true hero."[7] The task he performed was truly Herculean and required tricks as cunning as those of Hercules himself. Solie seems to have hidden from Taylor facts that flatly contradicted the deputy director's conclusions. In reality there were significant "conflicts" between what Nosenko reported and "the information and opinions Golitsyn . . . provided." And an "other defector," Peter Deriabin, had cast an indelible stain of doubt on Nosenko's bona fides. Deriabin was outraged by Taylor's statement.

A question inevitably arises in the mind of anyone who knows of the accumulated doubts described in previous chapters. How, in the face of all that, could CIA have ever believed in Nosenko?

The answer must lie partly in the human psyche—our incurable penchant to believe what we want to believe and to reject what we don't. (I discuss that general problem in Appendix C.)

So desperately did CIA's leaders desire to be rid of the ugly implications that underlay the Nosenko affair—KGB penetration of CIA and perhaps breaking of American ciphers—that they embraced a shaky, corrupt, and unsubstantial report—offered by an ill-qualified investigator—that fed that desire. Solie's report would deserve attention if for no other reason than to illustrate the power of desire over reason. But it is no mere curiosity; the Solie report led to CIA's final conclusion on the Nosenko case. It was crucial; its impact was permanent. Only through this corrupt gateway would future CIA officers gain access to the Nosenko case. It was declassified to make its wisdom accessible to trainees in counterintelligence. This is all that later CIA officers came to know, which is why they repeat its nonsense as fact in their memoirs today.

So it merits attention.

Solie began by adopting the (dubious) position that all he needed to do to prove Nosenko's innocence was to discredit the general conclusions of the SB report. Then he carefully selected the questions he would deal with, sidestepped some major anomalies as if they had never existed, and falsely assured his readers, in the passive voice, that "all areas of major significance have been examined."[8]

Despite its bulk, Solie's report presented no significant new information, though he and Nosenko had adjusted some details. It amounted essentially to a fresh interpretation of selected parts of the old data—an interpretation based on credulity rather than skepticism. Inevitably, the way Solie chose to explain one contradiction would conflict with the way he would explain a different one, but he did not call attention to this. And if he could not find any way to explain an oddity, he would fall back on this comforting thought: if the KGB *had* dispatched Nosenko, they would have surely prepared him better—ipso facto, the KGB *had not* dispatched him.

Among the "areas of major significance"—all of which Solie claimed to have examined—was how Nosenko's reporting touched on the case of Oleg Penkovsky. In this one case, aside from all the others, Nosenko had twice exposed the KGB's blundering hand on him—first in erring by a whole significant year about Abidian's visit to Penkovsky's dead drop, and second by mentioning (and later forgetting) "Zepp." How did Solie manage these hurdles? He simply ran around Zepp—didn't mention it at all. He struggled desperately to explain the dead drop visit and Nosenko's failure to mention it in 1962, exposing the absurd quality of this whole whitewash:

- Solie accepted as "not implausible" Nosenko's preposterous suggestion (to Solie, never to us earlier) that he had failed to tell us in 1962 because "the stakeout had long been dropped"—so long that he had forgotten all about it. But only a couple of paragraphs earlier Solie had recognized that Abidian's visit actually occurred only at the end of 1961. Thus Nosenko's stakeout, by his own account, would have been *still active when he departed for Geneva in March 1962 and would be fresh in his mind when, in June, he told us about Abidian and Moscow surveillance.*
- Or maybe, Solie and Nosenko agreed, Nosenko had somehow got confused and only *imagined* that he had been getting stakeout reports.
- Perhaps, instead, he had only "been advised" of the stakeout by other KGB officers. And maybe only after he had met CIA in 1962—perhaps at the time of the Penkovsky publicity. (How then could Nosenko have failed to relate the drop to Penkovsky when he told of it?)
- Or possibly Nosenko "consciously exaggerated his involvement with the visit and its aftermath." (How then did he know the details?)
- Or maybe "the evident distortions arose from honest confusion"—without explaining how.

- Anyway, Nosenko's errors and contradictions prove that he is *genuine.* "If dispatched, Nosenko presumably would have had the date right."
- Then Solie had one wonderful, final argument: it wasn't Nosenko's fault, but the fault of his CIA interrogators who had "confused matters to the point where complete clarification appears impossible."[9] In pushing out such nonsense, Solie must have assumed that his readers would not know that Nosenko had given, and repeated in detail, his stories of Abidian, of the drop, and of the stakeout *long before any interrogation began.*

Solie then exposed his intent—whitewash, not professional assessment: he dismissed the whole issue. The fact "that Nosenko is not able to properly date the visit of Abidian to Pushkin Street is in no way indicative of KGB dispatch."

Aside from its nonsense, the very structure of Solie's report amounted to a trick. By focusing on the SB report's (unproven) conclusions it skirted the impossible task of explaining the specific inconsistencies, contradictions, and lies that had led to those conclusions. The uninformed reader would never know they had existed.

Other aspects of his report were similarly questionable.

- When giving Nosenko's now "true" version of one story or another, Solie neglected to mention it was often a third or fourth version, nor did he describe the earlier, conflicting versions—or speculate on why there had *been* so many changes.
- Solie implied that thanks to his new, nonconfrontational manner Nosenko had become cooperative, consistent, and "relaxed" as never before and that Nosenko's "material assistance to the interviewer" (including writing reports) was a major departure from the past. In reality, Nosenko had invariably been cooperative except when cornered. He had written many reports for us. And his stories might have seemed consistent back then, too, had they not been challenged. Solie's role was not to challenge or question, but with Nosenko's help to shape some plausible explanation.
- Solie sought to discredit earlier investigations. At least ten times he referred to points he said had not been looked into or to situations in which he said his predecessors had misunderstood what Nosenko had been trying to say. Solie was wrong each time—but a reader with no access to the record would not know that.
- Again and again Solie made assertions as definitive as they were

unfounded. He usually couched them impersonally, often in the passive voice, to hide the fact that they were nothing more than his own opinions. He proclaimed, for example, "The information Nosenko gave *is commensurate with his claimed position.*"[10] "Nosenko," he wrote, "has furnished adequate information so that his claimed assignment during 1953–1955 *is considered sufficiently substantiated.*"[11] Nosenko's knowledge of the office of the Military Attaché supports his claim "that he was an officer of the First Section with the indicated assignment as related by him."[12] Yet again: "The *only* unresolved problem *considered of any significance* in regard to the 1955–59 period is the [XYZ] case,"[13] whereas in fact that particular case posed only minor problems compared with others.

- Solie failed to mention most of the other Soviet sources whose bona fides were also doubted, or about their connections to Nosenko's case.

Solie even administered a new polygraph test in 1968 and cited it as proof of Nosenko's truth—though Nosenko had been polygraphed prior to detention with contrary findings. Solie was ignoring, too, the chief polygraph specialist of the Office of Security, who had decreed in 1966, after CIA had made extended use of the polygraph as an interrogation tool, that no polygraph test of Nosenko after his detention would be valid or could be presented as evidence one way or the other.

Solie accepted as true things Nosenko said that were actually unthinkable in the real Soviet and KGB world of which Solie knew so little. As he hacked away at the SB report's conclusions, avoiding its details, Solie failed to clarify the new picture he was thus composing. If Nosenko were now telling Solie the whole truth, the reader would have to accept (as CIA did, in its desperation) things like these:

- that the KGB actually operated under procedures different than those reported by all earlier (and subsequent) defectors,
- that what Nosenko told Solie about his life was the final truth—even though it was a fourth or fifth version and still full of unlikely events and would later undergo further changes by Nosenko and contradiction even by Soviet sources,
- that a ten-year veteran staff officer of the KGB need not know or remember how to perform routine tasks he must have been doing daily, such as sending telegrams, distinguishing between different kinds of files, entering buildings, and using elevators,

- that a KGB operative need not remember any details of his own operations, not even the names of agents he had handled for years,
- that an officer responsible for the KGB's coverage and knowledge of the American Embassy building needn't himself know about it, or about his own service's measures to counter the technical spying the Americans were doing from that building—or even that that technical spying was being done at all,
- that an English-speaking rising star in KGB operations against the American Embassy would never appear in any of the many approaches the KGB is known to have made to Embassy personnel during his time, nor even have heard of them,
- that a supervisor of operations against the American Embassy would be setting up homosexual compromises of visiting *tourists*, and giving low-level assistance to an officer of another department,
- that a newly appointed supervisor of KGB operations against tourists inside the USSR would be sent abroad—twice—for *months' long* work ensuring the security of a conference delegation, work normally done by a department specifically set up for the purpose.

CIA was accepting Nosenko as genuine because this one man Solie would accept such nonsense and was unable (as he himself confessed) to "perceive any evidence of KGB deception or of any Soviet objective which might have justified their dispatching Nosenko." Someone knowing a bit more:

- might have recalled KGB deceptions whose goals could not have been perceptible to their victims,
- would have noticed the signs of source protection in many of Nosenko's reports, such as 1) his contradiction of Golitsyn's pointers to KGB recruitment of American code clerks, 2) his misleading story about Kovshuk's trip to Washington, and 3) his accounts of how Popov and Penkovsky were caught,
- would have recognized the many other signs of deception that smeared Nosenko's reports, such as his probing about Zepp; his story of Penkovsky's Pushkin Street dead drop; his unlikely multiplicity of contacts with the Lee Harvey Oswald case; and his claim of seeing a KGB file in Geneva showing they knew nothing about CIA there,
- would have seen that all of Nosenko's major leads—"Andrey," Sergeant Johnson of the Orly courier station, the British Admiralty source, Dejean, Gribanov's French businessman agent Saar Demi-

chel, the microphones in the American Embassy, and others—bore the marks of deceptive "chicken feed" in that 1) Nosenko could never get straight how he learned these hot items and 2) the KGB knew that all of them had previously been exposed or had lost their value to the KGB;

- might not have dismissed so offhandedly the only deceptive aim that Solie could envisage: that the KGB might be trying to saturate Western security services, busying them with leads to minor and useless KGB agents to keep them off more valuable ones. In fact, some FBI officers thought that at least in New York the anti-Soviet operatives *had* been saturated. More than fifty percent of their time, they later calculated, had been spent pursuing innocuous leads provided by Kulak and Polyakov. Solie never mentioned these sources or their connections with the Nosenko case.

The twisted and shaky edifice that Solie thus constructed would not stand up even to the gentlest breeze of skepticism, much less to professional or even scholarly appraisal. But it was never intended to endure either. It needed only seem solid to an uninformed and casual reader, for with few exceptions this was the only kind of reader it would ever reach. Future CIA officers would be taught its conclusion but would never see the data on which it was based.

Had it not been for Jim Angleton I might never have seen this "Solie report" and been left wondering what miracle had resuscitated Nosenko. Those who had salvaged Nosenko didn't want me to see the flimsy and corrupt way they had done it, and my "need to know" could be said to have expired with my assignment abroad. But during my routine visit to Headquarters in late 1968 Angleton took the initiative of showing it to me, along with the SB report it attacked (which I then saw for the first time).

I was appalled. In the vain hope of resuscitating that fleeting chance we had had to dig behind Nosenko's tales, I wrote a long rebuttal, containing the objections mentioned above and many more, and sent it to Angleton in January 1969 from my field station. My rebuttal was ignored, except in the Counterintelligence Staff, which was unable or unwilling to fight the case further.[14]

As soon as Solie's report and Taylor's memo had cleared Nosenko, CIA moved him to the Washington area and soon took him in as a consultant for its and the FBI's Soviet counterintelligence operations.[15] Eventually he began lecturing regularly at counterintelligence schools of the CIA, FBI, Air Force, and other agencies and from the mid-1970s often entered the CIA Headquarters building in Langley, Virginia.

Nosenko is said to have boosted CIA and FBI operations. He pointed to recruitment targets among Soviets in the United States, and in the 1970s one of them was successfully recruited.[16] As the director of Central Intelligence later described it to all CIA personnel, Nosenko had "conducted numerous special security reviews on Soviet subjects of specific intelligence interest, and . . . proven himself to be invaluable in exploring counterintelligence leads."[17]

In defending Nosenko later against the implication in a TV docudrama that there might be some substance to the old accusations that he was a phony, a CIA counterintelligence leader came to his defense. Among other things, Leonard McCoy expressed outrage that Nosenko's "dignity, self-respect and honor are once again casually impugned by this film," and that therefore "it is fitting that CIA recently called him in and ceremoniously bestowed a large check on him." Speaking for all CIA officers past and present, McCoy concluded, "Any claim we may have left to having served in an honorable and dignified profession dictates that we accept the Agency's judgment in this case—that Nosenko was always bona fide, and our colleagues made a terrible mistake. Thank you, Yuri Nosenko, for ourselves, for our Agency, and for our country."[18]

Nosenko had won—but voices continued to rise both against him and in his defense. The debate was decided, but not the truth.

CHAPTER 20

Lingering Debate

After they had decided once and for all that No-
senko genuinely defected and was telling the truth, CIA insiders spread the
happy word that they had received "convincing" confirmation from later
KGB sources.

"All of the KGB defectors since 1964—who were in a position to know
about the Nosenko case and whose bona fides have been absolutely verified by the CIA—have strongly supported Nosenko," they told an investigative journalist in the 1980s. They numbered "more than fifteen in all" and
were "uniformly incredulous to learn from the Americans that Nosenko
was ever doubted."[1] An official CIA spokesman was later to tell Congress
the same story.[2]

Fifteen confirmations might make a convincing case—but not these
fifteen. In actuality these sources had not been "in a position to know," nor
were their "bona fides absolutely verified." Five of them had never mentioned Nosenko at all, and others were not even in the KGB when Nosenko
defected.[3] Not one of the fifteen had firsthand knowledge, much less had
any of them been in a position to learn of the KGB's tightly compartmented
deception operations. Those who were not lying or fabricating were presumably repeating what they had been told either officially or by corridor
gossip—and in fact false accounts were being circulated. Another KGB
officer was told that no fewer than "forty colonels" had been fired as a result of Nosenko's defection—but after reflection and discussion with other

officers recognized the story to be false and an intentional plant within the KGB.[4] Three KGB veterans who talked with me after the Cold War seemed to believe these planted tales or rumors because they assumed (wrongly, as later events would show) that the KGB would never use one of its staff officers as a defector. One Illegal, alias "Rudy Herrmann," reported that he had been told to try to find Nosenko in the United States—but he could not know why. (The KGB must have been wondering why Nosenko had dropped off their radar screen.)

To label all these sources "absolutely verified bona fide" was grotesque. Suspicions hung over six of the fifteen.[5] If even one of those six was a KGB plant, a skeptic might wonder *why* the KGB, through that plant, had vouched for Nosenko.

There were, outside this list, more authoritative KGB sources, with more direct knowledge. What did *they* say about Nosenko—especially in the more relaxed conditions after the end of the Cold War? Some said flatly that Nosenko was lying, others inadvertently revealed it by contradicting Nosenko's stories, and the best-informed felt sure the KGB had planted him on CIA. For example:

- In his 1995 memoirs, Filipp Bobkov, deputy chief of KGB counter-intelligence (Second Chief Directorate, or SCD) and Nosenko's boss at the time, twisted the facts and ignored Nosenko's 1962 meetings with CIA, by then well known even to the public. He wrote that Nosenko went to Geneva for "serious operational tasks"—not the way the KGB describes delegation watchdogging. The KGB chairman at the time, Vladimir Semichastniy, said Nosenko had been sent to Geneva to work on "some woman" with an aim to recruit her. (Nosenko apparently did not know this.) Semichastniy said Nosenko had been "expelled from every school he attended" and had got into the KGB only with the help of (then deputy) chairman Ivan Serov. (Nosenko did not know this, either; he named a different high-level sponsor, equally unlikely.)[6]
- A later KGB chairman, Vadim Bakatin, along with former KGB foreign-counterintelligence chief Oleg Kalugin, told the chief counsel of the House Select Committee on Assassinations that Nosenko had "exaggerated and lied about his knowledge of Oswald."[7]
- Oleg Kalugin reported that Nosenko did not serve in the American Department of the SCD in 1960–1961.
- A veteran of the SCD's American Department at the time said No-

senko had served only one year, from 1952 to 1953, in the American Department. He had performed badly and was shunted off to the nonoperational department that handled routine liaison with other Soviet institutions.

- A KGB veteran told me after the Cold War that Nosenko did not hold the KGB jobs he listed for CIA and that the circumstances suggested to him that the SCD (specifically, its 14th Department, for operational deception) had dispatched Nosenko to deceive CIA.

Quite a different story came from a clumsy KGB effort to support and enhance Nosenko's image in American eyes. In the early 1990s they put an official file on Nosenko into the hands of KGB veteran Colonel Oleg Nechiporenko. It was ostensibly to help him write a memoir of his encounter with Lee Harvey Oswald in Mexico City a few weeks before Oswald assassinated President Kennedy—never mind that Nosenko was entirely irrelevant to this subject. Nechiporenko thereupon devoted *fifty pages*— under the title "Paranoia vs. Common Sense"—to make the point that CIA (and specifically me, Pete Bagley) had been stupid not to recognize the great good luck that had fallen into CIA's lap with Nosenko's defection. Like others, he stressed the "colossal damage" that this defection had done to the KGB and the near-panic it caused to high-level KGB chiefs and to Khrushchev himself. But the attempt backfired. That KGB file contradicted a lot of what Nosenko had told us about his early life and entry into the KGB, and Nechiporenko's book told things about Oswald that Nosenko must have known if he had really had access to Oswald's file—but did not know.[8]

Nechiporenko revealed that books like his own were actually parts of ongoing KGB operations. A West German editor complained to him, at about the time Nechiporenko's own book was appearing, that another author, Oleg Tumanov, was refusing to fill in the details in his manuscript recounting his twenty years as a KGB penetration agent inside Radio Liberty. You are naïve, Nechiporenko replied, to expect details. Tumanov, he explained, "was a link, a part of an operation. . . . And this operation isn't completed." If the author were to tell all, "CIA would know what the KGB was doing today and tomorrow. The KGB is not dead."[9]

Even if this still-living KGB was carrying on an unfinished operation, its use of Nechiporenko to attack me was like using a battering ram against an open door. CIA itself had disowned my position, had used some of the same words as Nechiporenko to denigrate me (and others who had distrusted Nosenko), and had been happily employing Nosenko for a quarter century. Why then this late, gratuitous assault? Could they still fear that CIA might reverse its position on Nosenko and finally look into the implications underlying his case? As far as I know, the KGB need have no fear on that front.

Nechiporenko's position in this ongoing KGB game contrasts oddly with the new line on Nosenko that was emerging in Moscow. After years of vilifying Nosenko for the damage he did the KGB and condemning him to death, KGB spokesmen were beginning to suggest that Nosenko did not defect at all. Their new line was that he fell into a trap and was kidnapped by CIA. After the assassination of President Kennedy, so this story goes, CIA learned (through what a KGB-sponsored article fantasized as a far-flung agent network in Russia) that a KGB officer named Nosenko had inside knowledge about Lee Harvey Oswald. So when that target came to Geneva (to recruit a woman connected with French Intelligence) a CIA "action group" under Pete Bagley, working on direct orders from CIA director Richard Helms and Soviet Division chief David Murphy, drugged and kidnapped him, in order to pump him for information about Oswald's sojourn in Russia.[10]

One can only speculate on the KGB's purpose in creating such a fantasy. Might they be preparing Nosenko's return to Russia without punishment like the later "CIA kidnap victim" Yurchenko? Whatever the reason, this change of posture reflected Moscow's growing readiness to admit that Nosenko's defection was not as previously presented. Finally, CIA will be left alone in believing in Nosenko.

For a few years after the Agency in 1968 made its official finding in Nosenko's favor, CIA did not speak with a single voice. The leadership of its Counterintelligence Staff under James Angleton judged Nosenko to be a KGB plant, and its operations chief Newton S. ("Scotty") Miler continued to probe into what lay behind the KGB's operation.

Two former KGB officers, Peter Deriabin and Anatoly Golitsyn, after learning about Nosenko's case in detail (Deriabin had even questioned him personally—see Appendix A) were certain that Nosenko had been dispatched by the KGB and was lying about his KGB activities and career. As Deriabin put it, *any* KGB officer knowing the facts would be equally convinced. He was right. After the Cold War a KGB officer, after reading some of CIA's questions and Nosenko's answers, laughed out loud and asked me an unanswerable question, "How could your service *ever* have trusted such a person?"

Helms never considered the doubts truly resolved and viewed the Agency's formal acceptance as a matter of convenience. Nosenko had to be released, and one way to do it was to clear him, at least officially.[11]

These doubts faded in the second half of the 1960s with the advent of Kochnov and the departure from Headquarters of myself and Dave Murphy. The man who replaced Murphy as Soviet Bloc Division (SB) chief, Rolf Kingsley, had not previously focused on Soviet matters and had little patience with counterintelligence. He called for a fresh review of the case by "more neutral" officers, who concluded that Nosenko was probably genuine.[12] Finally, when William E. Colby became director of Central Intelligence in September 1973, the Agency's approach to counterintelligence changed and the shadows over Nosenko were cleaned away. (At this time I had already retired, so I learned of these events only later from those who lived through them.)

Colby gave a strong push to the growing myth surrounding the Nosenko affair (see Appendix B). In his memoirs he asserted that some former CIA people believed in an all-knowing KGB that was well on the way to dominating the world. "The [SB] Division produced operations and intelligence," Colby wrote, "but the [counterintelligence] staff believed that those operations and intelligence were controlled by the KGB . . . to mislead the United States in a massive deception program."[13]

Colby also derided a "paralysis" that he claimed had overtaken Soviet operations. "I sensed a major difficulty," he wrote. "Our concern over possible KGB penetration, it seemed to me, had so preoccupied us that we were devoting most of our time to protecting ourselves from the KGB and not enough to developing the new sources and operations that we needed to learn secret information. . . . I wanted to consider the KGB as something to be evaded by CIA, not as the object of our operations nor as our mesmerizing nemesis."[14]

If one were to believe one of its later chiefs, the Soviet Division in that dark earlier time "had been turning away dozens of volunteers, Soviets and Eastern Europeans who had contacted American officials with offers to work for the United States."[15] In reality the caution that Murphy—not Angleton—introduced into CIA's efforts to recruit Soviets was never allowed to hinder the acceptance of a single Soviet volunteer, nor did it

preclude any well-considered recruitment approach. None of these assertions of "paralysis" has cited a single rejection of a volunteer, defector, or
proposal for action. Ironically, it was these latter-day critics who themselves started turning away Soviet defectors—on the grounds that CIA had
all it needed or could handle. Among those whom CIA turned away—on
specific orders from Headquarters—was Vasily Mitrokhin, who had stolen
and stashed a large hunk of KGB operational archives.[16]

While paying lip service to the need for vigilance, Colby saw counterintelligence mainly as an impediment to intelligence collection. His impatience and disinterest came out in the form of simplification and sarcasm.
"I spent several long sessions doing my best to follow [Counterintelligence
Staff chief Angleton's] tortuous theories about the long arm of a powerful
and wily KGB at work, over decades, placing its agents in the heart of allied
and neutral nations and sending its false defectors to influence and under-
mine American policy. I confess that I couldn't absorb it, possibly because I
did not have the requisite grasp of this labyrinthine subject, possibly because Angleton's explanations were impossible to follow, or possibly because the evidence just didn't add up to his conclusions. . . . I did not
suspect Angleton and his staff of engaging in improper activities. I just
could not figure out what they were doing at all."[17]

Colby soon got to work reorganizing the Counterintelligence Staff and
divesting it of some of its components. Then in 1974 the *New York Times*
exposed the fact that in apparent violation of the Agency's charter, Angleton's staff had been checking international mail to and from some left-
wing Americans. This gave Colby the ammunition he needed to rid himself
of this nuisance. At the end of that year he demanded Angleton's resignation and was glad to see Angleton's chief lieutenants Raymond Rocca,
William Hood, and Newton Miler follow him into retirement.

To steer a less troubling course, Colby appointed to head the Counterintelligence Staff George Kalaris, a man without experience in either
counterintelligence or Soviet bloc operations, and, as his deputy, Leonard
McCoy, a handler of reports, not an operations officer, who had already
distinguished himself as a fierce advocate for Nosenko.

Now began an extraordinary cleanup inside the Counterintelligence
Staff—and the disappearance of evidence against Nosenko. Miler's carefully accumulated notes on this and related cases were removed from the
files and disappeared, along with a unique card file of discrepancies in
Nosenko's statements.[18]

Shortly afterward Colby appointed an officer to review the files anew.

John L. Hart was assisted by four officers. They worked for six months, from June to December 1976. I caught a glimpse of their aims and work methods when Hart came to Europe to interview me. He had not bothered to read what I had written (though he said nothing new had come to light on the question of Nosenko's bona fides) and seemed interested only in why, eight years earlier, I had warned that bad consequences might flow from Nosenko's release. I saw that his aim was not to get at the truth but to find a way to clear Nosenko, so I refused to talk further with him.

As I later learned, Hart's team did not even interview the Counterintelligence Staff officers who had analyzed the case and maintained files on it for nine years. Among them were two veteran analysts who, having come "cold" to the case, had concluded on their own that Nosenko was a plant—and had written their reasons.

Hart then wrote a report that affirmed total trust in Nosenko.[19]

Having decreed their faith and gotten rid of disbelievers, the CIA leadership banned further debate. One experienced officer in the Soviet Bloc Division—my old colleague Joe Westin, who knew so much about this case—took a late stand against Nosenko's bona fides. He was told by higher-ups, "If you continue on this course, there will be no room for you in this Division"—and his future promotion was blocked. Peter Deriabin, who kept trying to warn Agency officials about Nosenko, was told to desist or his relations with CIA would be threatened (see Appendix A).

Nosenko's rescuers then set out to discredit those who had distrusted him. They first labeled them as paranoid (a charge always difficult to refute) and then moved on to distort the record.

One of Nosenko's now well-placed friends told an investigative reporter that Angleton's successor Kalaris had made the appalling discovery that the bad Angleton had ticked off the FBI's Soviet Military Intelligence source code-named "Nicknack" as a provocateur and thus had locked away his important leads to spies abroad. The good Kalaris, said this insider, proceeded to dig out one of those leads and personally carried it to Switzerland, where the Swiss Federal Police quickly identified the spy as a brigadier named Jean-Louis Jeanmaire. They convicted him of betraying military technological secrets to the Soviets.[20]

The accusation was pure invention. Angleton was impressed with Nicknack's leads to spies abroad and had asked William Hood to be sure that they were acted upon. Hood then—not Kalaris years later—personally carried the Swiss item to Bern.

Other misrepresentations were tacitly abetted. For instance, the new

Agency leadership did little to counter Nosenko's claim that he was drugged. This canard played for years in the media, and was allowed to circulate even in the halls of CIA. CIA director Stansfield Turner even hinted that it might be true, although his own subordinates had submitted to Congress—as sworn testimony on his behalf—a list of every medicament ever given to Nosenko, which proved the contrary. As I know, Nosenko was never drugged.[21]

The flimsy structure of CIA's defense of Nosenko was shaken in 1977 when investigative reporter Edward Jay Epstein got wind of the Nosenko debate. While researching a book on Lee Harvey Oswald he came upon the fact, until then hidden, that a defector named Nosenko had reported on Oswald and that some CIA veterans questioned that defector's bona fides. Digging into this potentially explosive subject, Epstein interviewed former CIA director Richard Helms, James Angleton, Newton "Scotty" Miler, and, on Helms's recommendation, me.

Thus in my retirement did I come back into the debate on Nosenko. I told Epstein some of the things in the preceding chapters. His book *Legend. The Secret Life of Lee Harvey Oswald* came out in 1978.

With its evidence that Nosenko was a KGB plant, the book logically concluded that what he told the Americans about Oswald—though presumably true in its basic message that the Soviets had not commanded Oswald's act—was a message from the Soviet leadership.

Coincidentally, the U.S. House of Representatives at this point appointed a Select Committee on Assassinations (HSCA) to reinvestigate the assassinations of President Kennedy and Martin Luther King. It interviewed Nosenko five times about his knowledge of Oswald's stay in the Soviet Union—and simply could not believe him. In its final report the committee stated flatly, "Nosenko was lying."[22]

Aware of the HSCA's doubts, and by now committed to a different image of Nosenko, CIA director Turner designated a personal representative to testify. It was none other than the man who had most recently whitewashed Nosenko, John Hart.

Hart spent his entire prepared testimony of an hour and a half defending Nosenko and degrading his own colleagues who had suspected him. He attacked me viciously, to the point of accusing me publicly of contemplating murder, though he knew it was nonsense.[23]

To the amazement of the HSCA members the CIA director's designated representative did not even mention the name of Lee Harvey Oswald. When they asked him why, Hart admitted that he "knew nothing about

Oswald's case, but hoped that by explaining misunderstandings within the Agency" and by attesting to Nosenko's "general credibility" he could "clear up the committee's problems with Nosenko" so that "allegations concerning [Nosenko] would go away."

But the committee's problem was not with Nosenko, but with what Nosenko had said about Oswald. So they forced Hart to address this question. Thereupon even he admitted that he found Nosenko's testimony "incredible," "hard to believe," and "doubtful."

"I am intrigued," House committee member (later Senator) Christopher Dodd said to Hart, "as to why you limited your remarks to the actions of the CIA and their handling of Nosenko, knowing you are in front of a committee that is investigating the death of a President and an essential part of that investigation has to do with the accused assassin in that case. Why have you neglected to bring up his name at all in your discussion?"

Hart replied that the Agency had asked him to talk "on the Nosenko case" and had accepted his unwillingness to talk about Oswald, of whom he knew nothing. "So," concluded Dodd, "really what the CIA wanted to do was to send someone up here who wouldn't talk about Lee Harvey Oswald."[24]

Still, the congressmen could not understand why a CIA officer, acting on the orders of the CIA leadership, would "throw up a smoke screen and get the Agency in the worst possible light as far as the newspapers are concerned." Why would he attack his own colleagues and create "smashing anti-CIA headlines?" "Puzzled and mystified," one congressman called "the whole scenario totally unthinkable." He added, "no one I know in the Agency has come up with any sensible explanation."[25]

While Hart was in the process of attacking his own organization—and me especially—I got a phone call in the middle of the night, European time. "They're crucifying you, Pete!" cried Yuri Rastvorov, who was watching the HSCA proceedings on C-Span television in the United States. This KGB veteran, who had defected in 1954, was outraged, having learned enough about the Nosenko case to have concluded on his own that Nosenko must be a KGB plant. I thanked him for the warning, went back to bed, and then waited while another friend fast-shipped to me the transcript of Hart's statement.

Reading this intensely subjective attack and the discussions that followed it, I could sense the committee's skepticism and wondered why they hadn't called on me to present my side—all the more when I learned that Helms, in his testimony, had recommended that they do so. Fearing that someone in CIA might be trying to prevent my appearing, I wrote the HSCA subcommittee chairman, Congressman Richardson Preyer, a rebuttal to Hart's testimony, asking for the opportunity to answer in public what had been a public attack. On the side, suspecting that the subcommittee's counsel was cooperating to keep me out, I contacted Congressman Preyer directly. Thus I was finally invited and flew from Europe to testify, pointing out Hart's untruths and evasions. Though I appeared only in executive (closed) session, Preyer courteously saw to it that my testimony (as "Mr. D. C."—for "deputy chief" of the Soviet Bloc Division) was included in the published record of the hearings.

Now I was back in the debate, though still carrying on my business activities in Europe and writing, with Peter Deriabin, a book on the KGB. In early 1981, when newly elected President Reagan appointed William E. Casey as director of Central Intelligence, I saw it as an opportunity to reopen the case and addressed a long report to him (to which Deriabin contributed what appears in this book as Appendix A). It was judged inadequate to overcome the Agency's evidence supporting Nosenko.

In 1987 I was interviewed by English playwright Stephen Davies, who was writing a semifictional drama on the Nosenko case. When the film appeared on television the CIA retirees' association published a review of it in their quarterly newsletter.[26]

Neither the film nor the reviewer took a position on the basic question —was Nosenko a KGB plant? But to the CIA at that time it was heresy even to leave a wisp of suspicion hanging over the hero of the myth. Leonard McCoy jumped to Nosenko's defense. In a passionate letter to the editor he lauded Nosenko and attacked the earlier handlers of the case in such splenetic terms that the editor (as he told me) refused to publish it until it had been toned down. McCoy's letter was full of misstatements, as I pointed out in a rebuttal.

Both Hart and McCoy knew Nosenko personally and had studied the case from positions of direct authority. Hart boasted of his own "standards of scholarship" and told Congress that he would never "go beyond the bounds of certainty" nor "extrapolate from facts." As for McCoy, on whose statements the writer Tom Mangold relied for his book *Cold Warrior*, Mangold described him as "a mature and meticulous intelligence officer, with an obsession about factual accuracy in all matters." So one might expect these two to dismantle any opposing argument point by point, using sure and accurate facts. Instead, both of them twisted the very nature of the affair and concealed major aspects of it. In Hart's sworn testimony were no fewer than thirty errors, twenty misleading statements, and ten major omissions, and dozens in McCoy's article.[27]

They (and CIA) had made an act of faith, perhaps not the best base for judging a complex counterintelligence question. Hart stated that Nosenko had *never* intentionally lied—never mind that Nosenko himself had admitted in writing a years-long inability to tell the truth to CIA. McCoy—as deputy head of CIA's Counterintelligence Staff—epitomized the Agency's position by writing that if by any mischance Nosenko had told a few fibs, *"They were not [spoken] at the behest of the KGB."* CIA's deputy director certified this act of faith, making it the Agency's official position that "there is *no reason* to conclude that Nosenko is other than what he has claimed to be."

Soon after the debate in the CIA retirees' newsletter, Nosenko and his defenders presented their case to investigative journalist Tom Mangold, who incorporated it in a book attacking James Angleton as a paranoid. Mangold acknowledged his debt to McCoy, who had "left an indelible imprint on every one of these pages."[28] His book accurately reflected CIA's defense of Nosenko and was thus studded with error, omission, misrepresentation, and invention, and colored by emotional bias for Nosenko and against his detractors.

These misstatements congealed into a myth that by its frequent repetition has become conventional wisdom inside and outside CIA. Consecrated by the sworn testimony of high CIA officials, it is treated as serious history. It is a tale of how a band of buffoons and demons—paranoid "fundamentalists"—tried wickedly and vainly to discredit a shining hero. It has been taught—without the facts on which it is supposedly based—to CIA trainees who, thinking it true, have passed it on to later generations of CIA people. Today, a generation later, one can see it repeated in their memoirs as an "inside" fact.

To create this myth its makers had to do some fancy twisting and inventing. Dismissing massive evidence to the contrary, they asserted that Nosenko always told the truth. Not only was and is he truthful, but he has been a veritable cornucopia of "pure gold," vast quantities of valuable information. To give substance to this wild claim, the mythmakers resorted to pure invention. They transfigured poor "Andrey" the mechanic, for example, into a code clerk who enabled the Soviets to break America's top-secret codes and moved dangerously into the code-breaking National Security Agency. They had Nosenko pinpointing fifty-two microphones in the American Embassy, something no one outside the KGB's technical services could even pretend to do. They gave color to their tales by the breathtaking misstatement that Nosenko told more, and of far greater value, than had the earlier defector Golitsyn. (Golitsyn, this story goes, never uncovered a single spy in the West.)

The mythmakers dismissed onetime suspicions of Nosenko as nothing but the product of potted preconceptions and wild theorizing by since-disgraced colleagues, incompetent and paranoid "fundamentalists."

The myth makes no mention of the underlying issues: the signs of penetration of American government and ciphers. Its focus, instead, is the pathos of the fate of a stupidly misunderstood, genuine defector who had been cruelly and duplicitously treated—until his saviors came along.

Finally, the mythmakers ridiculed as "nonsense" the idea that the Soviets would mount a deceptive operation of this magnitude—at least, after the first decade or two of Bolshevik rule—and labeled the very idea a delusion of some "monster plot." As a corollary, the myth asserts—without a trace of evidence—that this paranoia "paralyzed" CIA's intelligence operations against the Soviet Union.

Because it has become history, the myth's creation, its details, and the motives of its creators deserve attention (see Appendix B).

This myth enveloped CIA in a warm blanket of complacency (and aversion to "mole hunting") that later contributed to the Agency's long failure to deal effectively with even more glaring evidence of treason in its midst—that of Aldrich Ames.

PART SIX

Late Light

CHAPTER 21

Hiding a Mole, KGB-Style

Out of sight of other Russians, a man maneuvered himself close to a CIA officer and offered information. He revealed himself as a KGB officer from the American Department of the KGB's counterintelligence directorate, working against the American Embassy in Moscow. He could answer a question that was nagging CIA—how its spies in Russia had been caught—and he was willing to stay in secret contact in Moscow.

Was this Yuri Nosenko coming from KGB service against the American Embassy, telling CIA in Geneva how the KGB captured Pyotr Popov and Oleg Penkovsky?

No, this was a quarter-century later and not in Geneva but on a train rolling through the Russian night. The Russian's name was not Nosenko, but Aleksandr Zhomov—and unlike Nosenko, Zhomov would subsequently be exposed and admitted, even by the KGB itself, to have been a KGB plant.[1]

But they had similar KGB missions—to divert CIA's attention from a KGB mole in its midst—with this difference: Nosenko's mission succeeded and CIA found no mole, while Zhomov's, though it gained time for the later mole Aldrich Ames, ultimately failed.

Times had changed since Nosenko. When Zhomov surfaced, the KGB had a lot more arrests to explain than the two—Popov and Penkovsky—of Nosenko's time. In the meantime, CIA had been enjoying a windfall. As the Soviet Union rotted away, its officials turned ever more readily to the West for rescue or refuge when they became overwhelmed by disillusion, frustration, troubles, or greed for a better life. In the twenty years before the final breakdown of the system more KGB and Soviet Military Intelligence officers defected to, or began secret cooperation with, the West than in all the preceding fifty years.

Then things turned bad. In 1985 and 1986 these new spies began to disappear one after another in quick succession—caught by the KGB. So many fell in such a short time that not even the most obtuse or sanguine of CIA overseers could fail to ask, might there be a traitor in our midst?

CIA had to ask itself who could have betrayed these operations—who knew of all of them, who knew of each of them? That would require a painstaking, time-consuming effort, and to avoid alerting a mole if there was one, it must be carried out with extreme discretion, thus by only a few people. Even they would probably have to carry on their routine work as well, and at the same time they would have to—indeed, *want* to—look for other, less painful explanations for the debacle.

For instance, might our own operatives have blundered while communicating with these spies in the face of Moscow's stern, ever-vigilant security regime? With the few investigators available, it took time to comb so many files looking for such slips.

Or maybe our secret premises in the American Embassy in Moscow had been surreptitiously entered. There had recently been a fire and the KGB had tried to enter in the guise of firemen. Even more disturbing, Marine guard Clayton Lonetree had confessed to being compromised and recruited by the KGB; the possibility that he had let KGB people in, despite his denials, demanded a review of the files held there, to see if their contents could have compromised the lost agents.

A new source told CIA, too, that the Soviets had penetrated a CIA communications center. This could be part of the answer—and required urgent attention.

A different answer was suggested early on—from a defector fortuitously emerging from within the KGB. Colonel Vitaly Yurchenko brought startling news: a CIA officer had gotten into secret contact with the KGB and had revealed spies working inside the USSR. Yurchenko did not know the traitor's name, he said, but he had learned enough about him that CIA quickly identified Edward Lee Howard, who had been Moscow-bound and already briefed on important spies inside Russia before CIA fired him for misconduct. Might this, along with one or more of those other factors, explain the debacle?[2]

Apparently not. The analysts kept running into blank walls and finally came to the end of the road, facing the fact that no combination of the above factors could explain *all* the losses. The failed investigation ground to a halt.

Then Langley's guardian angel woke up, saw their plight, and sent a miracle from heaven in the form of a new, genuine source from inside the KGB. He pointed them toward a KGB mole in CIA's ranks.[3]

Finally then, after betraying with impunity throughout the whole *nine years* of the investigation's wanderings, Aldrich Ames, who had been head of counterintelligence against the Soviets and thus aware of almost every CIA spy against Russia, was arrested in February 1994. He confessed his treason and was sentenced to life imprisonment.

Fragments of information seeped out into public view and gradually co-alesced into a relatively coherent image of what had been transpiring during those nine years. Though the image remains vaporous and hazy (as it will remain until the unlikely day when all secret files spring open) it reveals a long, underground struggle of the KGB's practitioners of "aggressive counterintelligence" trying to nudge CIA's investigators onto rabbit paths off the track of Aldrich Ames while those investigators moved ponderously, almost reluctantly, toward whomever or whatever had betrayed CIA's agents in Russia.

The KGB actors of this drama were laboring under a huge disadvantage: they had to trick people who were already alert. With insouciant disregard for the safety of the precious mole, their leaders had ordered the arrest of CIA spies almost as soon as Ames uncovered them. Alarm bells clanged in Langley, again and again. In this daunting situation the KGB professionals evidently tuned up their long-practiced skills of aggressive counterintelligence. In the snippets of information that have seeped out, an onlooker can discern them launching deceptive games, one after another, sacrificing secrets, strewing lures and diversions to confuse, delay, and mislead the inevitable CIA investigation.

Act after act of this drama played out, year after year, with the KGB deceivers gradually prevailing, confusing their adversaries and stalling their investigation—only to be thwarted in a dramatic final act not by any failure of their cunning but by the arrival of a deus ex machina from offstage.

An epilogue, too, becomes hazily visible: a mischievous hint that the play had a different ending from the one we have seen. The KGB may have lost the fight onstage and failed in the long run to save Ames, but has the audience seen everything? While losing that fight, might the KGB have been winning a different one—successfully hiding another mole? We learn from insiders in both camps that neither Ames nor a combination of Ames and Howard and the KGB's mole in the FBI, Robert Hanssen, could have undone all the lost CIA spies. The curtain falls on the suggestion that another mole still lurks, undiscovered.[4]

The play has a prologue to whet the audience's anticipation: the events of the 1960s, when other KGB staff officers pretended to work for CIA and for the same reason—to hide and protect moles. In the events about to unfold on stage, the audience sees that the new KGB actors will have more difficulty covering up their discoveries of American spies. In the prologue there were fewer arrests (only Popov and Penkovsky), they took place three years apart, and there was no last-minute apparition to give away the game.

The drama thus emerging can be seen only hazily, but it is no illusion. The KGB confirmed, even boasted, about how it had been "confounding the CIA," as KGB colonel Victor Cherkashin put it. We in the KGB had sent out so many KGB officers to deceive CIA that one would have a hard time, this insider claimed, even to count how many *real* spies Ames ever betrayed. "Some names chalked up to him were double agents—loyal KGB officers who made the CIA and FBI believe they spied for them."[5] Another KGB officer was even told by colleagues closer to the operations that "most" of the KGB defectors had been sent out by Moscow Center to mislead the Americans and the British.[6]

One of them was that KGB apparition on the train in Russia in May 1987. "Alexander Zhomov, an SCD [Second Chief Directorate] officer, [had] staged an elaborate double-agent operation in Moscow in the late 1980s to protect Ames," admitted Cherkashin.[7] Zhomov played directly with CIA's Moscow Station chief—sending him surveillance photos and arranging communications via the CIA officer's own automobile. He proved his inside status by naming the CIA spies who had disappeared—the first confirmation of CIA's fears that they had been arrested. He demonstrated his ostensible goodwill by giving CIA advance notice of four planned KGB provocations, false volunteers to the Americans, who duly appeared.[8]

These were all parts of the KGB's game—and so, too, was Zhomov's "false information about how some of the CIA agents had been arrested."

He led CIA to believe that the KGB had caught each of the spies only "through sheer luck and hard work."⁹

"Sheer luck and hard work." These words might have stirred CIA memories. That's how Nosenko explained the KGB's "chance" detection of Popov and Penkovsky—by lucky but skillful and persistent Moscow surveillance of Western diplomats. And CIA was "confounded" then, too—with its guardian angel sound asleep.

Zhomov's game played on for three years. (CIA code-named him "PRO-LOGUE," though he acted in what was, in effect, an "epilogue" to the earlier Nosenko affair.) All that time Aldrich Ames continued blithely to betray. The game ended when CIA started planning to exfiltrate Zhomov from Russia. This being no part of the KGB's plan, Moscow brought the case to an end. This raised an eyebrow or two in CIA. They even wondered whether PROLOGUE might have been a KGB plant—but on a question with such unpleasant implications, they couldn't agree.

The KGB launched these games with confidence. We knew, the KGB colonel admitted, that "the CIA was all but certain that we never risked dangling one of our own staff officers. CIA would almost certainly take [Zhomov] for a real spy. It did."

The KGB was evidently aware of the prevailing CIA doctrine. The chief of CIA's Soviet operations division, Burton Gerber, had looked into the old files of Nosenko and related cases of the 1960s and had decided that the paranoid "sick think" of that earlier time "didn't stand up to scrutiny." Gerber concluded that "there was no evidence that the Soviets had ever allowed a serving KGB staff officer to approach the CIA as a double agent." He "developed a rule of thumb that had become accepted wisdom within the CIA: The KGB never dangles one of its own staff officers. When a KGB staff officer volunteers to become a spy, he's not a double agent."¹⁰

Another ploy in the KGB series had bedazzled CIA even before Zhomov did. An anonymous letter was dropped into the automobile of a CIA officer in Bonn, West Germany, in March 1986, ostensibly from a KGB officer. Six more letters followed from this "Mr. X," as the CIA dubbed him. He threw out (false) hints that one of CIA's lost spies (whom Mr. X named) had been betrayed to the KGB by the CIA case officer handling him. That called for a careful—and time-consuming—look.

The letter writer asked for (and got) $50,000 and then proceeded to send CIA down yet another rabbit path. He told them that "Moscow was intercepting cables sent from the secret CIA communications center in Warrenton, Virginia." This led CIA into a time-consuming series of tests of its communications security before it finally concluded that Mr. X was a KGB provocateur.[11]

Even after that, the KGB calculated that "the Americans couldn't be completely certain of their conclusions. The possibility always existed that something had gone unchecked or been misinterpreted, or that key facts remained unknown. In that sense—spreading uncertainty and tying up resources—the KGB's post-1986 operations were highly successful."[12]

In the summer of 1985, soon after Ames had identified the near totality of CIA's Soviet spies, emerged center stage of this drama (as already mentioned) a new defector from the KGB—the highest-ranked ever, it was said. Colonel Vitaly Yurchenko's principal contribution (no other important one has ever been publicly revealed) was to tell about two important spies in the American camp. He said he did not know their identities, but gave enough details to ensure that the Americans could identify them (and feel as if they had done it by their own clever investigation).

They were both important spies—or had been. Ronald Pelton had worked in the National Security Agency (NSA), the American center for making and breaking ciphers. This discovery could explain leaks in this field. Edward Lee Howard had worked in CIA's Soviet operations division. That could explain the arrest of CIA spies in Russia.

But Pelton and Howard had one disturbing characteristic in common. From the KGB viewpoint, both cases were stone cold dead. Pelton had already left NSA under a cloud and could never return. Howard had gone to the Soviets only after being fired from CIA, and he had told the KGB all he knew by the time Yurchenko fingered him.

Then, after a few weeks in the West and having delivered his messages, Yurchenko, though guilty in his own country of the capital crime of treason, returned to Moscow.

Having pursued defectors for the KGB, Yurchenko knew better than anyone else the fate of Soviet intelligence officers who had gone over to the adversary and betrayed state secrets. They could expect no mercy. Those caught while spying in place were shot. Those who had fled to the West were condemned to death in absentia and, if possible, assassinated.

Not Yurchenko. He was restored to duty in the KGB and received a medal for his brave act.

To explain this incredible turn of events the KGB leaders circulated a curious tale. They had accepted, they said, Yurchenko's claim that he had not defected at all. As the KGB story goes, Yurchenko said that he had been drugged and kidnapped by CIA in Rome. When he came to his wits in the United States he spun the Americans a few innocuous tales to gain their confidence and a measure of freedom—then cleverly eluded them and took refuge in the Soviet Embassy in Washington. KGB chairman Kryuchkov decorated Yurchenko for his daring.[13]

Some in the ranks of the KGB, while suspecting the truth, pretended to believe this impossible tale. It seemed career enhancing to follow the lead of Chairman Kryuchkov, who spread it. Kryuchkov was perhaps unwilling to admit to his Politburo superiors that he had sent Yurchenko into American hands.

Independent-minded KGB veterans treated the fable with contempt. I disingenuously asked one veteran who had been in a position to know, "Did Yurchenko genuinely defect?" Apparently taken aback by the naïveté of the question, but unwilling to go on record, he just stared at me for a moment, then rolled his eyes heavenward. Another veteran I approached shrugged, "I guess not." And yet another, who had seen Yurchenko in the KGB after his return, wrote of the "fake defection" for which Yurchenko received the Order of the Red Star.[14]

When sending a provocateur to the West as a "defector," the KGB necessarily had a plan of how to accept him back when his mission was completed. In the 1960s their plant Yuri Loginov (mentioned in an earlier chapter) returned after betraying some relatively unimportant and generally known KGB activities. A board "reviewed his case" in 1969 and, because this was in "the liberal times instigated by Khrushchev," decided that he did not deserve punishment.[15] The journalist defector Oleg Bitov, after contacting British and American intelligence and publicly denouncing the Soviet system for a year, returned to Moscow in 1984 with a story identical to the one Yurchenko would use—"drugged and kidnapped." He not only was forgiven (by a board on which Yurchenko claimed to have sat) but was promoted on the staff of the important newspaper from which he had defected. Another of their ilk, Oleg Tumanov, after twenty years of treason as an anti-Soviet broadcast editor of Radio Liberty in Munich, returned to Russia in 1986—to be "forgiven" because of his "repentance."

Perhaps the most revealing aspect of the Yurchenko defection is the American debate about him. Was he a genuine defector or not? In their own books and interviews with journalists, senior CIA officials have certified that Yurchenko gave too much information to be a plant, that the

KGB does not send staff officers as defectors, and that there is "no doubt" that his defection was genuine. This avoided the embarrassment of admitting to having been duped.

More importantly, it avoided the ugly demands of a contrary conclusion. It would be deeply troubling to inquire into *why* a KGB provocateur would have given away a CIA staff officer, Howard, and an NSA cipher breaker, Pelton, even if they were burnt-out cases.

To avoid doing that, CIA was even ready to swallow Yurchenko's absurd stated reasons for returning to certain death or jail and disgrace in Russia: first, because news of his defection had leaked to the press; second, because a onetime lady friend (married) refused to run off with him, and third, because he learned in the West that he was not, as he had feared, about to die of stomach cancer.

The incurable human penchant for self-deception was—not for the first time in history—lending a hand to hostile deceivers.

CHAPTER **22**

The Other Side of the Moon

In my school days I had an astronomy textbook with the memorable and categorical statement, "We will never see the other side of the moon." That's what I used to think during the Cold War about the "other side" of our Cold War encounters with the KGB.

Then, in late 1991, the dissolution of the Soviet Union offered an unexpected opportunity to see the other side. I seized it and sought contact with former Soviet intelligence and counterintelligence officers who might now talk more freely about a past we had lived through as adversaries. I found them, and in friendly discussions—usually outside the direct purview of this book—many threw light on these matters, each from his particular vantage point. Their answers to my questions, when taken together, told much about their side of our counterintelligence struggles.

Taken separately, what any one individual told me might not seem pertinent to my subject, so I have assembled it all into a single narrative. There is another, more compelling reason to do this: to protect individual interlocutors from accusations of (at least) indiscretion and (at most) disloyalty. This might seem unnecessary, since all were loyal to their country, would not betray secrets, and reminisced only about long-past events and individuals thoroughly known to both Eastern and Western services. But in Putin's Russia the KGB mindset lives on. Secrets are more severely defined and more jealously guarded than during that short period I enjoyed immediately after the Soviet collapse. Even some documents that were de-classified in those heady days have been *re*-classified as the Russian Federation's definition of "state secrets" slips back toward the absurd restrictiveness of Soviet times. KGB veterans have become more wary of Western contacts, and their security men keep a closer eye on who talks with whom.

They felt no need to go into detail that they (correctly) assumed I knew, and some of their allusions might seem almost cryptic to a layman. So I have inserted some interpretations and facts of my own to show how their revelations relate to my subject. These I have surrounded with brackets to distinguish them from what the sources themselves said. I record here only statements that appeared to be made spontaneously and were consistent internally and when compared with other sources.

Here is some of what these KGB veterans revealed.

From the mid-1950s Oleg Gribanov was chief (and before that deputy chief) of the KGB's Second Chief Directorate (SCD), responsible for counterintelligence inside the USSR. He was eager—some in foreign operations (First Chief Directorate—FCD) thought dangerously overeager—to emulate the successes of deception operations that occupied such an honored place in KGB history [for instance, "Trust" and "Syndikat-2" and "Throne"]. Responsible as he was for defending Soviet security against foreign intelligence and subversion, Gribanov set out with these aggressive techniques to unmask, mislead, entangle, confuse—and penetrate—the Western intelligence services. He was untroubled (one said even stimulated) by the fact that this would inevitably extend his range outside the Soviet sphere and put him into competition with the FCD, responsible for counterintelligence and deception operations abroad. FCD experts, on the other hand, knowing the meticulous preparation and attention to detail that deception operations demand, viewed Gribanov as overly bold, careless of detail, and likely to blunder.

Supporting—and sometimes inspiring—Gribanov's aggressive "games" were past KGB "damage assessments" (as they were commonly called in the American intelligence community). These were records that had been prepared by the various KGB commissions set up to determine what secrets a defector from the Soviet regime had exposed or could have exposed to Western adversaries. By the late 1950s—after the defections of KGB officers Peter Deriabin, Yuri Rastvorov, Vladimir Petrov, Nikolay Khokhlov, and others, and the treason of GRU officer Pyotr Popov—these reports had accumulated into a vast pool of former secrets that, reused at no expense, could not only furnish bulk to the reporting of a later, false defector but also increase his credibility in the eyes of the West, for these items would be "confirmed."

With the approval of the KGB chairman in each case, the SCD could run such operations against foreign intelligence services without the knowledge of the FCD. In practice, however, the SCD normally kept one or two top FCD leaders (not necessarily including the FCD's foreign-counterintelligence chief) informed of developments. To manage this activity Gribanov used (one source said "formed") a special department for "operational deception," designated as the 14th Department of the SCD. It consolidated functions that had in the past been carried out by varying units or by special or ad hoc staffs. Gribanov kept a tight personal grip on it. "Make no mistake," one veteran told me, "no matter who was formally the department chief, it was Gribanov himself who ran that department. It was his baby."

Though Gribanov had little luck in obtaining permanent slots in FCD residencies abroad, he sent his officers out on temporary missions to handle the foreign aspects of his games. And for another reason: they often had to make initial contacts abroad with foreigners returning to the West after being recruited inside the USSR by Gribanov's SCD. The FCD was usually reluctant to expose its officers in residencies abroad to such recruits until, in the West, they had demonstrated their willingness and usefulness. Because they had usually been recruited by compromise and blackmail, the FCD expected that as soon as they would get home and away from whatever lure or threat had forced them to promise collaboration, they were likely to evade contact or even turn themselves in to their own authorities and become double agents against the KGB.

[One such SCD mission abroad, evidently, was that of Vladislav Kovshuk and "Aleksandr Kislov."] In its operations against foreign embassy personnel in Moscow in the mid-1950s, Kovshuk of Gribanov's SCD had recruited the CIA representative Edward E. Smith [who apparently betrayed the CIA agent Lieutenant Colonel Pyotr Popov of Soviet Military Intelligence, the GRU].

One of the early chiefs of the 14th Department, Valentin V. Zvezdenkov, had led the investigation of Popov in East Germany and conducted his interrogation in Moscow. From Popov's confession Zvezdenkov had in hand, by the first half of 1959, the vast amount of information on the GRU that Popov had exposed to CIA. This enabled [perhaps inspired] Gribanov to launch a major deception operation involving the GRU (for whose security the KGB was responsible) to mislead and expose CIA and FBI work against the USSR. Gribanov's SCD dispatched a GRU officer, Dmitry Polyakov, to New York with the mission of becoming an American agent. In early 1962 Gribanov was preparing additional deceptive "games" involving dispatch to the West of false defectors. The timing and circumstances suggested to one of my KGB acquaintances that Yuri Nosenko might have been one of them.

In 1958, in one of his periodically convened meetings of chiefs of Warsaw Pact counterintelligence services, Gribanov proposed a joint operation. All at the same time, each of these services would expose publicly (on one pretext or another) a lot of Western spies they had caught and turned or whom they themselves had planted. This, Gribanov thought, would sow dismay and confusion in Western intelligence services, inhibit further spying, and tie them up in time-consuming and useless investigations.

Gribanov's proposal was not adopted. It caused (unspoken) outrage among the Eastern European chiefs because they, not the KGB, were to make the bulk of the sacrifices and because they doubted it would have long-term effect.[1]

Here one could see Gribanov's way of thinking [at about the time he was planning the Nosenko operation]: his impetuousness, his aggressiveness, and his readiness to sacrifice his own unneeded helpers.

The KGB labeled certain of its sources as "valuable" and gave them especially tight security protection, restricting knowledge strictly to the handlers, sometimes preserving few written reports and those in a file accessible only with the personal authority of the KGB chairman or directorate chief. In this category were, among others, the KGB's sources of foreign code secrets, penetrations of major Western intelligence services, and counterintelligence "plants." [This helps explain why so many KGB veterans had no idea, and even denied, that the KGB had dispatched Nosenko as a plant.] Other KGB sources were carefully protected and compartmented, but without the extraordinary precautions given to "valuable" agents. Outside these categories lay a pool of KGB spies who never had, or who had lost, their access to Western secrets, or who had been compromised by defectors from KGB or GRU ranks, or who were not trusted, even suspected (or known) to be acting as hostile double agents. Many had been swept into the net simply because the KGB got an opportunity for blackmail. These became fodder for Gribanov's schemes—KGB "spies" who could, with no real cost, be exposed by a false KGB defector sent by Gribanov into the hands of American Intelligence. This sacrifice of its own assets contradicted the KGB's principle of loyalty to its agents and therefore was kept unknown to KGB officers not directly involved. [The sacrifice of Ludwig Albert in the West German BND, to protect a more important penetration agent, Heinz Felfe, was one example. Nosenko's exposure of Sergeant Robert Lee Johnson was another—and both were fatal for the victims. Albert committed suicide and Johnson was stabbed to death by his own son visiting him in the prison to which his exposure by Nosenko had condemned him.]

[An unexpected crisis delayed Gribanov's project with Polyakov, who was already at his station in New York.] In mid-1961 the KGB discovered a real Western spy in the GRU—Oleg Penkovsky. Before Polyakov would make his first contact with American Intelligence, this potential threat to the new operation had to be (in the words of one source) "taken care of."

The KGB stopped Penkovsky's travels to the West and covered him and his apartment with intense physical and long-range photographic surveillance. Gribanov prepared to arrest him, but in a way that would hide the true source of the KGB's discovery.

Nosenko had been serving in the SCD's *vedomstvo* (other-agency liaison) department—a link from SCD headquarters to KGB officers stationed within various Soviet ministries and enterprises—having been shunted off to this nonoperational liaison work for incompetence after a brief and unsuccessful stint from 1952 to 1953 in the SCD American Department. [This contradicts the career story that Nosenko recounted to CIA.]

[Preparations for Nosenko's dispatch must have been under way by 1960, perhaps as early as 1959.] A member, later chief, of the SCD's 14th Department was Vladimir D. Chelnokov [whom Nosenko described to CIA as the chief of the 7th (Tourist) Department. Chelnokov in 1960 took Nosenko with him to his meeting in Odessa with "F," an American travel agent who frequently escorted tours to the Soviet Union. Apparently this introduction had two purposes: first, to show Nosenko as a real KGB officer (Nosenko in 1962 identified F to CIA as a KGB agent, so F, when queried by the Americans, could confirm it), and second, as Nosenko inadvertently revealed in 1964, to establish a channel for CIA contact with Nosenko in the USSR. (After firmly refusing in 1962 any contact with CIA inside the USSR, Nosenko later chided me for not trying. "You could have contacted me through F," he said. Indeed, in March 1963 F had traveled again to Odessa —and was met there by Nosenko.]

[Gribanov was confronted with an unexpected glitch in his plan to dispatch Nosenko.] In mid-December 1961 the KGB officer Anatoly Golitsyn defected. The KGB urgently set up a special commission consisting of the KGB chairman, the head of the KGB Cadres (personnel) Department, and the FCD chief, to assess what secrets Golitsyn could expose to the West. Their helpers looked into all files to which Golitsyn had had access and ordered interviews of his colleagues and friends in Moscow and abroad to determine what they might have inadvertently revealed to Golitsyn.

One of my KGB-veteran interlocutors said, "The commission told me Golitsyn had uncovered me."

"You mean," I said, "that they had determined that Golitsyn knew you and *presumably* identified you to the Americans."

"No. I mean what I said. They said Golitsyn *had*. They *knew*."

[This startling indication of penetration of the CIA staff is, as far as I know, unknown to CIA. It deserves investigation.]

The commission completed its work within about six weeks, by late January 1962. [It seems to have found that Golitsyn had hearsay knowledge of the SCD's recruitment of American Embassy code clerks. This alerted the KGB to its need to act urgently to divert Western investigations.]

[Conveniently, Nosenko was standing by, already prepared for a provocative mission. But if he were to divert these Golitsyn leads (and reuse other Golitsyn information so as to seem more knowledgeable) Nosenko's career legend would require amending. Now he would claim that through 1960 and 1961 he had supervised operations against American Embassy code clerks and security officers. One must suppose that the KGB figured CIA to be too stupid to wonder why Nosenko was claiming *tourist* operations, like F, during this period.]

Gribanov dispatched Nosenko to Geneva in mid-March 1962 in the company of an officer of the 14th Department traveling under the pseudonym Aleksandr Kislov. [Kislov had participated in Gribanov's investigation of Popov and had accompanied Kovshuk to the United States on the trip that led to the uncovering of Popov. In Geneva Kislov roomed with Nosenko in a small hotel far away from the delegation whose security Nosenko was ostensibly protecting.]

In Geneva was stationed (in one of Gribanov's handful of SCD slots abroad) Yuri Guk, a 14th Department officer with experience in provocative counterintelligence games that stretched back to his young days in postwar Berlin. He and Kislov together would prepare Nosenko for his contact with CIA. Guk made a trip back to Moscow for final preparations [and after Guk's return to Geneva Nosenko was sent into contact with CIA, shortly before the conference ended].

At that moment the KGB was preparing to arrest Penkovsky. In order to protect its source abroad who had really uncovered him a year earlier, the KGB wanted the West to believe that it had only stumbled upon Penkovsky's treasonous contacts while routinely tailing Western diplomats in Moscow. [This was evidently one of Nosenko's tasks. He regaled us with the skill and advanced technology of surveillance squads—and after Penkovsky's arrest, he "authoritatively" reported the surveillance version.] This was true only insofar as the footpads knew in advance whom to follow.

KGB insiders made it clear that Nosenko lied to CIA. Vladimir Semichastniy, KGB chairman at the time, said (and Gribanov's deputy Filipp Bobkov wrote in his memoirs) that Nosenko was in Geneva on a serious operational mission—in other words, he was not delegation-watchdogging. He had gone there, Semichastniy said, to recruit "some woman." According to another insider, it was while meeting that woman, who was connected with French Intelligence, that CIA "kidnapped" him in the Geneva area. Gribanov was coming to Geneva in early February 1964 to meet Nosenko per arrangements made by Nosenko, but arrived only after Nosenko had defected. [Nosenko told CIA of Gribanov's impending visit but never hinted that it concerned him in any way.]

A KGB-sponsored article about Aleksey Kulak, the longtime FBI (and later CIA) source inside the KGB, called this case "one of the greatest mysteries in the annals of modern espionage." It hinted tongue-in-cheek that this onetime war hero, Kulak, had perhaps "fallen victim to intrigues between the special services."[2] That was surely right. The FBI had concluded on its own in 1977 that the KGB had planted Kulak on them, and this article was the KGB's veiled admission that the FBI had been right. Only a KGB game could explain the KGB's "failure" to detect Kulak's treason for twenty years, *five of them after he had been exposed in the U.S. press.* Only a KGB game could explain the "coincidence," revealed by these KGB articles, that just when the KGB belatedly "discovered his treason," this wartime Hero of the Soviet Union had died of cancer and been buried with military honors in the presence of party dignitaries.

Bit by bit the "other side of the moon"—the KGB side of these aggressive counterintelligence games of the 1960s—was becoming known. But whatever the CIA and FBI have learned has apparently not inspired them to look back and examine *why* the KGB had launched such risky and expensive deceptions.

CHAPTER 23

Boomerang

Deception is a potential boomerang. If its intended dupe is alert and detects the fraud and looks into its purpose with open eyes not blinded by assumptions and desires, he may see the very truth it was designed to hide.

This truism—with all its "ifs"—is vividly illustrated by Operation Bodyguard, the Allies' deception of the Germans about the time and place of the impending landings on D-Day, 1944. The stakes were gigantic. On this hoax depended the success of the landings, and on the landings depended at least the duration and perhaps the outcome of the whole Second World War.

Bodyguard sought to convince the Germans that the Allies would use the narrowest crossing route and disembark in the Pas de Calais area, and at least a month later than actually planned for going ashore at the true site, in far more distant Normandy.

In a multitude of stratagems the Allies passed small bits of misinformation that would permit the German High Command to piece together for themselves the desired picture. "Secret" papers were leaked, individuals in neutral countries spoke "indiscreetly" to people known or suspected of German sympathies, rumors were spread, controlled spies sent secret messages to their German handlers, a British "4th Army" was invented, ostensibly ready to invade Norway. A huge force (FUSAG—First U.S. Army

Group) was formed under the famous battle commander George Patton. It "assembled" in southeastern areas favorable to a departure toward the Pas de Calais, with radio circuits busy for the benefit of German radio-intercept analysts. Dummy landing ships were moored in areas adjacent to the route to the Pas de Calais, for the benefit of German aerial reconnaissance. Spies were dispatched on spurious missions. Ships and aircraft and troops moved in ways that would convey the desired impression, and on and on.

Inevitably small mistakes—an unlikely report, an anomaly, a contradiction—would stir doubts in some German's mind. But he was unlikely to make these stirrings known to his superiors—to avoid disturbing them with probably insignificant detail or violating their firmly based assumptions or to avoid calling into question the value of a source upon whose performance his or their careers or prestige depended. If he happened nevertheless to do so, he would be calmed by more mature heads able to rationalize or shrug off any unwelcome doubt—or be told to keep his unsubstantiated and paranoid suspicions to himself.

The Allied deceivers did make mistakes and mishaps did occur. For instance, in managing British-controlled German spies, the agent handlers made slips that might have exposed the game. But even if the German handlers noticed these missteps, they managed (as one of the British officers controlling the British handlers later wrote) to find

> far more credible explanations of what had occurred than the true explanation that the agent was a double cross. They thought he had been misled and had exaggerated what he had seen; they thought that the plan had been adopted but had later been abandoned; most likely of all they thought that the honest agent had himself been deceived. . . . It was far more reasonable to suppose that he had been misled by the British than that he had over a period of years tricked and deceived his German paymaster. In short, it was extremely, almost fantastically difficult to "blow" a well-established agent. On one occasion an agent was deliberately run in order to show the Germans that he was under control, the object being to give them a false idea of our methods of running such an agent and thus to convince them that the other agents were genuine. . . . The gaffes [we] committed were crass and blatant, but [our] object was not achieved, for the simple reason that the Germans continued to think of the agent as being genuine and reliable![1]

Think of the consequences had the Germans been more alert or had their High Command overcome its preconceptions and concluded that the observed anomalies were symptoms of enemy deception. Had they then asked themselves what such a deception might be hiding, the hidden truth would have leaped out at them. If the invaders would not strike at the Pas de Calais, the most feasible other site was Normandy. The Germans could then have transferred there the tanks of the 15th Army Group defending the Pas de Calais, along with divisions from Norway and the Balkans, and they could probably have driven the landing force back into the sea. The Allies would need years to mount another attempt. Faced with a tired and heavily bled public, they might even have agreed to a negotiated peace, leaving Hitler dominating Europe.

The German dupes could also have detected the deception if they had had better sources of intelligence. Just one undiscovered German spy circulating in certain areas of England or in informed Allied circles might have revealed, for instance, that those landing ships moored in the Thames estuary were wood-and-canvas dummies, or might have failed to find any sign on the ground of the tens of thousands of troops of the "First U.S. Army Group."

The Allied deceivers, on their side, needed not just better but near-perfect intelligence. They had to *know*, not just hope or assume, that the Germans had no such spy. Without that knowledge it would have been self-defeating to launch the deception. But how can one know what spies the enemy does *not* have? For that, one must know all the spies he *does* have—and the Allies had that amazing capability. They were deciphering German military and intelligence radio communications—the now famous "Ultra" that remained a closely guarded secret until nearly thirty years after the war's end. Such inside knowledge is a sine qua non for any risky attempt to deceive.

In the late 1960s CIA let itself be duped just as the wartime German High Command had been. The deceiver this time (the KGB's SCD operational-deception department) committed transparent blunders. In Nosenko's case alone they dispatched a false defector amid scores of circumstances *any one or two of which* could cause Western suspicion and the collapse of their whole operation. But CIA, like wartime Germans faced with the Allies' blunders, preferred to rationalize and shrug them off as anomalies—and like Operation Bodyguard, the KGB deception succeeded.

Happily, the consequences were less painful to these latter-day dupes than to those of the Second World War—so much less, in fact, that the victims never even felt the pain. For this they can thank the good fortune that the Cold War did not turn into a hot one.

If CIA instead had admitted the evidence of deception that these blunders were revealing, and then looked behind them for the purpose of the deception, it could probably have uncovered Soviet success in breaking American military ciphers. It would thus have robbed a potential enemy of what the chief of U.S. Naval Intelligence (referring to the later treason of the Walker family of cipher clerks in the U.S. navy) called "a war-winning capability." Behind Nosenko's legend of having supervised the KGB's Moscow operations against American Embassy cipher clerks lay these three *specific* points:

1. *American cipher clerk, probably military, recruited in Moscow some time around 1949.* In 1962 when I asked Nosenko in what year the KGB in Moscow had recruited Sergeant "Andrey," a cipher machine mechanic—the KGB's "most important" recruitment—he unhesitatingly replied (and later repeated) "1949–1950"—that is, before Nosenko entered the KGB. In 1964, without referring to what he had said in 1962, Nosenko said (correctly) that Andrey was recruited some time between 1953 and 1955. This was evidently what he was supposed to tell CIA in 1962.

But what lay behind Nosenko's 1962 version? He did not dream it up. He was evidently confusing Andrey with some other recruit he had been told of, presumably also a code clerk or comparable and also military, someone who had really been recruited before Nosenko joined the KGB. Perhaps Nosenko learned this from his KGB handler in Geneva, Yuri Guk, who had been operating against the American Embassy in those earlier times. Might Guk, while briefing Nosenko to tell CIA the Andrey story, have told him about this other case?

The KGB in Moscow was running hard in that direction at the time. A military code clerk, Sergeant James McMillin, had defected from the American Embassy.[2]

After the Cold War I learned that the KGB in Moscow did indeed recruit an American Embassy military code clerk in the late 1940s. That spy was never uncovered, nor has the damage he did been assessed.

2. *American military code clerk (here called "Will").* A Moscow KGB officer indiscreetly told his KGB colleague Anatoly Golitsyn that he had

successfully recruited an American Embassy code clerk (unnamed, even by service). After Golitsyn's defection to CIA, Nosenko came along and said he himself had supervised this KGB operation and had even befriended one of the principals. He named the (military) code clerk target and proclaimed, with direct authority, that the recruitment attempt had failed. We came to realize that Nosenko had not held the KGB job that ostensibly gave him access to this case, so his report on Will must have come from the KGB deceivers, evidently trying to negate Golitsyn's information. That the KGB would take this trouble implies that they did in fact succeed in recruiting Will. And Will, according to our checks of security records at the time, did not report any KGB approach to him, whether he refused it or not. Because CIA and FBI chose to believe Nosenko, they did not investigate this lead. Will was not interviewed.

3. *American Embassy communications specialist (here called "Mott")*. Nosenko (falsely) claimed to have directly supervised the work of KGB Moscow case officer Vadim Kosolapov throughout 1960 and 1961. He apparently did not know (hence his KGB sponsors evidently did not want him to report to CIA) that during this period Kosolapov had gone out to Helsinki to ride back to Moscow with an arriving American Embassy communications supervisor. Kosolapov told his colleague Golitsyn in Helsinki that the KGB had high hopes of recruiting Mott by exploiting financial and marital difficulties the KGB knew he had suffered at his previous posting abroad. Nosenko knew nothing of this promising case.

Mott did not report any KGB approach to him, nor did he report the encounter on the train. Because both FBI and CIA believed in Nosenko, Mott was neither investigated nor interviewed.

Behind the Nosenko deception were also signs that the KGB had recruited one or more CIA officers. These signs were not followed up because CIA accepted Nosenko as being truthful.

1. *The betrayer of GRU Lieutenant Colonel Pyotr Popov (see Chapter 7)*. By looking behind Nosenko's story of his boss Kovshuk's trip to Washington, we identified Kovshuk's target as Edward Ellis Smith of CIA. (After the Cold War the KGB confirmed their recruitment of Smith.) But when CIA converted to faith in Nosenko it saw no reason to investigate Smith. Had he been interviewed before he was accidentally killed in 1982, Smith might

at least have thrown light on why the KGB was trying so hard, five years after he had left CIA, to hide his recruitment. (See next item.)

2. *A KGB recruitment in CIA known to, or helped by, Edward Ellis Smith?* It was noteworthy that the KGB made a major effort in 1962 to hide Smith as the target of Kovshuk's KGB assignment to Washington (and as the betrayer of Popov) because by then Smith had been out of CIA for five years. Did they have some *current* reason to prevent CIA from tumbling to this old recruitment? Had Smith pointed them toward a vulnerable recruitment candidate among officers he had worked with in the Soviet Division of CIA? However speculative these questions, they merited close examination, which they never got.

3. *The betrayer of CIA's agent, GRU Colonel Oleg Penkovsky* (see Chapter 14). Nosenko told tales that related to the KGB's investigation of Oleg Penkovsky and promoted its mole-hiding cover story that it had uncovered Penkovsky's treason only by chance while routinely surveilling diplomats in Moscow.

After the Cold War several KGB insiders revealed that the story was false. Penkovsky had actually been betrayed at the very outset of his spying by a KGB source abroad. The source was so important that the KGB permitted Penkovsky to continue his dangerous spying for more than a year until it could firmly plant the cover story.

While this still-unknown source might have been British, Nosenko's story of the dead drop on Pushkin Street pointed toward CIA—and (along with his "Zepp" probe) reduced the number of potential suspects.

As long as Nosenko was accepted as a genuine and truthful defector, there was no need to look into this "discredited theory."

4. *The KGB's "guarantee" that CIA had no source inside the KGB.* It became clear during our investigation and interrogation of Nosenko (see Chapter 15) that he had not held the jobs he claimed inside the KGB, particularly not as deputy chief of the section working against the American Embassy in 1960 and 1961. (KGB veterans confirmed this after the Cold War.) The KGB could not have based a deception operation on such transparent fiction unless it was certain that CIA could not check it inside the KGB. But how could the KGB know what assets CIA did *not* have in Moscow? For that they would have to know all the assets the CIA *did* have—and there

were not many people, even inside CIA's Soviet operations division, who could tell them that.

Other aspects of Nosenko's story similarly seemed to conceal other KGB successes, perhaps involving recruitments of Americans—Embassy officials, journalists, businessmen, and tourists. However, these were too speculative for mention here. They would, however, have produced a number of investigations had Nosenko not been cleared.

CIA avoided such unpleasantness by making an act of faith in Nosenko's truthfulness. Top Agency officials stated and restated this faith in words that, though already cited, deserve recall. "There is no reason to believe that Nosenko is other than what he has claimed to be"; he "defected of his own free will [and] had not sought to deceive us"; any contradiction in his case "is in no way indicative of KGB dispatch"; any untruths "were not at the behest of the KGB."[3]

Such conclusions, in the face of so much (never disproved) evidence to the contrary, would be possible only if one suppressed that evidence and created a new official "truth" (as described in Chapter 19 and Appendix B).

But *why* would any intelligence service voluntarily put on blinders?

Part of the answer must be institutional. If CIA were to recognize Nosenko as a KGB provocateur it would have to deal with the implications. The KGB was hiding things behind Nosenko's stories, evidently including KGB breaking of American ciphers and penetrations of American Intelligence. These are things no intelligence service wants to discover. If it should happen to find a mole in its ranks (always a possibility in the real world), it can expect no praise for the alert counterintelligence and security measures that helped it clean its own nest but, instead, public criticism, ridicule, and loss of confidence, credibility, and stature.

At the institutional level the motives are thus fairly clear. But on the personal level they are less so. Why did professional intelligence officers create a myth and bury the truth?

Part of the answer lies in the human penchant for self-deception—our minds unconsciously screening out the unpleasant and filtering in the pleasant. One writer called it "the universal inability to distinguish true from false, right from wrong, when the false is cast in the image of the world's desire and the true is nothing that the world can fathom, or wants to."[4] Thus, no doubt, some who purveyed the myth truly believed in its falsehoods—because they wanted to, and because others believed; it is easier to repeat what higher-ups say than to think for oneself. Group-think, careerism, and indifference play their roles.

That said, one cannot fail to wonder whether the KGB was able to influence CIA's official views in deeper ways than by sending false messengers. Nosenko's stories seemed to be hiding KGB penetration of CIA ranks—might one such have been in a position to exert such influence? The question hangs there among all the others.

What of the man himself, Yuri Nosenko?

KGB sources have recounted things about his life in the KGB before his defection—although, significantly, they do not give details and dates of his actual career. They describe him as a well-connected playboy who organized hard-drinking sex orgies for colleagues and that this, discovered in the course of the investigation following his defection, caused firings and demotions of those who had enjoyed them. SCD chief Oleg Gribanov, they said, was fired for his sponsorship of Nosenko within the KGB—not for the (temporary) failure of his deception operation during the time Nosenko was incarcerated by CIA. One source colored the tale by recounting his personal encounter with Gribanov, whom, he said, had become a hopeless, babbling, drunken wreck.[5] (This fabrication was exposed after the Cold War when a high-ranking former Chekist told me of his cheerful reunion with the healthy Gribanov during which Gribanov gave him his business card from his successful post-KGB employment.)

Of Nosenko's later history I have heard only bits of hearsay. He stayed in the United States, became an American citizen, counseled CIA, lectured to its counterintelligence students and other parts of the intelligence community, came occasionally into CIA Headquarters in Langley, and, as a director of Central Intelligence put it, "conducted numerous special security reviews on Soviet subjects of specific intelligence interest" and had proven to be "invaluable in exploring counterintelligence leads."[6] CIA thus became co-sponsor, with the KGB, of a shiny, fictional image of what, in reality, was a self-contradicting, lying (and inept) carrier of KGB messages.

It was said that he had settled successfully into a small American town and added two American wives to his previous Soviet three. He had visitors from Russia, and they apparently coached him to straighten out his tangled stories. Their task was hopeless: though he told journalists in the 1980s and 1990s different versions of earlier tales, these were no more consistent or believable than those he told in the past.

Nosenko must never have confessed his KGB mission because even a

CIA embarrassed by its past misjudgment could not then have failed to examine the implications. He would have had to recount the truths he had learned while the KGB was shaping his legend and preparing his mission—and not a single such revelation has come to light.

A day in the 1990s must count as one of the extreme low points of CIA counterintelligence. When this KGB provocateur and deceiver concluded a lecture to CIA staff personnel in their Langley auditorium, the audience—all professional American intelligence officers—rose as one, eager-faced and thrilled, to give Yuri Nosenko a standing ovation.

A KGB Veteran's View
of Nosenko

Former KGB Major Peter Deriabin, a CIA employee, questioned Nosenko personally. He was uniquely well qualified to do so because he knew intimately the Moscow environment in which Nosenko claimed to have lived and worked.

After serving as an investigator in a regional office of State Security, Deriabin became a personnel officer in KGB Headquarters at the time Nosenko claims to have entered the KGB. Having served earlier as a wartime officer of SMERSH (military counterintelligence) of the Soviet navy (assigned there after his fourth combat wound), Deriabin was well placed to assess Nosenko's accounts of his naval service. In the KGB Deriabin supported foreign-counterintelligence operations from a Moscow desk and while stationed in Vienna had watched over the conduct of Soviet officials abroad—the sort of work Nosenko claimed to have done in Geneva and elsewhere. Deriabin long served as Communist Party and Komsomol secretary in the army and KGB so could professionally judge Nosenko's accounts of party and Komsomol activity.

Those in the American intelligence and academic communities who knew Deriabin during his long years in the West honored his unequaled knowledge of the KGB, his sharp intelligence, his professional judgment, and his personal integrity. Deriabin talked with Nosenko twelve times, in sessions lasting as long as three hours. He also observed, via closed-circuit television, interrogations of Nosenko based on questions he himself had proposed. He had earlier transcribed the tapes that recorded all Nosenko's meetings with CIA in Geneva, and had studied the files on this and related cases.

He reported fully on the results of his interrogations and much later, after CIA had cleared Nosenko and taken him in as a consultant for its Soviet operations, repeated some of them in a message to the CIA leadership. This message contains barely a fraction of the points that Deriabin had noted and reported in the mid-1960s, so some of those other points have been added here as an annex to his own 1981 report.

It may be asked, did Deriabin later find reason to change his dark view of Nosenko, especially after later KGB defectors certified Nosenko's authenticity? CIA put this question to him in the 1980s and his answer was unequivocal: "There is no 'opinion' to change. I know the facts and I talked to the man. Nosenko was a KGB plant and whatever your 'official opinion' may be, he is certainly a KGB plant today."

Views on the Nosenko Case
by Peter Deriabin

My position about Nosenko's bona fides has been consistent ever since I first learned the details of the case, and is fully reported in CIA files.

I have long wanted to make known again my strong views on this case, especially since the hearings in 1978 of the House Select Committee on Assassinations. Nosenko's testimony there was no trivial matter; it was the president of the United States who was killed, not a chicken on the road. I testified briefly before that committee but CIA then told me to stop. When I later expressed my opinion to my superiors, I was warned to keep quiet because it might harm my position with the CIA.

Now retired, I still hope that CIA will change its wrong and dangerous position on Nosenko.

I am certain that the man known to CIA as Yuri Nosenko is a KGB plant. I make this statement on the following authority:

- I was a KGB officer in counterintelligence, personnel, and security, and as a party secretary, for more than ten years.
- I served in Moscow Headquarters at the same time Nosenko claims to have served there in 1953.
- My knowledge of KGB personnel, procedures, buildings, administrative matters, and operational activities has been well demonstrated in my twenty-seven years' service to my adopted country. During my long service with CIA most of my time was devoted to the continuing study of the KGB. Without false modesty I think I understand the KGB better than any other employee of the United States government.
- I had access to all information on the Nosenko case through 1966. I transcribed all the tapes of the predefection meetings held with Nosenko in Geneva in 1962 and 1964, and the tapes of his debriefings after his defection.
- I studied and submitted detailed comments on cases related to the Nosenko affair: Popov, Penkovsky, Golitsyn, Loginov, Krotkov, and others.
- In twelve long sessions I personally discussed the KGB with Nosenko. In addition I observed, via closed circuit TV, many other question sessions, some of them based on my questions.

Thus I am confident, as would be any other genuine veteran of the KGB who knew Nosenko's case in detail, that:

- Nosenko did not enter the KGB at the time he claimed, nor in the way he claimed.

- He did not hold the positions he claimed in the KGB, and was probably not a genuine KGB headquarters officer.
- He did not handle Lee Harvey Oswald's file, and knew only what the KGB, on orders of the Soviet leadership, briefed him to tell the Americans about Oswald.
- His information on KGB activities and operations was given to him by the KGB to support his legend and to distract our attention from important KGB activity.
- His life story, including education and military service, cannot be accepted as truthful.
- The way he explains his presence in Geneva, where he contacted CIA, cannot be true.

My reasons for these statements are included in hundreds of pages of reports to CIA through the years. I hope that these reports will be studied again, but in the meantime I recall here just a few of the points I made.

1. KGB entrance date:

Nosenko claimed several times before his detention that he entered the KGB in September 1952 (once saying 1951) and wrote this in his formal biography after defection. He later changed this story and had difficulty deciding on a new date but finally said mid-March 1953.

No genuine ex-KGB staff officer could be in doubt about at least the month of his entrance on duty. And it is impossible that anyone could forget whether it was before or just after Stalin's death. Moreover, no new employees were taken in during that troubled period except a few dozen officers who had worked there with Beria prior to 1947, all of them senior and experienced.

2. Conditions of his entrance into the KGB:

The way Nosenko claims to have entered the KGB is unthinkable to me as a personnel officer at that time. He admitted having been turned down as unsuitable in 1950. Then in 1953 (or 1952 or 1951) he was accepted. But at this time his status with the navy was unclear. He may have had active tuberculosis (depending on which of his stories one chooses to believe). He had a bad school record. His record showed a self-inflicted wound while in a naval preparatory school in wartime—this alone being enough to prevent the KGB from accepting him. He had failed the course in Marxism-Leninism at the Institute of International Relations. He had had a troublesome first marriage, and his father-in-law was in prison. (It does not matter that he was by then divorced.) His mother's noble family background would have been a negative factor, as would the fact that there was a KGB file of compromising material on his father and family. (Remember, this was still the Stalin-Beria time—not that KGB entrance requirements have become easier since then.) And at that time, as a rule, sons of ministers and generals were not accepted into the KGB.

I can state, having at that time recently left KGB personnel work, that this story is impossible.

Nosenko says it came about because of his father's status and because Bogdan Kobulov helped him. I knew Kobulov's case well and I doubt that he could have helped anyone into the KGB at the time Nosenko maintains. Nosenko claims to have entered in March 1953 and Kobulov's recommendation must have been made at least a month before. But before Stalin's death [5 March] Kobulov was not in any position to get KGB cooperation, least of all in accepting such a controversial candidate. Even if the story is true, the arrest of Kobulov three months later would have harmed Nosenko's position and in those rough days, with all the other negative factors on his record, would have caused his firing.

3. KGB career:

Nosenko's career as he described it is impossible. (Aside from the fact that he changed the story several times and admitted to lying about it.)

Nosenko stressed that he was, in his first three years in the KGB, worthless, inattentive, in trouble, badly regarded by his fellow officers, hardly conscious of his duties, and doing only low-level work. Then, in the second half of 1956—after his father died—he "found himself." In my opinion, Nosenko was practically admitting that he did not serve in the KGB during that time. His failure to answer many questions concerning the period confirms this impression.

But then his career took off. In less than two more years he was deputy section chief, a year and a half later he was shifted into a more prestigious section, and in two more years he made section chief. Only six months after that, three of them spent abroad on an irrelevant mission, he was yet again promoted, this time to the prestigious status of deputy department chief. But at the same time his rank promotions were being held up because his record was bad.

To the eye of a real KGB officer this is pure nonsense. It has nothing to do with the real Soviet Union.

4. Nosenko's KGB activities:

Nosenko claimed that he was a successful case officer against American and British tourists and American Embassy personnel, yet he could not give a single example of any successes, or even of any verifiable activities. In one case of compromise of a tourist ("B" in Kiev in 1956) he did appear, but in a role which I would attribute to an agent, not a case officer. When I questioned him about the case he did not know any of the operational procedures a case officer would have to know. He did not even know who first proposed action against this man. In the only other case where his presence could be confirmed, the American ("F") described Nosenko as a junior assistant—to my eye, the role played by an agent or interpreter.

5. Travel document:

Nosenko brought to Geneva a document authorizing his official travel to the town of Gorkiy in December 1963. It listed him as a lieutenant colonel. He claimed its purpose was to authorize his travel in the search for Cherepanov.

He was the wrong man to be chosen to search for Cherepanov. It was not his department's concern to do this search, whether he was working for the American Department or the Tourist Department.

Moreover, I know that such travel documents must be turned in when the trip is finished if the bearer is to be eligible to be paid at the next payday. And it would have to be turned in before any further travel is authorized. So how could Nosenko have brought the document to Geneva—and why?

In addition, he later confessed that he had never been a lieutenant colonel. When asked how the document had been issued in that rank, he said it was a clerk's mistake. Such "promotions" might be given to a traveler to improve his travel accommodations (a lieutenant colonel gets better treatment than a captain) but this is not how Nosenko explained it under careful questioning. And I am bothered by the coincidence that Nosenko was already lying to CIA about his rank a year before this "error" was made.

6. Vladimir inspection:
Nosenko claimed that in 1955 or 1956 he was part of a team investigating and helping the Vladimir region KGB in their operations against foreigners. Yet in other contexts Nosenko had stressed his inexperience and lack of qualifications during the period up to this time, just working on files and running file traces, badly considered in his service, in trouble for misuse of documents, venereal disease, etc., and having even been under house arrest. He was not even a member of the party or Komsomol. Thus to me his assignment to this inspection and educative mission is hardly thinkable.

7. Trip to Cuba:
Asked to explain how he was chosen to go to Cuba in October 1960, Nosenko could give no coherent answer. He said the CC CPSU said to the KGB, "You have Nosenko—he will go to Cuba." This is nonsense. Moreover, Nosenko could not say what he did in Cuba in any detail whatever. Asked why he used the name Nikolayev for this trip [whereas he had previously traveled to the area under the name Nosenko], he answered, "I don't know." This sort of vagueness is unthinkable for a KGB officer; such assignments are serious. And when the questioning on this trip became precise, Nosenko kept trying to change the subject and could not be made to give proper answers.

8. KGB name-checking:
Nosenko said that he hardly did anything during his first three years in the KGB except running traces and low-level file work. And it is true that any KGB officer holding the positions Nosenko claims would be frequently checking names of foreigners and Soviet citizens in the central archives and the archives of the First Chief Directorate. The procedures and forms would become second nature. However, Nosenko could not describe in detail how such a check is done in either place.

9. KGB documents and files:
Part of every KGB officer's life is work with files: putting documents into them, asking for them, studying them. He becomes thoroughly familiar with the various categories of KGB files. However, when I gave Nosenko examples of types of documents and asked him what sort of files they would be in, and gave him names of types of files in daily KGB use and asked him their purpose, he had no idea of most of them and could describe the others only superficially.

10. Security checks:
Nosenko claimed to be security officer of his delegations in Geneva in 1962 and 1964 and also of sports groups in earlier years. However, he could not even explain how Soviet citizens are checked for security before going abroad. This is simply unthinkable.

11. Telegrams:
Nosenko's KGB jobs would have required him to send telegrams to outlying KGB offices in the USSR. When asked exactly how such a telegram is prepared and sent, he could not even give a general account, much less details.

12. Komsomol:

Nosenko claims to have been Komsomol secretary of his KGB unit at one time. When questioned, however, he knew little or nothing about the Komsomol: the age limits of the time, dues collection, activities—and did not even understand the purposes of a Komsomol Congress. Finally I had to stop questioning on this subject because he was totally at a loss.

13. Party membership:

Nosenko said that when he left the Komsomol he did not become a member of the party right away. When told that this is impossible in KGB practice, he agreed but said that he was an exception—in fact, the only member of the KGB who, for the period of about a year, was neither a party nor Komsomol member. Given Nosenko's other problems at the time I can state, as a former Komsomol secretary and personnel officer, that his story is impossible. (I seriously doubt that he was ever a member of the Communist Party, in view of his ignorance of party procedures and his "forgetting" his membership card number. Remembering it was a strict rule.)

14. KGB procedures and daily life:

Nosenko knew so little about day-to-day procedures, things that any KGB officer would know like the fingers of his hand, that one can only conclude that he had never been a KGB officer, at least not in Moscow Headquarters.

Explaining his ignorance of restaurants and buffets in the KGB Headquarters building, Nosenko said that he had never eaten there. Shown ignorant about the KGB club, he said he'd only been in there once. Unable to locate the elevators in the new part of the Headquarters building, he said he'd never ridden one there. Asked about procedures for safe houses he himself supposedly used, he could not begin to answer. If he was telling the truth, he was not a KGB officer.

These impressions were reinforced by Nosenko's manner when questioned. When he did not know something, he would improvise an answer. These improvised answers were usually so naïve, so nonsensical, that no true KGB officer would ever dream of suggesting them, much less believe that they were real.

15. Promotion approvals:

When questioned, Nosenko said that his promotion to lieutenant colonel had been approved by the Central Committee of the CPSU. This is nonsense and every KGB officer knows it. Promotions at that level are approved within the KGB, usually by a deputy chairman. The first promotion requiring CC CPSU sanction (and decree of the Council of Ministers) is to General Maior. Never mind that Nosenko later admitted that he wasn't really a lieutenant colonel; any KGB officer would know this.

16. Nosenko's status:

On the basis of my study of the case and my talks with Nosenko, if he was telling the truth as best he knew it, I do not think that he was a KGB officer, at least not in the Moscow Headquarters. It is believable that from 1956 through 1960 he was closely connected, in some capacity, to the Second Chief Directorate, perhaps in a peripheral office. (His only two confirmed appearances occurred in the Ukraine during that time.)

The questions he answered best were about concentration camp jargon. His tattoos, partly effaced for reasons that made no sense, suggested to me that he had been a prisoner. His performance under American detention confirmed this idea.

It is most likely that Nosenko, sent by the KGB in 1962 to contact CIA, was not originally intended to defect and undergo such thorough questioning. Even after his defection, until he was detained, he evaded any detailed questioning.

17. Presence in Geneva:

There is *no* possibility that a newly appointed chief of section (or other Tourist Department officer) would be assigned to a months-long conference as security officer of the Soviet delegation, unless he had a specific operational mission related to his Moscow responsibilities. Nosenko admitted this, but said that he had wanted the assignments and arranged them through the benevolence of General Gribanov, his protector and head of the Second Chief Directorate. Aside from the fact that he later admitted that his relationship with Gribanov had not been this close, this explanation makes no sense. The Geneva trip appears even stranger when Nosenko claims that he was promoted only a few weeks before the 1962 trip and then promoted again two weeks after returning from it.

18. Security officer functions in Geneva:

Nosenko was unable to supply the sort of personality information on conference delegates which any security officer would have to have from deep study of the files.

Even less believable, Nosenko in Geneva lived far away from the hotel where the delegation was lodged. This is just not possible for a security officer responsible for keeping an eye on the delegates and protecting them. The rule is that he lives at the same place as his delegation.

This is but a small sampling of the hundreds of points of doubt raised by Nosenko in the eyes of a real KGB officer. Many more are contained in my earlier reports.

I am ready to cooperate in any new review of this case. I consider it very important, because I became convinced—on the basis of the Nosenko and related case materials and my other experiences—that the KGB has penetration of the American intelligence services.

(Signed) Peter S. Deriabin, 15 March 1981

Annex: Added Notes from Deriabin

Deriabin was selective in the above report in order to keep it short and simple. Here are a few of hundreds of the details he had noted but left out of the report.

1. Military service:

Deriabin questioned Nosenko about his alleged service in Naval Intelligence and—as a former officer in naval SMERSH (counterintelligence)—came out convinced that Nosenko had not been a naval officer. Aside from his changes of dates, places, and circumstances, aside from his attempts to change the subject whenever pinned down, he showed inexplicable ignorance of things that would be part of the daily life of such an officer. For example:

- He could not explain the most rudimentary naval terms.
- He could not clearly describe either his own title or his duties in the Baltic. He did not know the name of his own commanding officer there, or of the chief of intelligence of the Baltic Fleet.

- He could not begin to explain the requirements for local registration of military officers on leave. Only when he was told that there was such a requirement did he improvise the fact that indeed he did check in "seven or eight days after arrival"—which is wrong and would be punishable.
- He did not know in what regions were located the two bases at which he served. By insisting that Sovetskaya Gavan is in Primorsky Krai he made a mistake no one could make who had served there, and he had not even heard of Kaliningrad Oblast, in which his other base (Baltiysk) was located.

2. KGB procedures

In the main body of his report Deriabin mentioned his surprise at Nosenko's ignorance of several everyday KGB procedures. In fact, his questions uncovered many more, including these:

- Nosenko did not know what was contained in the secrecy statement signed by every KGB officer and in fact mixed it up with the secrecy oath required of informants.
- He was wrong about the hour that work began in KGB offices.
- He was, as noted above, ignorant of the KGB files he would have been dealing with every day of his career.
- He could not name the type of file the KGB maintains on organizations. When separately asked to explain a *liternoye delo* (the file on organizations), he had no idea, nor could he explain, what an agent file *(agenturnoye delo)* was. Though he was personally sent out on an All-Union search for Cherepanov, he did not know what a search file was.
- He did not know the purpose of a personnel document *(lichny listvo po uchet kadrov)*, which would be familiar to any supervisor.
- He did not know how to send a KGB telegram. Deriabin asked him, "Let's try, just go through the steps you'd take." Nosenko answered flatly, "I can't."
- He did not know how to make a file check in the KGB archives or those of its foreign directorate. He did not even know where the First Chief Directorate (foreign operations) archives were, much less how to get access to them to check on the foreign tourists who were supposedly his targets for seven years.

3. KGB and other buildings:

Nosenko did not know:

- What information was included on a KGB building pass.
- Of the existence of Entry No. 9 in Building No. 12, behind the main KGB building, known to *every* KGB officer.
- The location of the Chief Directorate of Militia, which a Second Chief Directorate officer would know like his own workplace.
- He stated that a certain restaurant *(Gastronom)* was across the street when he started work at the KGB (1952 or 1953, depending on the version of his story), and that he used to go there to eat. In fact it was not installed there until 1955 (as he himself quickly admitted when told).

4. KGB organization and personnel:

Nosenko proved similarly (and inexplicably) ignorant:

- He did not know the designation of the Kremlin Guards.
- He did not know what work was done by several prominent KGB institu-

tions with which he would have had dealings, such as the 4th and 5th *Spetsotdely* (Special Departments).

- He did not know the administrative subordination of Internal Troops, the Gulag, or other prominent organizations closely working with the KGB.
- He could not clearly distinguish between the functions of the three Soviet organizations servicing foreigners in Moscow: Burobin, UPDK, and UODK, all of which were directly responsive to the two KGB Second Chief Directorate departments in which he claimed to have held supervisory positions.
- He claimed to have entered the KGB directly into the Second Chief Directorate (internal counterintelligence) in 1952 or 1953—and was unaware that it was called *First* Chief Directorate at that time and was switched to Second only in 1954. He did not even know that any such switch had ever taken place.
- He made significant mistakes when asked about prominent KGB leaders. As chief of the First Chief Directorate during his first two years (ostensibly in the American Department, where dealings with that Directorate would be frequent), he named a person who did not become chief until 1955.

5. Komsomol:

As noted above, Nosenko claimed to have been Komsomol secretary in the Second Chief Directorate. In addition to his ignorance of the purpose of a Komsomol Congress (and one was held during his time) and his uncertainty about the maximum age for Komsomol membership, he could not name either the overall KGB Komsomol secretary or his own predecessor in the job.

6. KGB "serial number" and possible prison experience:

At one point Nosenko referred to his KGB serial number. In fact, KGB officers do not have and never have had serial numbers.

Those who *do* have serial numbers are prisoners, and this is but one of several indications Nosenko gave that he had spent time in prison (as noted in the body of this report). When Deriabin remarked on the skillful and practiced way Nosenko kept track of the days, and made chessmen and a chess board out of blanket wool, Nosenko admitted, "Prison experience was acquired" *(Tyuremnyy opyt otrabatyvala)* but refused to say what he meant.

In the same context, Deriabin disbelieved Nosenko's disingenuous explanation of what had been effaced from his tattoo (just "VMU"—*Voyenno-morskoye uchilishche,* or naval preparatory school). Nosenko could not coherently explain why he had gone to the pain and trouble to get rid of such an innocuous designation. Tattoos are in fact extremely common among common-law prisoners in Soviet prisons, camps, and labor units.

A Myth and Its Making

The conventional wisdom about the Nosenko case within CIA and in the public press stands on an apparently firm foundation of authenticity. Built as it is upon official documents, sworn testimony, and the statements and memoirs of respected CIA insiders and repeated for nearly forty years, it has gained the stature of serious history. But in reality it is a jumble of inventions, distortions, and misstatements. It is fiction—a myth.

It is a myth worth reviewing against the facts I have outlined in this book, as an example of how history can be written by the victors (and survivors) with little regard to reality. The novelist Josephine Tey played on this theme in her book *The Daughter of Time*, comparing what (little) was really known about King Richard III of England as against the image created by the Tudors, whose dynasty defeated his and wrote the history. From his hunched back to his murder of the little princes in the Tower of London, the "facts" in that history may have been fiction. So it is today with James Angleton's paranoia and Yuri Nosenko's noble observance of the truth.

Here is the myth, in the words put on the record by its creators. I have put these words into italics to distinguish them from truth. Subsequently I will describe how it was constructed and maintained.

It was an earlier defector, Anatoly Golitsyn, who caused CIA to doubt the genuineness of Nosenko's defection.

Golitsyn was only "a low-level fantasist," "clinically diagnosed" as paranoid, beset by "outlandish theories and fanatic beliefs" and "mind-boggling pipe dreams." His pointers to spies in the West were frequently inexact and misleading—some said intentionally—and not one of them was important. Golitsyn "never compromised any important Soviet agent."[1]

Nevertheless he somehow managed to cast a spell over the CIA's Counterintelligence Staff chief, James Angleton. "Angleton was astoundingly open to Golit-

syn's nonsensical assertions" because of a "deep personal trauma . . . developed when his close friend Kim Philby [a British intelligence officer] was unmasked as Moscow's most important spy in the West." It caused him "almost paranoid suspicions of every Soviet contact."[2]

Golitsyn had even "managed to convince . . . Angleton that every Soviet defector was probably a KGB double agent"—to the point that Angleton "actually thought that CIA could not have a bona fide Soviet operation." Angleton and Golitsyn even "convinced the agency that Colonel Penkovsky, probably the most important spy the West ever recruited in the Soviet Union, was just another KGB plant."[3]

Angleton and his followers "had turned away honest people who were offering to become spies for CIA" and thus had "paralyzed" CIA's anti-Soviet operations. They turned away "scores" of them.

Golitsyn entertained the "fantastic idea" that the KGB would send out someone to misdirect Western investigations of his pointers to KGB spies in the West. Angleton jumped to the conclusion that Nosenko must be the KGB plant that Golitsyn had foretold.[4]

Angleton's mind was "befuddled" with intricate theories, partly stemming from Golitsyn, of a "monster plot," "a massive deception program" against the West in which the KGB, endowed with vast resources, "was able to deceive the West . . . because it had penetrations at high levels . . . within the intelligence services of these countries, including [CIA]." Angleton had spun these crazy ideas from "a lot of historical research" into long-ago KGB operations that had no current relevance. "The so-called plot was sheer nonsense."[5]

Svengali-like, Angleton persuaded the officers handling Nosenko (in CIA's Soviet operations division) that their newfound source was a phony. They were receptive to his notions because they themselves had noticed some oddities in Nosenko's account of his life and, more importantly, what seemed to them a suspicious degree of overlap between Nosenko's reporting and Golitsyn's. (They failed to see the obvious explanation for this coincidence, i.e., that Golitsyn had spent some time in Nosenko's directorate.) Later they even fretted about Nosenko's exaggeration of his KGB rank, though this was obviously nothing more than a self-serving boast, unrelated to the question of his bona fides.

By the time Nosenko came west again in early 1964 his CIA controllers had already prejudged him a fake and were unwilling to take his reports at face value. This became particularly important because Nosenko was now bringing news about Lee Harvey Oswald, who only weeks earlier had assassinated President John F. Kennedy. He said he'd personally participated in Oswald's affairs in the Soviet Union and had read the KGB's only file, and it showed it had had little interest in and no contact with Oswald. Piling this on top of their earlier suspicions, CIA fundamentalists became convinced that the KGB had sent Nosenko out to pass this information.

"It was only Nosenko's reports on Lee Harvey Oswald that brought suspicion upon him." Nosenko's involvement in Oswald's case "determined his fate" and caused CIA's "scandalous handling of him." Had Nosenko brought different news about Oswald, Nosenko "would probably have been spared the most miserable years of his life."[6]

These CIA paranoids, suffering from "sick think," also put their jaundiced eye on the fact that Nosenko—contrary to what he'd said earlier—now wanted to stay in the West, abandoning his family. This and his readiness to testify before the Warren Commission investigating the president's assassination made these fundamentalists certain that Nosenko was a plant.

But because Washington ordained it, they had to accept Nosenko's defection and fly him to the United States.

There, from behind the scenes, the earlier defector Golitsyn "was masterminding the examinations [of Nosenko] in many ways." "Angleton showed Golitsyn all the CIA's reports of Nosenko's debriefing, from which [Golitsyn] concocted a wide range of accusations to challenge Nosenko's reliability. This achieved its purpose so completely that the agency turned on its defector [Nosenko]." "Angleton led [others] to the light: Golitsyn infallible, Nosenko phony" and Golitsyn's theories became "the definitive view." "For six years whatever Yuri [Nosenko] said was submitted for final judgment by" Golitsyn.[7]

These "anti-Nosenko plot adherents . . . prejudged Nosenko's bona fides before they ever debriefed him." Their "treatment of Nosenko was never . . . devoted to learning what . . . Nosenko said. What they really wanted was only to break him." They made a "convoluted effort to make Nosenko the living incarnation of [their] theory." They set out to "prepare a case against Nosenko . . . not to get information but to pin on [him] the label of a KGB agent sent to deceive us."[8]

To make their case, these sick-thinking CIA fundamentalists subjected Nosenko to a hostile interrogation. Of course—because he was innocent—Nosenko failed to confirm their theories. So they put him in a "torture vault" or "dungeon" for years, and drugged him.

There were wiser and cooler heads in CIA who opposed this mistreatment of an honest defector, so an "internal warfare" ensued that "split the CIA" for several years until CIA director Richard Helms's "intervention brought it to an end" and common sense and professionalism finally prevailed. The "fundamentalists" were removed and more reasonable CIA officers set out to re-question Nosenko and re-examine the case against him. They found logical explanations for "all" the apparent discrepancies in Nosenko's stories, particularly "the two most controversial ones" involving the recall telegram and his KGB rank. They also found that the "fundamentalists" had "deliberately suppressed" solid leads from Nosenko.

In sum, the Nosenko "case" boils down to a simple matter of incompetent CIA handling. "Even the most cursory examination would have demonstrated Nosenko's innocence."[9]

Happily, after years of confusion, CIA finally arrived at the truth: the whole case against Nosenko had been "sheer nonsense."[10]

In early October 1968, after months spent reviewing the case and consulting with Nosenko, CIA security officer Bruce Solie submitted a long report that wiped out all doubts about Nosenko. Within hours, evidently without taking the time to assess the validity of the report, CIA made its "final decision." Its deputy director ruled "that Nosenko was a legitimate defector. . . . [He] has not knowingly and willfully withheld information from us and there is no conflict between what we have learned from him and what we have learned from other defectors or informants that would cast any doubts on his bona fides."[11]

This decision was validated by yet another CIA review of the Nosenko case in 1976. Just how firmly it supported Nosenko's bona fides was demonstrated two years later when the CIA director sent the leader of that review process to testify for him before Congress in September 1978. As described above, the director's spokesman (John L. Hart) testified under oath to Nosenko's complete honesty and the incompetence and failure of those who distrusted him.[12]

CIA's adamant state of denial was baldly expressed by one of its top counterintelligence officials. He declared flatly that if Nosenko ever told fibs, they *were not [spoken] at the behest of the KGB*" but only "to inflate his personal prestige, . . . self-serving braggadocio . . . [to make himself] more important, more decent, perhaps more like what his father would have wished him to be."[13]

To these findings a director of Central Intelligence, Stansfield Turner, gave his top-level authority. He proclaimed to CIA personnel in writing that "it was eventually determined that [Nosenko] had defected of his own free will, had not sought to deceive us and had indeed supplied very valuable intelligence information to the U.S. Government. The hypothesis which had led to the original . . . [conclusion that Mr. Nosenko had defected under KGB orders] was found to have been based on inadequate evidence." In his memoirs, moreover, Turner described those who had distrusted Nosenko as "a group of Agency paranoids."[14]

How did this happen? How did truth get buried and fiction become doctrine?

The first, essential step for anyone anxious to believe in Nosenko and to clear him of suspicions was to *suppress the facts of the case.*

Not one of Nosenko's defenders addressed the questions raised by, for example, Nosenko's association with Guk and Kislov in Geneva, or the clash between Nosenko's (authoritative) account and the real circumstances of Kovshuk's trip to Washington, or the connections of Nosenko's stories with the KGB's uncovering of CIA's great spies Pyotr Popov and Oleg Penkovsky. In presenting a "true" version of Nosenko's life and career they failed to mention that it was a sixth or seventh version (and not the last).

Ignoring the inconvenient aspects, the mythmakers fabricated a wholly new picture. They did this by 1) misrepresenting Nosenko the man and his truthfulness, 2) grossly exaggerating the value of his reporting, 3) building a straw man of (false) reasons for suspecting him, then knocking the straw man down rather than addressing the real reasons, 4) vilifying CIA colleagues who suspected Nosenko, 5) diverting attention from the real issues, and 6) ridiculing the very idea of Soviet deception.

1. Misrepresenting Nosenko's truthfulness:

Nosenko's defenders abandoned objectivity, consistency, and truth in extolling his personal qualities. One wrote of the "fundamental nobility" of his nature while another testified under oath that "anything that [Nosenko] has said has been said in good faith." Nosenko "neither embroidered nor distorted" and "had no knack for lying or dissembling." Indeed it had been his very honesty that had caused his temporary downfall at the hands of CIA. There is "no reason to think that [Nosenko] has ever told an untruth," except due to forgetfulness, ignorance, or drunken exaggeration. Any little white lies, as noted above, were mere braggadocio. Though Nosenko's defender Hart found him "hard to believe" on the subject of Oswald, he falsely called that a one-time aberration. Though he had studied the file, he could not remember anything substantive that Nosenko said that had been proven to be incorrect.[15]

In fact, Nosenko's sworn testimony on Lee Harvey Oswald was so evasive and contradictory that the congressional committee, having questioned him at length, recognized and officially declared that Nosenko was lying. Ten years afterward his defenders tried to wipe that out, evidently relying on the ignorance or forgetfulness of readers. No, Hart wrote, Nosenko's testimony on Oswald was not at all incredible. On the contrary, Nosenko "was telling the truth about his involvement in Oswald's case."[16]

Had Nosenko's reporting on Oswald been the only aberration in an otherwise normal performance, as the CIA spokesman testified that it was, it might indeed have been shrugged off. But CIA officers who interviewed Nosenko encountered the same sorts of evasion, contradiction, and excuses from Nosenko whenever he was pinned down on practically any subject—just as the House Select Committee on Assassinations did on his Oswald story. This included his KGB career and activities, his travels and contacts, how he had learned what he told us, and even his private life.

Nosenko himself admitted that he had lied repeatedly about KGB activities and about the career that gave him authority to tell of them. In a written statement dated 23 April 1966 he said he had simply been unable to tell the truth throughout 1964 and 1965. But he was never willing to tell which of his statements were lies, except his KGB rank and certain of his claims to have recruited foreigners and the commendation these acts had earned him. This confession in no way inhibited his continued lying. He proceeded to tell tales no more believable than the earlier ones. Moreover, several witnesses from Moscow since the Cold War have belied Nosenko's KGB career *and* his claimed knowledge of Oswald.

2. Misstating the value of Nosenko's reporting:

Nosenko, said one of his defenders, was "the most valuable defector from the KGB yet to come over to the West." He provided a "solid layer of counter-intelligence gold." Another delivered, under oath, the breathtaking misstatement that Nosenko provided "quantitatively and qualitatively" far greater information than Golitsyn did.[17]

Nosenko's defenders cite his uncovering of John Vassall, the British Admiralty employee, as a great contribution although they knew that Golitsyn had previously exposed Vassall. To explain that away, they went further in inventiveness: the British weren't really on Vassall's track at all, they said. *Had it not been for Nosenko's information the British might have mistaken Golitsyn's lead to Vassall for a totally different Admiralty source, the Houghton-Gee-Lonsdale network earlier uncovered by Goleniewski.*[18] In fact, no such confusion was even remotely possible.

They pumped up Sergeant "Andrey," Nosenko's most important lead in 1962, to unrecognizable proportions. So little access to secrets did the sergeant really have that the KGB had dropped contact with him even before he retired from the army and American authorities found that he could not have betrayed secrets and saw no reason to prosecute him. But Nosenko's cleansers magically transformed this KGB reject into *a "code clerk" who "had supplied the Soviets with top secret U.S. military codes," permitting the KGB to break "the most sensitive U.S. communications. [Even worse:] 'Andrey' had later transferred to the super-sensitive communications agency NSA that would give him even greater access to cipher information."*[19]

In fact, Nosenko uncovered nothing that truly harmed the Soviet regime. He did not uncover a single KGB asset that the KGB could not have sacrificed—not one that had current access to NATO governmental secrets, was actively cooperating at the time, and had previously been unsuspected by Western counter-intelligence agencies.

3. Distorting the reasons Nosenko fell under suspicion:

Nosenko's CIA defenders repeated publicly that their CIA predecessors had wrongly "prejudged" him even before debriefing him and without "even the most cursory examination," which would have demonstrated Nosenko's innocence. Essentially, they "fabricated a case" to incriminate Nosenko.[20]

They only suspected Nosenko because of paranoid theorizing by the earlier defector Anatoly Golitsyn. Having adopted Golitsyn's theories, Nosenko's handlers didn't even try to find out what Nosenko had to say but simply set out to break him.[21]

This aspect of the myth required its creators to invent a role for Golitsyn in the Nosenko investigation. One of the mythmakers testified under oath that Golitsyn had "a substantial influence on the case" and "was masterminding the examinations [of Nosenko] in many ways. It is with this in mind that we have to approach everything that happened." Golitsyn was "made part of [the anti-Nosenko] investigating team," Golitsyn had current access to the debriefing of Nosenko, and "for six years whatever Yuri [Nosenko] said was submitted for final judgment by" Golitsyn.[22]

Pure invention. No member of the "investigating team" (which was in SB Division) ever saw Golitsyn or asked or got information or comment from him. He was being handled by the CI Staff and even they did not give him details of the case before 1967, aside from the fact of Nosenko's defection and his claimed biography. This was long after the Soviet Bloc Division's interrogation and conclusions. Even then Golitsyn declined to comment because he had not read the file. How, then, could he have ever exercised even an influence, much less a "final judgment"?

It was not until 1968 that Golitsyn reviewed transcripts of meetings. Then he stated unequivocally that Nosenko was a plant.

Because there is no substance to the myth's claim that Golitsyn participated or influenced anything, we need not dwell here on the mythmakers' denigration of Golitsyn—as a paranoid with "mind-boggling pipe dreams" and "outlandish theories." However, it is worth noting their own truly mind-boggling falsehood, that Golitsyn "never compromised any important Soviet agent."[23]

The mythmakers never revealed details of how Nosenko's reports overlapped those of Golitsyn. They dismissed the question by claiming Golitsyn learned a few facts from his brief orientation period in Nosenko's directorate, all of which Nosenko naturally knew better. This was a subterfuge: in reality, the Golitsyn tips that Nosenko diverted had nothing to do with Golitsyn's "orientation period" but were from his service in Finland and his handling of reports from spies within NATO governments.

The mythmakers reached out even further to misrepresent why Nosenko fell under suspicion.

- Drunkenness: One, under oath, testified that CIA came to suspect Nosenko because he had made some drunken misstatements. Yet the only time in all those years that Nosenko might have been drunk while reporting anything whatsoever to CIA was during one meeting in 1962, and even then he showed no sign of being under the influence.
- Language problems: In sworn testimony the representative of CIA's director asserted that language difficulties in Geneva caused "crucial misunderstandings." Yet he knew that a native Russian speaker had been present at all but the first meeting and even during that meeting the only misunderstandings involved one school Nosenko claimed to have attended and one

detail about his father. The FBI had no problem debriefing Nosenko in English.[24]

- Faulty transcripts: CIA's representative testified that "discrepancies" in the transcriptions of the recordings of the 1962 meetings were "very important in the history of this case because [they] gave rise to charges within the Agency that Nosenko was not what he purported to be."[25] But the witness, who had studied the case, must have known that no discrepancies ever gave rise to any such charge. Moreover, any errors in the transcripts were early detected and corrected by Peter Deriabin.

4. Vilifying those who suspected Nosenko:

Why, asked a congressman in 1978, would CIA director Stansfield Turner let his representative "create smashing anti-CIA headlines" by publicly attacking his own former colleagues?

The answer was that, lacking substantive arguments, CIA's spokesmen fell back on ad hominem attacks on Nosenko's detractors.

In sworn testimony the director's personal envoy publicly accused his former colleagues of fabricating a case, torturing, misusing Agency techniques, and contemplating murder. He rated their performance as "zero," "miserable," and "abominable." They were "naive," "utterly insensitive," "extremist," prone to "fanatic theories," blindly biased, "paranoid," and of "muddled mind."[26] Lumped into a never-defined category of "fundamentalists," they were derided as "zealots" and "true believers." A CIA director ticked off Nosenko's early handlers—whom he had never met—as "a group of Agency paranoids."[27]

So far gone in paranoia was this "group" that they thought "CIA could not have a bona fide Soviet operation" and turned away honest people who were offering to become spies for CIA. Nosenko's defenders never cited a single example because in fact CIA had never turned down any volunteer from a Soviet bloc government who met normal security criteria. It even accepted ones it *knew* to be provocateurs, like the Soviet lieutenant of the "Sasha and Olga" case I mention in Chapter 4, simply to get their stories.

John Hart, a former division chief in CIA, was under oath when he told Congress that the two top officers of the Soviet Division (David Murphy, its chief, and me, its deputy chief) "had been discredited" for their work on the Nosenko case and that this had "caused them to be transferred out . . . to foreign assignments."[28] But as the Headquarters supervisor of both these posts abroad, Hart knew that we had both opted for those challenging and prestigious assignments long before any "discrediting" began.

Never did Nosenko's defenders mention any positive results of the hostile interrogation. Indeed, the CIA director's spokesman testified that it had "failed miserably." In fact, it was by confronting Nosenko under circumstances he could not evade and where he could get no outside coaching that CIA established firmly that Nosenko was a KGB plant and documented some of the KGB's purposes in planting him.

5. Diverting attention from the underlying issue:

Nosenko's defenders presented his case as essentially "a human phenomenon" and that the "human factors involved have a direct bearing on some of the contradictions which have appeared in the case." As one put it, any questions of Nosenko's truthfulness are "poignantly overshadowed by Nosenko's personal tragedy, arising from CIA's handling of his defection." "We may not allow our-selves to forget," he wrote, "that this story deals with a living person."[29]

The central issue of the case, they were implying, was CIA's mistreatment of Nosenko. They expressed outrage that "duplicity" had been practiced against Nosenko and that the polygraph machine had been used more as an instrument of interrogation than as a fair test of Nosenko's truth. They misrepresented the reason Nosenko was incarcerated. They raised a horrifying vision of his being thrown into a "torture vault," as one put it, or a "dungeon," in another's words. By 1989 the former CIA senior officer John Hart had so lost touch with the truth that he asserted in writing that the interrogators had deprived Nosenko of sensory stimuli for more than three years, and another told an investigative reporter that Nosenko had been starving and close to death.[30] They must have been aware that Nosenko had regular (as I remember, weekly) visits by a doctor to ascertain his health and the adequacy of his diet. He was never ill, much less "close to death."

They were contradicting the documented record. CIA director Richard Helms and Nosenko's former handlers testified under oath that Nosenko had been in-carcerated only to prevent him from evading questions about contradictions and anomalies in his stories. (These were the ones that touched upon Oswald, the possible breaking of American ciphers, and penetration of American Intelli-gence.) We were preventing what happened in 1985, when the later defector Vitaly Yurchenko walked out and back to the KGB.

Whereas this case had damning interconnections with other cases like that of Kulak/"Fedora," Nosenko's defenders avoided this subject. One mentioned the cases of Cherepanov and Loginov only to imply that they, like Nosenko, were innocent individuals whom CIA had stupidly misunderstood.[31]

6. Ridiculing the "theory" of Soviet deception:

CIA spokesmen conveyed the idea that Soviet deception was a figment of paranoia. Golitsyn, said one, "was given to building up big, fantastic plots, and he eventually built up a plot . . . which was centered around the idea that the KGB had vast resources which it was using to deceive . . . Western governments. This plot was able to deceive the West . . . because [the KGB] had penetrations at high levels . . . within the intelligence services of these countries, including our own." They displayed contempt for those who believed in such a crazy idea as "a plot against the West," an idea that stemmed only from "historical research." "I don't happen to be able to share this kind of thing," said one. "The so-called plot was sheer nonsense."[32] Thus did CIA's official spokesman dismiss as mad fantasy the documented history of *sixty years* of such KGB "plots" of the sort described in Chapters 10, 11, and 12 of this book.

A top CIA counterintelligence officer attacked this "historical research" from a different angle. He admitted that Soviet deception operations had indeed taken place—but by Nosenko's time they were irrelevant. The classic prewar deception operation "Trust," he wrote, had existed "in a 'totally different KGB and a totally different world." He pointed out that in those distant days [the KGB] had had to deal with large-scale resistance from elements of the population who got support from emigration groups abroad. But both the resistance and the groups had since dwindled away—and with them, the need for this sort of operation.[33]

This denial became CIA doctrine—but not the KGB's. As set out explicitly in the KGB's in-house secret history of 1977, there was an unbroken continuum from "Trust" to the present day. The KGB was teaching today's officers that this "aggressive counterintelligence" was the *best* way to succeed in counterintelligence work.

The myth thus created was accepted not only by investigative reporters who could not know the truth but also by reputable historians—and even CIA personnel.

A writer in the 1990s, after talking to Agency insiders, could say with no fear of being contradicted, "Although *[Nosenko] was in fact a genuine defector,* Angleton became convinced that he was a fake."[34] A BBC interviewer asked a reputable British historian about the doubts that had circulated concerning Nosenko's bona fides. The historian answered confidently that there had never been genuine doubts but only paranoid views that had been fully discredited. Later this same historian wrote that CIA's suspicions of Nosenko were a "horrendous misjudgment" and its investigation "appallingly mishandled."[35]

Another prestigious historian in 1994 described "Lieutenant Colonel" Nosenko as "the highest-ranking officer of the KGB to fall into CIA hands." Though CIA had kept Nosenko "in sub-human conditions for five years, his evidence is now regarded as far more reliable than all that Angleton's protégé Golitsyn ever provided."[36]

The myth became doctrine within CIA itself. So deeply rooted did this fiction become that even later chiefs of the Soviet operations division adopted it and passed it on with their special authority. Two successive chiefs had so little knowledge of the Nosenko case that they propagated the myth that *"Angleton . . . persuaded others at the CIA that [Nosenko] had been sent by Moscow to tie them in knots about Oswald and dozens of other sensitive cases. He was encouraged in his paranoia by an earlier KGB defector, Anatoly Golitsyn, who had told Angleton that every defector after him would be a double agent. . . . Angleton had managed to co-opt key officials in the Soviet Division, convincing them that virtually all of the spies they were running were double agents sent against them by the KGB. . . . Those who . . . challenged the prevailing paranoia were in danger of coming under suspicion of being Soviet agents themselves. . . . The end result of these mind games was virtual paralysis in the CIA's operations against the Soviet Union. . . . CIA officers largely stopped trying to target Soviets [and] the Soviet Division had been turning away dozens of 'volunteers,' Soviets and Eastern Europeans [. . . offering] to work for the United States."*[37] As stated in Chapter 20, this was unfounded nonsense, and not a single Soviet volunteer was turned away.

Other CIA officers, without access to the files, typically knew only what they had been taught. One wrote, "The KGB defector Yuri Nosenko was badly and illegally mistreated . . . because James Angleton and the CIA were mesmerized by the paranoid ravings of a previous defector, Anatoly Golitsyn."[38]

Wrote another CIA veteran a generation afterward, "When Nosenko offered a version of Lee Harvey Oswald and the Kennedy assassination that didn't fit the agency's corporate view, he was sent to solitary confinement . . . for three years."[39]

With historians accepting it and CIA insiders reciting it, and with its high-level sponsorship, the myth has prevailed. Wishful thinking triumphed.

Self-deception—Bane of Counterintelligence

The most amazing part of the story of Arthur Orton, the imposter better known as "the Tichborne claimant," is that he nearly prevailed.

The butcher's apprentice Orton (if this was really who he was—he never admitted it) sailed from Australia to pose as the long-missing heir to the fortune and title of the Tichborne family in Victorian England. He was undeterred by his ignorance; he later proved unable to name a single one of the real heir's boyhood friends or schoolteachers. Also, he could not say what was written in a letter that the heir had left behind with his best friend and could not speak French although the heir had spent his boyhood in Paris. Whereas the heir was well educated, the claimant could not spell or write grammatically; worse, he was older, fatter, and looked quite different.

To compensate for all that, Orton had going for him the con man's equipment: a confident and persuasive air, quick thinking, skill in playing back information given to him, and—most important of all—the natural gullibility of others.

He managed to persuade the heir's own mother that he was her son and got more than eighty witnesses from the heir's army service, school, and other circles to certify that they recognized him. His claim caught the public's imagination, won organized support, and proved so difficult to judge that Orton's trial—which finally condemned him—spanned a total of 827 days and stands in the *Guinness Book of Records* as the longest in British history.[1]

Is this really so amazing? Frauds have succeeded with even less foundation. A late-eighteenth-century forger managed to convince renowned scholars that his hastily turned out letters and manuscripts were really written by Shakespeare despite errors and anachronisms that to one expert revealed "forgery palpable to the meanest capacity." Inspired by a drawing of the ancient British King Vortigern that hung prominently in his father's study, William Henry Ireland proceeded to write "Shakespeare's" manuscript of a play by that name. When his father told visitors the stunning and quite unbelievable news that this play had been unearthed, they simply considered it an "enchanting coincidence [that] Ireland should so long have owned a drawing on the same subject."[2]

"How willingly," the forger recognized, "people will blind themselves on any point interesting to their feelings. Once a false idea becomes fixed in a person's mind, he will twist facts or probability to accommodate it rather than question it."[3]

Among such con men and imposters feeding at the trough of human credulity are more dangerous predators: traitors and provocateurs, stealing not just money but the safety of nations. Not surprisingly, governments maintain organizations of specialists to detect and thwart them. What is surprising is that gullibility and self-deception flourish among these professional skeptics almost as extravagantly as along the patent medicine trail.

Looking back at the long string of successful Soviet bloc provocations from the "Trust" operation of the 1920s, we might suppose that naïve Westerners are the natural dupes of ruthless Eastern guile. Nothing of the sort: wily Russian conspirators too (as we shall see) have been undone by almost transparent dupery. Gullibility respects no frontiers or organizational fences; while the British in World War Two were cunningly manipulating Nazi agents in England in the famous "Double Cross" operations, other British were at the same time being duped on the continent by the Nazi counterespionage services.

The colorful and never-ending history of fraud continues to unfold in our daily newspapers with stories of innocent oldsters being gulled—and professional intelligence services as well. A defecting Cuban intelligence officer startled CIA in the late 1980s by revealing that every CIA spy in Cuba was working under the control of the Soviet-trained Cuban counterintelligence service. Defectors during the Prague Spring of 1968 gave CIA the unwelcome news that Czechoslovak officials the CIA thought had been successfully recruited by one of its fast-rising operatives in Asia had actually been pushed into CIA's overeager and underskeptical nets by Czech-Soviet controllers.

Clearly, this tendency to deceive ourselves deserves the attention of any student of counterintelligence.

We cannot and need not try to cover the whole subject of dupes and duplicity. That would lead us far back in history, far out in geography, and deep down into abstruse realms of psychology and epistemology. But we can usefully recall to mind some famous disasters and the human foibles that made them possible. We cannot help wondering whether the CIA handlers of those Cuban and Czech double agents—and others we will meet here—might have averted trouble for themselves and their organizations had they remembered their adversaries' penchant for deception and their own penchant for self-deception.

Among the plotters trying to overthrow the tsarist regime in Russia, none were more active than the Socialist Revolutionaries, and among these SRs none were more dangerously exposed than the members of their terrorist wing, the so-called combat organization. They lived with nerves stretched and sensitive to any unusual occurrence because they knew that the Okhrana, the Tsarist political police, was trying to insert agents provocateurs into their ranks.

How strange it seems, then, that they blinded themselves to the most threatening evidence. When their plans went astray and their members fell into police traps, they failed again and again to draw the seemingly inescapable conclusion. They even rejected precise warning that came to them from within the Okhrana itself.

In early 1903 a friendly Okhrana agent slipped the word to Khristianinov, a member of the combat organization, that the Okhrana would refrain from raiding the organization's secret weapons assembly shop "because it has an agent there already." Now, only a handful of the members even knew of the existence of that shop, so the finger pointed at the man who had set it up—their leader, Yevno Azev. But after Khristianinov had ineptly presented the facts and Azev, on the contrary, had defended himself lucidly and convincingly, an investigating group concluded that all was well and that Azev (who had, after all, organized the assassination of the tsarist Interior Minister Plehve) stood above suspicion.

Three years later came an anonymous letter from within the Okhrana, giving the names of two members of the combat organization who were police spies: "T., an ex-convict, and the engineer Azev who recently arrived from abroad." The SRs took this warning seriously enough; they immediately recognized "T" as Tatarov and checked, interrogated, and verified the accusation, and killed him. But with half the Okhrana message proven correct—excluding the ever-present menace of false denunciations—the SRs still could not bring themselves to accept the other half. Not even when, after another year, they got more news from inside the Okhrana. Their friend, the journalist and historian Vladimir Burtsev, confirmed that there was a traitor high in the SR leadership and even gave his police pseudonym, "Raskin." Despite the earlier warning, and despite the growing signs of betrayal from within, the SRs chose to treat Burtsev as "a ridiculous and harmful maniac." They accused him of trying to disrupt the revolutionary movement by discrediting Azev, its most formidable terrorist, and they warned him to desist. Lacking legal proof, Burtsev stood alone and helpless.

Again and again the SR combat organization's missions failed, and its members were arrested, but still the leaders rejected Burtsev's pleading as "idle chatter," the more so because the accused Azev was at that moment planning an assassination attempt against the tsar himself.

Finally Burtsev got the proof he needed. In Germany he met the retired, discredited Okhrana chief Lopukhin and, while telling him something that Lopukhin had not known, that Azev had masterminded Plehve's assassination—tried out on him the pseudonym "Raskin." In that dramatic moment in a train compartment Lopukhin answered, "I know nobody by the name of Raskin but I have met the engineer Yevno Azev several times."

Now Burtsev forced the SR party leadership to react by printing an open letter to it, accusing Azev. So how did they react? They sought to silence Burtsev by putting him on trial for libeling Azev. The judges were cold and hostile until he finally revealed Lopukhin's words, and even then one of them called it "slander." Finally they began the investigation of Azev that confirmed his guilt and in January 1909 precipitated his flight from the country. But this happened six years after the necessary evidence had been at hand, too late to restore the will and cohesion of the shattered combat organization.[4]

Lenin could also be deceived, despite the rosy view expressed by his wife and closest associate Krupskaya: "Of our entire group Vladimir Ilyich [Lenin] was the best prepared in the field of conspiracy; he knew his way about and was able to dupe spies superbly."

In 1912 this paragon of wariness promoted Roman Malinovsky to membership in the Bolsheviks' first Central Committee and made him his deputy inside Russia and the leading Bolshevik of the Social Democrat (SD) representation in the tsarist parliament (Fourth Duma). When Lenin's close collaborators Bukharin and Troyanovsky gave him solid reasons to suspect that Malinovsky was a tsarist police provocateur, Lenin angrily rejected the charges and threatened that if Bukharin joined this "dark campaign of slander" Lenin would publicly brand him a traitor. (Bukharin desisted.)

At the Duma Malinovsky gave the SDs' first major speech of the parliamentary session. Though its main purpose was to present two major platform items, Malinovsky (on Okhrana instructions) omitted precisely those two items. He explained afterward that he had been nervous in his maiden speech and had lost his place. When the SD newspapers then printed the passage that Malinovsky had omitted, the police confiscated the whole issue. Sill Malinovsky was able to brush suspicions aside. He even survived a later, more blatant episode: in February 1914 a new Okhrana chief, appalled at the potential scandal of running an opposition parliamentary deputy as a spy, forced Malinovsky to resign his Duma post without any logical excuse. To many this meant that Malinovsky must be a traitor. But not to Lenin.

By June of that year the Menshevik leaders Martov and Dan were "convinced beyond any doubt" that Malinovsky was a traitor and that the Okhrana controlled the internal Bolshevik organization around the newspaper *Pravda,* which Malinovsky had helped set up (with capital provided by another tsarist provocateur). But Martov recognized that "whether we shall succeed in proving it is another question, because we are handcuffed by our own people." How right he was; Lenin again refused to investigate these "dark rumors" and again turned on the accusers: "We do not regard them as honest citizens." As late as 1916 he was still speaking of the "dirty fabrications" against Malinovsky. He said that the "party leadership" had reached "the unqualified and unshakable conviction that . . . the legend of his being an agent provocateur was invented by conscious calumniators." Still later he called the charges "absolutely absurd."[5]

When the Okhrana files were opened after the tsar's fall in February 1917, Malinovsky was revealed, of course, to have been a provocateur from the outset. After the Bolshevik coup d'état, Lenin had him shot.

Leon Trotsky, old conspirator and co-founder of the Bolshevik state, was no more astute than Lenin in this way.

Outmaneuvered by Stalin, exiled and driven from one country to another, some of his helpers killed, Trotsky could not fail to be wary—but he proved unable to read the warnings he was getting. His faithful Dutch follower Sneevliet gave him good reason to believe that Mark Zborowski, the closest associate of Trotsky's son Leon Sedov in the Paris-based International Secretariat of the movement, was an NKVD (early designation of the KGB) provocateur. Trotsky, instead of ridding himself of Zborowski, called for a tribunal to condemn Sneevliet for sowing discord. It must have jolted him two years later, when his son died mysteriously in a Paris hospital; few beside Zborowski had even known Sedov's whereabouts. (Indeed, as was later learned, the KGB, with Zborowski's help, had found and murdered Sedov.)

Two years later, an anonymous source from inside the NKVD (identifying himself after his defection as Aleksandr Orlov, a senior official) sent a message telling Trotsky that Zborowski was an NKVD agent. Trotsky derisively rejected the warning as an NKVD effort to spread suspicion in his organization.

Orlov's message also told Trotsky that Stalin was trying to have him killed. Confirmation, if any was needed, came in the spring of 1940 when a team of assassins raided Trotsky's house in Mexico and sprayed seventy-five bullets into his bedroom, miraculously missing him and his wife. As a result, every morning thereafter Trotsky is said to have exulted, "Another lucky day; we are still alive."

All this was still not enough to alert him to the suspicious signs that his future assassin was scattering about. Ramon Mercader had insinuated himself from nowhere, introduced by his Trotskyite girlfriend, into Trotsky's guarded household. He was known to be using a false passport and the life story he gave, even his identity documents, could not withstand the most superficial check. And his character changed, too; once inside Trotsky's circle this formerly apolitical and ignorant drifter became so sharp and involved that Trotsky thought he might become a useful member of the movement.

Two days before the killing, in an almost blatant rehearsal, Mercader oddly kept his hat on while in Trotsky's study and, despite the warm weather, kept his coat (which would later hide the murder weapon) under his arm while he sat impolitely close by Trotsky's side rather than apart in a chair. This irritated rather than alarmed Trotsky, who complained to his wife that night, "I don't like the man." She remarked, moreover, that "he never wears a hat." When Mercader appeared at the house two days later, he appeared to Mrs. Trotsky strangely pale and troubled. But he was allowed in, again with his hat and coat, this time hiding the fatal ice axe.[6]

The success of the much-publicized Soviet deception operation called the "Trust" has been attributed to the cunning of its perpetrators in the KGB (then called OGPU), but it depended as much upon the gullibility of its victims.

These were people who, more than others, should have been wary. Military exiles driven from Russia after long civil war and terror, they knew the ruthless hand of the OGPU and knew it would reach out and try to neutralize them in their places of refuge abroad. Their clubs in Paris and Germany and their paramilitary units in Yugoslavia should be bastions of disenchantment, sprouting antennas sensitive to the slightest hostile move or beguilement from Soviet Russia, and ready to react with skepticism and outrage.

Nothing of the sort. They responded with simple joy when, hardly a year after their military defeat, a messenger brought news of a resistance to Bolshevik rule growing secretly in the form of a "Monarchist Organization of Central Russia" (MOCR), with secret sympathizers inside the OGPU and other Soviet agencies. They admired the uncanny ability of these new "friends" to move into and out of the tightly policed country, to procure false identities backed by authentic Soviet documentation, and even to spring co-conspirators from jail. When the MOCR set up "windows" for couriers to pass through the borders of Poland, Finland, or Estonia, the emigrés spent less time asking how were the wires cut or the guards bribed than in exulting over these openings to the homeland. Even in Paris their "secret" plots were the talk of the cafes, but they deluded themselves that unbeknownst to the OGPU whole roomfuls of conspirators could safely meet in Moscow and Petrograd.

Western intelligence services were sucked in, too. Neglecting Machiavelli's warning about emigrés, they saw this "resistance organization" not as a trap but as an opportunity to get information from the forbidden land.[7] After a while some recognized Trust's intelligence as spurious, and others drew back after experienced operatives Sidney Reilly and pre-Revolutionary SR terrorist Boris Savinkov (Azev's onetime deputy) had gone to their doom in Soviet Russia through MOCR "windows." But even these deceived themselves long enough to permit the

OGPU to close out the hoax at a time of its own choosing and to use this closure to open yet another trap—into which the outsiders again leaped.

This and similar KGB provocations neutralized resistance to Bolshevik rule in its early years. But even after they were exposed, their victims' embarrassment was still not intense enough to cure gullibility. The Poles, for example, had been among the first to recognize that the Trust's information was useless and deceptive, but hardly twenty years later some of these same individuals, by then in emigration themselves, allowed themselves to be duped by a carbon copy of the Trust. The same Soviet manipulators organized a new "resistance" to Soviet rule, this time in Poland with Polish communist helpers, in an organization called "WiN" (Polish initials for "Freedom and Independence"). It accomplished its Soviet aims for five years but then the Soviets chose to close it down at the end of 1952 in order to use its closure, as they had that of Trust, as part of another Soviet operation.[8]

The British in World War Two used captured spies as double agents to mislead the Germans concerning the time and place of the Allies' 1944 invasion of Europe—and were playing a risky game. A single mistake might be enough to alert the German handlers and expose what the British were hiding: the real invasion plans.

In fact, the British controllers of the double agents did make some slips, and mishaps did occur. But they were protected by the adversaries' gullibility. If the German handlers noticed (wrote one of the British officers involved), they managed to find "far more credible explanations of what had occurred than the true explanation that the agent was a double cross. . . . It was far more reasonable to suppose that he had been misled by the British than that he had over a period of years tricked and deceived his German paymaster. . . . It was extremely, almost fantastically difficult to 'blow' a well-established agent."[9]

Not only the Germans were gullible. While the British were deceiving them, they were deceiving the British. Whole networks of Allied agents dedicated to sabotage in occupied Europe were taken under German control. The German handling of these double agents was flawed—more than one managed to radio to London the prearranged signal that he had fallen under German control—but like the Germans, the British "found more credible explanation for what had occurred than the true explanation that the agent was a double cross." So at the end, as Allied armies advanced through Europe, the last German-controlled message from the ostensibly British "North Pole" agent network in Holland, addressed by name to the British handlers in London, shed crocodile tears of "regret" that "we [Germans] have acted for so long as your sole representatives in this country."

In 1941 the German battleship *Bismarck*, having intercepted and sunk the British battle cruiser *Hood*, and having fought off other warships, escaped into the vast Atlantic. In a surprisingly short time a huge force assembled and then intercepted and sank the *Bismarck*. The German naval command asked itself, might the British have broken the Germans' ciphers? (Indeed they had, in the now famous "Ultra" affair.)

No, decided the German board of inquiry. "It is not necessary to put the blame on a breach of security as regards the code and cipher tables." There is the defensive reaction of almost any organization: "not necessary," meaning in effect not easy, not pleasant.

The question kept popping up. Some convoys supplying Rommel's corps in the North African desert from across the Mediterranean were spotted with suspicious speed (one as it emerged from dense fog) and were attacked and sunk from sea and air. The Germans were forced again to ask themselves about the security of their ciphers. Then U-boat losses to Allied aircraft rose startlingly. In mid-1943 they were being spotted suspiciously often in many different areas (in fact, thanks to Ultra). Again a German board reviewed communications security. Each of these reviews concluded smugly that the ciphers were safe. As late as 1959 Grand-Admiral Doenitz still refused to believe they were not, and ascribed his navy's losses to the excellence of British radar.

This kind of self-deception joined with a lack of courtroom-quality proof to grant to Kim Philby many extra years to do the work that has since caused him to be labeled (perhaps prematurely) as "the spy of the century."

Philby's career was jolted on 25 May 1953 when British diplomats Guy Burgess and Donald Maclean fled England to the USSR just after Burgess had returned to London from Washington, where he had lived for a year with Philby, and just three days before Maclean was to have been interviewed by British counterintelligence. As MI6 chief in Washington, Philby had been one of the few people to know of the impending move against Maclean (exposed by a break of KGB ciphers code-named "Venona"). Now the CIA and FBI refused to deal further with Philby, so he was recalled to London and questioned about "indiscretions" and "misconduct."

His interrogators, Milmo and Skardon, considered Philby a traitor and they had better reasons than the "third man" warning to Burgess and Maclean. One was Philby's communist first wife, another was "the nasty little sentence in Krivitsky's evidence" (as Philby later called it). NKVD operative Walter Krivitsky, after defecting in 1937, had told the British that the NKVD had sent a young English journalist to Spain during the civil war there. This had caused Philby no problem at the time because many fit this description. But the lead hung there waiting for a cross-bearing.

Pointing more directly toward Philby were four fingers left behind by the ghost of Konstantin Volkov. This British-desk NKVD officer had contacted the British Consulate in Istanbul in August 1945 offering information about Soviet spies in the British government. His information could have uncovered Philby, Maclean, and Burgess (and doubtless others) but fate—and Soviet manipulation—had placed Philby across his path. Philby had become head of counterintelligence work against the USSR and was the logical choice, as he pointed out, to handle the case. He quickly alerted the NKVD, which removed Volkov before he could make his next contact. But these pointers remained:

- Volkov had told the British Consul that a "head of a British counterespionage organization" was an NKVD agent. Philby was now head of a recently formed MI6 organization to counter Soviet espionage.
- Within MI6 Philby had handled the Volkov matter almost single-handedly. Any suspicion that a leak might have caused Volkov's untimely disappearance would necessarily point toward him.

- Philby had so dragged his fee and delayed the British response to Volkov's appeal that the British Consul correctly concluded that unless Philby was criminally incompetent, he must be a Soviet agent.
- "Two days after the Volkov information reached London," as Philby learned from his British interrogator Milmo, "there had been a spectacular rise in the volume of NKVD wireless traffic between London and Moscow, followed by a similar rise in the traffic between Moscow and Istanbul."

But this had not been enough. It took the Burgess-Maclean flight, *eight years later,* to halt Philby's rise toward the top of MI6. And even that was not enough to make him confess. MI6 dropped him for errors of judgment, not for treason, and a few years later, in what may have been an accident of parliamentary procedure, he was publicly cleared by Foreign Secretary Harold Macmillan. So those icebergs of suspicion gradually melted in the warm waters of organizational self-deception and forgetfulness—and Philby sailed on. Incredibly, MI6 rehired him. Its chiefs, like many MI6 officers, had scoffed at the very thought that Philby might be a traitor, and at the paranoid idea that the Soviets might have penetrated their ranks. Now they set him up as a journalist in Beirut where they thought his contacts would prove useful.

Useful they were, but mainly for the KGB. Though removed from MI6's central files, Philby kept in touch with former colleagues and other Westerners of interest to KGB recruiters. These Westerners still trusted Philby; even those who thought he might have warned Burgess and Maclean did not suspect he had done it on the KGB's behalf. A former CIA official in the area wrote, "When I went to Beirut in 1957 to set up a consulting firm I was told by both CIA officers and SIS officers that Philby was still suspect, although he had been formally cleared of any connection with Burgess and Maclean, and that I would be doing a great service to my country were I to keep an eye on him. I did, as did other British and American laymen who were friends of his. *Like all the others, I didn't have the slightest suspicion that he was a Soviet agent and, in fact, wouldn't believe it until he surfaced in Moscow. . . . Believe me, it was a terrible shock."*[10]

Finally, in 1962 new information pointed unmistakably at Philby, and MI6 had to act. A longtime colleague, Nicholas Elliott, got a partial confession from him, but then he fled to the Soviet Union and until his death in 1988 kept on helping the KGB damage the West.

Alger Hiss was another beneficiary of willful neglect of the obvious. His secret collaboration with Soviet Intelligence was known to Western authorities long before he moved up to play a substantive role in conferences where America's posture toward the Soviet regime was being worked out, and more than a decade before he was finally brought before a court. Here is how:

- In 1937 the Soviet defector Walter Krivitsky, when he met the former Soviet diplomat Alexander Barmine in Paris, named Hiss as an agent.
- In September 1939 French Intelligence passed to American Ambassador Bullitt information (presumably from Krivitsky) that Alger and his brother Donald Hiss were Soviet agents. Bullitt told President Roosevelt soon thereafter.
- On 2 September 1939 the journalist Isaac Don Levine, Krivitsky's friend, escorted Whittaker Chambers to the home of Assistant Secretary of State Adolph Berle, where Chambers gave details of his Soviet and Communist

Party of the United States of America (CPUSA) intelligence activity and clandestine contacts with Alger and Donald Hiss. Berle took notes and reported to President Roosevelt—who laughed it off. Others also told Roosevelt about the suspicions, but neither he nor Berle passed the information to the FBI.

- In 1941 the FBI got its first news of Hiss directly from Chambers. Despite their initial interest, they neglected to follow up.
- In April 1945 at the San Francisco Conference, which founded the United Nations, Soviet Foreign Minister Gromyko indiscreetly told American Secretary of State Stettinius that he would be "very happy to see Alger Hiss appointed temporary secretary general, as he had a very high regard for Hiss, particularly for his fairness and impartiality."
- In August 1945 the GRU code clerk Igor Gouzenko defected and reported that an assistant to Secretary Stettinius was a Soviet spy.
- In November 1945 Elizabeth Bentley, a communist underground courier, named to the FBI Soviet spies in government, including some who had been previously named by Chambers. She had been told about Hiss. FBI director J. Edgar Hoover asked President Truman for permission to take action against Hiss, but Truman remained "stubbornly antagonistic" to the allegations.

Hiss's career path to the top was blocked only when Congress took an interest in him after a 1946 grand jury in New York had begun looking into Soviet espionage. This finally forced the State Department to remove him from access to secrets. In mid-1948—more than ten years after he had first been exposed—the spotlight finally shone on him. The House Un-American Activities Committee called Chambers to testify and arranged his dramatic confrontation with Hiss. Chambers then revealed the famous "pumpkin papers" that documented Hiss's treason. He denied under oath having ever known Chambers, but when confronted with contrary facts began to back off and equivocate. The committee "kept Hiss on the stand, leading him point by point over his past testimony, leading him to dodge, bend and weave—a spectacle of agile and dogged indignity —through his discrepancies and contradictions, but never bringing him completely to lose his footing or to yield an inch in his denials." To one committee member Hiss's testimony appeared "clouded by a strangely deficient memory."

Nevertheless the press echoed public sympathy for Hiss ("tall, handsome, well-educated, a brilliant law student") and skepticism and contempt for Chambers: "Not only was he untidy," commented a biographer of President Truman, "but he had had an erratic career and was clearly far gone into paranoia."

In 1977 the writer Allen Weinstein, helped by Hiss and intending to prove his innocence, set out to review all the data. But he was an honest man and the facts he found convinced him (as they do any reader of his book) that Hiss was guilty. Still some journalists kept suggesting that Hiss had been diabolically framed.[11]

Why do we fall prey to hoaxes, deceptive tricks, impostures, lies, and misrepresentations that seem obvious to others less emotional or less involved? Why, once duped, do we then hang on to our misconception, sometimes against the evidence of our senses? Why, when supplied with that evidence, are we more likely to attack its suppliers—a Burtsev, Bukharin, Martov, Sneevliet, or Chambers— instead of the deceiver?

And why do professional intelligence officers, trained to expect such hoaxes and paying fulsome lip service to alertness, fall again and again into traps? Why does the harsh light of skepticism so often diffuse into a rosy glow of wishful thinking?

You might blame a training that fails to instill skepticism, or you could criticize bureaucratic structures that let responsibility fall between stools, but that would be too easy. The reason lies deeper—far down in the recesses of the human mind. It is not our eyes and ears that shape our reality but our brain, which filters and translates their perceptions, a brain produced by a unique set of needs and desires so that different people may make different interpretations and draw different conclusions from the same evidence.

Here we touch upon the classic conflict between mind and heart, reason and emotion, sun and moon, a conflict which, as we are reminded by ancient poems and aphorisms, is as old as humanity. Scientific enlightenment has not resolved that conflict. Our brains still filter in the perceptions they desire and filter out those they do not. They still lead us unconsciously toward "reasonable" choices that favor our self-interest or our ease and—in defiance of warning, instruction, or experience—lead us away from those that bother or threaten. Hence we suffer from that "universal inability to distinguish true from false, right from wrong, when the false is cast in the image of the world's desire and the true is nothing that the world can fathom, or wants to."[12]

Alger Hiss knew this and cynically built it into his defense. In essence, he asked the committee to disregard the evidence and follow its emotions. "It is *inconceivable* that there could have been on my part, during fifteen years or more in public office . . . any departure from the highest rectitude without its becoming known. It is *inconceivable* that the men with whom I was intimately associated during those fifteen years should not know my true character better than this accuser. It is *inconceivable* that . . . [etc.]" How right he was: we have seen two presidents finding it inconceivable, Roosevelt "laughing it off" and Truman "stubbornly antagonistic."

Trained and experienced intelligence officers are only human. As a KGB (then OGPU) officer said to calm the nerves of a Trust provocateur he was dispatching to contact Western Intelligence, "You'll have no problem. They *want* to believe and trust you."[13] Indeed "they" do—as they showed through the decades by falling for hoax after Soviet hoax, false defectors, double agents, and operational traps, and by failing to recognize penetration agents in their midst.

Perhaps those German case officers noticed oddities in their agents' reports from England, but their own careers and prestige depended on these agents and obscured their concern for winning the war. Those SR conspirators genuinely could not imagine that Azev would betray them. Those MI6 leaders could not believe Philby to be a traitor, because that would annul all their hard work and devoted careers.

If Americans are not alone in suffering this form of blindness, they are particularly predisposed to it. Whittaker Chambers wrote of that "invincible ignorance, rooted in what was most generous in the American character, which because it was incapable of such conspiracy itself, could not believe that others practiced it. It was rooted, too, in what was most singular in the American experience, which because it had prospered so much apart from the rest of the world, could not really grasp . . . why [Communists] acted as they did." Regarding the sincere belief of Hiss's lawyer, Marbury, in Hiss's innocence, Chambers concluded that Marbury "knew that my charges could not be true because . . . Communists simply could not occur in [his] social and professional world. . . . Marbury's mind was closed to certain possibilities and a part of its natural acuteness blunted—a condition that would seem to be almost as dangerous to a lawyer as to a general in the field."[14]

This, perhaps, helps explain why many American intelligence officers refuse to accept the idea of Soviet deception operations. After a lifetime in intelligence work, former director of Central Intelligence William Colby seemed proud to admit that he "could just not figure out at all" what [his own counterintelligence staff] were doing."[15] A veteran supervisor of CIA operations abroad dismissed sixty years of KGB deception operations as a sort of paranoid fantasy and admitted with candor, "I don't happen to be able to share this kind of thing."[16]

Having committed himself to an erroneous position—having been duped—a person is likely to react to contrary evidence in the same way as those German handlers of the "double cross" agents: by refusing to admit it. "Faith, fanatic Faith," a poet wrote, "once wedded fast/To some dear falsehood, hugs it to the last." Samuel Ireland, father of that faker of Shakespeare, was a renowned expert and collector of Elizabethan manuscripts. Ridiculed for (unwittingly) lending his prestige to his son's forgery by publishing it, he never to his death allowed himself to believe they were false, despite expert evidence and even his son's repeated confession. President Truman, having labeled the Hiss investigation a red herring, felt the need to repeat it in the face of mounting evidence and was finally driven to declare at a press conference the patent absurdity that "no American secret ever was leaked to the Russians."

If the individual alone is vulnerable, he becomes even more so when he works closely with others. Yale psychology professor Stanley Milgram demonstrated that, consciously or not, we give way to social pressures rather than trust in our own powers. He often repeated an experiment in which, pretending to test the acuity of the eye, he laid out before four people a paper on which three lines had been drawn, and asked them which was the longest. Of these people the first three had been secretly briefed to choose a line that was quite obviously not the longest. And in no fewer than half the cases, the fourth person followed the others rather than believe his own eyes—and chose the same wrong line.[17]

The individual tends to conform to the views of people he admires and emulates, the careerist to those who write his fitness reports. One CIA officer expressed it well when asked to explain his radical turnabout from what, before the political winds had shifted, seemed to be his unshakable conviction. "After all," he said, "we working-level types have to work within the general framework set by the chiefs."

To the individual's hang-ups are added the organization's own. For its power and prestige (and perhaps its budget) it tends to repel any suggestion that it has erred or been duped or manipulated.

No organization wants to discover a Philby in its ranks; the cure may seem more harmful than the illness. The Hiss case may have eliminated a Soviet spy network within sensitive parts of the U.S. government, but Secretary of State Dean Acheson described it as "something approaching national disaster, lending as it did support to a widespread attack throughout the country upon confidence in government itself."[18] Chambers, painfully breaking away from Soviet espionage and offering lists of spies within the U.S. government, faced a wall of disbelief and apparent disinterest. After years of trying to alert the government to its danger, he "concluded that there were powerful forces within the Government to whom such information as I had given [Assistant Secretary of State Adolf Berle in 1939] was extremely unwelcome. . . . I had been warned repeatedly that the brunt of official wrath was directed, not against Alger Hiss as a danger, but against me for venturing to testify to the danger [and] that if I made myself troublesome, any action taken would be taken against me." He became certain that the administration was more interested in suppressing his story than in discovering the facts.[19]

A storm of criticism and ridicule falls upon an intelligence service that— acting responsibly and professionally—discovers a traitor among its trusted employees. A French intelligence officer pushed hard to get his service to investigate the leads provided in 1962 by the KGB defector Anatoly Golitsyn, to clean out moles from the French government and intelligence services. To his amazement and dismay, Philippe Thyraud de Vosjoli encountered only resistance and hostility from his superiors. He was ordered "in peremptory tones" to stop. When he went ahead and informed his foreign ministry of its security problem, his own service leaders were furious about his "indiscretion in divulging so sensitive a topic." Later, when he got further clues to spies, "not a question was asked, no one wanted to know about any other Soviet agents." "Nobody really wanted the truth to come out," he concluded, and his chief admitted that the service "could not stand a scandal at this time."[20]

Here bureaucracy has a point. Even the most routine security precautions can damage an organization's morale. Trotsky complained that the rules imposed by his guard force to save his own life—searching visitors for concealed weapons, preventing visitors from talking alone with him in his study—would create "mutual suspicion [which] was a disintegrating force much worse than the inclusion of a spy in the organization."[21]

An intelligence agency tends to jettison whatever slows down its information gathering. "CIA is not primarily out there to contest the KGB," said one former director. "It's got *a much more important job*, which is to find out what's going on at the political and strategic levels of foreign thinking and Soviet thinking."[22] Those wartime German case officers were collecting "important" reports from England; those wartime British were busy weakening the enemy by sabotage and armed resistance; neither side wanted to waste time worrying about possible enemy control of that work.

This breeds scorn for those who do worry about such things. A onetime head of CIA's Soviet Russia Division, forgetting how often it had been victimized by the KGB, resented what he called the "counterintelligence clique" and "high priesthood of secrecy." Another CIA executive ticked off counterintelligence as "little more than operations for operations' sake," while others accused it of paranoia, of "suspecting every defector to be a deception agent."[23]

And an organization, even quicker than an individual, can forget what it has learned. "Permanent files" it may have, but it can wipe out this memory and experience by simply transferring or retiring a few veterans. Their younger replacements are likely to be disinclined, or kept too busy, to delve into written records that their superiors dismiss as "ancient history."

The organization's compartmentalization—the indispensable security principle of "need to know"—makes it harder to bring together related facts in ways that, to an individual brain, create understanding and insight. It hides from one professional what another has learned or suffered, how others tumbled into traps like Trust and WiN and the Cuban and Czechoslovak double agents—and so leaves its employees naked before their enemies.

None of this will change. All these tendencies are firmly rooted in the human psyche and the bureaucratic character. No amount of education, goodwill, or even bloody experience will eradicate any one of them.

But they can be fought—by being kept in mind. Faced with an opponent skilled in deception and provocation, an intelligence officer can stop and think about Roman Malinovsky, about the Trust, about CIA's debacle in Cuba, and about those years of treason handed unnecessarily to Alger Hiss and Kim Philby and Aldrich Ames. One can wonder whether those German case officers might have staved off the D-Day landings, and whether a more skeptical Trotsky might have lived on to oppose Stalin—if only they had overcome their human penchant for self-deception.

Glossary

Names and Code Names (asterisks denote individual listings)

Abidian, John: U.S. State Department employee, Security Officer of the American Embassy in Moscow from early 1960 to early 1962. There he performed some operational tasks for CIA*, including checking the dead drop established by Penkovsky*.

Agee, Philip: CIA* officer in the 1950s and 1960s. He left CIA in 1968, contacted the KGB and its Cuban affiliate, and then for years did all he could to hamper and discredit CIA by publicly exposing its personnel and operations.

Ames, Aldrich: CIA* officer beginning in 1962 who contacted the KGB in Washington in 1985 and, for large amounts of money, betrayed more than a dozen Soviet citizens whom CIA had recruited. Those whom he named were then arrested and some shot. It was later learned that several had already been betrayed by Robert Hanssen*. CIA investigated but it took nine years and a new source from the KGB to catch Ames. Arrested in February 1994, he was sentenced to life in prison.

Andrey: Soviet code name for an American sergeant, cipher-machine mechanic in Moscow from autumn 1951 to autumn 1953. The KGB recruited him just before returning to the United States but did not recontact him until October 1957. The two KGB officers who then met him in the Washington area, one of whom was Vladislav Kovshuk*, recognized that he had no access to secrets, for the KGB never met him again. Then, in 1962, six months after he had left the army, Yuri Nosenko* exposed him (falsely) as the target of Kovshuk's 1957 trip to Washington, about which CIA* had just learned from the defector Anatoly Golitsyn*. In 1964 Nosenko gave different data that finally made it possible to identify "Andrey."

Angleton, James J.: Chief of CIA's* CI (Counterintelligence) Staff* who believed that Yuri Nosenko and certain others were planted on American Intelligence by the KGB. He was fired by CIA Director William Colby* in December 1974 and was later vilified by his critics as a paranoid.

Artamonov, Nikolay Fedorovich: Soviet naval officer (destroyer captain) who defected in the 1950s and moved to the United States where (under the assumed name of Nicholas Shadrin) he worked as a consultant for the U.S. navy. Agreed to work as a double agent for the Americans and thus allowed himself to be "recruited" by KGB officer Igor Kochnov*. In the course of the operation the KGB kidnapped and inadvertently killed him.

B: American university professor recruited by KGB in the Ukraine in 1956 through homosexual compromise. Yuri Nosenko claimed to be the principal recruiter but later changed his story and proved to be ignorant of the details of the case. B's version revealed Nosenko to be a low-level assistant or agent and not the principal case officer.

Barnett, David: CIA* officer from 1958 to 1970 who served in Indonesia. In 1976 he volunteered his services to the KGB and betrayed CIA operations and personnel. He rejoined CIA in 1979 but was soon betrayed by a KGB officer working as a spy for the Americans, and in January 1981 was given a long prison sentence. The KGB man who betrayed Barnett was later himself betrayed by Aldrich Ames* and shot by the Soviets.

Blake, George: British Intelligence (Secret Intelligence Service*) officer who while interned in Korea in 1950 volunteered to spy for the KGB. From 1953 to 1961 he met the KGB in London, Berlin, and Beirut and betrayed many British intelligence activities until he was uncovered by Michal Goleniew-ski* and recalled and sentenced to forty-one years in jail. He escaped from Wormwood Scrubs Prison in 1966 and lives in Moscow.

Caesar (Cezary): Polish Communist state security service, or UB* code name for a deception operation (1947–1952) centered on an anti-Communist resistance movement called WiN*.

Chelnokov, Vladimir Dmitryevich: KGB officer, said by Yuri Nosenko* to have been chief of the SCD* 7th (Tourist) Department in the late 1950s and early 1960s. Nosenko worked with him as a junior assistant in his meeting with an American tour organizer, F*, despite the fact that Nosenko claimed to have been at the time a supervisor in a different department. After the Cold War it was learned that Chelnokov had been a senior officer of the SCD's section for operational deception.

Cherepanov, Aleksandr Nikolayevich: Former KGB SCD* officer who in November 1963, while working in the International Book firm in Moscow, passed to the American Embassy, via a visiting American businessman, a bundle of secret KGB draft documents. He was presumably preparing to begin a clandestine relationship. But the Embassy, fearful of provocation, turned over the documents to the Soviet Foreign Ministry. The KGB identified Cherepanov as their source and reportedly hunted him down and shot him for treason. Yuri Nosenko* claimed to have participated in the hunt. About half the "Cherepanov papers" related to the Popov* affair.

Chernov, Nikolay (code name Nicknack): GRU technician who collaborated with the FBI during trips to the United States in 1963 and 1972. He uncovered important GRU agents in Western countries including Great Britain, France, and Switzerland.

Chin, Larry Wu-tai: A Chinese-born, naturalized American citizen who was a translator for CIA's* Foreign Broadcast Information Service in the Far East and Washington. He spied for more than thirty years for Chinese Communist Intelligence from the early 1950s until he was betrayed by a Chinese defector in 1986. He was tried and convicted, and he committed suicide while awaiting sentencing.

Colby, William E.: CIA* officer with Far Eastern experience who in September 1973 became director of Central Intelligence (until January 1976). Inexperienced in either Soviet or counterintelligence matters, he resented and distrusted the influence and ideas of James Angleton* and fired him in December 1974. Colby played a major role in downgrading and discrediting counterintelligence in CIA and in dispelling doubts about Yuri Nosenko*.

Deriabin, Peter (Pyotr): KGB officer who defected to the Americans in Vienna in February 1954 and became a valuable consultant to CIA* and other U.S. agencies. Participated in interrogation of Yuri Nosenko* in 1964–1966 and wrote numerous detailed reports explaining his unshakable conviction that Nosenko was a KGB plant. Died in 1992.

F: American travel agent and tour organizer who frequently visited and sojourned in the USSR. Recruited and handled, according to Yuri Nosenko*, by KGB Colonel Chelnokov*, who was then (again according to Nosenko) chief of the KGB's anti-tourist department. Nosenko assisted Chelnokov in one meeting with F in Odessa in 1960 (though he was working in a different department at the time) and met F alone during a later visit, in 1963—possibly anticipating a CIA* effort to contact him through F. After the Cold War Chelnokov was revealed to be a leader of a special operational-deception unit inside the Second Chief Directorate*.

Felfe, Heinz: Wartime member of German Nazi intelligence (SD) who in 1951 joined West German Intelligence—then the Gehlen* Organization, which became the BND*—and became head of all its counterespionage operations against the Soviet Union. Throughout his entire service he worked as a penetration agent for the KGB until his arrest in 1961 as a result of information given to the Americans by Michal Goleniewski*. Released from prison in 1969.

Gehlen, Reinhard: Senior German intelligence officer for the Russian Front in the Second World War, who afterward established an intelligence service under American aegis. Called the Gehlen Organization, it became in 1955 the West German Federal Intelligence Service (BND)*.

Goleniewski, Michal: High officer of Polish state security who in March 1959 began a German-language correspondence with American Intelligence, hiding his identity and nationality behind the code name "Heckenschuetze" (Sniper). With information learned as a trusted contact of the Soviet KGB, he uncovered the important Soviet moles Heinz Felfe* and George Blake*, and other Soviet bloc spies in Western institutions. Within a year the KGB learned of this activity and was closing in on him when he fled to the West at the end of 1960.

Golitsyn, Anatoly: KGB officer who was stationed in Austria in 1953–1955 and defected to CIA* in Helsinki on 15 December 1961 after years of memorizing cases and documents that had come to his attention. His pointers exposed active KGB spies in several Western governments, including three intelligence services.

Gordievsky, Oleg: KGB colonel who agreed in 1974 to collaborate with British Intelligence in Copenhagen. While he was serving in London in the 1980s the KGB learned of his collaboration and recalled him to Moscow, where he was interrogated but did not confess. He managed to flee the USSR and subsequently made his life in England.

Gribanov, Oleg Mikhailovich: First deputy chief, then chief, of KGB Counterintelligence (Second Chief Directorate) in the 1950s and first half of the 1960s. Supervisor of the arrest and interrogation of CIA's* spy Pyotr Popov*. Sponsor of Nosenko's trips to the West and his promotions. He was allegedly fired because of Nosenko's defection. Died in the early 1990s.

Gryaznov, Gennady: Officer of American (1st) Department of KGB's SCD* in the 1950s and 1960s. Responsible for operations against American code clerks. Traveled to Helsinki for one of these operations. Yuri Nosenko* claimed to be his direct supervisor throughout 1960 and 1961.

Guk, Yuri Ivanovich: KGB officer who served twice abroad, in Washington 1955–1957, where he operated with Vladislav Kovshuk* and Aleksandr Kislov*. In Geneva 1961–1963, he was the companion of Yuri Nosenko* before and after the latter's meetings there with CIA* in June 1962. After the Cold War it was learned that he was a member of a special operational-deception unit inside the SCD*. Died in the 1990s.

Hanssen, Robert Philip: FBI officer who betrayed to the GRU* and KGB* the secret activity and agents of the FBI's New York field office from about 1979 until a KGB defector uncovered him in 2001.

Hart, John L.: CIA* officer who had served in the Far East and later became head of its European division. With assistants, he reviewed the Yuri Nosenko* case in 1976 and cleared Nosenko of any suspicions lingering after the Bruce Solie* report of 1968. In 1978, as personal representative of CIA director Turner, testified to HSCA* during its review of President Kennedy's assassination—instructed (as he admitted under oath) not to talk about the assassin Oswald but to denigrate CIA personnel who had doubted Nosenko's bona fides.

Howard, Edward Lee: CIA* officer who defected to the Soviets in 1985 after being fired from CIA. After the KGB had debriefed him he was uncovered by the KGB defector Vitaly Yurchenko*.

Johnson, Robert Lee: American army sergeant who for money provided the KGB* with top secret U.S. Air Force documents he smuggled out during his night duty in 1962 in a courier center at Orly Airport near Paris. By late 1962 or early 1963 Johnson had lost access to any classified information, and his wife was telling friends that he was a Soviet spy. The KGB dropped contact in 1963. Yuri Nosenko* uncovered his treason in February 1964. Johnson was arrested, tried, and sentenced to twenty-five years' imprisonment—and stabbed to death by his son during a prison visit.

Kalugin, Oleg: KGB* officer who served in the United States in the 1960s and later became chief of foreign counterintelligence department. Tried vainly to get the KGB reformed, and became a member of the Russian parliament. After the Cold War moved to the United States and wrote a book about his career and often spoke publicly about the KGB. His friendly counsel to Americans caused the KGB to brand him a traitor, which he was not. He brought an eyewitness account of the KGB kidnapping and accidental killing of Nikolay Artamonov*.

Kampiles, William: CIA* officer for a brief period in 1977 and who, in 1978, sold to Soviet Intelligence a top-secret manual on a new and important American reconnaissance satellite, permitting the Soviets to evade its eye. Betrayed by a Soviet intelligence defector to the Americans, Kampiles confessed his misdeed and in 1978 was sent to prison.

Kislov, Aleksandr Konstantinovich (probably a pseudonym): Served in United States as TASS (Soviet news agency) journalist from January 1957, and quickly began clandestine operations in Washington with KGB officers Yuri Guk* and Vladislav Kovshuk*. Immediately after his return to Moscow in January 1959 Kislov met socially the American Embassy officer, George Winters, who had just mailed a CIA* operational letter to Popov. Accompanied Yuri Nosenko on the Soviet delegation to arms conference in spring 1962 in Geneva, and roomed with him in a small hotel far removed from the delegation, which Nosenko was supposedly protecting. Nosenko reported Kislov had no connection with KGB*.

Kochnov, Igor: KGB officer who volunteered to work for CIA* while he was on a temporary mission to Washington in June 1966. To promote his KGB career CIA and FBI allowed him to "recruit" his target, Nikolay Artamonov*. His prospects to rise in the KGB* disappeared, as indeed so did he a couple of years later. He uncovered no spies who were arrested, but told CIA his other KGB assignment was to locate the important defectors Golitsyn* and Yuri Nosenko*. This convinced some in CIA, including Bruce Solie*, that Nosenko was genuine.

Kopatzky, Aleksandr: See Orlov, Igor.

Kosolapov, Vadim: Officer of the KGB SCD* section working against the American Embassy in Moscow during the late 1950s and early 1960s. In 1960 he went to Helsinki to ride back to Moscow on the train with an arriving American communications officer whom the KGB had high hopes of recruiting. Anatoly Golitsyn* reported this, CIA* confirmed it, and Nosenko knew nothing of it. The communications officer did not report any KGB contact or recruitment attempt.

Kovshuk, Vladislav (alias Komarov): KGB* counterintelligence officer, head of its section working against the American Embassy in Moscow in the 1950s and 1960s. Stayed in the United States for ten months in 1957 on an operational assignment in which he worked with Yuri Guk* and Aleksandr Kislov* while still holding down his Moscow job. His trip (under a pseudonym) had escaped American notice until revealed in December 1961 by Anatoly Golitsyn*. Yuri Nosenko* in June 1962 provided a (demonstrably false) explanation for the trip. Died in the 1990s.

Kulak, Aleksey: KGB* officer in New York who walked into the FBI in March 1962 and began a long career as a spy for the FBI (with the code name "Fedora") and for CIA* after he was transferred back to Moscow. Kulak supported Nosenko's* bona fides in several ways. In 1977 the FBI reviewed his case and decided that Kulak was a KGB plant and had deceived the FBI throughout his nearly fifteen years' service in New York. The KGB claimed to have failed to detect Kulak's treason until his death from cancer in 1983.

McCoy, Leonard V.: CIA* reports officer who handled information coming into SB Division* from Pyotr Popov* and later Oleg Penkovsky*. Later became deputy chief of the Counterintelligence Staff. He became a ferocious defender of Yuri Nosenko's* bona fides and published and fed to investigative reporters false information promoting this viewpoint and attacking those with differing views.

Mott: Nickname (for "Man-On-The-Train") for an American Embassy communications officer in Moscow from about 1960. The KGB had already targeted him for recruitment because of his financial and other difficulties at his previous posting. KGB* officer Vadim Kosolapov* went to Helsinki to board the train on which Mott was to arrive, to establish a relationship with him as part of the KGB recruitment plan. Kosolapov told Anatoly Golitsyn* that the prospects for KGB success were bright. Mott never reported any KGB or other Russian contact. Nosenko claimed to have directly supervised all Kosolapov's activities at the time, but knew nothing of this promising operation or of any trip of Kosolapov's abroad.

Nosenko, Yuri Ivanovich: KGB* officer who approached CIA* in Geneva at the end of May 1962 and gave information over the course of a few meetings before his visiting delegation returned to Moscow. Came back to Geneva in late January 1964 and defected six days after several more meetings with CIA. His good faith came under suspicion but CIA later certified him as a genuine defector. Has since resided in the United States.

Orlov, Igor: CIA* agent in Berlin (1951–1961), of Russian origin and German citizenship, later naturalized American. Parachuted by Soviet Intelligence behind German lines, he was captured and turned against the Soviets, working for the Germans under the identity they provided him: Aleksandr ("Sasha") Kopatsky. After the war Orlov worked in Germany for a Russian emigré organization and the Gehlen* organization, then with CIA until he emigrated to the United States in 1961. CIA ignored many signs that he was a KGB* penetration of their operations in Germany. In late 1961 Anatoly Golitsyn* gave pointers to a KGB penetration of CIA whom he thought was code-named "Sasha"*. CIA investigation pointed to Orlov, and this suspicion was later confirmed by Igor Kochnov* and Oleg Kalugin*. Orlov died in 1982.

Oswald, Lee Harvey: Assassin of President John F. Kennedy in Dallas on 22 November 1963. Because he had defected to USSR in 1959 after service in the U.S. marines, then changed his mind and returned to the United

States in 1962 with a Soviet wife, the question was raised as to whether the Soviets had a hand in the assassination itself. Within weeks, Yuri Nosenko* brought authoritative evidence that the Soviet government had had no interest in, or operational contact with, Oswald.

Pelton, Ronald William: Employee of the NSA* from November 1965 to July 1979. In January 1980, soon after leaving government service, he offered his knowledge to the Soviets and the KGB* subsequently debriefed him on his knowledge of American COMINT* during sessions in Vienna in 1980 and 1983. After Pelton broke contact with the KGB in 1985, the (temporary) KGB defector Vitaly Yurchenko* gave information that led to Pelton's arrest. He was convicted and jailed.

Penkovsky, Oleg Vladimirovich: Colonel of GRU* who volunteered and began a long series of meetings with CIA* and MI6* in London in April 1961, again in London, and a third time in Paris (September 1961) but was then banned from further travel abroad. In Moscow, however, he passed secret documents on microfilm about ten times to British or American contacts in Moscow before he was arrested in September or October 1962. He was sentenced in May 1963 and shot.

Philby, H. A. R. ("Kim"): British intelligence officer who became an ideological recruit to Communism in the mid-1930s, rose to high rank in the SIS*—overseeing its work against Soviet Intelligence—all the time betraying its secrets to the KGB. Under deep suspicion as "the Third Man" after the flight of British traitors Guy Burgess and Donald Maclean in 1951, he was finally uncovered only in the early 1960s, whereupon he fled to Moscow and continued to help the KGB until his death in April 1988.

Pitovranov, Yevgeny Petrovich: Top-level KGB* officer long experienced in deception operations. He was an organizer of the Caesar* operation in Poland from 1947, chief of SCD* until the fall of 1951, briefly chief of FCD* from late 1952, then chief of the KGB apparatus in Karlshorst, East Berlin. Died in the 1990s.

Polyakov, Dmitry Fedorovich: Colonel, later General-Major, of GRU*. In 1957 he escorted a GRU Illegal* named Margarita Tairova* from Moscow to Berlin, where Popov* would handle her onward dispatch to the United States. In 1959 assigned to New York though by then it was known that Popov had revealed to the Americans Polyakov's intelligence functions. In December 1961 in New York he volunteered to spy for American Intelligence and gave information on GRU operations in the United States. Though he continued to spy for twenty-seven years while serving in four later posts, he was not arrested until eight years after Robert Hanssen* betrayed him to the KGB and three years after Ames later did. The FBI examined his case in 1977 and was unable to conclude that he was a genuine source (or a plant). But CIA* claimed that he had been its most important human source of Soviet information during the entire Cold War.

Popov, Pyotr Semyonovich: Lieutenant Colonel of GRU* who volunteered to CIA* in late 1952–early 1953 in Vienna and provided vital military secrets there and during a later assignment in Germany until the KGB*, suspecting him, recalled him from Berlin to Moscow in November 1958. But according to Nosenko* and others, it was not until late February 1959 that the KGB finally discovered Popov's treason, by spotting an American Embassy employee named George Winters* mailing a letter to him. This story was hiding a penetration of CIA.

Sasha: Nickname of Igor Orlov* and KGB code name of a recruited American army officer who served in Germany in the 1960s. Anatoly Golitsyn* thought this was a code name, and the resulting confusion led to several errors in Western publications including the unfounded allegation that Yuri Nosenko* had told CIA* that there was a mole in its ranks code-named "Sasha." It is generally agreed, on the basis of confirmations by Igor Kochnov* and Oleg Kalugin* that Orlov was the KGB agent at whom Golitsyn had pointed. Nosenko had never heard of him, but in 1964 said he had heard that the KGB had recruited an army captain in Germany code-named Sasha (no further details, and too vague to permit identification). That U.S. army officer was later identified by Kochnov*.

Shadrin: See Artamonov.

Smith, Edward Ellis: CIA* operative in the American Embassy in Moscow who was supporting CIA's contact inside Russia with Pyotr Popov*. Vladislav Kovshuk* compromised Smith and tried to recruit him in the fall of 1956, at which time CIA recalled and fired him because of his delay in reporting and because it disbelieved his account. Yuri Nosenko* claimed in 1962 to have participated with Kovshuk in approaching Smith, then in 1964 denied any knowledge of the affair. A Russian book on the KGB in 2000 listed Smith as the KGB's first successful recruitment of a CIA officer.

Solie, Bruce: CIA security officer who worked on personnel security matters. Was assigned as case officer for Igor Kochnov* in 1966 and came to believe Yuri Nosenko* was a genuine defector. Criticized the 1967 report by CIA's* SB Division* and then spent months devising a new story with Nosenko. Solie wrote a report that, by 1 October 1968, finally cleared away CIA official doubts about Nosenko's bona fides.

Swiatlo, Josef: Polish colonel of the KGB-run UB*, who defected in 1953. Gave important and high-level insights into Soviet operations and techniques. His service in the department that spied on the leadership of the Polish ruling party itself gave him access to some of the most sensitive and compromising information ever leaked to the West. This information, sent to Poland by leaflet and radio, shook the regime and led to reforms that, developed in later years, made Poland a factor in the eventual collapse of Soviet Communism.

Tairova, Margarita: GRU* Illegal* whom the GRU dispatched to the United States in 1957, where her husband (also an Illegal) was already in place. The Moscow officer Dmitry Polyakov* escorted her to Berlin, where he turned her over to Pyotr Popov* for onward dispatch to the United States under a different identity. In the New York area she and her husband reportedly detected FBI surveillance and fled back to the USSR. Her misadventure cast suspicion onto Popov. As learned after the Cold War, the case was regarded among some KGB insiders as mysterious, and it may have had still-hidden implications.

Tuomi, Kaarlo: GRU* Illegal* and former KGB* agent who in 1959 was uncovered by chance in the United States and compelled to work on behalf of the FBI. He managed to signal to his GRU sponsors that he was under FBI control, and after Dmitry Polyakov* began to work for the FBI at the end of 1961, Tuomi identified him as one of his earlier GRU trainers.

Walker, John A., Jr.: Warrant Officer in U.S. navy communications who sold cryptographic material to the KGB* from 1967 until his arrest in 1985. He recruited his son Michael and a friend, Jerry Whitworth, both also in the navy, to carry on his KGB work. His information permitted the Soviet Union to break most naval and some other ciphers which, according to the chief of U.S. Naval Intelligence, gave the USSR a "war-winning capability."

Will: Nickname used in this book for an American Embassy code clerk. The Moscow KGB* case officer Gennedy Gryaznov* told Anatoly Golitsyn* in Helsinki that the KGB had successfully recruited Will thanks to the help of an agent of the Helsinki residency named Preisfreund. Yuri Nosenko*, claiming to have directly supervised Gryaznov and this operation, named Will and said the recruitment attempt had failed. Nosenko had supervised and made friends with Preisfreund during the failed attempt.

Winters, George: U.S. State Department employee who was co-opted by CIA* for the period of his tour in Moscow 1958–1960 to perform support tasks (mailing letters, etc.). By mistake he mailed an unnecessary letter to Pyotr Popov* in February 1959. Shortly after mailing the letter he met socially with Aleksandr Kislov*, who had just returned from the United States where he had worked with Vladislav Kovshuk* on the case of E. E. Smith*. Winters remained in Moscow until the end of his tour in 1960.

Wynne, Greville: British businessman in overt contact with Oleg Penkovsky* in 1960–1962 in the latter's cover capacity as member of the Soviet State Committee on Science and Technology. Arranged the initial contact between Penkovsky and MI6* and CIA* in London, and subsequently met with Penkovsky in Moscow and carried some of his microfilmed information to the West. Wynne was kidnapped in Budapest in November 1962, tried with Penkovsky, sentenced to eight years in jail, and liberated a year later in a spy swap.

Yurchenko, Vitaly: High-ranking KGB* officer who defected to the United States from Italy in 1985. While being debriefed in Washington—after giving information that led to the uncovering of burned-out KGB spies Ronald Pelton* and Edward Howard*, and confirming the importance of John Walker* and his son Michael—Yurchenko walked out and went to the Soviet Embassy and returned to the USSR, where he was restored to his KGB status. He was still working in the KGB in 2002.

Zvezdenkov, Valentin Vladimirovich: KGB* officer who interrogated Pyotr Popov* after his arrest. As was learned only after the Cold War, he was a senior officer of the SCD's* operational-deception unit, involved in deceiving the Americans about how the KGB had detected Popov's treason.

Organizations, Terms, Initials

AK: *Armija Krajowa* (Home Army). The Polish armed resistance to Nazi occupation during the Second World War.

BfV: *Bundesamt fuer Verfassungsschutz* (Federal Office for the Protection of the Constitution). The West German (later German) counterintelligence service.

BND: *Bundesnachrichtendienst,* the West German (later German) Federal Intelligence Service. Though it assumed this official designation only in 1955 when West Germany regained full sovereignty, it was originally founded under American aegis by the wartime German intelligence officer Reinhard Gehlen* as the "Gehlen Organization." Its headquarters were in Pullach, near Munich.

CI: Common abbreviation for counterintelligence and counterespionage. The exact sense of, and distinction between, CI and CE have been debated through the years without definitive resolution.

CI Staff: A component of CIA's* Directorate of Operations with advisory and liaison functions, headed for some twenty years, until late 1974, by James Angleton.

CIA: Central Intelligence Agency. From its formation in 1947 its clandestine intelligence and counterintelligence functions were carried out by its OSO*. In 1952 it absorbed OPC* in a joint Clandestine Services, under the Directorate of Plans (later Directorate of Operations).

COMINT: Communications Intelligence. The interception and decipherment of foreign encrypted communications. The principal U.S. agency for this work is the NSA*. The Soviet equivalent was the 8th Chief Directorate of the KGB* and (for recruitment of secret sources on Western communications) the 16th Department of the FCD*.

FCD: English-language initials of the KGB's* First Chief Directorate (*Pervoye Glavnoye Upravleniye* [PGU]), responsible for foreign intelligence gathering. It controlled stations abroad (each known as a *rezidentura**). After the fall of the Soviet Union it became the SVR*.

FSB: *Federalnaya Sluzhba Bezopastnosti* (Federal Security Service). Post–Soviet era designation of the counterintelligence and security arm (SCD*) of the former KGB*.

GRU: *Glavnoye Razvedivatelnoye Upravleniye* (Chief Administration of Intelligence of the Soviet General Staff). The Soviet Military Intelligence Service.

HSCA: The U.S. House of Representatives Select Committee on Assassinations, which conducted hearings in 1978 on the assassinations of President John F. Kennedy and Reverend Martin Luther King. It issued its final report on 29 March 1979. It repeatedly interviewed Yuri Nosenko* and "was certain Nosenko lied about [Lee Harvey] Oswald*."

Illegal: Soviet intelligence personnel of either KGB* or GRU* serving abroad under assumed foreign identities, normally operating and communicating with Headquarters without any direct connection to official (or "legal") residencies (see *rezidentura*). Illegals mentioned in this book include Yuri Loginov, Kaarlo Tuomi*, and Margarita Tairova*.

KGB: *Komitet Gosudarstvennyye Bezopastnost'* (Committee of State Security of the USSR), the designation (1954–1991) of the Soviet state security service. Earlier designations (as special commission, people's commissariat, or ministry) bore such initials as Cheka, OGPU, NKVD, MGB, and MVD, but it was always one and the same organization, founded in December 1917.

MI6: British Intelligence, also known as SIS (Secret Intelligence Service).

NSA: National Security Agency, the American government's principal organization for COMINT* and developing cipher systems.

OPC: Office of Policy Coordination, a euphemistic designation of the U.S. organization established in 1949 to carry out clandestine political action in support of American foreign policy. In 1952 merged with the OSO* as a component of CIA.

OSO: Office of Special Operations, a component of CIA* responsible for clandestine intelligence and counterintelligence abroad. It became part of CIA's Clandestine Services when merged in 1952 with OPC*.

OSS: Office of Strategic Services, the World War Two American intelligence organization that was disbanded after the war. Some of its functions were assumed by CIA* when the latter was established in 1947.

Rezidentura: A Soviet intelligence station, or residency, of KGB* or GRU*. "Legal" rezidenturas used the cover and facilities of official Soviet representations abroad. There were also "Illegal" ones (see Illegal).

SB Division: Soviet Bloc Division, the operating unit of CIA's* Directorate of Plans (later Directorate of Operations) as it was called after a merger of its Soviet (SR) division and Eastern European (EE) divisions in 1966. It was responsible for conducting espionage and counterintelligence operations against the Soviet bloc.

SCD: Abbreviation for an English-language translation (Second Chief Directorate, sometimes translated as Second Main Administration) of the KGB's *Vtoroye Glavnoye Upravleniye*, responsible for counterintelligence inside the Soviet Union. Watched foreign embassies and recruited as spies foreigners stationed in or visiting the USSR. Such recruits were normally handled abroad by the FCD*. Since the collapse of the Soviet Union the SCD has been known as the FSB* (*Federalnaya Sluzhba Bezopastnosti*—Federal Security Service).

SIS: Secret Intelligence Service, a designation (along with MI6*) of British Intelligence.

SVR: Post–Soviet era designation of the foreign intelligence component (FCD*) of the former KGB*. Stands for *Sluzhba Vneshnaya Razvedka* (Foreign Intelligence Service).

UB: An old and commonly used abbreviation for *Urzad Bezpiecestwa*, or Security Directorate, the Polish Communist state security service. It was established and supervised initially by the KGB* (then NKVD) in the last phase of the Second World War, and later became the Ministry of Public Security and a part of the Ministry of Internal Affairs.

VENONA: Code name given by Western intelligence services to Soviet intelligence communications intercepted during the Second World War and deciphered in the immediate postwar years. These decrypts, long kept secret, led to the uncovering of, among others, Soviet atomic spies Klaus Fuchs and the Rosenbergs, and the penetration of Western governments and intelligence services by spies such as Donald Maclean and Guy Burgess.

WiN: *Wolnosc i Niezawislosc* (Freedom and Independence). Polish anti-Communist organization formed after the Second World War from the remnants of the AK*. Fell under the control of the KGB* and UB* in 1947–1948 and was publicly disbanded in December 1952.

Notes

Chapter 3. A Visit to Headquarters

1. Headquarters had code-named Nosenko as "Barman," which, though it fit the carousing Nosenko, had been picked simply as the next available on an arbitrary list of words. In conversation and correspondence he was always referred to by this or subsequent cryptonyms. To avoid confusion I use his name throughout.

Chapter 4. En Route

1. He even had "spy" credentials of his own, a cloak and dagger presented by the president. Upon creation of the Central Intelligence Group in 1946, Truman convoked to the Oval Office Leahy and Rear Admiral Sidney W. Souers, designated as the first Director of Central Intelligence. There the president playfully presented each of them with a black hat, a cloak, and a wooden dagger, and pasted a black mustache on Leahy's lip and presented a certificate commissioning them respectively as "Personal Snooper" and "Director of Centralized Snooping."

2. Soon thereafter, in a normal rotation, Richardson was replaced by Bronson Tweedy.

3. Peter Deriabin and T. H. Bagley, *KGB. Masters of the Soviet Union* (New York: Hippocrene Books, 1989).

4. *Wiener Kurier,* 8 February 1955, "Sowjetkonsul als Lockvogel."

5. One of these was released for publication in a magazine article on Deriabin's revelations. *Life* 23 (March 1959): 116.

6. Here I cannot resist jumping ahead to an extraordinary moment after the Cold War. In eastern Berlin I, who some forty years earlier had been the case officer of the CIA operation that uncovered Blake, found myself in the backseat of a little car being driven by former East German intelligence chief Markus Wolf, while in the front passenger seat was Blake's KGB case officer, Sergey Kondrashev, helping us find the exact spot where the

Soviets uncovered the tunnel at its eastern end—using the sketch Blake had drawn for the KGB at the time, exposing the route of the tunnel even before it was dug.

7. A Soviet "Illegal"—the word here capitalized as we commonly did in CIA to distinguish its special meaning from the more general one—was a specially trained officer or agent operating in a foreign country under false name, nationality, and life story (legend). Illegals stayed rigidly away from Soviet installations and official representatives, who were routinely watched by Western security services. Illegals should not be confused with Western services' use of "non-official cover," whereby the operatives retain their personal and national identity while simply covering their relationship to the government.

Chapter 5. New Job, Under Clouds

1. Jerrold L. Schecter and Peter S. Deriabin, *The Spy Who Saved the World* (New York: Charles Scribner's Sons, 1992).

2. Oleg Penkovsky, *The Penkovsky Papers*, trans. Peter Deriabin (Garden City, N.Y.: Doubleday, 1965).

3. Harry Rositzke, *The CIA's Secret Operations* (New York: Reader's Digest Press, 1977), 68–69.

4. For simplicity the organization will be called "KGB" throughout this book, and this will not violate reality. Whether called a "Special Commission," "directorate," "people's commissariat," "ministry," "committee," or, today, "service," it began and remained one and the same organization throughout Soviet history. It was always headquartered in the same buildings and its unbroken succession of officers pursued the same basic tasks throughout Soviet history. Today, long after the fall of the Soviet Union, its members still proudly call themselves "Chekists," from the Russian initials of that early "Special Commission," Che-Ka. Today's Russian histories of the KGB begin in 1917, nearly forty years before those particular initials applied. Though ostensibly created only after the fall of the Soviet Union, Russia's SVR and FSB (post–Soviet era designations of the foreign intelligence component and the counterintelligence and security arm of the former KGB, respectively) officially celebrated their *eighty-eighth* birthday in 2005.

5. David Doyle, *Inside Espionage* (London: St. Martin's Press, 2000), 200–2.

Chapter 6. Bombshell

1. Frequent KGB practice was to have one or more other officers supporting an agent handler who was meeting an important agent. Several operatives working together can better detect and confuse hostile surveillance, and the one who meets and receives documents from the spy (evidence that could be used against him in case he is arrested) can quickly pass it to a nearby colleague before sitting down to talk with the spy.

Chapter 7. Popov's Ghost

1. Peer de Silva, *Sub Rosa. The CIA and the Uses of Intelligence* (New York: Times Books, 1978), 68–69 and 94–96. De Silva, who was the Soviet Division operations chief at the time, had himself recruited and assigned Smith to Moscow in 1953 in the event that Popov should be unexpectedly transferred there from Vienna. Smith's story is told by Richard H. Smith in

"The First Moscow Station: An Espionage Footnote to Cold War History," *International Journal of Intelligence and Counterintelligence* 3, no. 3 (1989): 333–46.

2. In his account of Smith's dalliance with the maid, de Silva lapses into an exaggeration favored by less informed writers and refers to the enchantress as "a KGB Major." In actual practice an attractive field-grade KGB officer is not assigned as a housemaid and laundress for even the few weeks needed to get a target into bed, thence to star in a form of pornographic film subsequently to be viewed by her colleagues of the officers' mess. In real life, the nubile maids came from a lesser stratum of Soviet society.

3. These files had been entrusted to the Tsarist ambassador in Paris, Vasily A. Maklakov, who much later gave them to the Hoover Institute to be sealed until his death. He had just died, in 1957. On the basis of his study, Smith wrote a book (*The Young Stalin* [New York: Farrar, Straus and Giroux, 1967]) that presented persuasive circumstantial evidence that Stalin had secretly cooperated with the Tsarist *Okhrana* at least from 1906 to 1912.

Smith was killed by a hit-and-run driver while standing on a pedestrian crosswalk in the San Francisco Bay area in the spring of 1982. The driver later turned himself in and the police found no reason to suspect that it was other than a genuine accident.

4. A. Kolpakiki and G. Prokhorov, *Vneshnyaya Razveda Rossii* (Russian Foreign Intelligence) (Moscow: Olma-Press, 2000), 70.

5. This was the thrust of a three-hundred-page study by CIA analyst Renée Peyton, according to Tom Mangold, *Cold Warrior. James Jesus Angleton: The CIA's Master Spy Hunter* (New York and London: Simon and Schuster, 1991), 387 n 40.

6. David E. Murphy, Sergey A. Kondrashev, and George Bailey, *Battleground Berlin* (New Haven: Yale University Press, 1997), 267–68 and (for the student case) 276.

7. Ibid., 276–77.

8. Some of these details, and others in the following paragraphs, were reported in *Battleground Berlin*, 279–80. I have seen the actual note.

9. The KGB may not yet have decided to attribute Popov's uncovering to the letter mailing because, as noted elsewhere, it did not fit the circumstances—surveillance had already seen Popov's contact with CIA.

10. Murphy, Kondrashev, and Bailey, *Battleground Berlin*, 277.

11. Report of the President's Commission on the Assassination of President John F. Kennedy (Washington: Government Printing Office, 1964), 268.

Chapter 8. Defection

1. House Select Committee on Assassinations, 95th Congress, Hearings (Washington: Government Printing Office, 1979), Vol. VI, 528.

2. Richard Helms with William Hood, *A Look over My Shoulder* (New York: Random House, 2003), 240–41.

Chapter 9. Impasse

1. Charles E. Bohlen, *Witness to History 1929–1969* (London: Weidenfeld and Nicolson, 1973), 346. Bohlen could not, of course, know of the KGB's (successful) recruitment of Andrey.

2. HSCA Hearings, Vol. XII, 521–22.

3. HSCA Hearings, Vol. XII, 507.

4. Oleg M. Nechiporenko, *Passport to Assassination* (New York: Birch Lane Press, 1993), 32–34, 43–44, 50–51, 55, 62–63.

5. Nosenko later spun tales to journalists. To Tom Mangold he claimed to have given details on "Soviet personnel in Geneva who were the best candidates for recruitment" (Tom Mangold, *Cold Warrior. James Jesus Angleton: The CIA's Master Spy Hunter* [New York and London: Simon and Schuster, 1991], 145). He did not.

6. Bruce Solie, asked by Newton S. Miler. Miler to the author.

Chapter 10. "Guiding Principle"

1. *Istorii organov sovetskikh gosudarstvennoy bezopastnosty* (History of Soviet State Security) (Moscow, Vyshaya Krasnoznamennaya Shkola KGB imeni F. E. Dzerzhinskogo [Dzerzhinsky KGB Red Banner Institute], 1977). The definitions come from *Kontrrazvedyvatel'nyy Slovar* (Counterintelligence Dictionary) (same publisher, 1972), 172 and 114.

2. The first citation is from *Ocherki Istorii Rossiyskoy Vneshney Razvedki* (Sketches from the History of Russian Foreign Intelligence) (Moscow: International Relations Publishing House, 1996), 8. The second is from Sergey Z. Ostryakov, *Voyennye Chekisty* (Military Chekists) (Moscow: Military Publishing House, 1979), ch. 1.

3. Among the sources the Chekists used was an *Okhrana* document dated 1907 and updated in 1916, titled "Instructions for Organizing Internal Observation." The Chekists consolidated these lessons in two manuals instructing their men to work this way (*Istorii*, ch. 2, pt. 3). The quote is from *Ocherki*, 7–8.

4. "Left-Wing Communism, an Infantile Disorder," 1920.

5. *Izvestiya*, 22 October 1918, cited in L. Gerson, *The Secret Police in Lenin's Russia* (Philadelphia: Temple University Press, 1976), 306 n9.

6. *Istorii*, ch. 4, pt. 5. I have inserted the word "opposition" in place of the then-current appellation "White Guard."

7. *Ocherki*, 8.

8. KGB veterans confirmed this after the Cold War. Pavel Sudoplatov, deputy head of the KGB (then NKVD) foreign intelligence operations in the 1930s, in Pavel Sudoplatov, Anatoly Sudoplatov, and Jerrold and Leona Schecter, *Special Tasks* (Boston: Little, Brown, 1994), 156. Former KGB foreign-counterintelligence chief General Oleg Kalugin also told of KGB penetrations of the emigration: Oleg Kalugin, *The First Directorate* (New York: St. Martin's Press, 1994), 55, 193.

Chapter 11. Deceiving in Wartime

1. Robert Stephan, *Stalin's Secret War. Soviet Counterintelligence Against the Nazis, 1941–1945* (Lawrence, Kan.: University Press of Kansas, 2004), 52–53 and 83.

2. David Thomas, "Foreign Armies East and German Military Intelligence in Russia, 1941–1945," *Journal of Contemporary History*, no. 22 (1987): 190.

3. Reinhard Gehlen, *The Service* (New York: Times Mirror World Publishing, 1972), 109.

4. H. Höhne and H. Zolling, *The General Was a Spy* (New York: Coward, McCann and Geoghegan, 1972), 21–22 and 43.

5. Walter Schellenberg, *The Labyrinth* (New York: Da Capo Press, 2000), 263.

6. Several different Soviet units controlled these double agents, though the deception they passed to the Germans was centrally coordinated in the top military staff. Among their commanders were military counterintelligence (SMERSH) chief Viktor Abakumov, Partisan Directorate leader Pavel Sudoplatov, and regional State Security commanders in the affected zones, among them the later prominent Yevgeny Pitovranov. Some of these spymasters wrote accounts of these operations, including Pavel Sudoplatov, Anatoly Sudoplatov, and Jerrold and Leona Schecter, *Special Tasks* (Boston: Little, Brown, 1994), and Dmitry Tarasov, *Bolshaya Igra* (The Great Game) (Moscow, 1997.)

7. To the author from Arnold M. Silver, who interrogated Baun in 1945 at the U.S. army's interrogation center at Camp King in Oberursel, near Frankfurt. See also Silver's article, "Questions, Questions, Questions: Memories of Oberursel" *Intelligence and National Security* 8, no. 2 (April 1993): 208.

8. From October 1943 to May 1944 Soviet Counterintelligence, according to its own secret history, sent 345 agents, of whom 57 succeeded in getting themselves recruited and trained to go back, or getting positions in the German intelligence and training groups, where they proceeded to recruit 69 more.

9. *Istorii organov sovetskikh gosudarstvennoy bezopastnosty* (History of Soviet State Security) (Moscow, Vyshaya Krasnoznamennaya Shkola KGB imeni F. E. Dzerzhinskogo [Dzerzhinsky KGB Red Banner Institute], 1977), ch. 9, pt. 4. The Partisan Directorate statistic comes from Sudoplatov et al., *Special Tasks*, 160. The KGB's total is cited by Tarasov, *Bolshaya Igra*.

10. *Istorii*, ch. 9, pt. 4.

11. This operation is described in *Istorii*, ch. 9, pt. 5, and in Sudoplatov et al., *Special Tasks*, 152–60.

12. Sudoplatov et al., *Special Tasks*, 158–59.

13. Ibid. See also the article by Lev Bezymensky, Winfred Mayer, and Pavel Sudoplatov, "Geyne po imeni Maks" (Heine alias Max), in *Novaya Vremya*, no. 41, Moscow, 1993.

Chapter 12. Postwar Games

1. As listed in NKVD orders of 28 November 1940 and 25 April 1941 for their first takeover of Lithuania, cited in Aleksey Myagkov, *Inside the KGB* (Richmond, U.K.: Foreign Affairs Publishing, 1976), 15.

2. Josef Swiatlo's access to this and other tightly guarded secrets stemmed from his rare position in the UB, spying on the Communist leadership itself. Some of his revelations about Soviet wartime collaboration with the Gestapo in Poland were published in *News from Behind the Iron Curtain* 4, no. 3 (March 1955), esp. 14–16 and 19–20.

3. Stalin had ordered the jailing of Pitovranov shortly after that of his boss, Viktor Abakumov, in about August 1951, along with scores of other KGB officials, in connection with intrigues that are only beginning now, more than a half century later, to be clarified. See Jonathan Brent and Vladimir P. Naumov, *Stalin's Last Crime* (London: John Murray, 2003).

4. *Istorii organov sovetskikh gosudarstvennoy bezopastnosty* (History of Soviet State Security) (Moscow, Vyshaya Krasnoznamennaya Shkola KGB imeni F. E. Dzerzhinskogo [Dzerzhinsky KGB Red Banner Institute], 1977), ch. 10 (Conclusions and pts. 3 and 4).

5. Some of these operations are described in Tom Bower, *The Red Web* (London: Aurum Press, 1989), and in *Istorii* and *Ocherki Istorii Rossiyskoy Vneshney Razvedki*

(Sketches from the History of Russian Foreign Intelligence) (Moscow: International Relations Publishing House, 1996).

6. David E. Murphy, Sergey A. Kondrashev, and George Bailey, *Battleground Berlin* (New Haven: Yale University Press, 1997), 24–26.

7. Fabrichnikov's operational career was summarized on a Russian Internet site: http://wwii-soldat.narod.ru/fabrichnikov.htm. Former foreign operations directorate counterintelligence chief Oleg Kalugin confirmed to me his deputy Fabrichnikov's transfer to head the Second Chief Directorate 14th Department.

Chapter 13. Symbiosis: Moles and Games

1. *Istorii organov sovetskikh gosudarstvennoy bezopastnosty* (History of Soviet State Security) (Moscow, Vyshaya Krasnoznamennaya Shkola KGB imeni F. E. Dzerzhinskogo [Dzerzhinsky KGB Red Banner Institute], 1977), ch. 5, pt. 4.

2. Ibid., ch. 3, pt. 3.

3. Vitaly Pavlov, *Dela Sneg* (Operation Snow) (Moscow: Geya, 1996), last page. Pavlov was aware, of course, that these onetime Communist penetrations of OSS had been discovered and dismissed before they could move into the new CIA. See also Allen Weinstein and Alexander Vassiliev, *The Haunted Wood* (New York: Random House, 1999), 238ff, on this move from idealism to treason and on penetrations of OSS.

4. Oleg Kalugin, *The First Directorate* (New York: St. Martin's Press, 1994), 167.

5. James Critchfield, *Partners at the Creation* (Annapolis, Md.: Naval Institute Press, 2005), 194.

6. CIA had obtained KGB secret orders along these lines, and senior KGB veterans (such as General Vitaly Pavlov in *Dela Sneg*) have confirmed it since the end of the Cold War.

7. Reinhard Gehlen, *The Service* (New York: Times Mirror World Publishing, 1972), 246.

8. Viktor Cherkashin with Gregory Feifer, *Spy Handler. Memoir of a KGB Officer* (New York: Basic Books, 2005), 183.

Chapter 14. Dead Drop

1. Penkovsky proposed this site in a letter passed to the American Embassy through an American student tourist whom he accosted on a Moscow street in August 1960 (Jerrold L. Schecter and Peter S. Deriabin, *The Spy Who Saved the World* [New York: Charles Scribner's Sons, 1992], 425–27). Penkovsky's letter was seen by four highly placed members of the Embassy and afterward by four CIA insiders in Washington. Only these individuals and our Moscow Station knew the details.

2. Abidian, conversation with the author.

3. The desperate and corrupt manner by which CIA and Nosenko later dealt with this anomaly—and with Nosenko's failure to mention this during the 1962 Geneva meetings—is described in Chapter 19.

4. Schecter and Deriabin, *The Spy Who Saved the World*, 262.

5. Ibid., 289. This book, based on the CIA case file, reported that the British, because they had successfully met Penkovsky on the 23rd, considered the phone call a false alarm and recommended against any visit to the drop.

6. Garbler's statement was reported by Joseph J. Trento, *The Secret History of the CIA*

(Roseville, Calif.: Prima Publishing, 2001), 246–47. Abidian, whose memory was clear and certain (and of course could or would never have gone without instructions to do so), told me the correct information about Garbler's uncertainty and recommendation.

7. For the "Zeph" matter as seen from the Western side, see Schecter and Deriabin, *The Spy Who Saved the World*, 151, 165, 221, and 336.

8. Ibid., 322.

9. The KGB had presumably got the same explanation from Penkovsky after his arrest in September or October 1962, and must have been relieved by Wynne's confirmation that this strange unknown was simply a bar girl.

10. Vitaly Pavlov, *Dela Sneg* (Operation Snow) (Moscow: Geya, 1996), emphasis added.

11. KGB General Yevgeny Grig, *Da, ya tam rabotal* (Yes, I Worked There) (Moscow: Geya, 1997), 14.

12. The questioner was the writer Jerrold Schecter, getting the KGB's cooperation on a book on the Penkovsky case (Schecter and Deriabin, *The Spy Who Saved the World*, 413, emphasis added).

Chapter 15. Code Clerks

1. Perhaps realizing how this contradicted his career story, Nosenko later forgot the metallurgical delegation and changed his story. He had gone there, he said, to teach the Cubans how to work against Western diplomats in Havana (an echo of his Sofia improvisation). Still later, he spun a tale of carrying back to Moscow Fidel Castro's correspondence to Khrushchev about Soviet military plans for Cuba. To this he added a dramatic note: passing through Holland on his way back, he had vainly tried to attract CIA's attention, already then seeking to establish a relationship (Tom Mangold, *Cold Warrior. James Jesus Angleton: The CIA's Master Spy Hunter* [New York and London: Simon and Schuster, 1991], 141). By that time he had apparently forgotten his earlier claim that his approach to us in 1962 was only to cover his misuse of operational funds.

Chapter 16. Connections

1. The KGB was spreading stories of its plans to assassinate Nosenko. The KGB counterintelligence chief in New York told his colleague Oleg Gordievsky in the late 1960s that his prime murder targets in the United States were Nosenko and Anatoly Golitsyn (C. Andrew and O. Gordievsky, *KGB: The Inside Story* [New York: HarperCollins, 1990], 585).

2. George Lardner, Jr., "FBI Says Its Spy in KGB Was a Fake," *Washington Post*, 3 September 1981.

3. John Barron, *KGB. The Secret Work of Soviet Secret Agents* (London: Hodder and Stoughton, 1974), 124.

4. According to a KGB document in the so-called Mitrokhin Archive, Cherepanov was arrested on 17 December 1963 on "the frontier with Turkestan" and "sentenced to death at a secret trial in April 1964." Christopher Andrew and Vasily Mitrokhin, *The Mitrokhin Archive. The KGB in Europe and the West* (London: Allen Lane/Penguin, 1999), 242.

5. It was possible that the KGB (using Polyakov) had dispatched Tairova –through Popov in full or partial awareness of Popov's treason, with one or both of two purposes: to test Popov (seeing whether a KGB mole in the New York Field Office of the FBI would confirm that the Americans knew in advance of her arrival) and/or to create a collateral

excuse to arrest Popov in a way that would hide a mole who actually betrayed him. If Tairova were to spot surveillance—or say she did—Popov would be the prime suspect for having betrayed her mission. And in fact she did report—falsely—that she had spotted surveillance (falsely, because she claimed she was followed all the way from Berlin, which she was not). And Popov did then "fall under suspicion."

6. Canadian Television, "The KGB Connections: An Investigation into Soviet Espionage Operations," late 1981.

7. Tom Mangold, *Cold Warrior. James Jesus Angleton: The CIA's Master Spy Hunter* (New York and London: Simon and Schuster, 1991), 206, named "important" GRU spies uncovered by Polyakov in his first year of cooperation (i.e., late 1961 through 1962). In reality, all had been previously known or were dead cases, or were falsely attributed to Polyakov. U.S. army Lieutenant Colonel William Henry Whalen had been under FBI suspicion and surveillance since 1959, suffered a heart attack in 1960, retired from the army in 1961, and was of no further use to the Soviets by the time Polyakov "uncovered" him—an ideal subject for KGB sacrifice. Similarly, army Sergeant Jack Dunlap, once an important source of communications secrets, had failed a polygraph test, retired from the service, and lost all access to secrets just before he was fingered to the Americans. The British Air Ministry employee Frank Bossard was actively spying for the GRU when uncovered—but uncovered by another source, Nikolay Chernov, FBI code name "Nicknack." Air force Sergeant Herbert W. Boeckenhaupt did not begin spying for the GRU until June 1965, and he did so in Germany while Polyakov was stationed in Burma.

Chapter 17. Crunch Time

1. John Vassall, *Vassall. The Autobiography of a Spy* (London: Sidgwick and Jackson, 1975), 132–34.

2. Oleg Kalugin, *The First Directorate* (New York: St. Martin's Press, 1994), 57–58.

3. We foresaw—and forestalled—what was to happen twenty years later. After a few weeks in the West the ostensible KGB defector Vitaly Yurchenko, having betrayed "secrets," walked out on CIA in Washington and returned to Moscow, not to be punished as a traitor but to resume his KGB employment and to be given a medal.

Chapter 18. Face-off

1. House Select Committee on Assassinations, 95th Congress, Hearings (Washington: Government Printing Office, 1979), Vol. II, 483; Vol. IV, 97–98.

2. "The Analysis of Yuri Nosenko's Polygraph Examination," testimony of Richard O. Arther, president, Scientific Lie Detection, Inc., New York, N.Y., and director, National Training Center on Polygraph Science, to the Select Committee on Assassinations, U.S. House of Representatives, 95th Congress, Second Session, March 1979, paragraphs 33, 34 and 35. Mr. Arther rejected the argument by some analysts that it was invalid because of the added device.

3. Not having the transcripts of the interrogation I am compelled to reconstruct the questions and answers from informal notes, but all these questions were asked and his answers were as here given.

4. The FBI's source in the New York KGB rezidentura, Aleksey Kulak, heard in his office that "Lieutenant Colonel" Nosenko had defected in Geneva when he was recalled to

Moscow by a telegram from the Center. Later, after Nosenko's own admission of this fact, Kulak reported that he had now heard that Nosenko was not really a lieutenant colonel but only a captain.

5. In his early weeks in the United States I had invited him to my house and introduced him to my family, and had spent part of his Hawaiian vacation with him there. He knew most other officers only by pseudonyms, as was routine in early handling of defectors.

6. CIA failed to include Deriabin's report when in the late 1970s it transmitted to the House Select Committee on Assassinations a supposedly comprehensive documentation of Nosenko's case as it applied to his reporting on Lee Harvey Oswald. This documentation gave no hint of Deriabin's intervention or of his conclusion that "Nosenko did not handle Lee Harvey Oswald's [KGB] file."

Chapter 19. Head in the Sand

1. Angleton told me many years later that he and Helms had thought to brief me personally at the time, but decided against it because to ask me to keep such an operation secret from my own boss, the chief of SB Division, might cause a conflict of loyalties. Indeed it would have.

2. As Helms became director of Central Intelligence, the chief of Naval Intelligence, Vice Admiral Rufus L. Taylor, was coming in as his deputy. Taylor had been acquainted with Artamonov, who had supplied the U.S. navy with fresh and important information from his (demonstrated) experience as a destroyer captain.

3. A decade later this case, at first so secret, came to be widely publicized, beginning in May 1978 with an article by Strobe Talbott in *Time*. The case has since been treated in books in varying ways: sketchily by D. C. Martin in *Wilderness of Mirrors* (New York: Harper and Row, 1980), seriously by Henry Hurt in *Shadrin. The Spy Who Never Came Back* (New York: Reader's Digest Press, 1981), and with basic errors and vacuous speculation by W. R. Corson and S. and J. Trento, *Widows* (New York: Crown, 1989), and by J. Trento, *The Secret History of the CIA* (New York: Forum/Prima, 2001).

4. The then head of the KGB's foreign counterintelligence operations, Oleg Kalugin, asserted that it was only in the Canada meeting, six years after the case began, that the KGB first realized that Artamonov was under American control. As a test, he said, the KGB sent Artamonov to meet in Canada to see whether the Americans would inform the Canadian security service, where the KGB had a mole who would hear of it (Oleg Kalugin, *The First Directorate* [New York: St. Martin's Press, 1994], 95–96 and 152–58).

5. House Select Committee on Assassinations, 95th Congress, Hearings (Washington: Government Printing Office, 1979) (hereafter HSCA Hearings), Vol. II, 450–51.

6. Memorandum for the director, from Deputy Director of Central Intelligence Rufus Taylor, 4 October 1968. HSCA Hearings, Vol. 4, 46.

7. These words were used to describe Solie when his report was declassified in the 1990s to show learners how to do truly professional counterintelligence analysis.

8. The Nosenko Report, declassified 1994. CI Online, Counterintelligence Center's Counterintelligence and Security Program (CISP$), Section II.3.

9. Ibid., Section IV.E, 5–8.

10. Ibid., II.D.1 (emphasis added).

11. Ibid., III.B.4 (emphasis added).

12. Ibid., IV.C.3.

13. Ibid., IV.D (emphasis added).

14. The rebuttal has remained hidden but was implicitly declassified when CIA declassified Solie's report in 1994.

15. As CIA reported to the HSCA in 1978. HSCA Hearings, Vol. II, 458–59, 485; Vol. IV, 37–38, 60–61, 77–78, 93–94.

16. A senior CIA official told me this in 1981.

17. "Notes from the Director," no. 30, 21 September 1978, declassified.

18. Leonard V. McCoy, "Yuri Nosenko, CIA," *CIRA Newsletter* XII, no. 3 (Fall 1987): 22.

Chapter 20. Lingering Debate

1. Of the fifteen, thirteen are named: "Kitty Hawk" [Igor Kochnov], Ilya Dzhirkvelov, Yuri Loginov, Aleksandr Cherepanov, Vitaly Yurchenko, and apparently Yuri Krotkov, as well as Vladimir Kuzichkin, Viktor Gundarev, Ivan Bogatyy, the Illegal "Rudolf Herrmann," Vladimir Vetrov (alias "Farewell"), Oleg Gordievsky, and Oleg Lyalin. Tom Mangold, *Cold Warrior: James Jesus Angleton: The CIA's Master Spy Hunter* (New York and London: Simon and Schuster, 1991), 365 n53.

2. House Select Committee on Assassinations, 95th Congress, Hearings (Washington: Government Printing Office, 1979) (hereafter HSCA Hearings), Vol. 4, 60.

3. Those five were Cherepanov, Loginov, Krotkov, Lyalin, and Vetrov. Loginov, as mentioned elsewhere, heard of an "important defection" that (by its date) presumably referred to Nosenko's, but he claimed not to know who it was, nor did he claim any other knowledge about the incident.

4. Stanislav Levchenko to Peter Deriabin; Deriabin to the author, in conversation, 1981.

5. In this book alone can be found some of the reasons to suspect Cherepanov, Loginov, Krotkov, Yurchenko, and Kochnov, while Dzhirkvelov fabricated his account of personal knowledge of Nosenko and Gribanov.

6. Filipp Bobkov, *KGB I Vlast'* (KGB and State Power) (Moscow: Publishing House "Veteran MP," 1993), ch. 22. He wrote that Nosenko went out in 1964—not 1962—to get medicine for his daughter's illness, and on "serious operational business," not delegation watchdogging. Semichastniy's statements are from his memoirs, cited in *Krasnaya Zvezda* (Red Star), 6 September 2002.

7. *Washington Post*, Outlook Section, 7 November 1993. Kalugin later confirmed this to me.

8. Oleg M. Nechiporenko, *Passport to Assassination* (New York: Birch Lane Press, 1993), 214–64 and especially 225–26 and 233–35.

9. Henno Lohmeyer, foreword to Oleg Tumanov, *Tumanov. Confessions of a KGB Agent* (Chicago, Berlin, Tokyo and Moscow: edition q, 1993), x.

10. This nonsense, presumably sponsored and undoubtedly cleared by the KGB (currently called FSB and SVR), appeared under the title "Predatel'stvo ili—Pokhishcheniye?" (Treason or–Abduction?) in *Krasnaya Zvezda* (Red Star), 29 August, 6 September, 11 September, and 19 December 2002. Its stated author, Aleksandr Sokolov, was a onetime KGB counterintelligence officer in Washington. The "trap" citation is from Nosenko's boss; Bobkov, *KGB I Vlast'*, 227–29. Another contributor to the kidnapping theme, equating the kidnapping of Nosenko with the later "kidnapping" of Vitaly Yurchenko in Rome, was KGB General V. N. Udilov, in *Zapiski Kontrrazvedchika* (Notes of a Counterintelligence Officer) (Moscow: Yaguar, 1994), 201–6.

11. For Helms's testimony on this subject see HSCA Hearings, Vol. IV, 33–34, 61–63, 96, 99. He said the same thing in an interview with David Frost, 22–23 May 1978 (*Studies in*

Intelligence, Special Unclassified Edition, Fall 2000, 130). Helms expressed this view again in 2001.

12. Mangold, *Cold Warrior,* 175.

13. William E. Colby and Peter Forbath, *Honorable Men. My Life in the CIA* (New York: Simon and Schuster, 1978), 244–45.

14. Ibid., 364. Rolfe Kingsley, Murphy's successor as Soviet Division chief, described this (imaginary) "paralysis" in Mangold, *Cold Warrior,* 242.

15. Burton Gerber, cited by his deputy Milton Bearden. Milton Bearden and James Risen, *The Main Enemy* (London: Century, 2003), 23.

16. Christopher Andrew and Vasily Mitrokhin, *The Mitrokhin Archive. The KGB in Europe and the West* (London: Allen Lane/Penguin, 1999).

17. Colby, *Honorable Men,* 364.

18. It was McCoy who took the files, as I heard from a member of the Counterintelligence Staff who was there. Presumably this was a part of his large-scale destruction of the files that he himself described to a journalist (Mangold, *Cold Warrior,* 306).

19. HSCA Hearings, Vol. II, 490.

20. Mangold, *Cold Warrior,* 320–21.

21. HSCA Hearings, Vol. XII, 543. While questioning Nosenko we asked a specialist whether the much-touted "truth serum" sodium amytal would help, but were told it was basically ineffective. This has been misrepresented in some writings as a request to use it which was denied. I made no such "request" and am sure no one else did.

22. Report of the Select Committee on Assassinations of the U.S. House of Representatives, Findings and Recommendations (Washington, D.C., Government Printing Office, 20 March 1979), 102.

23. Hart's testimony is in HSCA Hearings, Vol. II, 487–536. My rebuttal to that testimony was printed in HSCA Hearings, Vol. XII, 573–644. The murderous thoughts Hart attributed to me were contained in a penciled note I jotted while mulling over possible ways to resolve Nosenko's status. I had thought of about ten or eleven things to do—possibly turning him back, handing him to another Western service, locating him in another country, or resettling him in some remote area of the United States. I also amused myself by giving vent to frustration in the way a baseball fan might shout, "Kill the umpire!" and stuck in this list such impossible and impractical things as killing him or rendering him crazy. Of course I never sent or showed or even discussed these thoughts with anyone. I must have inadvertently dropped my penciled jottings into the file, where Hart, with evident delight, found them. He edited out the more serious alternatives as "insignificant" and presented the facetious but compromising ones to the HSCA as evidence of actual CIA planning. I had completely forgotten the note (or the ruminations) and learned of its full contents only through the courtesy of a member of the subcommittee staff.

24. HSCA Hearings, Vol. II, 509, 511.

25. HSCA Hearings, Vol. XII, 623, 642.

26. "Yuri Nosenko, KGB," British Broadcasting Company (BBC), first shown in the United States by Home Box Office (HBO) on 7 September 1986. Issued as DVD under the title "Yuri Nosenko, Double Agent."

27. HSCA Hearings, Vol. II, 490, 515, 522. The original review by Mark Wyatt of the BBC/HBO telefilm "Yuri Nosenko, KGB" appeared in the *CIRA Newsletter* (Spring 1987), and McCoy's defense of Nosenko appeared that fall in Leonard V. McCoy, "Yuri Nosenko, CIA," *CIRA Newsletter* XII, no. 3 (Fall 1987): 22. I answered McCoy in the edition of Spring 1988 (vol. XIII, no. 2). See also Mangold, *Cold Warrior,* 270. My general appraisal of Hart's testimony is in HSCA Hearings, Vol. XII, 593.

28. Mangold, *Cold Warrior,* vi.

Chapter 21. Hiding a Mole, KGB-Style

1. Viktor Cherkashin with Gregory Feifer, *Spy Handler. Memoir of a KGB Officer* (New York: Basic Books, 2005), 206. Milton Bearden and James Risen, *The Main Enemy* (London: Century, 2003), 202–3 and 297ff.

2. CIA veterans described these various paths of investigation in memoirs or in talks with investigative reporters. See, for example, Pete Earley, *Confessions of a Spy* (New York: G. P. Putnam's Sons, 1997), 222; Bearden and Risen, *The Main Enemy*, 377–78; David Wise, *Nightmover* (New York: HarperCollins, 1995), 164–65; and David Wise, *The Spy Who Got Away* (New York: Random House, 1988); Ronald Kessler, *Escape from the CIA* (New York: Pocket Books, 1991).

3. That new KGB arrival was never identified publicly and in 2005 was still being sought by Russian Counterintelligence. His advent was revealed by Ron Kessler, *The FBI* (New York: Pocket Books, 1993), 433; Brian Duffy and Edward T. Pound, "The Million Dollar Spy," *U.S. News and World Report* (7 March 1994): 61; Peter Maas, *Killer Spy* (New York: Winner Books/Time Warner, 1995), 134, 164; David Wise, *Nightmover*, 227–28; Tim Weiner, David Johnston, and Neil A. Lewis, *Betrayal* (New York: Random House, 1995), 234; Bearden and Risen, *The Main Enemy*, 526. It got KGB confirmation by Colonel Viktor Cherkashin (Viktor Cherkashin with Gregory Feifer, *Spy Handler. Memoir of a KGB Officer* [New York: Basic Books, 2005], 203).

4. Bearden and Risen, *The Main Enemy*, 527; Cherkashin, *Spy Handler*, 253.

5. Cherkashin, *Spy Handler*, 206.

6. Alexander Kouzminov, *Biological Espionage* (London: Greenhill Books, 2005), 59.

7. Cherkashin, *Spy Handler*, 259 and 206.

8. Bearden and Risen, *The Main Enemy*, 302–3.

9. Cherkashin, *Spy Handler*, 206 and 261.

10. Bearden and Risen, *The Main Enemy*, 23 and 303–4.

11. Cherkashin, *Spy Handler*, 259; Bearden and Risen, *The Main Enemy*, 175–76 and 197–98.

12. Cherkashin, *Spy Handler*, 260.

13. The most detailed and authoritative elaboration of this fairy tale was given by Victor Cherkashin, who had supervised Yurchenko and undoubtedly knew better (*Spy Handler*, 166–73). Several memoirs by senior KGB officers have also supported the humbug, such as Kryuchkov, *Lichnoye Delo* (Personal File) (Moscow: Olma, 1996), 122ff, and V. N. Udilov. *Zapiski Kontrrazvedchika* (Notes of a Counterintelligence Officer) (Moscow: Yaguar, 1994), 202–5. The latter even suggested that such a "kidnapping" was what really happened to Yuri Nosenko twenty years earlier.

14. Kouzminov, *Biological Espionage*, 107.

15. Tom Mangold, *Cold Warrior. James Jesus Angleton: The CIA's Master Spy Hunter* (New York and London: Simon and Schuster, 1991), 203–4, citing Oleg Gordievsky, who had sat on the review board. The decision was surely based less on "liberal times" than on high-level, eyes-only instructions to the review board chairman.

Chapter 22. The Other Side of the Moon

1. Two of its Eastern European participants confirmed to me this conference that Michal Goleniewski had reported in his "Sniper" correspondence.

2. "The Agent Named 'Fedora.' Did Hero of the Soviet Union Aleksey Kulak Work for the FBI?" by Vladimir Snegirev, in three installments in *Trud*, Moscow, 5, 8, and 9 December

1992, translated and published in FBIS-USR-92–163. The case was later mulled over in a speculative article—preserving the mystery intact—by KGB American-operations specialist Yuli N. Kobyakov in the newspaper *Sovershenno Sekretno* (Top Secret), no. 5, 2002, 23–24, as part of a "forthcoming" book, "A New Look at Old Spy Cases," that has still not been published, perhaps a victim of the tightening security precautions in Russia.

Chapter 23. Boomerang

1. J. C. Masterson, *The Double Cross System in the War of 1939 to 1945* (New Haven: Yale University Press, 1972), 30–31.

2. American Ambassador Walter Bedell Smith, *My Three Years in Moscow* (Philadelphia: J. B. Lippincott Company, 1950), 187. Also Jack Anderson, "What Happens to American Traitors?" *Parade Magazine,* 4 December 1960.

3. These statements, already cited in earlier chapters, were made by authoritative sources: a CIA deputy director, a CIA director, a senior officer who requestioned Nosenko extensively, and a former deputy chief of CIA's Counterintelligence Staff.

4. Whittaker Chambers, *Witness* (New York: Random House, 1952), 770 (paraphrase).

5. Ilya Dzhirkvelov, *Secret Servant. My Life with the KGB and the Soviet Elite* (London: Collins, 1987), 280–81.

6. Stansfield Turner, *Notes from the Director no. 30,* 21 September 1978, declassified.

Appendix B. A Myth and Its Making

1. John L. Hart, *The CIA's Russians* (Annapolis, Md.: Naval Institute Press, 2003); Leonard V. McCoy, former deputy chief of Counterintelligence Staff, in Leonard V. McCoy, "Yuri Nosenko, CIA," *CIRA Newsletter* XII, no. 3 (Fall 1987): 22.

2. Obituary of John L. Hart in *Guardian Unlimited,* 7 June 2002 (hereafter Hart obituary).

3. Tom Mangold, *Cold Warrior. James Jesus Angleton: The CIA's Master Spy Hunter* (New York and London: Simon and Schuster, 1991), presumably from Counterintelligence Staff deputy chief Leonard McCoy, whom the author acknowledged to have "left an indelible imprint on every one of these pages"; Hart obituary.

4. Sworn testimony of John L. Hart, representing the director of Central Intelligence, House Select Committee on Assassinations, 95th Congress, Hearings (Washington: Government Printing Office, 1979) (hereafter HSCA Hearings), Vol. II, 494–95.

5. Hart, HSCA Hearings, Vol. II, 495, 519, 535; 581; and 586, and his book *The CIA's Russians;* McCoy, "Yuri Nosenko, CIA," 22; Mangold, *Cold Warrior,* 39–40; Colby, *Honorable Men,* 244.

6. Hart, *The CIA's Russians,* 146. Elsewhere Hart had testified that it was Golitsyn who caused all Nosenko's troubles.

7. Hart, HSCA Hearings, Vol. II; Hart obituary; McCoy, "Yuri Nosenko, CIA," 22; Hart, *The CIA's Russians,* 139.

8. Hart, HSCA Hearings, Vol. II, 495.

9. Hart obituary; Mangold, *Cold Warrior,* 175.

10. Hart, HSCA Hearings, Vol. II, 519.

11. Memorandum of deputy director of Central Intelligence Rufus Taylor, 4 October 1968. HSCA Hearings, Vol. IV, 46.

12. HSCA Hearings, Vol. II, 508, 510, 526, 527.

13. McCoy, "Yuri Nosenko, CIA," 22.

14. Stansfield Turner, *Notes from the Director*, no. 30, 21 September 1978, and his *Secrecy and Democracy—The CIA in Transition* (Boston: Houghton Mifflin, 1985).

15. Hart, HSCA Hearings, Vol. II, 508, 510, 526, 527. "Fundamental nobility" were the words of Leonard McCoy, deputy head of CIA's Counterintelligence Staff, in McCoy, "Yuri Nosenko, CIA," 22.

16. McCoy, "Yuri Nosenko, CIA," 22.

17. McCoy, "Yuri Nosenko, CIA," 22, 18; Hart, HSCA Hearings, Vol. II, 495.

18. McCoy, "Yuri Nosenko, CIA," 22.

19. Mangold, *Cold Warrior*, 145 (as noted elsewhere, this book acknowledges McCoy's imprint on its every page).

20. Hart, *The CIA's Russians*.

21. Hart, HSCA Hearings, Vol. II, 495.

22. Ibid.; Hart, *The CIA's Russians*, 139.

23. McCoy, "Yuri Nosenko, CIA," 22.

24. FBI testimony, HSCA Hearings, Vol. XII, 539.

25. Hart, HSCA Hearings, Vol. II, 492.

26. Hart, *The CIA's Russians*.

27. Turner, *Secrecy and Democracy*.

28. HSCA Hearings, Vol. 2, 496.

29. Hart, HSCA Hearings, Vol. II, 490; McCoy, "Yuri Nosenko, CIA," 22.

30. Hart, *The CIA's Russians*; Mangold, *Cold Warrior*.

31. McCoy, "Yuri Nosenko, CIA," 22.

32. HSCA Hearings, Vol. II, 494, 519, 535; Vol. XII, 581 and 586.

33. McCoy, "Yuri Nosenko, CIA," 22; Mangold, *Cold Warrior*, 39–40.

34. Mangold, *Cold Warrior*, 3.

35. Christopher Andrew, speaking on the BBC and in two other books in which he quoted Nosenko in ways that demonstrated the author's complete confidence in the myth.

36. Peter Grose, *Gentleman Spy. The Life of Allen Dulles* (Amherst: University of Massachusetts Press, 1994), 551.

37. Milton Bearden, talking of himself and Burton Gerber. Milton Bearden and James Risen, *The Main Enemy* (London: Century, 2003), 20–23.

38. Frederick L. Wettering, "Counterintelligence: The Broken Triad," *International Journal of Intelligence and Counterintelligence* 13, no. 3 (Fall 2000): 267. The author is there described as "a retired . . . [CIA] operations officer [who] managed clandestine operations in Europe and Africa."

39. Robert Baer, *See No Evil. The True Story of a Ground Soldier in the CIA's War on Terrorism* (New York: Crown, 2002), 256–57.

Appendix C. Self-deception—Bane of Counterintelligence

This is an edited version of an article by Tennent H. Bagley, titled "Bane of Counterintelligence: Our Penchant for Self-deception," that appeared in *International Journal of Intelligence and Counterintelligence* 6, no. 1 (1993). Reprinted by permission.

1. The *Guinness Book of Records*, 22d ed., 191, notes that the civil hearing began on 11 May 1872 and lasted 103 days, while the criminal hearing for perjury lasted 188 days with sentencing on 28 February 1874.

2. Bernard Grebanier, *The Great Shakespeare Forgery* (London: Heinemann, 1966), 143.

3. William Henry Ireland's confession, 1805, cited in A. Klein, *Grand Deception* (Philadelphia and New York: Lippincott, 1955), 120.

4. Azev's fellow conspirator Boris Savinkov, *Vospominaniya Terrorista* (Moscow, 1909), English translation: *Memoirs of a Terrorist* (New York, 1931); and Boris Nicolaevsky, *Aseff the Spy. Russian Terrorist and Police Stool* (Garden City: Doubleday, Doran, 1934). These citations are drawn from the French translation of Savinkov (*Souvenirs d'un terroriste* [Paris: Editions Champ Libre, 1982], 325–55), and from Nicolaevsky, 4–7, 268–87.

5. John S. Reshatar, Jr., *A Concise History of the Communist Party of the Soviet Union* (New York: Praeger, 1960), 17; Bertram Wolfe, *Three Who Made a Revolution* (New York: Dial, 1948), 547–48; David Shub, *Lenin* (New York: Mentor, 1961), 119–20; Edward E. Smith, *The Young Stalin* (New York: Farrar, Straus and Giroux, 1967), 404 n546; G. Aronson, *Rossya nakanune . . .* (New York: 1962), 53–55.

6. The Sneevliet incident was reported by Georges Vereeken, *The GPU in the Trotskyist Movement* (Clapham, England: New Park Publications, 1976), 292–93, 364. Peter Deriabin testified before Congress that he had heard inside the KGB that it had killed Sedov. Other congressional testimony pointed to Zborowski as supplying the necessary information. Alexander Orlov later testified to the anonymous note, and David Dallin testified to Trotsky's derisive rejection of it. For Mercader, see Isaac Don Levine, *The Mind of an Assassin* (New York: Farrar, Straus and Cudahy, 1959).

7. Citing examples drawn by Titus Livius from the time of Alexander the Great, Machiavelli warned of "the danger of trusting to the representations of men who have been expelled from their country." "As to their vain hopes and promises," he wrote, "such is the extreme desire to return to their homes that they naturally believe many things that are not true, and add many others on purpose; so that, with what they really believe and what they say they believe, they will fill you with hopes to that degree that if you attempt to act upon them you will incur a fruitless expense, or engage in an undertaking that will involve you in ruin" (Niccolo Machiavelli, *The Prince and the Discourses* [New York: Modern Library, 1940]; *Discourses*, Second Book, Chapter XXXI, 388–89).

8. Stalin's closing-out of Trust as part of his 1927 "war scare" provocation, and his similar closure of WiN in 1952 as part of his preparations for a major purge, are mentioned in Chapter 12 of this book, as well as in Peter Deriabin and T. H. Bagley, *KGB. Masters of the Soviet Union* (New York: Hippocrene Books, 1989), 262–65.

9. J. C. Masterson, *The Double Cross System in the War of 1939 to 1945* (New Haven: Yale University Press, 1972), 30–31.

10. Miles Copeland, *The Real Spy World* (London: Weidenfeld and Nicolson, 1974), 187–88 (emphasis added).

11. These citations come from Whittaker Chambers, *Witness* (New York: Random House, 1952), and Allen Weinstein, *Perjury* (New York: Vintage, 1979).

12. Chambers, *Witness*, 770 (paraphrase).

13. Lev Nikulin, *Mertvaya Zyb* (Deadly Swell) (Moscow: Ministry of Defense, Military Publishing House, 1965), 111.

14. Chambers, *Witness*, 763 and 731.

15. William E. Colby and Peter Forbath, *Honorable Men. My Life in the CIA* (New York: Simon and Schuster, 1978), 364.

16. Sworn testimony of John L. Hart, representing the director of Central Intelligence, House Select Committee on Assassinations, 95th Congress, Hearings (Washington: Government Printing Office, 1979), Vol. 2, 494, 519.

17. Stanley Milgram, *Obedience to Authority* (New York: Harper and Row, 1974).

18. Cited by Merle Miller, *Plainly Speaking* (New York: Berkeley, 1974), 411.

19. Chambers, *Witness*, 707, 739.

20. Philippe Thyraud de Vosjoli, *Lamia* (Boston: Little, Brown, 1970), 313–16.

21. Levine, *Mind of an Assassin*, 109.

22. Former Director William Colby, in "CIA Round Table" of 24 March 1978, published in *The Washington Quarterly*, Autumn 1978. Compare the opposing view of former director of Central Intelligence Richard Helms on the same occasion: "Any secret organization must necessarily focus both on the recruitment of foreign agents and on counterintelligence methods which constantly scrutinize the reliability of agents abroad and protect us against espionage agents at home. . . . The theory that counterintelligence can just be tucked away in a back room in a world dominated by KGB and other hostile agents is simply naïve."

23. These quotes come, respectively, from John M. Maury, "What Hinders CIA from Doing Its Job?," *Washington Star*, 3 December 1978, and Victor Marchetti and John Marks, *The CIA and the Cult of Intelligence* (New York: Knopf, 1974), 214. The field operative Joseph B. Smith called counterintelligence "paranoia made systematic by a card index" (Joseph B. Smith, *Portrait of a Cold Warrior* [New York: Putnam, 1976], 132).

Index